Marek Nekula

FRANZ KAFKA AND HIS PRAGUE CONTEXTS: STUDIES IN LANGUAGE AND LITERATURE

CHARLES UNIVERSITY IN PRAGUE
KAROLINUM PRESS 2016

CATALOGUING-IN-PUBLICATION – NATIONAL LIBRARY OF THE CZECH REPUBLIC

Nekula, Marek
Franz Kafka and His Prague Contexts : Studies in Language and Literature / Marek Nekula; parts translated by Robert Russell, Carly McLaughlin. – First English edition. – Prague : Charles University in Prague Karolinum Press, 2016
Translated from Czech
ISBN 978-80-246-2935-3

821.112.2(437.3) * 82:81–26 * 81:82 * 316.347 * 316.72 * 316.73 * 81'373.45 * 82.07 * (437.311)
– Kafka, Franz, 1883–1924
– Prague German literature – 20th century
– language of literature
– language and literature
– national identity
– cultural identity
– culture's influence
– language influence
– interpretation and reception of literature
– Prague (Czechia) – 1901–1930
– monographs

830.9 – German literature (on) [11]

ISBN 978-80-246-2935-3
ISBN 978-80-246-2992-6 (pdf)

CONTENTS

FOREWORD

It is now taken for granted that Franz Kafka has become one of the most published German-language writers, that he is a world literary figure, that his fragmentary texts with their polyphony and rich ambiguity exemplify the procedures of literary modernism, and that his writings address the key questions of the modern age. There are several editions of his complete works in German alone, while the critical edition strives to reconstruct faithfully the genesis of his texts and their variants, elucidating the contexts from which they emerged in exhaustive commentaries. Besides Kafka's literary works, diaries and letters, the critical edition also includes the letters he received. Even the correspondence and official reports he wrote or may have written at work, whether alone or as co-author, have been published and annotated. And alongside the constant flow of new studies analysing his literary works from various angles, there has been (and continues to be) a plethora of specialized studies and monographs concerning the books Kafka possessed or read, the films he saw, the family he was born into, the women he knew, the sanatoria he was treated in, the pubs he frequented, and the factories he had dealings with in his work.

Yet paradoxically, given this flood of secondary literature relating to Kafka's life and work, authors seeking a new perspective increasingly do not take for granted that he can be written about. The question: What should a new study of Kafka be about? thus becomes: Can it in fact say anything new about him? Does it serve any purpose? Moreover, by devoting so much attention to Kafka do we not displace other writers to the periphery and distort our perception of the literary field of the time? These questions are of particular relevance for this collection of Kafka studies initiated by the Karolinum Press, which I have called *Franz Kafka and His Prague Contexts*.

After all, 'Kafka and Prague' is hardly an original subject. Indeed, the conjunction is so obvious that it has prompted many efforts to 'ground' the writer in his home city and interpret him 'from the Prague perspective'. After the years of Czechoslovak socialist realism in the 1950s, when the supposedly 'decadent' Kafka had been considered taboo, Germanists in Czechoslovakia began to appropriate him on the evidence of his family background and topographical links with Prague.

What is new in my book, I believe, is its critical view of the apparent self-evidence of such appropriation. That is why it opens with the essay 'Suppression and distortion: Franz Kafka "from the Prague perspective"', which challenges the self-evidence of the biography- and sociology-based view of Kafka associated with the Liblice conference which, with its over-simplified data, research interests and interpretations of Kafka's texts, persists in some studies of Kafka to this day. As the 2008 conference *Kafka and Power 1963 – 1968 – 2008* and studies by Vladimir V. Kusin and Michal Reiman have reminded us, the Liblice conference was more significant from the point of view of cultural policy than of literary studies. The part played by Liblice in shaping 'readings' of Kafka in the wider context of his reception has been examined by Veronika Tuckerová. In this regard, my study focuses on the role of Kafka's family language in interpretations of his work 'from the Prague perspective' and on the resulting distortion of authentic readings of Kafka's Czech texts that helped sustain the 'Prague interpretation'. This view relied less on his texts and more on external sources, including the testimony, not always genuine, of contemporaries who knew him or met him. At the time of the Liblice conference Kafka still was a part of communicative memory and thus fell victim to the self-interest of story-tellers such as Gustav Janouch and Michal Mareš.

The opening study in the present volume, first published in 2014 in *Franz Kafka – Wirkung, Wirkungsverhinderung* (Franz Kafka – Reception and Reception Blocks), has two aims. The first is to demonstrate how an ideology-driven approach to Kafka led to the distorting of the authentic shape of Kafka's language in his texts and thus to the reinforcing of a particular interpretation of his literary works. The second is to exemplify the approach I have adopted in the other studies in this collection and which gives the book its unity – although these are concerned with linguistic as well as literary issues. The other studies, too, address questions that may be considered self-evident or already settled, challenging, for instance, the widely accepted myth of 'Prague German' and its supposed influence on Kafka's literary style, or revisiting the seemingly obvious question of Kafka's natural ('organic') language – to which the answer is in fact far from obvious. Studies of the form of language used in Kafka's texts go back wherever possible to the authentic versions of his texts with their unretouched idiosyncrasies, mutations and multiple corrections and variants. The present studies contextualize these idiosyncrasies, whereby their author is the first to admit that their sources and interpretations, given Kafka's social milieu and the linguistic situation in his day, may be multifarious. The studies of the literary texts, in turn, go back to a 'close reading' of the actual text – not in an attempt to imprison it in one of its possible readings, as was proposed by Marxist scholars with their 'Prague perspective', but to uncover in a 'wide reading' the polysemy of

Kafka's texts and the plurality of their readings, out of and into which lead 'textual threads' that connect them with the literary and public discourse of the period. While the opening chapter offers an external outline of Kafka's identity in German Studies, the essays that follow look at the discursive negotiation of that identity (or identities) from within his literary and non-literary texts. These are read, in the modus of New Historicism, in contrast not only with each other but, in the context of contemporary discourses, with other, non-literary texts. Overall, my intention in these studies is to extricate Kafka from the one-sidedness of partisan interpretations, which tended from the outset to marginalize other perspectives and approaches to Kafka within German Studies and ignore the relevance of other literary and public discourses that he – if we are to believe Julie Kristeva's dictum that writing is a re-reading of other texts – assimilated both as reader and author. Such narrowness distorted not only the polyphony of Kafka's texts but the way we view the literary field in which he was active.

Thematically, this collection of my studies is devoted to the actual language of Kafka's texts as well as the fictive languages we encounter within his literary works – such as those spoken by the builders of the Tower of Babel, or by the nomads who chatter like jackdaws – taking into account the prevalent language situation, the function of language(s) in the public space, and contemporary discourse on the language question. I have adapted these studies so that they form chapters of a book that I hope is coherent in both form and content. Partly, I take up themes discussed in my 2003 monograph *Franz Kafkas Sprachen: '...in einem Stockwerk des innern babylonischen Turmes...'* (Franz Kafka's Languages: '...on a Floor of the Inner Tower of Babel...'), which was published in both German and Czech. There I examined Kafka's written language in both his Czech and German texts, taking into account his language biography as well as the status of the two languages in public institutions and, in general, the role of language in the formation of collective identity and the way it is negotiated in Kafka's texts. The form of both languages found in his texts was reconstructed and viewed in the context of the linguistic usage of his day. Similarly, Kafka's acquisition of each language and its use in his family was contextualized with regard to the prevailing language situation. Notwithstanding certain idiosyncratic features that Kafka's German undoubtedly displays, I confined myself in that work to a critical interpretation of empirical material, taking issue with Eisner's 'triple ghetto' thesis and its more recent variants, and with the attribution of Kafka's literary language and style to the 'poverty' (*Armut*) of 'Prague German', a consequence of its supposed isolation.

In *Franz Kafkas Sprachen* I drew on textual and archival material as well as biographical works by Klaus Wagenbach, Anthony D. Northey, and Alena Wagnerová, but also on specialized studies by Pavel Trost, Kurt Krolop, Josef

Čermák, Jürgen Born and Hartmut Binder. For my analysis of the historical status of languages and ethnicities and the language situation in Prague, I was indebted to the work of the historians Hannelore Burger, Gary B. Cohen, Jaroslav Kučera, Robert Luft and Jiří Pešek; and with special reference to the Jewish context to Andreas Kilcher and Hillel J. Kieval. I was also able, thanks to my collaboration in the course of preparing the Czech complete edition of Kafka's works and the German critical edition with Hans-Gerd Koch, Benno Wagner, Kafka archivists and his surviving relatives, to present a more precise picture of the language of Kafka's Czech texts, as well as providing new or newly contextualized material and, by drawing attention to the specific character of Kafka's Czech and German and the function of each language in his family and in the wider social context of the time, identifying a new area of research for Kafka scholarship. By focussing on how Kafka acquired his knowledge of the Czech language and Czech literature at school as well as on the content and context of his Czech reading (bearing in mind the quantitative and qualitative differences between his Czech, German and Jewish reading), my book provided a counterbalance to the simplistic restriction of Kafka to the German linguistic, literary and cultural context and an alternative view of Kafka's reading of Jewish texts and the Jewish reading of Kafka. The latter is also significant in the light of his 'Character sketch of small literatures' and thus of his aesthetic conception and understanding of the function of literature and writing.

I have referred at length to my earlier monograph partly because much of this English edition of my Kafka studies is derived from it, in particular the chapters 'Franz Kafka at school: Kafka's education in Czech language and literature' and 'Kafka's Czech reading in context', which are updated English translations of the corresponding chapters in that book. The chapter 'The "being" of Odradek: Franz Kafka in his Jewish context' is a revised and abridged conflation of two chapters from my earlier work that investigates the languages used by Kafka's parents in the wider context of language assimilation among Bohemian Jews and shows how Kafka's attitudes to Yiddish and Hebrew evolved over time.

The chapter 'Franz Kafka's languages' is new, although that too draws on material collected and treated in the earlier volume. In addition to a discussion of Kafka's Czech and German and interference from Yiddish in his idiolect, it also considers his other languages, including Hebrew, referring to the work of Alfred Bodenheimer and others. The sections devoted to Czech, German and Yiddish also contain new material, with a more thorough discussion of those languages in the context of research on language contact and bi- or multilingualism. In these sections Kafka's multilingualism is discussed in the context of his parents' bilingualism and multilingualism in the Kafka household. Here I draw not only on my own research, but also on studies and monographs produced by a group of PhD students as part of my project *Language and Identity: Franz Kafka in a Central European Linguistic and Cultural Context*, which ran from 2004-07 and was financed by the Fritz Thyssen Foundation. To their and my own publications, which were also jointly published as conference proceedings, I refer the reader in notes in the chapter 'Franz Kafka's languages' as well as in the final bibliography.

While working on that project I also began to consider, besides the actual language(s) of Kafka's texts, the fictive languages contained in some of them, namely that of the builders of the Tower of Babel or the nomads who chatter like jackdaws, relating them to contemporary discourse on the language issue. Here I was able to build on the work of the literary scholars Andreas Kilcher, Axel Gellhaus and Benno Wagner, and of the historian Kateřina Čapková. Kafka's treatment of the language question within his literary texts is a subject I dealt with in my interpretation of the figure of Odradek in the short story 'The householder's concern', also in my 2003 monograph. The text 'Kafka's "organic" language: Language as a weapon', an abridged version of a paper delivered at the 2010 Oxford conference *Kafka, Prague, and the First Word War*, considers primarily the stories 'Report to an Academy', 'In the penal colony' and 'A page from an old manuscript'. These I read through the prism of New Historicism in the wider context of discourses on language, specifically manifested in texts of the contemporary philosophy of language as well as in antisemitic discourse. The image of an 'organic' language, which we find in Kafka's letter to Brod about the 'mauscheln' of German-speaking Jews, takes up the theme of the preceding chapter 'Franz Kafka's languages' while shifting its focus from the way Kafka used language to the way he thought about it, placing it within the debate on collective identity. In their choice of particular language categories, however, Kafka's literary texts interact with his non-literary texts, thus widening their scope, as noted above, to engage in the language discourse of the day.

'Divided city: Franz Kafka's readings of Prague', the last of the chapters devoted to literature, also addresses the theme of language discourse in its interpretations of the texts 'The city coat of arms', 'The Great Wall of China', 'Silence of the Sirens' and 'The hunter Gracchus'. By analysing the conceptualization and literarization of Prague public space, it shows how public discourse on language, permeating through its 'textual threads' the literary discourse, invaded the public space of the city, and how discursive reality intersected with non-discursive reality. This text dates from 2006, when I spent a sabbatical at the Davis Centre for Russian and Eurasian Studies at Harvard University, and has been abridged and revised for the present volume.

This brings me to the institutions and individuals who have made the publication of these texts and this book possible. My thanks are due to the Fritz Thyssen Foundation for their support of the aforementioned project, and to the Davis Center for Russian and Eurasian Studies for the undisturbed sabbatical I spent there in an inspiring environment. I also wish to thank my publishers Karolinum Press for generously facilitating the translation of my Czech and German texts into English, the translators Robert Russell and Carly McLaughlin for their patience with my reformulations of their work, Robert Russell and Peter Zusi for their careful reading of and comments on the final manuscript, and Veronika Tuckerová and Kateřina Čapková for comments on various parts of the text. I am also deeply indebted to Hans-Gerd Koch for his constant support and generous permission to reprint illustrative material from the archive of the German critical edition of Kafka's works. Thanks, too, to the various institutions who allowed me to reprint other reproductions and who are credited separately under each one, as well as to the publishers of the journals and anthologies in which my texts first appeared for their kind permission to reuse and translate them.

I should also like to express my gratitude to Franz Kafka's nieces, not only for the information they imparted to me but also for the meetings we had in the course of my research, which for me were unforgettable experiences. When, a few days after I had submitted the English manuscript, I received notice that Věra Saudková, the last member of Franz Kafka's family who still personally remembered him, had died on the very day I had submitted, I could not help reflecting that something had come to an irrevocable end, not only on the personal level. Henceforward Kafka will exist only in our cultural memory. This should remind literary scholars of the necessity of concentrating on Kafka's texts, with the aim not simply of preserving them but of ensuring that their ambiguous and multilayered meaning will never be reduced to a single canonical interpretation or lost in the myth of the 'Prague perspective'. That is my public wish. On a personal note, I should like to dedicate this book to the memory of Věra Saudková and Marianne Steiner, to whom Fate was kinder than to other members of their family, allowing them to pass on their memories of Franz Kafka, his family and his world to our shared cultural memory.

SUPPRESSION AND DISTORTION: FRANZ KAFKA 'FROM THE PRAGUE PERSPECTIVE'

RETURN OF A COUNTRYMAN

A very good overview of Franz Kafka's reception in Czechoslovakia has been provided by Josef Čermák.[1] His first publications on this topic date back to the 1960s.[2] My study picks up precisely where his study of 2000 left off, namely in 1963, although admittedly I do not get far beyond 1963. It is in this year that Kafka's Czech-language texts were first published. I am going to focus on the inclusion of these published texts in academic and journalistic discussions, which goes hand in hand with the interpretation of Kafka 'from the Prague perspective'. The – albeit only fragmentary – publication of Kafka's unknown Czech texts was, in the context of Kafka's reception, an entirely new phenomenon;[3] in the Czechoslovak context, however, this was also true to an extent of Kafka himself and his work as a whole. The Czech translations of his works were, after all, banned from 1948 until 1957. From the perspective of socialist realism Kafka's writings were regarded as formalist and decadent; stigmatised as a representative of the bourgeoisie, Kafka became a taboo author.[4] Even in 1957 the slowly burgeoning reception of Kafka faced strong ideolog-

---

1 See Josef Čermák, Die Kafka-Rezeption in Böhmen (1913–1949) (Kafka's reception in Bohemia 1913–1949). In: Kurt Krolop – Hans Dieter Zimmermann (eds), *Kafka und Prag* (Kafka and Prague). Berlin, New York: de Gruyter 1994, pp. 217–237; Josef Čermák, Die Kafka-Rezeption in Böhmen (1913–1949) (Kafka's reception in Bohemia 1913–1949). *Germanoslavica* 1 (1994), pp. 1–2, pp. 127–144; and Josef Čermák, Recepce Franze Kafky v Čechách (1913–1963) (Franz Kafka's reception in Bohemia (1913–1963). In: *Kafkova zpráva o světě* (Kafka's Report on the World). Prague: Nakladatelství Franze Kafky 2000, pp. 14–36.

2 See Josef Čermák, Česká kultura a Franz Kafka: Recepce Kafkova díla v letech 1920–1948 (Czech culture and Franz Kafka: Reception of Kafka's work 1920–1948). *Česká literatura* 16 (1968), pp. 463–473.

3 See Franz Kafka, Neznámé dopisy Franze Kafky (Unknown letters by Franz Kafka). Translation by Aloys Skoumal. Introduced by Jiří Hájek. *Plamen* 5 (1963), No. 6, pp. 84–94; Jaromír Loužil, Dopisy Franze Kafky Dělnické úrazové pojišťovně pro Čechy v Praze (Franz Kafka's letters to the Worker's Accident Insurance Company). *Sborník Národního muzea v Praze*, Row C, Literary history 8 (1963), No. 2, pp. 57–83. The Czech passages in Kafka's *Briefe an Milena* are mainly quotations from Milena's letters. See Franz Kafka, *Briefe an Milena* (The Letters to Milena). Frankfurt am Main: Fischer 1952.

4 These categories persisted, resulting in the view of Kafka as representative of the 'Prague German-Jewish bourgeoisie'. See Pavel Reiman, 'Proces' Franze Kafky (Franz Kafka's *The Trial*). In: Franz Kafka, *Proces* (The Trial). Prague: Československý spisovatel 1958, pp. 207–225, p. 211.

ical opposition from those who went on to shape the cultural politics of the Czechoslovak *Socialist* Republic, which was officially declared in 1960. The social and territorial 'grounding' or proletarianisation of Kafka, the process of making Kafka 'one of us' and his representation 'from the Prague perspective'[5] surmounted the ideological barriers of 1963 but not without excluding or overlooking other aspects of the author, such as the Jewish dimension of his work.

Why 1963 is of greater importance than any other year should be obvious. It marks – along with the Liblice conference initiated by Eduard Goldstücker[6] – an important turning point in Kafka's reception, the implications of which were relevant also outside of Czechoslovakia. Although this phase of his reception also saw him being appropriated by various contemporary discourses, this time it did not result in a ban of his work. Rather, it transformed Kafka – at least in Czechoslovakia – into a cult author of the 1960s. This turning point in Kafka's reception has, however, less to do with the 'internal' (implicit) or 'external' (biographical) author and much more with the 'image of the author'.[7] The 2008 conference *Kafka and Power 1963–1968–2008* focused precisely on the myth surrounding the Liblice conference and the effect it had well into the 1960s, not least on the Prague Spring. Kusin has

---

5 See Eduard Goldstücker – František Kautman – Pavel Reiman (eds), *Franz Kafka: liblická konference 1963* (Franz Kafka: Liblice Conference 1963). Prague: ČSAV 1963; Eduard Goldstücker – František Kautman – Paul Reiman (eds), *Franz Kafka aus Prager Sicht 1963* (Franz Kafka from the Prague Perspective 1963). Prague: ČSAV 1965.

6 The question of the 'initiation' of this conference is contentious; nevertheless, the conference's organisation highlights the central role of Eduard Goldstücker and Pavel/Paul Reiman/Reimann. The conference was organised by the Czechoslovak Academy of Sciences, Charles University and the Czechoslovak Writers' Guild in Liblice Castle on 27 and 28 May 1963. Over twenty speakers, from Czechoslovakia, the GDR, Poland, Hungary, Yugoslavia, France (Roger Garaudy) and Austria (Ernst Fischer) participated in the conference. The following authors appear in the conference proceedings: O. F. Babler, Josef Čermák, Zdeněk Eis, Dagmar Eisnerová, Ernst Fischer, Pavel Trost, Ivo Fleischmann, Norbert Frýd, Roger Garaudy, Jiří Hájek, Klaus Hermsdorf, František Kautman, Jenö Krammer, Alexej Kusák, Dušan Ludvík, Josef B. Michl, Werner Mittenzwei, Pavel Petr, Jiřina Popelová, Petr Rákos, Pavel Reiman, Helmut Richter, Ernst Schumacher, Ivan Sviták, Pavel Trost and Antonín Václavík.
For more see Michal Reiman, Die Kafka-Konferenz von 1963 (The Kafka conference of 1963). In: Michaela Marek – Dušan Kováč – Jiří Pešek – Roman Prahl (eds), *Kultur als Vehikel und als Opponent politischer Absichten. Kulturkontakte zwischen Deutschen, Tschechen und Slowaken von der Mitte des 19. Jahrhunderts bis in die 1980er Jahre* (Culture as Medium and Opponent of Political Programs: Cultural Contact between Germans, Czechs and Slovaks from the middle of 19th Century to the 1980s). Essen: Klartext 2010, pp. 107–113, or Ines Koeltzsch, Liblice. In: Dan Diner (ed.), *Enzyklopädie jüdischer Geschichte und Kultur* (Encyclopaedia of Jewish History and Culture). Vol. 3 (He – Lu). Stuttgart, Weimar: Metzler 2012, pp. 511–515.

7 For more on the terminology used here see Petr A. Bílek, Obraz Boženy Němcové – pár poznámek k jeho emblematické funkci (The image of Božena Němcová – some remarks on its emblematic function). In: Karel Piorecký (ed.), *Božena Němcová a její Babička* (Božena Němcová and her *Babička*). Prague: Ústav pro českou literaturu 2006, pp. 11–23.

also looked at the role of the Liblice conference for the reform movement.[8] For the same reason, scholars such as Goldstücker or Kusák, among others, have also looked back on this from their perspective as key participants.[9] To read the contemporary clash over 'Spring, swallows, and Franz Kafka' – in which Kurella uses swallows as well as other black bird species with less positive connotations to build up his polemical arguments[10] – is to encounter the imagery and rhetoric of both the Prague Spring and of 'Normalisation', making the teleological perspective of the *Kafka and Power 1963–1968* [...] conference easily understandable. The election of Eduard Goldstücker as Chairman of the Czechoslovak Writers' Guild seems to complete an arc which began with the Liblice conference and ended with the Prague Spring. In the 1970s the proximity of these two events as well as the accusation of his 'bourgeois decadence' from the 1950s proved to be disastrous for Kafka's reception:

> [...] it made the civil servant J. furious that the Kafka motto 'I write differently from how or what I speak, I speak differently from what I think, I think differently from the way I ought to think, and so it all proceeds into deepest darkness'[11] had been retained in the translation. And not only because the motto was deceitful, but also because it had been penned by Kafka, the writer who had been condemned and whose name 'was not to appear anywhere'. [...] The point of this story is, however, in true Švejk style utterly stupid: three months later I saw 18 copies of the Kafka book by Brod [...] lying on the desk of the antiquarian bookshop in Ječná Street... the unsold remains of the print run which had [now] been released for sale.[12]

In order to understand the ethos of the Kafka reception of 1963, we need to go back a few years. Following the advent to power of the communists in 1948 there was a glaring hiatus in the official reception of Kafka which would last

8 See Vladimir V. Kusin, *The Intellectual Origins of the Prague Spring. The Development of Reformist Ideas in Czechoslovakia 1956–1967*. Cambridge (MA): Cambridge University Press 2002.

9 See Eduard Goldstücker, *Prozesse. Erfahrungen eines Mitteleuropäers* (Trials: Experiences of a Central European). Munich: Knaus 1989; Eduard Goldstücker, *Vzpomínky* (Memoirs) Vol. 2: 1945–1968. Prague: G plus G 2005; Alexej Kusák, *Tance kolem Kafky: Liblická konference 1963 – vzpomínky a dokumenty po 40 letech* (The Dance around Kafka: the Liblice Conference of 1963 – Memories and Papers 40 Years on). Prague: Akropolis 2003.

10 See e.g. Alfred Kurella, Jaro, vlaštovky a Franz Kafka (Spring, the swallows and Franz Kafka). *Literární noviny* 12 (1963), No. 40, p. 8, and Ernst Fischer, Jaro, vlaštovky a Franz Kafka (Spring, the swallows and Franz Kafka). *Literární noviny* 12 (1963), No. 41, p. 9. See further Čermák, Recepce Franze Kafky, p. 28, which contains the revealing reference to Howard Fast's Czech edition. See Howard Fast, *Literatura a skutečnost* (Literature and Reality). Translation by Zd. Kirschner and Jaroslav Bílý. Prague: Svoboda 1951. Fast also sees Kafka not as a swallow but a repugnant bird ('Kafka' literally means jackdaw) which sits atop 'the cultural dungheap of reaction'.

11 *Franz Kafka to Ottla*, 10 July 1914. – See Franz Kafka, *Letters to Friends, Family, and Editors*. New York: Schocken Books 1977, p. 109.

12 Jan Zábrana, *Celý život: Výbor z deníků 5. listopadu. 1976 – července 1984* (A Whole Life: Selected Passages from the Diaries, 5 November 1976 – July 1984). Vol. 2. Prague: Torst 1992, p. 567.

until 1957, a much longer hiatus, then, than that between 1939 and 1945. The absence of an official normative reception should, however, not be mistaken for an interruption of the reception in itself, as Jan Zábrana's diary entry describing the decentralised, individual reception of Kafka makes clear. Nevertheless, it is clear that this reception, too, had an ideological frame and was formulated in reaction to the official ideological discourse on Kafka and the exclusion of his writings from the official literary sphere:

> For the young, non-conforming Prague intellectuals of the 1950s who skulked around the literary scene or who themselves wrote, it was common for each of them to have a couple of Franz Kafka's short stories at home which they had translated themselves and which they lent to friends and acquaintances or read them out at get-togethers. [...] It was somehow the done thing. I heard and saw several Kafka stories in perhaps twenty handwritten translations doing the rounds. Where did all these cobbled-together translations disappear to? They were an expression, a reflection of the longing for the knowledge of the forbidden, outlawed world of true writing which Kafka at the time embodied for them. That it was only ever a couple of stories, one, two, three – never a whole book –, was simply evidence of the authentic love of *amateurs* rather than of superficiality. They were not professionals; they were not capable of more, had not the staying power; they were mostly timid lovers of an illusion which Franz Kafka embodied for them at the time. My memories of those evenings when somebody somewhere would read out Kafka's stories are filled with great melancholy. All of these stories were later published in book form, making sure that it could never be the same again.[13]

However, the criticism of the cult of personality in 1956 made it possible for Kafka's writings to be published again. The breakthrough came in 1957 with the publication of *Doupě*, the Czech translation of Kafka's story 'The burrow'. It was published in the magazine *Světová literatura* (World Literature) alongside an essay on Kafka by its translator Pavel Eisner in which he picked up once again and elaborated on his concept of the triple (linguistic, social and religious) ghetto.[14] As Čermák remembers, the publication must have 'resonated powerfully' with his readers.[15] Reactions in the press to Pavel Eisner's ventures as well as to the publication of the Czech translation of Kafka's novel *The Trial* in the following year, also translated by Pavel Eisner, were however – in comparison with the response to Kafka that was to follow in

13 Zábrana, *Celý život*, p. 886.

14 Franz Kafka, Doupě (The burrow). *Světová literatura* 3 (1957), pp. 132–153; Pavel Eisner, Franz Kafka. *Světová literatura* 3 (1957), pp. 109–129; Pavel Eisner, Německá literatura na půdě ČSR. Od r. 1848 do našich dnů (German literature on Czechoslovak territory. From 1848 to the present day). In: *Československá vlastivěda* (Encyclopaedic Information on Czechoslovakia). Vol. VII: *Písemnictví* (Letters). Prague: Sfinx 1933, pp. 325–277.

15 Čermák, Recepce Franze Kafky, p. 28.

1963 – scarce.[16] Čermák discusses each of the responses that did appear, positively evaluating the studies by Ivan Dubský and Mojmír Hrbek and Oleg Sus, and criticising Pavel Reiman and Jiří Hájek.[17] According to the international bibliography of Kafka's oeuvre and reception, there were also other publications on Kafka during this time.[18] I found yet other peripheral publications on Kafka, e.g. in the Christian Review,[19] but it would be another four years before the next translations of Kafka work were published.[20] Only rarely did someone venture forth, for example Goldstücker or Grebeníčková,[21] who reviewed Victor Erlich's study of Gogol's 'The Nose' and Kafka's 'The Metamorphosis' in the journal *Plamen* (Flame).

The reception of Kafka between 1956 and 1962[22] and its entanglement with contemporary political discourses can be summed up in a single visual image. In 1956 the military uniform on the body of the communist president Klement Gottwald, on display at the Czechoslovak Mausoleum of Revolution on Mount Vítkov, modelled on the Lenin and Stalin Mausoleum in Moscow, was replaced by civilian clothing. But it was not until 1962 that Gottwald's corpse was cremated and the monumental Stalin statue on Letná hill blown up.[23]

That year also saw the publication of the Czech translation of the unfinished novel *The Man who Disappeared*, although Pavel Reiman was still obliged to translate the novel in the shadow of an ideologically acceptable interpreta-

---

16 Franz Kafka, *Proces* (The Trial). Translation and afterword by Pavel Eisner. Prague: Československý spisovatel 1958; with commentary by Ján Rozner, Případ Kafka? Nad českým vydáním Procesu (The case of Kafka? On the Czech edition of *The Trial*). *Slovenské pohľady* 75 (1959), No. 2, pp. 125–140.

17 Ivan Dubský – Mojmír Hrbek, Kafkův Proces (Kafka's *The Trial*). *Květen* 3 (1958), pp. 620–623; Oleg Sus, Kafka – zmatení jazyků (Kafka – the confusion of tongues). *Host do domu* 6 (1959), pp. 139–140; Pavel Reiman, Společenská problematika v Kafkových románech (On the social issues in Kafka's novels). *Nová mysl* 1 (1958), pp. 52–63; Jiří Hájek, Spor o Franze Kafku (The dispute over Franz Kafka). *Tvorba* 24, 8. 1. 1959, No. 2, pp. 31–32.

18 Čestmír Jeřábek, Jubileum pražského básníka (Anniversary of the Prague writer). *Host do domu* 5 (1958), pp. 334–335; Čestmír Jeřábek, Kafkův Proces česky (Kafka's *The Trial* in Czech). *Host do domu* 5 (1958), pp. 373–374. See Maria Luise Caputo-Mayr – Julius Michael Herz, *Franz Kafka: Internationale Bibliographie*. Vol. 1–2. Munich: De Gruyter/Saur 1997 & 2000, here vol. 2, p. 255.

19 Oskar Kosta, Hledání a bloudění Franze Kafky (The searching and wandering of Franz Kafka). *Nový život* 10 (1958), pp. 784–786; Josef Svoboda, Bez víry? (Without faith?). *Křesťanská revue* 25 (1958), pp. 283–285.

20 The illustrated volume by Frynta published in the interim was only intended for a non-Czech readership. See Emanuel Frynta, *Franz Kafka lebte in Prag* (Franz Kafka Lived in Prague). With photographs by Jan Lukas. Translation into German by Lotte Elsner. Prague: Artia 1960.

21 Eduard Goldstücker, Předtucha zániku: K profilu pražské německé poezie před půlstoletím (Premonition of doom: On the profile of German poetry in Prague 50 years ago). *Plamen* 2 (1960), pp. 92–96; Růžena Grebeníčková, Gogolovy 'metamorphosis' na Západě (Gogol's 'metamorphosis' in the West). *Plamen* 2 (1960), pp. 126–128.

22 Starting with Ivan Dubský – Mojmír Hrbek, O Franzi Kafkovi (On Franz Kafka). *Nový život* 8 (1956), pp. 415–435.

23 See Hana Pichová, The Lineup for Meat: The Stalin Statue in Prague. *PMLA (Journal of* Modern Language Association of America*)* 123 (2008), 3, pp. 614–630.

tion.[24] For instance, he places the Stoker at the centre of the novel as a representative of the working class who finds sympathy in Karl Rossmann, who, as a member of the 'bourgeoisie', has realised that capitalism is on the verge of collapse. As a result of these sympathies he initially acts as the mouthpiece of the Stoker. Reiman also argues that Rossmann's downfall is due to the fact that he loses sight of the Stoker and, thus, of the working class. Among those who greeted this publication with reviews were Ivan Dubský in *Kultura* (Culture) and *Host do domu* (Guest at Home), Ivo Fleischmann in *Literární noviny* (Literary Newspaper), Pavel Grym in *Lidová demokracie* in (People's Democracy) and Eduard Goldstücker in *Tvorba* (Creation).[25] These covered the entire spectrum of periodicals concerned with the reception of cultural events. Nevertheless, according to the *Bibliografický katalog ČSSR – články v českých časopisech* (Bibliographical Catalogue of Czechoslovakia – Articles in Czech journals) apart from these and three brief articles by Zdeněk Kožmín, Agneša Kalinová and 'zf',[26] nothing else appeared in this year – except the translation of Franz Kafka's letter to his father in the journal *Světová literature* (World Literature).[27]

It was in Moscow, rather than in Prague, that the wall around Kafka in the Eastern Block was finally toppled – by Jean-Paul Sartre. In 1962, at the World Peace Congress in Moscow, the French thinker held a metaphor-laden speech with the title *La démilitarisation de la culture*,[28] in which he labelled Kafka as a 'weapon' used by the West and called for 'cultural demilitarisation' in the relationship between the East and the West.[29] At the same time he insisted on

---

24 Franz Kafka, *Amerika* (The Man who Disappeared). Czech translation by Dagmar Eisnerová. Prague: SNKLU 1962; Pavel Reiman, Úvod (Foreword). In: Franz Kafka, *Amerika*. Prague: SNKLU 1962, pp. 7–23.

25 Ivan Dubský, Kafkova Amerika (Kafka's *Amerika*). *Kultura* 6 (1962), 12, p. 4; Ivan Dubský, Amerika aneb Nezvěstný (Kafka's *Amerika* or *The Man who Disappeared*). *Host do domu* 9 (1962), 4, p. 181f.; Ivo Fleischmann, Kafkova Amerika (Kafka's *Amerika*). *Literární noviny* 11 (1962), No. 16, pp. 368–369; Eduard Goldstücker, Kafkův 'Topič' (Kafka's 'The Stoker'). *Tvorba* 27 (1962), No. 16, pp. 368–369; Gm [= Pavel Grym], Kafkův hrdina v labyrintu světa (Kafka's hero in the labyrinth of the world). *Lidová demokracie*, 16.2.1962, p. 3.

26 Zdeněk Kožmín, Marxistická monografie o Kafkovi (Marxist monograph on Kafka). *Host do domu* 7 (1962), pp. 223–225; Agneša Kalinová, Kafka v Bergamu (Kafka in Bergamo). *Literární noviny* 11 (1962), No. 40, p. 8; Zf, O Kafkovi trochu jinak (Harry Järve's bibliography of Kafka scholarship). *Lidová demokracie*, 8.4.1962, p. 5.

27 Franz Kafka, Dopis otci (Letter to his Father). *Světová literatura* 7 (1962), No. 6, pp. 84–112. Translation by Dagmar Eisnerová and Pavel Eisner, introduced by Klaus Hermsdorf.

28 See Jean-Paul Sartre, La démilitarisation de la culture: Extrait du discours à Moscou devant le Congrès mondial pour le désarmement générale et la paix. *France-Observateur*, 17.7.1962, pp. 12–14; Stephan Hermlin, Die Abrüstung der Kultur. Rede auf dem Weltfriedenkongress in Moskau. (The demilitarization of culture: Speech for the world peace conference in Moskau). *Sinn und Form* 14 (1962), pp. 805–815.

29 Veronika Tuckerová deals with the reception of Franz Kafka between the East and the West during the Cold War. I was unable to get hold of her dissertation. Veronila Tuckerová, *Reading Kafka in Prague: The Reception of Franz Kafka between the East and the West during the Cold War*. New York: Columbia University 2012.

the need for people in the East to finally be allowed to 'read' Kafka. His speech instigated an – in quantitative terms – influential, but at the same time politically chequered, reception of Kafka in the Eastern Block. In the following year there was a veritable flood of Kafka publications largely inspired by the Liblice conference – enabled, if not inspired, by Sartre's speech. In 1963, in addition to the Czech translation of Kafka's 'The Metamorphosis',[30] roughly seventy translations of Kafka's short works or journalistic texts made reference to,[31] amongst other things, Jean-Paul Sartre's reflections on Kafka, the Liblice conference, Kafka's birthday and publications. These, along with radio broadcasts and the Czech edition of the Liblice conference volume, rained down on the parched public sphere like a long awaited rainstorm.

If at the beginning many referred to the breakthrough instigated by Jean-Paul Sartre in order to support their own response to Kafka, their reception of Kafka did not align with Sartre's calls for a concentration on texts. Incidentally, over the course of the year explicit references to Sartre disappeared completely. Fischer, for example, devised the metaphor of spring and the swallow in 1963.[32] Goldstücker even went so far as to present Kafka, in view of the hiatus in his reception particularly between 1948 and 1957, as a 'victim of the cult of personality';[33] in doing so he may well have been projecting his own personal agenda on to Kafka. In 1951 Goldstücker had been sentenced to lifelong imprisonment in an antisemitic show trial, only to be rehabilitated and released in 1955.[34]

---

30 Franz Kafka, *Proměna* (The Metamorphosis). Translation by Zbyněk Sekal and afterword by Josef Čermák. Prague: SNKLU 1963.

31 See Marek Nekula, Einblendung und Ausblendung: Tschechoslowakische Kafka-Rezeption und Erstveröffentlichungen von Kafkas tschechischen Texten (From the shadow into light: The Czechoslovak reception of Franz Kafka and the first publication of his Czech texts). In: Steffen Höhne – Ludger Udolph (eds), *Franz Kafka – Wirkung, Wirkungsverhinderung* (Franz Kafka: Reception and Reception Blocks). Cologne, Weimar, Vienna: Böhlau 2014, pp. 61–91. This paper contains a list of sources which is based on my own research conducted with the help of the *Bibliografický katalog ČSSR – články v českých časopisech*, and related research by Jiskra Jindrová from the bibliographical department of the Czech National Library in Prague, and also draws slightly on Caputo-Mayr – Herz, *Franz Kafka: Internationale Bibliographie*. In my endeavour to document this 'flood' of sources, the bibliography has become very long; only some of these texts are quoted in this chapter.

32 Fischer, Jaro, vlaštovky a Franz Kafka.

33 Eduard Goldstücker, Jak je to s Franzem Kafkou? (How do things stand with Franz Kafka?) *Literární noviny* 12 (1963), No. 7, p. 4; Eduard Goldstücker, *Na téma Franz Kafka. Články a studie* (On the Subject of Franz Kafka: Essays and Papers). Prague: Československý spisovatel 1964, p. 62. See also Eduard Goldstücker, Vyděděnci a temný obraz světa (Outcasts and their dark image of the world). *Plamen* 3 (1961), No. 10, pp. 66–69.

34 On the show trial see for example Goldstücker, *Prozesse*, or Koeltzsch, Liblice. In 1956 Goldstücker became a lecturer at Charles University. He was completely rehabilitated and appointed professor in 1963.

The political language in which Kafka's reception was couched may well have had little to do with Kafka and his works, but it nevertheless became an important aspect of the author's image, and, consequently, of the contemporary interpretation of his works. In this time, Kafka became a reference point not only for the at this time more open-minded Marxist critics and historian of literature like Pavel Reiman, Eduard Goldstücker, Jiří Hájek and others, but also for the official newspaper of the communist party.[35] Furthermore, in the Czech, that is the Czechoslovak, context the appropriation of Kafka as 'one of us' was of central importance. Miroslav Kaňák used the title 'Ztracený a znovunalezený' (Lost and found) for his article published in the weekly Hussite newspaper *Český zápas* (The Czech Struggle),[36] in which he reflected on Franz Kafka's reception, superimposing the protagonist of *The Man who Disappeared* onto Kafka and in doing so characterising him as the prodigal son. Eduard Goldstücker's imagery also went along the same lines and marked an equally clear departure from Sartre and contextualised Kafka's texts to selective biography including his posthumous fortunes. In his speech on the occasion of the opening of the exhibition of Kafka's personal documents and book publications in the literary archive of the *Památník národního písemnictví* (Museum of Czech Literature), at the beginning of July 1963, Eduard Goldstücker welcomed the 'countryman born in Prague' on his return from 'a long and undeserved emigration'.[37] Of particular note here are the family semantics of the prodigal son ('lost and rediscovered') and of the homeland ('compatriot', 'undeserved emigration') which are in keeping with Goldstücker's call for the 'grounding' of Kafka and thus also with the interpretation of his work 'from the Prague perspective', to which I will return later.

The prodigal son and compatriot was also welcomed on the occasion of his eightieth birthday on 3 July 1963, around five weeks after the Liblice conference, right across the Czech media landscape, including the most official newspapers like *Rudé právo* (Red Justice), *Mladá fronta* (Young Front), *Práce* (Labour), *Svobodné slovo* (Free Speech), *Lidová demokracie* (People's Democracy) etc.[38] The women's magazine *Vlasta*, the youth magazine *Mladý svět*,

---

35 See e.g. Jiří Hájek, Kafka a marxistické literární myšlení (Kafka and Marxist literary thought). *Plamen* 5 (1963), No. 7, pp. 131–132, as well as A. Petřina, Jako v Kafkově 'Procesu' (As in Kafka's *The Trial*). *Rudé právo* 43, 10.8.1963, No. 219, p. 3.

36 Dr. M. K. [= Miroslav Kaňák], Ztracený a znovu nalezený (Lost and found). *Český zápas* 46 (1963), No. 34-35, p. 8.

37 Article on the exhibition in *Literární noviny* 12 (1963), No. 23, p. 13. The reflection of Kafka in terms of 'return' is present also in Ivan Dubský, Návrat Franze Kafky (The return of Franz Kafka). *Kulturní tvorba* 1 (1963), No. 26, p. 8; and Zdeněk Pešat, Kafkův návrat domů a literární věda (Kafka's homecoming and literary studies). *Literární noviny* 12 (1963), No. 17, p. 5.

38 See Eduard Goldstücker, Lidské poselství hledajícího člověka (Human legacy in search of people). *Rudé právo*, 3.7.1963, p. 5; Svatoslav Svoboda, Franz Kafka. *Mladá fronta*, 3.7.1963, p. 5; Josef

or the Magazine of Jewish Communities in Czechoslovakia also joined in.[39] The poet Ivan Diviš got carried away enough to write and publish a poem in the weekly literary publication *Literární noviny* titled 'Franz Kafka', which, unlike Louis Fürnberg's poem 'The Life and Death of Franz Kafka',[40] may mention Kafka's name but barely features him:

Only after years, close even to the moment where my backbone fractures,
only after years, struggling through the halls whose locks
hardened into sharp ice – I realised something I did not want to!
When they say to you at twenty: remember
a house can also be built as a warning –
You do not believe it, you crawl in, to, befuddled by booze,
Reel from non-father to non-mother, proud of your baboonish delirium
And, persisting in this confusion, like fly shit,
Hanging off the side of an avalanche! As if I would ever cry over you, Franz!
A rosary of empty nutshells!
Those are the years, when I was nowhere,
When I, teetering between Archimedes and Copernicus,
Gradually dissolved into adjectives
And only, thanks to a box around the ears from the storm, realised that he who walks before me
On wide legs – yes, now it's clear to me, is a woman!
Dirty, because she made the world. In her whole life
No booze passed her lips, and as earth lurched near
She merely whispered. I wouldn't have expected that from you –
And began to cry tiny tears
Like a quail in blood, before it's picked up.
That's what you've always said. And the would-be crucified
Walked the dreads of mysticism.[41]

Čermák, Franz Kafka, umělec naší doby (F.K., Artist of our age). *Práce*, 3.7.1963, p. 4; Vlastimil Vrabec, Fantastický svět Franze Kafky (The fantastical world of Franz Kafka). *Svobodné slovo*, 2.7.1963, p. 3; Miloslav Bureš, Franz Kafka u nás (Franz Kafka here with us, a list of the old and planned translations). *Svobodné slovo*, 9.7.1963, p. 3; Věra Poppova, Výročí Franze Kafky (Franz Kafka's anniversary). *Lidová demokracie*, 3.7.1963, p. 3.

39 See Vl. Moulíková, K nedožitým osmdesátinám Franze Kafky (On what would have been Franz Kafka's 80th birthday). *Vlasta* 17 (1963), No. 34, p. 6 f.; Franz Kafka, Poselství Franze Kafky (Legacy of Franz Kafka). With translations of 'First sorrow' and 'Poseidon' by Jiří Gruša. *Mladý svět* 5 (1963), No. 27, pp. 10–11. See also F. R. Kraus, K 80. narozeninám Franze Kafky (On Franz Kafka's 80th birthday). *Věstník židovských náboženských obcí v Československu* 25 (1963), No. 7, p. 6.

40 Louis Fürnberg, Život a smrt Franze Kafky (The Life and Death of Franz Kafka). Translation by Valter Feldstein. *Plamen* 5 (1963), No. 7, p. 108.

41 Ivan Diviš, Franz Kafka. *Literární noviny* 12 (1963), No. 27, p. 7.

Diviš' poem and its alienation of Kafka through Christian imagery may be somewhat odd, but the way that he projects his own poetic agenda onto the 'unknown' in a similar way to other interpreters makes it highly typical of its time. For however eloquently Kafka is denied in this poem, it is an excellent demonstration of the way in which others' agendas were superimposed onto Kafka at that time, as is seen, for instance, in the semantics of the 'prodigal son' or the discourse of destalinization, which featured prominently at the time.

MARXIST READINGS

The discourse of victimhood and rehabilitation projected onto Kafka certainly does not mean that people relinquished their Marxist – even crudely Marxist – approach to Kafka's work. Although in his paper at the Liblice conference Eduard Goldstücker referred to Eisner's biographical argument of the triple ghetto in relation to his question of why the signs of the crisis of bourgeois liberalism in Prague were felt so early and forcefully,[42] elsewhere his approach is actually closer to Pavel Reiman. Goldstücker, too, remains entrenched in a Marxist, biographical and sociological reading of Kafka, and simply casts Reiman's interpretation into a more positive light. For instance, he links Franz Kafka to Karl Rossmann and declares Kafka to be an utopian socialist; even the land surveyor K. in *The Castle* is hailed as a revolutionary.[43] At another point Goldstücker claims:

> Whenever we approach the extremely complicated organism of Kafka's work, it very quickly becomes clear that we would not get very far if we were to base our analysis on the texts alone, because it is immediately apparent that these are a crystallisation of his own personal set of questions and that the protagonists of his works, whether they are called Bendemann, Samsa, Raban, Gracchus, Josef K., land surveyor K. or something else, always signify Franz Kafka.[44]

---

42 See Eduard Goldstücker, Über Franz Kafka aus der Prager Sicht (On Franz Kafka from the Prague perspective). Translation by Kurt Krolop In: Eduard Goldstücker – František Kautman – Paul Reimann (eds), *Franz Kafka aus Prager Sicht* 1963 (Franz Kafka from the Prague Perspective 1963). Prague: ČSAV 1965, pp. 23–43, p. 32.

43 Goldstücker draws a direct connection between Kafka and 'utopian Socialism', and at the same time also establishes an analogy between Karl Rossman, the Stoker and the bosses (captain, shipping company) on the one hand and Kafka, customers of his insurance company and the management of his insurance company on the other. Similarly, he understands the 'surveyor' in accordance with the Marxist idea of 'land division' as a character preparing to carry out the 'distribution of property'. Goldstücker, Über Franz Kafka aus der Prager Sicht, 37, 43. See also Eduard Goldstücker, Kafkas 'Der Heizer'. Versuch einer Interpretation (Kafka's 'The Stoker': An attempt at an interpretation). *Germanistica Pragensia* 2 (1964), pp. 49–64, as well as Eduard Goldstücker, Doslov (Afterword). In: Franz Kafka, *Zámek* (The Castle). Prague: Mladá fronta 1964, pp. 306–313.

44 Goldstücker. *Na téma Franz Kafka*, p. 67.

This turn away from the text and the shifting of focus from the internal to the external author ('personal ... questions'; 'the protagonists of his works .... signify Franz Kafka') may well be entirely correct according to the Marxist theory of representation, but they lack depth because their Marxist glasses distort the crisis as a 'situation of modernity', and thus blind them to the treatment of contemporary discourses in Kafka's work. This accounts for the tendency to neglect a close analysis of his poetics.[45] This diagnosis of Czechoslovak Kafka scholarship was issued as early as 1964 by Grossman who one year after the Liblice conference caused a sensation with his dramatization of *The Trial*.[46] Nevertheless, the focus on the base runs as a common thread through Goldstücker's publications of 1963. Remarkably, Goldstücker frequently cites a decontextualized passage of Sartre's speech even though his approach is the complete opposite of Sartre's insistence on removing Kafka from discussions in his local context in order to focus solely on his work. Goldstücker instead invokes the social roots of artistic creativity, applying this to all literature and thus to Kafka's work:

> The depth of each work feeds off the depth of national history, of language, tradition, off the special and often tragic questions which time and space impose on the artist through their dynamic communion of which he too is an inextricable part.[47]

It is this view of art that provides the basis for Goldstücker's call for the 'grounding' of Kafka, which he understands in both a territorial as well as a social sense. Since Kafka's proletarianisation as well as his connection with 'the people' play an important role in the transformation of Kafka into a utopian socialist and revolutionary, Goldstücker later also reinterprets Hermann Kafka's biography in line with this. In doing so he forced a connection with the Czech substructure of Franz Kafka's work. Accordingly, he also claims that Hermann Kafka (1852–1931), whom he calls 'Heřman',[48] and whose 'Czech' surname he etymologises as jackdaw,

---

45 On modernity see Silvio Vietta, *Ästhetik der Moderne: Literatur und Bild* (Aesthetics of the Modern: Literature and Image). Munich: Fink 2001. On the treatment of discourses see Andreas Kilcher, Kafkas Proteus: Verhandlungen mit Odradek (Kafka's Proteus: Negotiation with Odradek). In: Irmgard M. Wirtz (ed.), *Kafka verschrieben* (Committed to Kafka). Göttingen, Zürich: Wallstein 2010, pp. 97–116; Marek Nekula, Kafkas 'organische' Sprache: Sprachdiskurs als Kampfdiskurs (Kafka's organic language: Language discourse as struggle discourse). In: Manfred Engel – Ritchie Robertson (eds), *Kafka, Prag und der Erste Weltkrieg. Kafka, Prague, and the First World War*. Würzburg: Königshausen & Neumann 2012, pp. 237–256.

46 Jan Grossman, Kafkova divadelnost? (Kafka's theatricality?). *Divadlo* 9 (1964), pp. 1–17.

47 Goldstücker, Jak je to s Franzem Kafkou?, p. 5.

48 See also Klaus Wagenbach, *Franz Kafka*. Reinbek bei Hamburg: Rowohlt [1964] 1991, p. 17, as well as Max Brod, *Franz Kafka. Eine Biographie* (Franz Kafka: A Biography). Frankfurt am Main: S. Fischer 1963, p. 7. According to Gustav Janouch, Franz Kafka himself also interpreted his name along these lines. See Gustav Janouch, *Gespräche mit Kafka. Aufzeichnungen und Erinnerungen*

> grew up in an exclusively Czech environment and all his life spoke better Czech than German.[49]

At the same time as this, Klaus Wagenbach also reinforced these Czech, folk-like motifs in his popular illustrated Kafka biography by labelling Hermann Kafka a 'Czech Jew' and having him come from a 'Czech-Jewish provincial proletarian' background.[50] According to Wagenbach, from his contemporary point of view, further indirect indications of Hermann Kafka's Czechness are 'language errors' in the letters he wrote in German to his future wife Julie Löwy, née Kafka, in 1882.[51] Wagenbach even made Hermann Kafka, using his 'Czech surname' to support his argument, a 'member of the executive board of the first Prague synagogue in the Heinrichsgasse in which sermons were held in Czech'.[52]

The appropriation of Hermann Kafka went so far in the Czech German Studies, that Wagenbach's relatively cautious claim that the everyday language of Hermann Kafka's childhood and youth in Osek was 'more likely Czech'[53] was in the Czech translation much more forceful: 'jehož mateřská řeč byla česká' (whose mother tongue was Czech).[54] This has also had consequences for the appraisal of Franz Kafka. Following this logic, Kafka would have lived in a Czech – or through his mother and father at least a bilingual – household, and thus learned to speak excellent Czech and German. This would also account for the declaration of both German and Czech as his 'mother tongue' in his first and second years at primary school. Wagenbach says of Franz Kafka:

> He was the only one [of the Prague-based German authors] who spoke and wrote Czech almost flawlessly, who had grown up in the middle of the old town, on the edge of the ghetto quarter, then still an architectonic unity. Kafka never lost this close link to the Czech people, never forgot this atmosphere of his youth.[55]

(Conversations with Kafka. Notes and Memoirs). Extended edition. Frankfurt am Main: S. Fischer [1968] 1981, p. 30.

49 Goldstücker, *Na téma Franz Kafka*, p. 7.

50 Wagenbach, *Franz Kafka*, p. 17, and Klaus Wagenbach, *Franz Kafka.* Prague: Mladá fronta [1965] 1993. Czech aspects in the family history are already a feature of his 1958 biography of Kafka. Klaus Wagenbach, *Franz Kafka: Eine Biographie seiner Jugend 1883–1912* (Franz Kafka: A Biography of his Youth 1883–1912). Bern: Francke 1958.

51 See Wagenbach, *Franz Kafka*, 1991, p. 16. I interpret them as specific local variants typical for Hermann Kafka's time. See Marek Nekula, Deutsch und Tschechisch in der Familie Kafka (German and Czech in the family Kafka). In: Dieter Cherubim – Karlheinz Jakob – Angelika Linke (eds), *Neue deutsche Sprachgeschichte. Mentalitäts-, kultur- und sozialgeschichtliche Zusammenhänge* (New German History of Language: Mentality, Culture and Social History). Berlin, New York: W. de Gruyter 2002, pp. 379–415.

52 Wagenbach, *Franz Kafka*, p. 16.

53 Wagenbach, *Franz Kafka*, p. 16.

54 Wagenbach, *Franz Kafka*, 1993, p. 15.

55 Wagenbach, *Franz Kafka*, 1991, p. 17.

Goldstücker adds that in his 'Character sketch of small literatures', which is concerned with Czech and Yiddish literature, Kafka looked back at the popular intellectual legacy of his forefathers.[56] Specifically, Goldstücker meant his Czech intellectual legacy, even though Kafka was actually more concerned – the mentioned text draws on Yitzchak Löwy – with the Jewish legacy.

The transformation of the representative of the 'Prague German-Jewish bourgeoisie'[57] – this label was Kafka's doom, ideologically speaking, during the Stalin era – into a son of the 'Czech-Jewish rural proletariat' was thus complete, while the Jewish aspect was pushed into the background. But how closely is this instrumentalised construction to actual reality? On this point the otherwise usually surreal Hugo Siebenschein sticks fairly close to the facts in his remarks on Kafka. Regarding language, for instance, he mentions that Hermann Kafka spoke 'perfect German' and that both languages (German and Czech) were 'equally satisfying and equally interchangeable means of communication'.[58] In the Czech original, Siebenschein's formulation 'lhostejný' (indifferent) makes clear that the interchangeability is also to be understood beyond Czech and German national identity. Other retouched details could also have done with being corrected in the same way.[59]

In turn, Hartmut Binder's German-centric account of Franz Kafka in his biographical overview of the author and his family omits 'Czech' elements and in doing so appropriates Kafka for German-language culture. Binder applies the label 'German Jew' to Hermann Kafka, for example when he says of Kafka's mother Julie: 'she is *also* to be included in the German-Jewish population of Bohemia'.[60] Here we are to understand 'also' as meaning just like Kafka's father. Elsewhere, on Kafka's father Binder writes: 'His mother tongue was German: the gravestone of Jakob Kafka also has a German inscription alongside the one in Hebrew'.[61] Binder also refers to the family's German tradition, which he sees confirmed in the names of Jakob Kafka's children

---

56 Goldstücker, *Na téma Franz Kafka*, p. 14f.

57 Reiman, 'Proces' Franze Kafky, p. 211.

58 Hugo Siebenschein, Prostředí a čas. Poznámky k osobnosti a dílu Franze Kafky (Milieu and time: Remarks on the personality and oeuvre of Franz Kafka). In: *Franz Kafka a Praha. Vzpomínky, úvahy, dokumenty* (Franz Kafka and Prague. Memories, Reflections, Papers). Prague: Žikeš 1947, pp. 7–24, p. 21.

59 For an analysis of languages in Kafka's family see Nekula in this volume or in Marek Nekula, *„...v jednom poschodí vnitřní babylonské věže..." Jazyky Franze Kafky* ('... on one Floor of the Inner Tower of Babel...': Franz Kafka's Languages). Prague: Nakladatelství Franze Kafky 2003, or Marek Nekula, Franz Kafkas Sprachen und Sprachlosigkeit (Franz Kafka's languages and the absence of language). In: *brücken. Germanistisches Jahrbuch Tschechien – Slowakei.* NF 15 (2007), pp. 99–130.

60 Hartmut Binder, *Kafka. Ein Leben in Prag* (Kafka. A Life in Prague). München: Mahnert-Lueg 1982, p. 13. My emphases.

61 Binder, *Kafka. Ein Leben in Prag*, p. 13.

(Philip/Philipp, Anna, Heinrich, Hermann, Julie, Ludwig) or those of Hermann Kafka (Franz, Georg, Heinrich, Gabriela, Valerie, Ottilie), ignoring the broader context of naming discussed in the next chapter. He also points out that German was the language of instruction at Jewish schools, which no doubt was also the case in Osek. Finally, Binder's explanation of the etymology of the surname 'Kafka' is different; he sees it as deriving from 'Kov-ke', the supposed Low German diminutive form of the name יעקב (Yaakov), which is said to have been used by Ashkenazic Jews.[62]

Of course, such categories imposed from the outside or projected outwards have very little to do with the reality. Wagenbach regards Hermann Kafka as a 'Czech Jew' on the basis of his supposedly preferred language whilst Kafka's mother is seen as a 'German Jew' on the basis of her language. However, of the texts that have survived, Hermann Kafka's papers contain only German writings,[63] whilst there is evidence that Julie Kafka also wrote letters in Czech to staff which were – phonetically at least – in flawless Czech. Furthermore, in her letters, Julie Kafka addressed her daughter, with whom she otherwise wrote German letters, using Czech names such as 'Otilko', 'Ellinko'.[64]

Goldstücker's 'grounding' of Kafka and – through this – his territorial, social and national appropriation of Kafka as 'one of us' reached its height in October 1963 when he presented the writer as 'attached to his homeland and his people' in an article in *Literární noviny*:

> For *us in Czechoslovakia* he [= Kafka] means more. He was born *in Prague*; his entire life and his entire oeuvre are *bound up with our capital city* and *our land*. [...] Memories and stories of Kafka in which truth and fiction are intertwined circulate amongst the *simple people* of Prague's old town. [...] his work [...] contains the imprint of *our* worries.[65]

This remark appeared in an essay written in response to the attack by his 'comrade' Kurella and it thus needs to be seen in the wider context of the debate around estrangement. Opinions were divided on whether estrangement was merely to be viewed as a temporary historical phenomenon in bourgeois society, as the representatives of German Studies in the German Democratic Republic were keen to understand it, or whether this concept

---

62 Binder, *Kafka. Ein Leben in Prag*, p. 31. There are also Hebrew etymologies like the double use of the initial כ and final letter ך (kaph, kaf, kav).

63 With the exception of the Czech letter to the Worker's Accident Insurance Company which Josef David wrote for his parents-in-law following Kafka's death. This is held in the Literární archiv Památníku národního písemnictví (Literary Archive of Museum of Czech Literature). See Nekula, Deutsch und Tschechisch in der Familie Kafka, p. 379.

64 See Nekula, Deutsch und Tschechisch in der Familie Kafka, pp. 407–409.

65 Eduard Goldstücker, Dnešní potřeby, zítřejší perspektivy (Today's needs, tomorrow's perspectives). *Literární noviny* 12 (1963), No. 40, p. 9. My emphases. See also Eduard Goldstücker, Kafka, oni a my (Kafka, them and us). *Literární noviny* 13 (1964), No. 26, p. 1.

could be applied elsewhere, as was claimed not only by the Czechoslovak Marxist literary scholars who took part in the Kafka conference but also by Ernst Fischer and Roger Garaudy.[66] This political engagement of Marxist literary studies led to a transgression of boundaries of scholarship which led to an aversion against Kafka amongst Marxist ideologues and regime yes-men, as is mentioned in Zábrana's diary. Criticism of Kafka also drew on non-literary arguments. For example, in the key Czech journal for theory and history of literature *Česká literatura* (Czech Literature) Vítězslav Rzounek compared Kafka and Jaroslav Hašek and rejected Kafka on the basis of biographical arguments for being decadent, for unlike Hašek, who participated in the revolution, Kafka had apparently opposed the revolution.[67] This is the kind of language that we are familiar with from the 1950s and which was rejected by Sartre. Yet in his article, quoted above, Goldstücker's piece is far from being merely an attempt at self-justification in the face of the attacks by the 'comrade' Kurella.[68] Rather, it presents an idea that is reinforced through the Czech press and culminates in Kafka's transformation into a 'Czech' author. Goldstücker had earlier called for a territorial, social and national 'grounding' of Kafka in the February issue of *Literární noviny*, cited earlier,[69] and in doing so had chalked out the development of Kafka's reception in 1963.

In his contextualisation of Kafka's works, Goldstücker also saw an opportunity to curb the proliferation of Kafka scholarship and to 'surmount the ambiguity' of the various interpretations of Franz Kafka. He thus precluded the possibility that the appeal of the author might actually lie precisely in his 'multiple voices', as is argued by Benno Wagner, who also writes of the 'poetic shorthand' by which Kafka 'records' the plurality of contemporary discourses in his work.[70] Goldstücker also defended his vague idea of the

66 See also Roger Garaudy, Kafka a doktor Pangloss (Kafka and Dr. Pangloss). *Literární noviny* 12 (1963), No. 40, p. 9; Roger Garaudy, O filosofii, Picassovi a Kafkovi (On philosophy, Picasso and Kafka). *Plamen* 5 (1963), No. 8, pp. 1–3. For a contemporary reflection on this polemic see Jiří Hájek, Alfréd Kurella a Franz Kafka, aneb o podmínkách principiální polemiky (Alfred Kurella and Franz Kafka, or on the conditions for a controversy over principles). *Plamen* 5 (1963), No. 10, 131.

67 Vítězslav Rzounek, Poznámka o pojetí stranickosti v epice (Remarks on the concept of party-mindedness in epic literature). *Česká literatura* 11 (1963), No. 3, pp. 188–192.

68 On the stance of German Studies on Kafka in East Germany and the interweaving of literature and politics in relation to 1968 see the article by Steffen Höhne, 1968, Prag und die DDR-Germanistik. Zur Verflechtung von Ideologie und Politik in der Kafka-Rezeption (1968, Prague and GDR German Studies: Ideology and politics in Kafka's reception). In: Wolfgang Adam – Holger Dainat – Günter Schandera (eds), *Wissenschaft und Systemveränderung: Rezeptionsforschung in Ost und West – eine konvergente Entwicklung?* (Scholarship and System Change? Reception Research in East and West: A Convergent Development?) Heidelberg: Winter 2003, pp. 225–244.

69 Goldstücker, Jak je to s Franzem Kafkou?, p. 4.

70 See Benno Wagner, Fürsprache – Widerstreit – Dialog: Karl Kraus, Franz Kafka und das Schreiben gegen den Krieg (Recommendation – conflict – dialogue: Karl Kraus, Franz Kafka and the

'grounding' of Kafka's writings, which met with a critical response from Ivo Fleischmann in *Literární noviny* in March 1963.[71] Drawing on Max Brod, Fleischmann described Kafka as a religious, metaphysical, transcendental writer who represents the life into which we are thrown as a trial that we lead with ourselves and with God and in which we – since of course we have to die – are always the losers. In true Marxist fashion, Goldstücker's response warned people against the illusion that

> an artistic work and its creator can be understood in their entirety without considering alongside the work the external, personal, social, historical circumstances in which the artist lived and out of which he created his art.[72]

This kind of 'grounding', that is, the localisation of Kafka in a Prague and Czech context, which supersedes the Jewish aspects – as in the polemic with Fleischmann – was also Goldstücker's main concern at the Liblice conference. His insistence on a Prague-based interpretation is clear in the circumscription 'from the Prague perspective' in the title of the conference proceedings. The Prague perspective, which consisted in the biographical localisation of Kafka, also echoed in the personal memory recounted by the Communist 'national artist' Marie Majerová during her opening speech:

> He spoke Czech and wrote in German; he often spent time with us although he remained distant. But as a Prague man he was one of us, a native of the old Prague lanes [...], a connoisseur of Czech literature. Whilst we, however, wandered in the still fresh traces of Neruda, he, so to speak, meandered in the 500 hundred-year-old footprints of Rabbi Lowe.[73]

---

writing against the war). In: Manfred Engel – Ritchie Robertson (eds), *Kafka, Prag und der Erste Weltkrieg. Kafka, Prague, and the First World War*. Würzburg: Königshausen & Neumann 2012, 257–278, and Benno Wagner, „Sprechen kann man mit den Nomaden nicht". Sprache, Gesetz und Verwaltung bei Otto Bauer und Franz Kafka ('It is impossible to speak with nomads'. Language, law and administration in Otto Bauer and Franz Kafka). In: Marek Nekula – Ingrid Fleischmann – Albrecht Greule (eds), *Franz Kafka im sprachnationalen Kontext seiner Zeit. Sprache und nationale Identität in öffentlichen Institutionen der böhmischen Länder* (Franz Kafka in the National Context of His Time. Language and National Identity in the Public Institutions of the Bohemian Crown Lands). Cologne, Weimar, Vienna: Böhlau 2007, pp. 109–128.

71 See Eduard Goldstücker, O přístupu ke Kafkovi (On the approach to Kafka). *Literární noviny* 12 (1963), No. 11, pp. 4–5, as well as Ivo Fleischmann, O čem psal Franz Kafka? (What did Franz Kafka write about?). *Literární noviny* 12 (1963), No. 13, pp. 4–5.

72 Eduard Goldstücker, O přístupu ke Kafkovi, p. 4 f.

73 Marie Majerová, Zahajovací projev (Opening speech). In: Eduard Goldstücker – František Kautman – Pavel Reiman (eds), *Franz Kafka: liblická konference 1963* (Franz Kafka: Liblice Conference 1963). Prague: ČSAV 1963, p. 9.

Tellingly, in her speech the Jewish aspect of Kafka's biography was mentioned in passing, only to be – as was largely the case in the other conference papers – superseded immediately, as if it was only the rhetorical anchoring of Kafka amongst the Czech people and Czech national literature (Jan Neruda) that counted. Then, after two further opening speeches (Eduard Goldstücker, Pavel Reiman),[74] it was Eduard Goldstücker's turn with his Marxist 'grounding' of Kafka in his paper 'Franz Kafka from the Prague perspective' in which he picked up on the aforementioned biographical topoi. He argued, among other things, that Kafka could only be fully understood by taking Prague as the starting point; that the Prague context forms the base out of which Kafka's works grow; that the author seeks out a connection with his people, to which his work also bears witness. He repeatedly declared his conviction that the 'Prague perspective' would prove that 'answers to some questions relating to Kafka's life and oeuvre could in fact be best provided by taking Prague as the starting point'.[75] He continued by arguing that Kafka's 'Prague-related life issues' were reflected in his work and, accordingly, that only the understanding of the wider historical-social context could form a steady 'base' for the understanding of Kafka's work, that is of the 'superstructure'. In Goldstücker's terms, it was precisely the 'fundamental scholarly [i.e. Marxist] illumination of the issues [...] encapsulated in the caption Kafka and Prague' that was the 'key' to Kafka.[76] This 'base' approach gave precedence to biographical and social factors over the 'superstructure' of his texts.

Goldstücker's paper was followed by František Kautman's presentation 'Franz Kafka and Czech Literature', which listed the affinities between Kafka's oeuvre and Czech literature and culture, but rated these rather as coincidental and fleeting.[77] This notwithstanding, he too was of the opinion that Kafka's oeuvre was inconceivable without the Czech context. The article published in

---

74 Pavel Reiman, Kafka a dnešek (Kafka today). In: Eduard Goldstücker – František Kautman – Pavel Reiman (eds), *Franz Kafka: liblická konference 1963* (Franz Kafka: Liblice Conference 1963). Prague: ČSAV 1963, pp. 13–20. Reiman also had a presentation and closing words to the conference. See Pavel Reiman, O fragmentárnosti Kafkova díla (On the fragmentarity of Kafka's oeuvre). In: Eduard Goldstücker – František Kautman – Pavel Reiman (eds), *Franz Kafka: liblická konference 1963*. Prague: ČSAV 1963, pp. 213–218; Pavel Reiman, Závěrečné slovo (Closing words). In: Eduard Goldstücker – František Kautman – Pavel Reiman (eds), *Franz Kafka: liblická konferen"ce 1963*. Prague: ČSAV 1963, pp. 275–277.

75 Goldstücker, O přístupu ke Kafkovi, p. 5; Goldstücker, *Na téma Franz Kafka*, 64; Eduard Goldstücker, Über Franz Kafka aus der Prager Sicht, p. 26.

76 Goldstücker, *Na téma Franz Kafka*, p. 73.

77 František Kautman, Franz Kafka a česká literatura (Franz Kafka and Czech literature). In: Eduard Goldstücker – František Kautman – Pavel Reiman (eds), *Franz Kafka: liblická konference 1963* (Franz Kafka: Liblice Conference 1963). Prague: ČSAV 1963, pp. 39–75. For further early publications on this topic see František Kautman, Ještě jednou Franz Kafka z pražské perspektivy (Franz Kafka, once again from the Prague perspective). *Plamen* 6 (1964), No. 8, pp. 165–166, as well as František Kautman, Franz Kafka a Čechy (Franz Kafka and Bohemia). *Literární archiv* 1 (1966), pp. 179–197.

Literární noviny also judged these two plenary lectures to be of central importance.[78]

In this context the opinion of Václav Černý is particularly worth mentioning. Černý, who had begun to write about Kafka as early as the 1940s, saw in Kafka a forerunner of the existentialists and, following Sartre's impulse, took a philosophical approach to Kafka.[79] Tellingly, he was not invited to the Liblice conference where, it seemed, the 'comrades' preferred to stick to themselves with their 'grounding' of Kafka.[80] Nevertheless, the Liblice conference could hardly escape anyone's notice, and he referred to it in the following way:

> Here, the number of reviews began to rise dramatically in 1963, that is, at the time of the third Writers' Congress and of the largely unsuccessful international conference on Kafka in Liblice. Goldstücker was quite clumsy in his endeavours at the conference to bang Kafka into the size and shape of the social, if not socialist, poet. He had only been released from prison a short time before and the regime compensated him by securing him a chair at Charles University. Goldstücker did what he could and was also prepared to do what was not allowed to be done for others. Yet Kafka had been sanctioned – a sign of the changing times![81]

Sartre's foray into the reading of a literary work and his drive to liberate culture from the clutches of politics failed to make real inroads at the Liblice conference; Kafka's selectively narrated biography continued to take precedence in the endeavour to ground him in a local, social and national context. Nevertheless, his writings did get through to readers, even if they failed to secure a central position in the interest of literary scholars.

CZECH READINGS OF CZECH TEXTS

Alongside Kautman's paper, which under the circumstances of the period was a remarkable pioneering achievement, it was the first publications of Kafka's Czech letters in 1963, fragmentary as they were, which broke new ground for Kafka scholarship.[82] The first widely available book edition of Kafka's letters to his family and of his office writings, which includes Kafka's

---

78 The conference was also commented upon in Věra Macháčková, Konference o díle Franze Kafky (Conference on the work of Franz Kafka). *Rudé právo*, 31.5.1963, p. 3.

79 See Václav Černý, *První sešit o existencialismu* (The First Book on Existentialism). Prague: Václav Petr 1948, p. 24 f., or Čermák, Die Kafka-Rezeption in Böhmen, p. 232.

80 Černý published the same on Kafka in a Slovak journal. Václav Černý, Hrsť poznámok o kafkovskom románe a o kafkovskom svete (Some comments on Kafka's novel and on Kafka's world). *Slovenské pohľady* 79 (1963), No. 10, pp. 80–95.

81 Václav Černý, *Paměti 1945–1972* (Memoires 1945–1972). Brno: Atlantis 1992, p. 475.

82 See Kafka, Neznámé dopisy Franze Kafky, and Loužil, Dopisy Franze Kafky.

Czech texts published in 1963 in Czechoslovakia, were only published ten years later in Germany.[83] On the back of the 1963 publications Prague had an advantage in Kafka-related knowledge and scholarship. But despite what is to be gleaned from Eduard Goldstücker's polemical articles, these letters hardly made a solid case for the 'single correct interpretation' of Kafka's ambiguous writings; nor did they justify the claim that Kafka could only be interpreted 'from the Prague perspective'. Also the fact that Kafka was proficient in Czech was by no means new knowledge. Since, however, prior to the publication of Kafka's Czech texts in 1963 people had had to rely on witnesses rather than textual evidence to underpin their claims, this had left a lot of room for the imagination.

So it was, for example, in 1947, that Hugo Siebenschein in the otherwise respectable monograph *Franz Kafka and Prague* was able to claim somewhat surreally that Franz Kafka, whom he categorised as a 'surreal writer', sang only in Czech:

> The language of his political friends was Czech; it was only in Czech that he could be as carefree and curious as a child; it was only in Czech that he sang. More sceptical friends were surprised when they saw him amongst the crowd of Czech demonstrators singing nationalist, Sokol and Socialist songs. He was frequently caught singing at the top of his lungs 'Hey, Slavs', pale and excited, apparently oblivious to everything around him, his timid eyes aglow with enthusiasm.[84]

Another and no less problematic contemporary witness of Kafka and his relationship with his milieu – including his Czech setting – emerged in 1951 in the figure of Gustav Janouch.[85] A few years later, in 1958, Klaus Wagenbach's influential monograph was published in Germany which, drawing on the primary Prague sources, depicted Kafka's anarchism as well as, with reference to Hermann Kafka, the Czech blood running through Kafka's veins.[86]

The edition of Kafka's Czech texts did not just mean the next forays in this direction, however; they also brought new, unknown sources to light.

83 See Franz Kafka, *Briefe an Ottla und die Familie* (Letters to Ottla and Family). Edited by Hartmut Binder and Klaus Wagenbach. Frankfurt am Main: S. Fischer [1974] 1975; Kafka, *Letters to Friends…*; Franz Kafka, *Amtliche Schriften* (Office Writings). Edited by Klaus Hermsdorf. Berlin: Akademie-Verlag 1984.

84 Siebenschein, Prostředí a čas, p. 21f.

85 In the next edition of 1968 Janouch put further coals on the fire of the Czech bias by adding further details. See Gustav Janouch, *Gespräche mit Kafka* (Conversations with Kafka). Frankfurt am Main: S. Fischer 1951. For more details on this see Marek Nekula, Poznámky (Comments). In: Gustav Janouch, *Hovory s Kafkou* (Conversations with Kafka). Translation by Eva Kolářová, ed. by Marek Nekula, afterword by Veronika Tuckerová. Prague: Torst 2009, pp. 223–252.

86 See Klaus Wagenbach, *Franz Kafka. Eine Biographie seiner Jugend 1883–1912* (Franz Kafka: A Biography of his Youth 1883–1912). Berlin: Wagenbach 2006, p. 19, 23.

O. Beneš and P. Lecler, translators of these sources into French, expressed the impact of these letters with impressive precision in their decision to title their translation 'Kafka inconnu' (Unknown Kafka).[87] Kafka, and not his literary writings, takes centre stage here, and it is the desire to discover the unknown and even – in the Czechoslovak context – taboo Kafka which drives this obsession with revelation. It is also remarkable that both 'discoveries' of Kafka's Czech texts which show Kafka 'from the Prague perspective', and thus reinforce the impact of the Liblice conference, were made public independently of the conference, namely in the journal *Plamen* and the museum's journal. At the Liblice conference Josef Čermák reported on the 'unknown Kafka papers' – that is, on Kafka's letters to Ottla and his family. In the conference proceedings which were published in Czech in the very same year of the conference, Čermák referred explicitly to the publication of the letters in the July edition of *Plamen*,[88] but they were not reprinted in the conference volume. It was only after 1989 that these writings were published as part of the critical edition of Kafka's works.[89] This makes their publication from 1963 so important because they seemingly support the 'grounding' of Kafka.

At the same time we are dealing here – as is often the case with Kafka – with more than one paradox. Although the editing of the unknown letters in *Plamen* makes clear that Franz Kafka asked Ottla and her Czech husband Josef David to translate his letters to the Workmen's Accident Insurance Company from German into Czech, the private letters to Ottla, *née* Kafka, and Josef David published in 1963, which made a considerable contribution to the myth of Kafka's affinity with Czech language, culture and the people, because they were written in Czech. Then, the publication provided the Czech public and thus also Czech Germanists with proof that in these non-translated letters to his relatives Kafka's written (and spoken) Czech was largely impeccable. It was not too great a leap of imagination to claim that he was inextricably connected with Czech language and culture and thus was best understood 'from the Prague perspective'.

In reality, however, Kafka's Czech was by no means as flawless as this edition of his letters led readers to believe. On four small A5-pages of the Czech

---

87 Franz Kafka, Kafka inconnu. Translation by O. Beneš and Paul Lecler. *La vie tchécoslovaque* 11 (1963), No. 10, pp. 26–27.

88 Josef Čermák, Zpráva o neznámých kafkovských dokumentech (Report on unknown Kafka documents). In: Eduard Goldstücker – František Kautman – Pavel Reiman (eds), *Franz Kafka: liblická konference 1963* (Franz Kafka: Liblice Conference 1963). Prague: ČSAV 1963, pp. 249–252.

89 The edition in Franz Kafka, *Dopisy Ottle a rodině* (Letters to Ottla and Family). Translation, annotation and afterword by Vojtěch Saudek. Prague: Aurora 1996, is however not without errors and was only corrected in Franz Kafka, *Dopisy rodině* (Letters to Family). Translation by Vojtěch Saudek. Edited and commentary by Václav Maidl and Marek Nekula. Prague: Nakladatelství Franze Kafky 2005, and Franz Kafka, *Briefe 1914–1917* (Letters 1914–1917). Edited by Hans-Gerd Koch. Frankfurt am Main: S. Fischer 2005; Franz Kafka, *Briefe 1918–1920* (Letters 1918–1920). Edited by Hans-Gerd Koch. Frankfurt am Main: S. Fischer 2013.

text, there are 53 corrections to the original which present Kafka's Czech in the printed version in a more positive light. Here are just a few examples based on a comparison of the manuscripts held in the Bodleian Library (Oxford):[90] in the Czech edition from 1963 *z**ú**častnil* instead of the original *z**ů**častnil*, *lyža**ř**ský* instead of *lyža**r**ský*, *nád**ě**je* instead of *nád**e**je*, [ty] ***j**si* instead of [ty] *si*, *hebrejsk**y*** instead of *Hebrejsk**ý***, *toti**ž*** instead of *tot**í**ž*, *oprav j**í** to* instead of *oprav j**i** to*, *nep**ří**jemné* instead of *nep**ři**jemné*, *léka**ř**ské* instead of *léka**r**ské*, *děkuj**i*** instead of [já] *děkuj**í***, *n**a**bídku* instead of *n**á**bídku*, *půjde**š*** instead of *půjde**s***, *več**e**r* instead of *več**é**r*, *napíše**š*** instead of *napíše**s***, *nemá**š*** instead of *nemá**s***, *ke **mně*** instead of *ke **mě***, *s n**i**mi* instead of *s n**í**mi*, *ješt**ě*** instead of *ješt**e***, ***j**si chtěl* instead of *si chtěl*, *o **b**erl**í**nském* instead of *o **B**erl**i**nském*, ***b**erl**í**nské cen**y*** instead of ***B**erl**i**nské cen**ý***, etc.

The most significant example for this edition is the correction of an error in Kafka's use of the aspect, which is the best indicator of native or near-native proficiency in Czech. The Czech edition corrects the original *'buď bude třeba abych se dále léčil totiž buď bude nádeje že bych se mohl ještě dále **vy**léčit'* (on one hand it will be necessary to stay in the sanatorium which means, on one hand there is a hope that I might *further fully recover*) in *'buď bude třeba abych se dále léčil totiž buď bude nádĕje že bych se mohl ještě dále léčit'*[91] (on one hand it will be necessary to stay in the sanatorium, which means, on one hand there is a hope that I might recover further), because the original seems to be 'incorrect': the perfective ***vy**léčit* (fully recover) is in opposition to *dále* (further).

It was probably such unknown corrections that enabled Kafka to be seen as completely bilingual and encouraged people to cling to the belief in Kafka's inner affinity with the Czech language.[92] Thus, for example, Jaromír Loužil, editor of Kafka's official letters to the Workmen's Accident Insurance Company drafted or translated by Kafka's relatives, claimed, in spite of his knowledge and somewhat prematurely, that they prove his almost complete proficiency in the Czech language; according to Loužil we are most certainly dealing with much more than the version of Czech as we know it spoken by Austrian lawyers.[93] Yet with a few exceptions, these texts can hardly be considered authentic Czech writings by Kafka in view of the fact that

---

90 For further on this see, facsimiles of the texts in Nekula, *Jazyky Franze Kafky*, and ib. pp. 84–94. My emphases.

91 Kafka, Neznámé dopisy Franze Kafky, p. 93.

92 A similar approach can be found in Zdeněk Nejedlý's corrective interventions in the edition of letters written by Friedrich/Bedřich Smetana and member of his family; it was on the basis of this edition that he underpinned his assumption of the nationalist and purely Czech orientation of the Smetana family. See Marek Nekula – Lucie Rychnovská, Smetanova čeština v dobovém kontextu (Smetana's Czech in historical context). *Hudební věda* 47 (2010), No. 1, pp. 43–76.

93 Loužil, Dopisy Franze Kafky, p. 59.

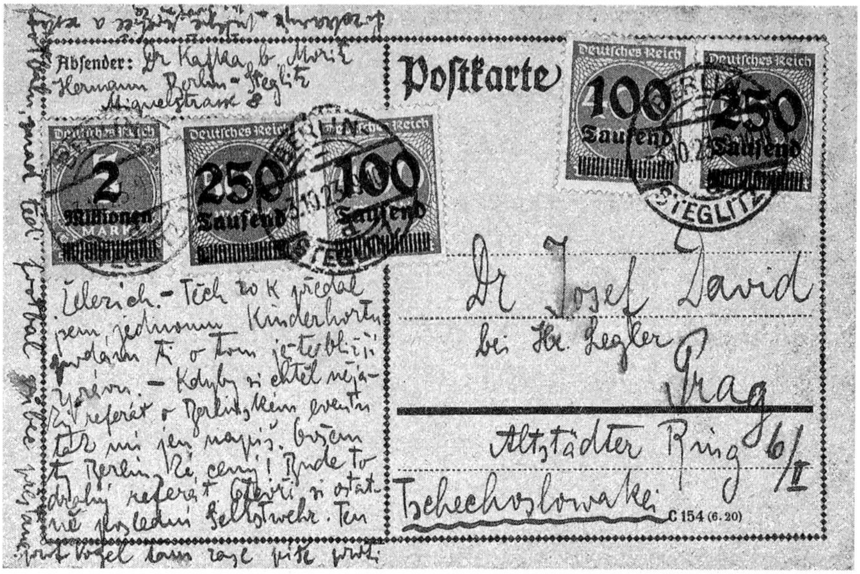

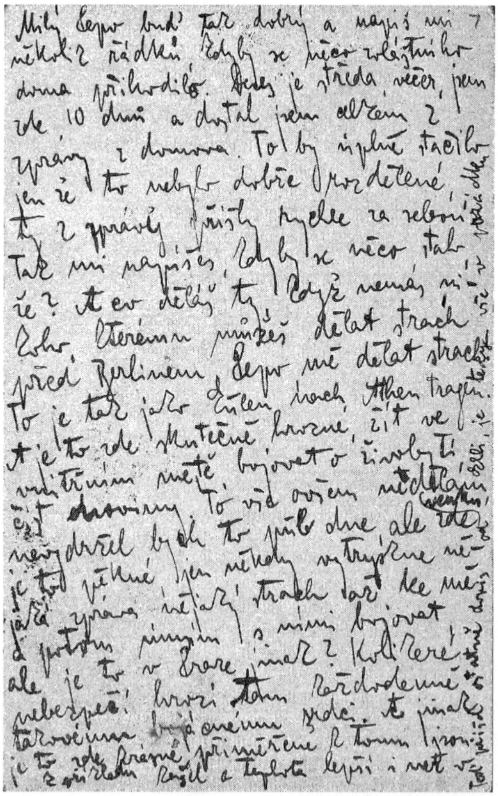

Franz Kafka to Josef David, 3 October 1923. Archiv Kritische Kafka-Ausgabe.

they were either drafted and proved for Kafka or translated from German into Czech.[94]

References to Kafka's affinity with the 'Czech element' also came from elsewhere. I am referring here to the memoirs of Anna Pouzarová, a Czech woman who as a 21 year old worked for the Kafka family as the governess of Kafka's sisters. These were published in 1964 in the journal *Plamen* (Flame) and the newspaper *Práce* (Labour) and were given a distinct slant by the editor's commentary.[95] The commentary tells the story of a little known love between the 'attractive and slim' Czech woman and the two-years-younger Kafka who would always urge Anna to read out loud to his sisters from *The Grandmother* by the Czech national writer Božena Němcová. In a single swoop, then, we have here the national appropriation of Kafka, not just in a linguistic but also in a literary and erotic sense.[96] More props to support this appropriation could have been garnered from letters to Milena, in which fragments of Czech from Milena's Czech letters flow into Kafka's German letters and in which there are scattered references to Czech authors (and which were published in 1966 in a popular edition).[97] Pavel Reiman did just this at the end of his afterword to the Czech edition of *The Trial*; his otherwise objective afterword ends by expressing his joy that this Franz Kafka novel has now been published in 'the language of his Milena Jesenská'.[98] The point is, however, that in the case of Anna Pouzarová we are dealing with a private matter and in Milena Jesenská's case with private letters, and not with literary texts. Although the reference to Němcová is important, it remains the case that in the 1960s – apart from the identification of such moments of affinity commendably compiled by Kautman[99] – there was a dearth of serious analyses of Kafka's writings that would and could show this side of Kafka 'from the Prague perspective' on the

---

94 Verified individually in Nekula, *Jazyky Franze Kafky*. Friedrich/Bedřich Smetana also proceeded in a similar fashion. He is another example of a figure co-opted for Czech culture, who, unlike Kafka however, became involved after 1861 in the national culture and its network of organisations. See Marek Nekula – Lucie Rychnovská, Bedřich Smetana's use of the Czech language. In: *Musicalia. Journal of the Czech Museum of Music* 1 (2012), No. 1–2, pp. 6–38.

95 Anna Pouzarová, Ze vzpomínek vychovatelky v rodině Franze Kafky (From the memoirs of the governess in Franz Kafka's family). Recorded by Hanuš Frank and Karel Šmejkal. *Plamen* 6 (1964), pp. 104–107; Frank Hanuš – Karel Šmejkal, Po stopách Franze Kafky do jižních Čech (On the trail of Franz Kafka in South Bohemia). A. Pouzarová's memoirs recorded by Hanuš Frank and Karel Šmejkal. *Práce*, 16.2.1964, p. 5.

96 Pavel Eisner is convinced that the idea of the erotic appropriation of another culture can even serve as a general model for German literature in Prague and Bohemia. See Pavel Eisner, *Milenky. Německý básník a česká žena* (Lovers. The German Writer and the Czech Woman). Prague: Dolínek 1930.

97 Franz Kafka, *Briefe an Milena* (The Letters to Milena). Edited and with an afterword by Willy Haas. Frankfurt am Main: S. Fischer 1966.

98 See Reiman, 'Proces' Franze Kafky, p. 225.

99 Kautman, Franz Kafka a česká literatura; František Kautman, Franz Kafka und die tschechische Literatur (Franz Kafka and Czech literature). In: Eduard Goldstücker – František Kautman – Paul

basis of his literary texts. Goldstücker's call for a 'grounding' of Kafka and his interpretative approach to Kafka 'from the Prague perspective' remained entrenched in biographical and sociological arguments.

A further problem arises in connection with this. The key term 'Prague' in 'from the Prague perspective' was not only bound up very strongly in the context of the Liblice conference but also in the press, which endorsed the arguments of the Liblice conference,[100] with the local context and, accordingly, also with Czech themes and a 'Czech perspective'. This is very clear in the Goldstücker quotation, cited earlier, which I shall repeat in these closing remarks in order to highlight his appropriation of Kafka as 'one of us' that emerges here:

> For *us in Czechoslovakia* he [= Kafka] means more. He was born *in Prague*; his entire life and his entire oeuvre are *bound up with our capital city* and *our land*.[101]

If we consider the actual proportion of Czech to Jewish elements in Kafka's real life, his circle of friends, correspondence, reading and writing, it becomes clear that the co-opting of the term 'Prague' in the motto 'from the Prague perspective' for the local social context as well as Czech national literature and language corresponds with a partial omission of the Jewish dimension of Kafka's biography and oeuvre. Nevertheless, the Liblice conference of 1963 may well be a part of Bohemian culture's return to its Jewish roots. For example, there followed in 1964 the renaming of the *Památník národního utrpení* (Monument of national suffering) to *Památník Terezín* (Terezín Memorial) and it was during this time that plans for a ghetto museum in Terezín were forged. This, however, has little to do with Kafka's texts and the Liblice conference of 1963 followed another path.

Reimann (eds), *Franz Kafka aus Prager Sicht 1963* (Franz Kafka from the Prague Perspective 1963). Prague: ČSAV 1965, pp. 44–77.

100 See, for example, Ivo Fleischmann (ed.), Franz Kafka a náš svět (Kafka and our world). Articles by Eduard Goldstücker, Ernst Fischer, Roger Garaudy, Ivan Sviták. *Literární noviny* 12 (1963), No. 23, p. 3; Karel Kosík, Hašek a Kafka neboli groteskní svět (Hašek and Kafka, or the grotesque world). *Plamen* 5 (1963), No. 6, pp. 95–102; Hanuš – Šmejkal, Z vzpomínek vychovatelky v rodině Franze Kafky; František Kautman, Boje o Kafku včera a dnes (Disputes over Kafka then and now). *Literární noviny* 14 (1964), No. 27, p. 5; František Kautman, Pražská německá literatura (German literature in Prague). *Literární noviny* 14 (1964), No. 48, p. 4.

101 Goldstücker, Dnešní potřeby, zítřejší perspektivy, p. 9. My emphases.

THE 'BEING' OF ODRADEK: FRANZ KAFKA IN HIS JEWISH CONTEXT

> Some say the word Odradek is of Slavonic origin and seek to trace its derivation on that basis. Others believe it was originally German and was merely influenced by the Slavonic. The uncertainty surrounding both interpretations, however, suggests that perhaps neither is correct, particularly since neither of them furnishes a meaning for the word.[1]

This passage concerning the uncertain origin of the word Odradek is from Kafka's story 'The householder's concern', written in 1916–17 and included in the collection *A Country Doctor: Short Stories*, published by Kurt Wolff in Munich and Leipzig on 12 May 1920. Not only is the origin of the word (and, incidentally, of the 'householder's concerns') unclear: there is no telling who or what Odradek actually is. Pavel Trost attempted to answer the second question by considering the first. Taking up the etymological challenge posed at the start of the story itself, Trost decided on the Czech option and, removing the apparently diminutive suffix *-ek* from the Czech neologism Odradek, interpreted the remaining O**D**RA**D** as a coded form of the name KAFKA.[2] In this way he connected the story about the 'concerns of the householder' with Kafka's own family life. It also makes sense if we read the fragment O**D**RA**D** in the Hebrew manner, from right to left; even more so if we see in Gregor SAMSA in 'The metamorphosis', as well as in *K.* in Josef K. in *The Trial* and in *The Castle*, an allusion to Kafka's name, which means 'jackdaw' and also plays a role in other stories, notably in 'A page from an old manuscript' and 'The hunter Gracchus'.

However, Trost's answer to the first question is imprecise, while any answer to the second, as to who Odradek actually is, is problematic. As the story itself indicates, the word *odradek* does not exist in any Slavonic language (and thus not in Czech), just as the being named *Odradek* has no real existence. But in principle it could very easily be a Czech word – and one with a fairly clear meaning. The root *odrad-* immediately suggests the verb *odradit*, which has the following approximate meanings: 1) to deter, discour-

1 Franz Kafka, The householder's concern. In: *Franz Kafka, Stories 1904–1924*. Translated by J. A. Underwood, with a foreword by Jorge Luis Borges. London: Abacus 1995, p. 206.

2 Pavel Trost, Franz Kafka und das Prager Deutsch (Franz Kafka and 'Prague German'). *Germanistica Pragensia* 2 (1964), 29–37, here p. 33. See also Pavel Trost, Der Name Kafka (The proper name Kafka). *Beiträge zur Namenforschung* 18 (1983), No. 1, 52–53.

age or spoil the pleasure or interest of someone in something, to take away someone's joy or resolve, to intimidate, to estrange someone from something; 2) to put someone off another person, to spoil someone's relationship with or liking for another person.[3] In this case, unlike in Trost's interpretation, the *-ek* is not a diminutive suffix but a suffix denoting the result of an action, analogous to words like *výrob-ek* (=product, from *vyrob-it*, to produce).[4] This would give the word *odradek* the meaning 'something created through discouragement or intimidation'. It is a peculiar feature of such formations that they denote only concrete or abstract objects, but not persons – that is, not sentient, thinking beings with the capacity to be discouraged or intimidated. Odradek, however, is an oddity. For the father (i.e. the 'householder') it is only a *Wesen* ('being') or *Gebilde* ('entity'), a mere *es* ('it') which therefore cannot die; yet at the same time it is clearly more than a mere 'it', since *er* ('he') can move around, laugh, talk and be silent. If we accept Trost's interpretation that there is a link between Odradek and Kafka, and the assumption that Kafka's story obliquely refers to his own relationship with his father, then the writer who created this word and mentions its 'derivation' must have had a very good knowledge of Czech.

While Czech etymology can make sense of the word,[5] any attempt at a German derivation is doomed to fail, notwithstanding the observation in the story that '*andere meinen, es stamme aus dem Deutschen, vom Slawischen sei es nur beeinflußt*' ('others believe it was originally German and was merely influenced by the Slavonic'). This is a paradox that points either to another language or beyond language altogether. But both 'some' and 'others' address the question of Odradek's existence only from an external point of view and in relation to language: Odradek is reduced to '*das Wort Odradek*' ('the word Odradek') and his/its existence to a matter of linguistic appurtenance. Here, too, it is not hard to read biographical allusions into the text: the 'word' as a cipher for Kafka's writing; the external assigning of linguistic identity as a metaphor for linguistic polarization in a land peopled by both Czechs and Germans. The Kafka family had to deal with this polarization at every school admission, at every census time, and in everyday reality, where the question of their linguistic identity ignored another reality, another identity. In contrast to all other members of the Kafka family, who declared Czech as their common language,

3 See Hugo Siebenschein, *Česko-německý slovník* (Czech-German Dictionary), vol 2. Prague: Státní pedagogické nakladatelství 1983, p. 700f.

4 For the formation of this group of Czech words, see Dušan Šlosar, Slovotvorba (Word Formation). In: Petr Karlík – Marek Nekula – Zdenka Rusínová (eds), *Příruční mluvnice češtiny* (Handbook of Czech Grammar). Prague: Nakladatelství Lidové noviny 1996, pp. 109–225, here p. 146.

5 Another interpretation of the word Odradek sees a possible analogy with the proper name Odkolek (also the name of a firm). See Johannes Urzidil, Von Odkolek zu Odradek (From Odkolek to Odradek). *Schweizer Monatshefte* 50 (1970), No. 1, pp. 957–972. There is also the village of Ostředek near Prague, though it is unlikely to have any significance for Kafka.

German was entered as the common language next to Franz Kafka's name in the 1910 census.[6] It is inconceivable that this disparity would not have led to a 'clash with the father';[7] Franz Kafka lived with his family in a single household and the declared language his father provided for the rest of the family was called into question by Franz Kafka's entry. This was one of the conflicts that came to a head in Kafka's family in and after 1910, besides his perceived lack of commitment to the factory and his Jewish 'rebirth'.

Not long after Kafka wrote 'The householder's concern', Max Brod addressed similar issues in his essay 'Jews, German, Czechs'. Writing in July 1918, he said:

> I do not feel myself to be a member of the German people, but am a friend of Germanness and also, by language and education [...], culturally related to Germanness. I am a friend of Czechness, yet am in essential ways [...] culturally detached from Czechness. I cannot find a simpler formulation for an existence in the Jewish diaspora of a nationally divided city.[8]

If 'the uncertainty surrounding both interpretations [...] suggests perhaps neither is correct, particularly since neither of them furnishes a meaning for the word', it might be better to move away from the linguistic derivation of Odradek and the external perspective of 'some' and 'others', and focus instead on the 'being' of Odradek, as Kafka did in his story.

In the second paragraph of the story, which considers Odradek's *Wesen* (being), he/it is described as a '*eine flache sternartige Zwirnspule*' ('a flat, star-shaped spool').[9] Under '*Spule*', Grimm's dictionary gives the Austrian dialect usage of the word (meaning No. 8) as '*Quirl*' ('a whisk'), a utensil which in its traditional Central European form has a star-shaped wooden head.[10] Grimm also lists the expression '*Zwirnstern*' ('a star-shaped spool').[11] The phrase '*eine flache sternartige Zwirnspule*' ('a flat, star-shaped spool') can thus be seen as

---

6 See Kurt Krolop, Zu den Erinnerungen Anna Lichtensterns an Franz Kafka. Ke vzpomínkám Anny Lichtensternové na Franze Kafku (On Anna Lichtenstern's recollections of Franz Kafka). *Germanistica Pragensia* 5 (1968), pp. 21–60.

7 Franz Kafka, *Kafka's Selected Stories*. Translated and edited by Stanley Corngold. New York, London: W. W. Norton 2005, p. 12.

8 First published in Max Brod, *Im Kampf um das Judentum. Politische Essays* (In the Struggle for Jewishness: Political Essays). Vienna, Berlin: R. Löwit Verlag 1920, p. 15. See also Marek Nekula, Theodor Lessing und Max Brod. Eine mißlungene Begegnung (Theodor Lessing and Max Brod: A failed encounter). In: *brücken. Germanistisches Jahrbuch Tschechien – Slowakei*. NF 5 (1997), pp. 115–122, here p. 118.

9 Franz Kafka, *Ein Landarzt und andere Drucke zu Lebzeiten* (A Country Doctor and Other Texts Published in his Lifetime). Ed. by Hans-Gerd Koch. Frankfurt am Main: S. Fischer 1994, p. 222.

10 Jacob Grimm, *Deutsches Wörterbuch* (German Dictionary). Vol. 10. Leipzig: Verlag von S. Hirzel, 1919, column 221.

11 Grimm, *Deutsches Wörterbuch*, vol. 16, 1954, column 1320.

referring to the Star of David, and hence to Jewishness in general. But this is no proud 'being', no unequivocal identity. The Star of David-shaped 'Odradek' is described in terms of 'rupture', 'fissure' and 'senselessness' – undermining any belief in a fixed, authentic, 'organic' and hence meaningful Jewish identity:

> At first it looks like a flat, star-shaped spool for thread, and in fact, it does seem to be wound with thread, although these appear to be only old, torn-off pieces of thread of the most varied sorts and colours [...] / It is tempting to think that this figure once had some sort of functional shape and is now merely broken. But this does not seem to be the case; at least there is no evidence for such a speculation; nowhere can you see any other beginnings or fractures that would point to anything of the kind; true, the whole thing seems meaningless yet in its own way complete.[12]

This interpretation is supported by others traits of Odradek – *'beweglich'* (nimble), *'nicht zu fangen'* (cannot be caught) and *'unbestimmter Wohnsitz'* ('of no fixed abode') recalling the rootlessness of the Jews as a result of repeated expulsions. This sort of 'being', which used to be called Jewish, is more than simply 'the householder's concern' in Kafka's story. The battle over Jewish identity was a problem in Kafka's relationship with his father as well as with respect to his civil identity. Thus 'beings' like Odradek were defined not only 'from within', but also 'from outside', as the allusion to the antisemitic figures, like 'of no fixed abode', in this story shows.

There are also other specific allusions in this story, such as the reference to Odradek's laugh, which sounded *'wie man es ohne Lungen hervorbringen kann'* ('[like the kind of laugh] that can be produced without lungs' and *'wie das Rascheln in gefallenen Blättern'* ('like the rustle of fallen leaves.'). This can be understood autobiographically as a recollection of the first symptoms of Kafka's pulmonary illness, which appeared in August 1917 and were diagnosed in early September. That is why in this chapter I shall, exceptionally, follow the biographical path taken by Trost and others and go back to the origins of Franz Kafka and his family, linking their story to that of the Jews' emergence from the ghetto and the struggle for Jewish identity.

OUT OF THE GHETTO

In Austria and Bohemia, it is customary to date the first crumbling of the ghetto walls to 1781, when Joseph II made life easier for non-Catholics in the Habsburg Empire. But the emancipation of the Jews did not proceed smoothly – neither at the political level nor in public life. The decree of 1781

12 Franz Kafka, *Kafka's Selected Stories*, p. 72.

relaxed legal restrictions on the Jewish population initially only in commerce. The regulations and directives that followed in the 1780s and 1790s were eventually codified in a systematic review of Jewish legislation (the *Judensystemalpatent*) in 1797.[13] Jewish inclusion in the community also entailed obligations, among them limitations on the role of religion. The abolition of rabbinical courts and use of German in 1784 was the first step in that direction. Jews in the Bohemian lands had to take non-composed non-Jewish (German) surnames (1787),[14] attend German-language schools,[15] use German in dealings with the authorities (e.g. in public registers and accounts books) and so on. The fears of some rabbis of a decline in the use of Hebrew and Yiddish (which Kafka's south Bohemian grandparents had still spoken) were already being realized in the first half of the 19th century.

Discrimination in its various forms – from the law limiting the number of Jews entitled to an official wedding ceremony (which included Kafka's grandparents) to restrictions on freedom of movement, continuing isolation in the ghettoes, low levels of tolerance, and stigmatization by the use of 'particular' surnames – disappeared only gradually. Thus the name *Kafka* (from *kavka* [kafka] = jackdaw) could be classed as one of those names that could stigmatize their bearers by referring to some supposedly typical characteristic such as hair colour or texture (*Kafka*, *Schwarz* (Black), *Roth* (Red); *Kraus* (Curly) etc.), nose shape (*Nossig* or *Nosek*) or pronunciation (*Khon*, *Khol* rather than *Kohn*, *Kohl*). When in 1836 Jews were given the option of dropping their hitherto prescribed, mainly Hebrew first names like *Moses* and *Sarah* and adopting neutral German names, many took it up. Kafka's forbears born before that year all had names like *Josef*, *Jakob*, *Isaak*, *Adam*, *Samuel*, *Sara*, *Salamon*, and *Jonas*, while members of Kafka's parents' generation tended to have 'German' names such as *Heinrich*, *Hermann*, *Ludwig*, *Alfred*, *Richard*, or *Philip*.[16] The right

---

13 See August Stein, O židovské obci v Čechách (On the Jewish Community in Bohemia). In: *Kalendář česko-židovský na rok 1887/1888*, pp. 131–165. See Michael K. Silber, Josephinian reforms. In: *The YIVO Encyclopedia of Jews in Eastern Europe* (online).

14 The names are not exclusively German. Besides the Kafkas, we can also find in Osek a family named Holub (in fact the headstone in the cemetery bears a Germanized form of the name, 'Hollub'), suggesting that Czech names and sobriquets soon became commonplace – a reaction against the 'unintelligibility' of Hebrew and Yiddish names and of the Hebrew script in general. More see Jiří Kuděla, Germanizace židovských jmen v Čechách (Germanization of Jewish names in Bohemia). *Židovská ročenka*, 2005, pp. 29–39.

15 See J. S. Kraus, Německo-židovské školy v Čechách (German-Jewish schools in Bohemia). In: *Kalendář česko-židovský na rok 1882/1883*, pp. 117–125.

16 See Kafka's family tree in Anthony Northey, *Kafkas Mischpoche* (Kafka's Mishpoche). Berlin: Wagenbach 1988; Anthony Northey, Die Kafkas: Juden? Christen? Tschechen? Deutsche? (The Kafkas: Jews? Christians? Czechs? Germans?) In: Kurt Krolop – Hans Dieter Zimmermann (eds), *Kafka und Prag. Colloquium im Goethe-Institut Prag. 24.–27. November 1992* (Kafka and Prague: Colloquium in the Goethe Institute in Prague, 24–27 November 1992). Berlin, New York: de Gruyter 1994, pp. 11–32.

to use Czech first names, introduced as part of the repeal of discriminatory legislation after 1848, had little effect on established practice, at least not for a while. Thus in the Kafka family, apart from Franz himself, there were his siblings Georg (1885–86), Heinrich (1887–88), Gabriela (1889–1941), Valerie (1890–1942) and Ottilie (1892–1943). An exception in that generation was Franz's cousin Zdeněk, son of his uncle Philip (or Philipp – both forms can be found in Hermann Kafka's letter of 25 July 1882) and his wife Klára Kafka, née Poláček.

The Kafkas' road out of the ghetto can be mapped not only through their names but in the ghetto itself and its dissolution. Johann Gottfried Sommer records that in the 1830s there were 50 houses and 382 inhabitants in the south Bohemian village of Osek near Strakonice, where Kafka's paternal grandfather and his family lived.[17] In regions of mixed nationality such as this, the majority of the population in rural communities was Czech while the elites and holders of administrative authority tended to be German. Sommer tells us there were twenty Jewish families in Osek in the late 1830s[18] – though that figure only included families approved under a law regulating the number of Jewish families. That means that in Osek – or rather Little Osek, in Jewish Street and around the Synagogue – there was a community of around a hundred. *Die Notablenversammlung der Israeliten Böhmens in Prag* (The Prague Compendium of Notable Jews in Bohemia) records 20 families and 95 community members.[19] An 1837 map shows nineteen houses in Jewish Street alone, with another sixteen beyond the synagogue on the road to Radomyšl; in the 'Christian' part of the village there were seventeen houses.[20] The land register for the year 1837 lists a total of 55 houses (including the castle), 94 'residential units' and 406 inhabitants – making an average of four people per household. That would mean 32.3 residential units in Jewish Street, a figure corresponding to that in the register (32) for households occupied by those engaged in the trades Jews were allowed to pursue before 1848. On this basis we can assume that 130–140 people lived in Jewish Street alone. Add to that

17 See Northey, Die Kafkas, p. 12, and Alena Wagnerová, *„Im Hauptquartier des Lärms." Die Familie Kafka aus Prag* ('In the Headquarters of Noise': The Family Kafka from Prague). Berlin: Bollmann 1997, p. 29f.

18 See Johann Gottfried Sommer, *Das Königreich Böhmen statistisch-topographisch dargestellt* (The Kingdom of Bohemia from a Statistical and Topographical Perspective). Vol. 8, Prague 1840, p. 103.

19 See Albert Kohn, *Die Notablenversammlung der Israeliten Böhmens in Prag, ihre Berathungen und Beschlüsse. Mit statistischen Tabellen über die israelitischen Gemeinden, Synagogen, Schulen und Rabbinate in Böhmen* (The Prague Compendium of Notable Jews in Bohemia, their Sessions and Resolutions. With Statistical Tables on Jewish Municipal Authorities, Synagogues, Schools and Rabbinates in Bohemia). Vienna: Verlag von Leopold Sommer, 1852, 411ff; quoted in Northey, Die Kafkas, p. 12.

20 My thanks to Pavla Kostková of the Prague Land Survey Office and Jindřich Zdráhal of the Strakonice Land Registry for providing copies of land records and maps from 1837 to 1914.

the houses and dwellings on the other side of the synagogue on the Radomyšl road and we arrive at an even higher figure. Taking into account the fact that one household (such as that of Hermann Kafka's parents) might consist of eight persons, the number of people living in Jewish Street could have been a lot higher and, combined with other Jewish families in the village, could have made up half the population of Osek. Either way, the picture we get is of a socially structured and relatively self-sufficient Jewish community.

Posten Nro	Namen der Catastral-Gemeinden.	Bevölkerung männlich.	Bevölkerung weiblich.	Bevölkerung zusammen.	Dieselbe ist vertheilt in Häuser.	Dieselbe ist vertheilt in Wohnpartheien.	Auf eine Wohnparthei kommen im Durchschnitte Köpfe.	Von den Wohnpartheien beschäftigen sich ausschliessend mit der Cultur des Bodens.	ausschliessend mit Gewerben.	mit der Cultur des Bodens und Gewerben zugleich.	mit keinem von beiden.
76	Jažowic mit Lhota	213	226	439	53	102	4	95	1	2	4
77	Třeschowic	103	123	226	32	60	4	55	4	1	. .
78	Turna, Gross	148	155	303	37	74	4	71	1	2	. .
79	Turna, Klein	90	91	181	25	42	4	20	4	18	. .
80	Wohrazenic	62	65	127	17	30	4	26	2	2	. .
81	Wojnic	118	116	234	35	55	4	52		2	1
82	Wollenic	255	274	529	72	111	5	90	2	15	3
83	Wossek	203	203	406	55	94	4	44	32	17	1
84	Zborowic Vorder	91	89	180	25	46	4	44	2		. .

Land records for Osek, 1837.
Strakonice Land Registry. Prague Land Survey Office.

At its centre was the synagogue, where the roads from Malá Turná (1 km) and Radomyšl (3 km) met, next to the village inn. The village butcher – Jakob Kafka (1814–1889), Franz's grandfather – lived in Jewish Street. In the 'next street', at right angles to Jewish Street, were a general store and a tailor's. Besides merchants and peddlers Little Osek also had its cobbler and its glazier.[21] Data from 1837 show that 44 households ('*Wohnpartheien*') in Osek were engaged in agriculture ('*mit der Cultur des Bodens*'), 32 in trades ('*mit Gewerben*'), 17 in both agriculture and trades ('*mit der Cultur des Bodens und Gewerben zugleich*'), and one in neither ('*mit keiner von beiden*'). The 32 households engaged in trades were presumably the non-privileged Jews in Jewish Street, for whom owning land and working it was hardly an option.

21 Based on the traditional names of the cottages in Jewish Street, where in 2000 I interviewed a number of men (average age 70) who had been born, grown up and lived in Osek. This is not a fully reliable source, of course; still, place names lodged in the memory do tell us something.

Alena Wagnerová believes there was also a privileged Jewish 'upper class' in Osek – leaseholders of the brewery, distillery, etc.[22] – an assumption supported by an 1837 record of a Jewish hospital near the synagogue.[23] This 'upper class', however, would probably have thought of itself as German, as the Czech-Jewish movement did not emerge with any force until the 1870s.[24] It can thus be assumed that German was spoken both in the synagogue and in religious instruction lessons. Hebrew was only used during the liturgy itself, while Yiddish in the culturally mixed community gradually diminished in importance – although Hermann Kafka, according to his son, continued to pepper his speech with Yiddish expressions even in old age.[25] We know that Osek had its own rabbi between 1823 and 1827;[26] otherwise it shared one with the similarly-sized Jewish communities of Písek and Strakonice. The district rabbi lived in Strakonice (about 10 km south of Osek), and the local rabbi in Horažďovice.[27] The community also had a *shamas* or warden to look after the synagogue, who doubled as a German teacher.[28] Merchants would seek trade not only in the immediate locality, but as far afield as Písek fifteen kilometres to the east, so it must be assumed that owing to the predominance of Czechs in the region the merchants, at least, must have spoken Czech. This was also true of Hermann Kafka and his relatives. Franz Kafka, writing of his sister Valli's wedding in a letter to Felice dated 13 or 14 January 1913, quotes his father's use of the Czech word 'kněžna' (princess) to describe the bride.[29]

The revolution and reforms of 1848, and in particular the March Constitution of 1849, brought an end to the visible ghetto. The administrative inclusion of Jews in rural communities was certainly a step forward in terms of emancipation, but it did not lead to full social acceptance or integration. Franz Kafka's father Hermann (1852–1931), who was born in Jewish Street in

---

22 See Wagnerová, *„Im Hauptquartier des Lärms"*, p. 30.

23 See Northey, Die Kafkas, p. 13.

24 See Hillel J. Kieval, *The Making of Czech Jewry. National Conflict and Jewish Society in Bohemia, 1870–1918*. New York, Oxford: Oxford University Press 1988.

25 Franz Kafka, *Zur Frage der Gesetze und andere Schriften aus dem Nachlaß in der Fassung der Handschrift* (On the Question of Laws and other Literary Remains based on the Handwritten Manuscripts). Ed. by Hans-Gerd Koch. Frankfurt am Main: S. Fischer 1994, p. 44. Kafka recalls Hermann Kafka calling Max Brod 'einen meschuggenen ritoch'. Julie Kafka, in a letter from Perštejn (Pürstein), uses the word 'Mišpoche'; in another letter dated on 12 July 1925, she writes 'Mischpoche' (Bodleian Library, Oxford). See Franz Kafka, *Tagebücher* (Diaries). Ed. by Hans-Gerd Koch, Michael Müller , Malcolm Pasley. Vol. 1. Frankfurt am Main: S. Fischer 1990, p. 214. See also Northey, *Kafkas Mischpoche*.

26 Northey, Die Kafkas, p. 13.

27 See *Seznam míst v království Českém* (Index of Villages and Towns in the Kingdom of Bohemia). Prague: Místodržitelská tiskárna (Governor's Printing Press) 1907, p. 503.

28 Northey thinks this public servant was Jakob Kafka, which would mean that German was spoken in the family. Northey, Die Kafkas, p. 18.

29 See Franz Kafka, *Briefe 1913 – März 1914* (Letters 1913 – March 1914). Ed. by Hans-Gerd Koch. Frankfurt am Main: S. Fischer 2001, p. 39.

Osek, still knew what it was like to live in the confines of a ghetto. Little Osek, as the Jewish quarter was known, was separated from the rest of the village by the castle, open land, ponds and marshland. From the synagogue, known locally as 'the church', it was a walk of eight or nine hundred metres to the little chapel outside the castle in the Christian part of the village. The fact that one had to walk around the castle and its grounds to get there only added to the isolation of the Jewish part of the village. From the castle there was a direct and shorter path to Little Osek, which went on to Turná, Radomyšl a Strakonice; but it was not a public road.

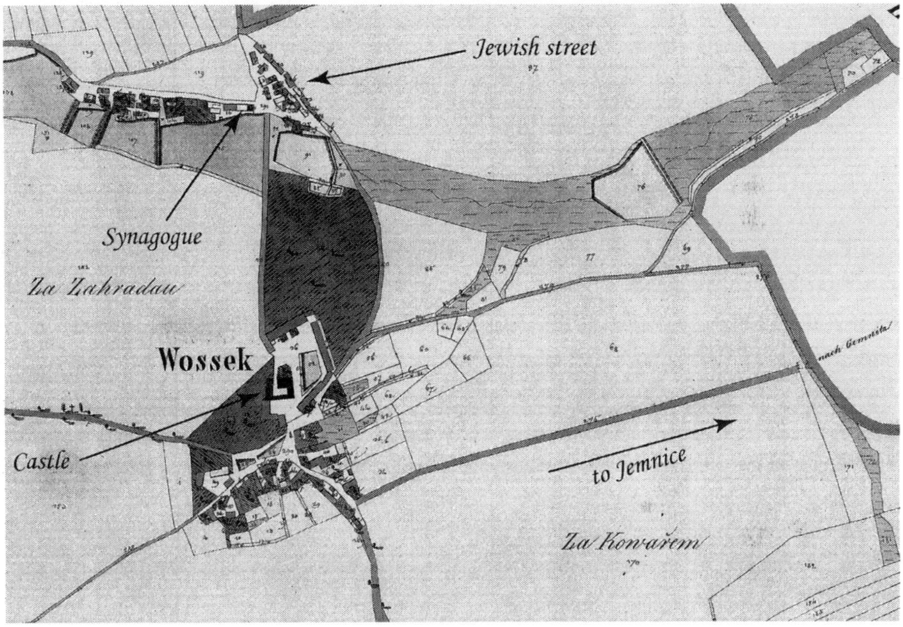

Map of Osek from 1837.
Prague Land Survey Office.

In many ways the Catholics of Osek led a quite separate life. They had their own inn and smithy, their own merchant, and so on. But there was no Czech school in the village, which meant that children requiring a Czech education had go to Jemnice, a walk of about two kilometres. The road there was on the other side of the village from the Jewish quarter, so that in the 1850s when Hermann Kafka was a boy neither the children nor the adults of Osek had much everyday contact with each other and people tended to look for partners within their own communities, be they Catholic or Jewish. Before his marriage Jakob Kafka lived in house No. 30, his bride Franziska Platowski in No. 35.[30]

30 For the situation in the Kafka household see Northey, *Kafkas Mischpoche*.

From the present perspective it is hard to say to what extent anti-Jewish sentiment impinged on daily life in Osek. We do know, however, that in 1861 in Strakonice, only ten kilometres away, there were anti-Jewish pogroms and that the army was called in to restore order.[31] We know equally, however, that besides their economic interaction the Jews kept themselves apart, within their own rhythms and routines and cultural confines. Kafka's mention of the ghetto in his Letter to Father is therefore very pertinent:

> You really had brought some traces of Judaism with you from the ghetto-like village community; it was not much and it dwindled a little more in the city and during your military service; but still, the impressions and memories of your youth did just about suffice for some sort of Jewish life [...][32]

The language laws proved particularly enduring. Although the March Constitution of 1849 and subsequent amendments gave Jews a free choice in declaring their children's first language when enrolling them for school, German remained the most common preference. There were various reasons for this: identification with German as the language of emancipation; German as a precondition for a good education, social advancement and better career opportunities; but also the lack of Czech schools, or their limited capacity. Under the Bach system in the 1850s 'teaching in the Czech language was restricted'[33] and it was not until the 1860s and 1870s that a proper network of both Czech and German schools began to emerge in linguistically mixed areas. One such area was Little Osek, where Hermann Kafka almost certainly attended a German school.[34]

German (Jewish) schools were usual at the time, even in areas with a predominantly Czech population.[35] One such school in nearby Strakonice survived until 1898.[36] A fairly sure indication that Hermann Kafka did indeed have a German education is the 'German' *Kurrent* script taught in the German schools of the time which he uses in his letters to his future wife Julie Löwy

31 At the same time there were similar incidents in Prague. See Kieval, *The Making of Czech Jewry*, p. 18.

32 Franz Kafka, *Dearest Father. Stories and Other Writings.* Translated by Ernst Kaiser and Eithne Wilkins. New York: Schocken 1954, p. 173.

33 Jan Křen, *Konfliktgemeinschaft. Tschechen und Deutsche 1780–1918* (Conflictive Community: Czechs and Germans 1780–1918). 2nd edition. Munich: Oldenbourg 2000, p. 111.

34 For the school in Osek, see also Wagnerová, *„Im Hauptquartier des Lärms"*, p. 40.

35 Hugo Hermann, *In jenen Tagen* (In those Days). Jerusalem: self-publication, 1938, p. 222. See also Krolop, Zu den Erinnerungen Anna Lichtensterns an Franz Kafka, p. 41.

36 See Rudolf M. Wlaschek, *Juden in Böhmen. Beiträge zur Geschichte des europäischen Judentums im 19. und 20. Jahrhundert* (Jews in Bohemia: Contributions to the History of European Jewry in the 19th and 20th Century). Munich: Oldenbourg 1997, p. 29.

(1854–1934) in 1882.[37] Czech schools, on the other hand, were already teaching a modified form of Latin script introduced in 1849.[38]

It is therefore quite likely that Hermann Kafka could not write Czech. A number of 'Czechisms' that appear in his German letters to Julie Löwy in German show that Hermann Kafka had – like his wife – considerable difficulty with Czech spelling:

> *Přibik* for 'Přibík', *Tabor* for 'Tábor', *Pisek* for 'Písek', *Budín* for 'Budyň', *Götzova* for 'Götzová', *Daňek* for 'Daněk', *Kc* for 'Kč' (Czech crowns), *Mseno* for 'Mšeno'.[39]

In the case of the word *Daňek* (instead of the correct *Daněk*) he fails to apply the spelling rule taught in the first class of elementary school that a palatalized /ň/ before /e/ is spelt *-ně-* not *-ňe-*. With the word *Budín* (instead of the correct 'Budyň' or 'Budyně') he fails to distinguish between the palatal /ď/ and the alveolar /d/, which requires the spelling *-dy-* rather than *-di-*. He also omits diacritics, or puts them in the wrong place.

It must be said that Hermann Kafka also had difficulty with German orthography, as a result of his inadequate schooling. For he had 'already at the age of ten to push a handcart round the villages even in winter and very early in the morning';[40] and 'aged seven I already had to take the handcart round the villages'.[41] In his dealings with customers in the villages he would have needed both languages.

But it was German that enjoyed the higher status in the Kafka family and generally in this time. German was essential for communicating with many of Hermann Kafka's clients and business partners in Prague and Vienna.[42]

---

37 These letters from 1882, along with his German notes on Julie Löwy's letters made in 1917, 1926 and 1929, are in the Bodleian Library, Oxford.

38 See for example the comparative tables of Czech spelling rules in František Čapka – Květoslava Santlerová, *Z dějin vývoje písma* (From the History of the Evolution of Writing Systems). Brno: Masarykova univerzita 1998.

39 Hermann Kafka to Julie Löwy, 9 June 1882, 6 July 1882, 11 August 1882; Julie and Hermann Kafka and Marie Wernerová to Elli and Karl Hermann, 24 March 1926. Bodleian Library, Oxford. – Hermann Kafka generally used German topographical names such as *Böhmisch Leipa* for *Česká Lípa*, so that his *Tabor* (Czech *Tábor*, German *Tabor*) may simply be the (correct) German spelling. *Budyně nad Ohří* is often called simply *Budyně* or *Budyň*. Antonín Profous, *Místní jména v Čechách. Jejich vznik, původní význam a změny* (Bohemian Toponyms: The Origins and Changes of their Meanings). Vol. 1. Prague: ČSAV 1954, p. 230.

40 Kafka, *Tagebücher*, p. 323.

41 Kafka, *Zur Frage der Gesetze*, p. 29.

42 For example, Hermann Kafka mentions Vienna in a letter to Julie Löwy written in 1882 (Bodleian Library, Oxford). For the Prague milieu, see inter alia Northey, Die Kafkas; or Marek Nekula, *„...v jednom poschodí vnitřní babylonské věže..." Jazyky Franze Kafky* ('... on one Floor of the Inner Tower of Babel...': Franz Kafka's Languages). Prague: Nakladatelství Franze Kafky 2003. For a more general study of Prague, see Jiří Pešek, *Od aglomerace k velkoměstu. Praha a středoevropské metropole 1850–1920* (From an Agglomeration to the Capital City: Prague and Central European Capital Cities 1850–1920). Prague: Scriptorium 1999.

It was also of central importance in his personal life, being the language of his correspondence with Julie Löwy before they were married. After his marriage and the birth of their children, who had German names and went to German schools, this tendency became even more marked. Hermann Kafka almost certainly spoke German with his wife and children; he and his family went to the German synagogue; he enrolled his children in German schools, read the newspapers *Bohemia* and *Prager Tagblatt*[43] and had various announcements published in the German press.[44] Letters to the children were also in German, though these were mostly written by their mother, who used Czech vocative and diminutive forms of their names such as *Liebste Ottilko!, Liebste Otilko!* and *Liebe Ottilko!*, or *Liebste Ellynko!, Liebe Ellynko*, etc.[45] – the same forms her husband had once used in his letters to her: *Vielgeliebte Julinko, Liebe Julinko* or simply *Julinko*.[46] For Julie Czech was not only a language of affection; she had a very thorough knowledge of spoken Czech.[47]

The privileged status of German in Kafka's parents' family can also be seen in the inscription on the gravestone of Hermann Kafka's father and Franz Kafka's grandfather Jakob – clearly a context of special emotional significance. On the upper part the gravestone there is a Hebrew inscription, and below it in German '*Friede seiner Asche*' (Peace to his ashes). All but two of the other gravestones in the forest cemetery at Osek (there are 39 in total) have only Hebrew inscriptions. David Hollub has both Hebrew and German, while Julie Auler has only German. A similar, though more striking illustration of the growing importance of German rather than Hebrew in such symbolic contexts, can also be found in other Jewish cemeteries, such as the one in Trebitsch/Třebíč. In practical daily life this trend was even more obvious. By 1900, 91% of the Jewish children registered at German schools in Prague,[48]

43 If Kafka really did recommend the Franklin biography to his father, Hermann Kafka most probably read it in the existing Czech translation. – See Kafka, *Zur Frage der Gesetze*, p. 45. See also Jürgen Born, *Kafkas Bibliothek. Ein beschreibendes Verzeichnis* (Kafka's Library: A Descriptive Index). Frankfurt am Main: S. Fischer 1990, p. 169.

44 Julie Kafka to Elli and Karl Hermann, 14 March 1926. Bodleian Library, Oxford.

45 Julie Kafka to Ottla Kafka, 20 July 1910, 9 August 1917, 24 August 1917, 6 July 1918, 14 November 1918, 20 November 1918, 1 December 1918; Julie Kafka to Ottla David, 1920ies, 13 May 1925; Julie Kafka to Hermann Kafka, 12 July 1925; Julie Kafka to Elli and Karl Hermann and Marie Werner, 1 August 1923. Bodleian Library, Oxford.

46 Hermann Kafka to Julie Kafka, 7 July 1882, 25 July 1882, 29 July 1882 (Bodleian Library, Oxford). See Marek Nekula, Deutsch und Tschechisch in der Familie Kafka (German and Czech in the Kafka family). In: Dieter Cherubim – Karlheinz Jakob – Angelika Linke (eds), *Neue deutsche Sprachgeschichte. Mentalitäts, kultur- und sozialgeschichtliche Zusammenhänge* (New History of the German Language: Mentality, Culture and Social History). Berlin, New York: W. de Gruyter 2002, pp. 379–415, here p. 386.

47 For an analysis of her Czech texts see especially Nekula, Deutsch und Tschechisch in der Familie Kafka, pp. 407–409.

48 See Gary B. Cohen, *The Politics of Ethnic Survival: Germans in Prague 1861–1914*. Princeton: Princeton University Press 1981, p. 224.

even though many came from predominantly Czech areas. Migration from rural areas to the cities and industrial and commercial centres,[49] which in the case of the Jews was connected with the disappearance of the vestiges of the old 'visible' ghetto, is reflected in the declining population of Osek detailed in the local land register. In fact Franz Kafka's grandfather was the last Jewish inhabitant of Osek to be buried in the Jewish forest cemetery, in 1889.[50] Čapková points out that 'whereas in 1872 there were 327 Jewish religious communities in Bohemia, in 1890 there were only 247' and that by 1921 69% of the Jewish population lived in towns of over 10,000 inhabitants.[51]

CZECHS? GERMANS? 'THE UNCERTAINTY SURROUNDING BOTH INTERPRETATIONS...'

The process of emancipation took place in a time of optimistic liberalism and growing indifference to religion,[52] the latter – more pronounced in Bohemia than elsewhere[53] – becoming particularly apparent towards the end of the century. Hermann Kafka, on an invitation dated 1896, paraphrases *barmizwe* of his son as *Confirmation*.[54] Julie Kafka, in a private family letter of 14 December 1917, writes of the *Weihnachts Feiertage*, and for Franz Kafka the word *Weihnachten* (Christmas) also has a personal resonance,[55] whereas Max Brod preferred the term *Chanuka*.[56] These are two different linguistic and cultural regimes coming together. Significantly, this acculturation was also reflected in language use. In the first phase of emancipation, acculturation

49 At the beginning of the 20th century Osek had only 53 houses and 279 inhabitants. *Seznam míst v království Českém*, p. 503.

50 This is the date on his gravestone, whereas Northey mentions 1888, see Family tree in Northey, *Kafkas Mischpoche*.

51 Kateřina Čapková, *Czechs, Germans, Jews? National Identity and the Jews of Bohemia, 1918–1938*. New York, Oxford: Berghahn Books 2012, p. 19.

52 See Wilma Iggers, *Die Juden in Böhmen und Mähren. Ein historisches Lesebuch* (Jews in Bohemia and Moravia: A Historical Reader). Munich: Beck 1986, p. 144 ff. With regard to Kafka see Northey, *Kafkas Mischpoche*.

53 See Kateřina Čapková, Tschechisch, Deutsch, Jüdisch – wo ist der Unterschied? Komplexität von nationalen Identitäten der böhmischen Juden 1918–1938 (Czech, German, Jewish – where is the difference? Complexity of national identities of Bohemian Jews 1918–1938). In: Marek Nekula – Walter Koschmal (eds), *Juden zwischen Deutschen und Tschechen. Sprachliche, literarische und kulturelle Identitäten* (Jews between Germans and Czechs: Linguistic, Literary and Cultural Identities). Munich: Oldenbourg 2006, pp. 73–84.

54 See reprint in Klaus Wagenbach, *Franz Kafka*. Reinbek bei Hamburg: Rowohlt 1991, p. 28 f.

55 Julie Kafka to Ottla and Franz Kafka, 14 December 1917 (Bodleian Library, Oxford), see also Franz Kafka, *Briefe an Ottla und die Familie* (Letters to Ottla and Family). Ed. by Hartmut Binder and Klaus Wagenbach. Frankfurt am Main: S. Fischer 1974, p. 61; Max Brod – Franz Kafka, *Eine Freundschaft. Briefwechsel* (A Friendship: Correspondence). Ed. by Malcolm Pasley. Vol. 2. Frankfurt am Main: S. Fischer 1989, p. 212, 451.

56 See Brod – Kafka, *Eine Freundschaft*, p. 209.

to German language and culture came quite naturally to the Bohemian and Moravian Jews. German was not only the language of their emancipation and an expression of their social aspirations; for seventy years – from the 1780s till the mid-19th century – they were required by law to use German in all stipulated spheres of public life. Both in Bohemia, where before 1848 Jews were also allowed to live in rural communities, and in Moravia, where they tended to settle in small towns, living side-by-side with the Czech-speaking population provided ideal conditions for acquiring Czech culture and language, though this did not happen as a matter of course. Acculturation to Czech culture became easier following new legislation after 1848 and in the 1860s[57] that granted Jews equal rights, including the right of choice of language in the school system. In Prague this trend became apparent in the mid-1870s, intensifying in the 80s and 90s when a new generation made its presence felt in cultural and public life – young Jews born after 1848 or those who had come to the capital to study or in search of work.

A milestone in the self-organization of the Jewish community in the secular sphere was the founding of the *Spolek českých akademiků židů* (Society of Czech Academic Jews) in 1876. The following years were characterized by the dynamic growth of the Czech-Jewish movement that continued until the mid-90s. Even in the First Czechoslovak Republic, this movement remained an important intellectual trend in the Jewish community.[58] 1881 saw the first publication of the *Kalendář česko-židovský* (Czech-Jewish Calendar), which from 1918 to 1920 was edited by Alfred Fuchs, whom Kafka knew personally. In 1883 a group was set up called *Or-tomid* (Eternal Light), which in 1886–87 successfully campaigned for the liturgical use of Czech. In the same period, Hebrew prayer books were published with Czech interlinear translations.[59] Sedláček's *Základové hebrejského jazyka biblického* (Biblical Hebrew Primer) came out in 1892. It was the first textbook of Hebrew language written in Czech for academic purposes, and Kafka owned a copy.[60] Shortly afterwards, another modern Czech textbook of Hebrew appeared, written by Richard Feder, a rabbi from Kolín, whose *Židovské besídky* (A Jewish Miscellany) also attracted attention. That too was a book Kafka possessed, as we shall see in the chapter on his reading. In 1893 the various Jewish organizations finally came together under the umbrella *Národní jednota českožidovská* (Czech-Jew-

57 See Josef Žalud, Zákonná ustanovení ohledně židů v Rakousku od r. 1867 (Legal regulations concerning Jews in Austria since 1867). In: *Kalendář česko-židovský na rok 1882/1883*, 96–104.

58 Čapková examines the work of various Jewish associations in post-1918 Czechoslovakia. (Understandably, assimilated Jews play only a marginal role in her study.) See Čapková, *Czech, Germans, Jews?*, as well as Kieval, *The Making of Czech Jewry*.

59 See Oskar Donath, *Jüdisches in der neuen tschechischen Literatur* (Jewishness in New Czech Literature). Prague: Privately printed 1931, p. 87.

60 See Born, *Kafkas Bibliothek*, p. 155.

ish National Unity), while in 1894 the *Českožidovské listy* (Czech-Jewish Newspaper), printed in Czech, appeared, first as a fortnightly then (from 1897) as a weekly. As the names of these societies and publications indicate, Czech-oriented Jews saw themselves as an integral part of Czech society, whereas those aligned with the German community were firmly integrated into German institutions of every kind such as the *Verein Deutsches Casino* (German Club), founded in 1862 and renamed as the *Verein Deutsches Haus* in 1916, or the *Lesehalle der deutschen Studenten in Prag* (Reading Hall of German Students in Prague), founded in 1848 and later renamed the *Rede- und Lesehalle der deutschen Studenten in Prag*, where they played an important if not a leading role.

Wagenbach, who claims that Hermann Kafka 'in his first years in Prague felt like a Czech and was regarded as a Czech',[61] locates him in the Czech-Jewish movement:

> Thus in this period he was a board member of the synagogue in Heinrichgasse (Jindřišská), founded in around 1890, the first Prague synagogue where services were conducted in Czech.[62]

The assertion proves problematic, however, when we realise that even in 1897 *Or-tomid* was still unable to fund a permanent synagogue.[63] True, the group did try in the late 1890s to raise money for a Jewish house of worship in Heinrichsgasse,[64] but it was not until 1905–06, following a decision made in 1898, that the first synagogue in this part of Prague was built, in nearby Jerusalem Street. Wagenbach's claim that Hermann Kafka was on the board of a 'synagogue' in Heinrichsgasse remains without support, either from contemporary testimony[65] or from written sources, and I have been unable to find the name Hermann Kafka in the Czech-Jewish Calendar for the period in question. Considering that the Calendar regularly printed lists of the members of the Society of Czech Academic Jews, the *Or-tomid* association, reading clubs, ball committees, etc., the 'omission' of a board member of a 'Czech synagogue' would have been almost unthinkable. But this is not the only evidence against Wagenbach's hypothesis.

---

61 Wagenbach, *Franz Kafka*, p. 16. – See also Klaus Wagenbach, *Franz Kafka. Eine Biographie seiner Jugend 1883–1912* (Franz Kafka: A Biography of his Youth). Bern: Francke Verlag 1958, p. 19.

62 Wagenbach, *Franz Kafka*, p. 16.

63 See *Kalendář česko-židovský na rok 1897/1898*, Prague 1897, p. 193. *Or-tomid* nevertheless rented a space there. See Kateřina Čapková, Raum und Zeit als Faktoren der nationalen Identifikation der Prager Juden (Space and time as factors of national identification). In: Peter Becher – Anne Knechtel (eds), *Praha – Prag 1900–1945: Literatur zweier Sprachen* (Prague 1900–1945: Literature of two Languages). Passau: Stutz 2010, pp. 21–30, here p. 27.

64 See *Kalendář česko-židovský na rok 1900/1901*, Prague 1900, p. 139.

65 Interviews recorded by the author with Kafka's nieces Marianne Steiner (March 1998) and Věra Saudková (February 1999).

On 25 December 1893 a general meeting was held in the 'Gypsy' Synagogue (at the time the Kafkas' local synagogue) at which the building of a new house of worship was discussed.[66] The invitation was acknowledged by 123 members of the Community, as their signatures testify (the names of three members are missing). Against the name 'Kafka H.' on page five of the invitation and page three of the actual list of names we find Hermann Kafka's signature: 'HKafka'. On the register of those present at the two-hour meeting his signature 'Herman Kafka' again appears, as number thirty-six out of only forty-nine Community members who attended.

The protocol of the meeting gives us a good idea of the content and character of the debate, which focussed on the 'asanation' (*asanace*), i.e. clearance and redevelopment of the inner city proposed by a law passed earlier that year, including the building of a new temple to replace the condemned 'Gypsy' Synagogue:

> Chairman Mr Jos. Inwald opened the meeting and gave the floor to Mr Gottfr. Weltsch, who read out the following resolution, unanimously passed by the whole committee on 23 December 1893:
>
> 'We the members of the Gypsy Synagogue, gathered on 25 December 1893 in an extraordinary general meeting, have conferred on our Board of Representatives Mr Josef Inwald, Mr Adolf Fischl and Mr Gottfr. Weltsch unlimited authority together to take all necessary steps and all relevant measures for the preservation of the Gypsy Synagogue, or that may be necessary for the construction of a new building in the form of a modern, large Temple sufficient to honour and grace the Jewish Community and to express, on the condition requested by Mr Jac. W. Pascheles that the divine service as practised until now will not be changed for a liturgy in any other language and that no national discord be conducted in the hitherto peaceful House of God, our fullest confidence in the Board in this matter that concerns us all.'
>
> Mr Reach asked to speak and expressed his objections to a new building; he would be in favour of keeping the capital that the Synagogue owns and warned against taking any ill-considered steps.
>
> Mr Pascheles opposed Mr Reach's speech and thanked him for his concern in the good cause; he is in favour of building a Temple for today for the needs of the young generation.
>
> Mr Weltsch also rebutted the ideas of Mr Reach and explained the Expropriation Law.

66 The following citations are from 'Einladung zu einer außerordentlichen General-Versammlung' (Invitation to an extraordinary general meeting), 'Protocoll der außerordentlichen Generalversammlung am 25. Dezember 1893' (Protocol of the extraordinary general meeting on 25 December 1893) and accompanying documents. – Archiv hlavního města Prahy (Prague Municipal Archives, Records of the Jewish religious community), Box No. 219.

Mr Inwald entered the debate and also explained the expropriation procedure if a decision to [re]build or not to [re]build the Gypsy Synagogue is not taken within two years; he explained to the Members the various [...] existing reasons for building, as well as the responsibilities of the Community to their Synagogue[s]; the question arises whether the Members want to build on the present site, or whether they would prefer to undertake a new building on another suitable site and purchase the necessary plots, for which it must be said funds are not available.

Mr Weltsch then argued in favour of building outside the Josefov district, in order to make it easier for the public to visit Divine Service, and moved that the meeting be closed, which was accepted.

In an open vote of 48 in favour and one against, the Members entrusted the Board with their full confidence to proceed independently in the matter, and the foregoing resolution proposed by the Committee was accepted!

Chairman Mr Inwald thanked the Members for their unanimous trust, after which, at 12 o'clock noon, the meeting was closed.

It may be assumed that the single vote against was cast by Mr Reach. In view of the tenor of the resolution and the relatively low number of congregants present (only about a third of those invited) it is quite possible that the 'national' polarization between supporters of the 'German' and 'Czech' liturgy was one reason why the general meeting was convened. We can also assume that many of those who failed to attend were advocates of the 'Czech' liturgy, of whose existence in Prague at that time there can be no doubt (in 1892 Josef Žalud tried to found a Czech-Jewish temple),[67] while among those present only one – Mr Reach – voted against the motion, albeit for different reasons. So presumably Hermann Kafka, along with the others, voted in favour of the regular liturgy and against the 'national' strife that was dividing not only the Jewish community – hardly the action of a committed member of *Or-tormid*.

Such an ideological U-turn from an alleged 'board member' of a Czech-Jewish synagogue 'around 1890' would be surprising to say the least. It might possibly have been a response to the new tough line taken by the imperial governor of Prague against Czech-Jewish associations.[68] But in the light of the above it seems more likely that Hermann Kafka's links with the Czech-Jewish movement are mere speculation. And although Čapková reminds us that it was not unusual for one individual to be involved in Jewish community activities that might seem contradictory, it would be extremely odd for Hermann Kafka to serve on the board of a 'Czech synagogue' so soon after he had enrolled his son in a German school in 1889. One of the Czech-Jewish

67 Kieval, *The Making of Czech Jewry*, p. 38.
68 Kieval, *The Making of Czech Jewry*, p. 59.

movement's primary aims, after all, was to ensure that Jewish children went to Czech schools, and successes in this endeavour were regularly reported in the Czech-Jewish Calendar.

On the other hand it is also true that in the census of 1890 the Kafkas gave their 'common language' as Czech, and that 'Heřmann Kafka' here appears in a hybrid form between German 'Hermann' and Czech 'Heřman'. The surnames of Julie, Gabriela and Valerie Kafka are given as 'Kafka', i.e. without the Czech feminine suffix *-ová*,[69] although Czech was declared as the Kafkas' 'common language'. This public inconsistency applies not only to spelling but to his attachment to national symbols. Wagenbach points out that under the name *kafka* – or *kavka* in standard orthography – on the family firm letterhead there is a sprig of oak leaves in the German version, while the Czech has a linden branch.[70] For the sake of his Prague customers Hermann Kafka made a point of employing Czech staff. When one of them handed in his notice, Franz Kafka was asked to act as mediator and sort out the situation.[71] Part of his negotiating strategy with the accountant was to speak to him in Czech (though not to present himself as a fellow-Czech):

> [...] the whole afternoon in Cafe City persuading Miška to sign a declaration that he was only a commis in the firm and not required to be insured, and that Father is not obliged to pay the large supplementary payments for his insurance. He promises to, my Czech is fluent, I even apologize for my mistakes elegantly, he promises to send the declaration to the shop on Monday, I feel if not loved then at least respected by him, but on Monday he sends nothing, is not even in Prague any longer but has left.[72]

Not only did Hermann Kafka argue with his domestic staff and shout at them[73] – he did so in Czech: *'To je žrádlo. Od 12 ti se to musí vařit'* ('This nosh is only fit for an animal. It must have been cooking since 12').[74] The choice of words may not be refined (*žrádlo* literally means 'animal food'), but they are nevertheless Czech – because some of the Kafkas' servants were Czech.

According to the Kafkas' 1890 census form, their household included the maid and cook Františka Nedvědová and the servants Marie Zemanová and Anna Čuchalová, the latter also a nanny;[75] in the 1900 census we find the names Božena Hořčičková and Anna Sedláčková, also 'servants'; and in 1910 Anežka

69 Women's names also appear in the non-derived form in the 1900 census declaration, whereas in the 1910 census they are written with the *-ová* suffix. – See Krolop, Zu den Erinnerungen Anna Lichtensterns an Franz Kafka, p. 56 f.

70 See Wagenbach, *Franz Kafka*, p. 17.

71 Diary, 16 October 1911. – See Kafka, *Tagebücher*, p. 84.

72 Diary, 25 November 1911. – See Kafka, *Tagebücher*, p. 271.

73 See Kafka, *Zur Frage der Gesetze*, p. 17, 19.

74 See Franz Kafka to Ottla, 19 April 1917. – See Kafka, *Briefe an Ottla und die Familie*, p. 33.

75 See Krolop, Zu den Erinnerungen Anna Lichtensterns an Franz Kafka, p. 56.

Ungrová. Judging by their names, places of birth and declared language we may assume they were all Czechs. A police report on another member of the household, however, the nanny Franziska Haas from Poděbrady, who in 1885 was called as a witness concerning the theft of a laundry-basket from the Kafka's home,[76] records her language as German. This was also the language of Elvira Sterk, Franz's sisters' governess, who worked for the Kafkas until 1902.[77] By then the 'French girl' Céline (or Josephine) Bailly from Monthiers en Bresse in Belgium[78] had also joined the household. And in early October 1902 the Kafkas engaged a new Czech governess, Anna Pouzarová, who was recommended by friends of Hermann Kafka's in Strakonice and stayed until October the following year.[79] In around 1910 '*slečna*' ('Miss') Marie Wernerová (1884–1941), whose family was Czech-Jewish,[80] began working for the family, and by 1921 at the latest she was living with them.[81] We know her dominant language was Czech, as both Franz Kafka and his mother addressed her in Czech when they wrote to her.[82]

A few lines of Czech written by her have been preserved, as well as one greeting in German. To Kafka's sister Ottla David (who married the Czech Josef David) she adds at the end of letters from Franz and Julie: '*Mnoho pozdravu* [sic] *zasila* [sic] *Marie Wernerová*' ('Marie Werner sends many greetings')[83] and '*Pozdravuji srdečně babičku Davidovou*' ('Give Granny David my warmest wishes')[84]. But in a PS on a letter to the German-speaking family of Elli, *née* Kafka, and Karl Hermann she writes in German: '[Mit] *besten Grüße*[n] *Fräulein / Marie Wernerova*'.[85]

---

76 See Wagnerová, *„Im Hauptquartier des Lärms"*, p. 81.

77 Copies of Julie Kafka's letters to Elvira Sterk are held in the Literary Archive of the Museum of Czech Literature in Prague (Literární archiv Památníku národního písemnictví). Letters from Kafka's sisters to Sterk are reprinted in Wagnerová, *„Im Hauptquartier des Lärms"*, p. 96 f.

78 In her registration with the directorate of police on 19 October 1889 (until 1904) her occupation is given as 'Erzieherin' (governess) in the employ of Mrs. Leonie Weil. From 1907, she is called a 'Lehrerin' (teacher or tutor). Státní ústřední archiv (State Central Archive, now National Archive), alphabetical records of the Police Presidium.

79 See Anna Pouzarová, Als Erzieherin in der Familie Kafka. In: Hans-Gerd Koch (ed.), *„Als Kafka mir entgegen kam..." Erinnerungen an Franz Kafka* ('As Kafka approached me.' Recollections of Franz Kafka). Berlin: Wagenbach 1995, pp. 55–65, here p. 55, 65.

80 See Wagnerová, '*„Im Hauptquartier des Lärms"*, p. 80.

81 See Franz Kafka, *Briefe 1900–1913* (Letters 1900–1913). Ed. by Hans-Gerd Koch. Frankfurt am Main: S. Fischer 1999, p. 637.

82 See a note to a letter from Franz Kafka to Elli Hermann, probably 16–19 January 1924; or a similar note added a letter from Julie Kafka to Elli and Karl Hermann, 1 August 1923. Bodleian Library, Oxford.

83 Postcard from Franz Kafka to Ottla, 27 November 1918. – See Kafka, *Briefe an Ottla und die Familie*, p. 60.

84 Similarly on the postcard from Julie Kafka to Ottla, 12 September 1923. Bodleian Library, Oxford.

85 Postscript in the letter from Julie and Hermann Kafka to Elli and Karl Hermann, 24 March 1926. Bodleian Library, Oxford.

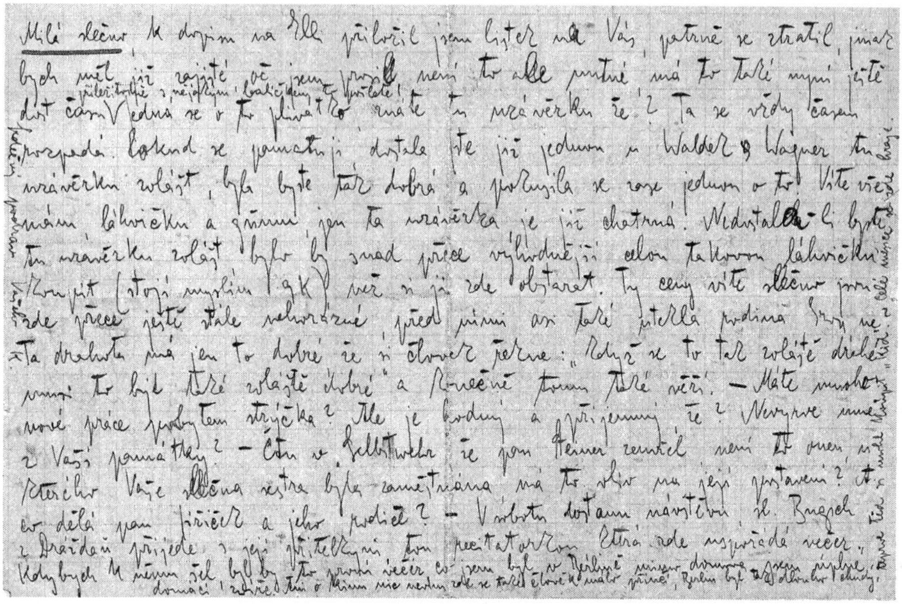

Franz Kafka to Elli Hermann, née Kafka, and Marie Wernerová, probably 16–19 January 1924. Archiv Kritische Kafka-Ausgabe.

So Hermann Kafka's declaration in the census that Czech was commonly used in his family was correct. And considering that respondents were only allowed to declare one of the two official languages, his decision was quite understandable, given the dominance of Czech in the city administration and the politicization of the whole language question. A ruling by the Administrative Court that the language declared by a person in the census has no bearing on their national identity, and is therefore not binding when it comes to their children's schooling,[86] tells us, first, that information provided in the census was not anonymous and, secondly, that interpretations of such data could if necessary be challenged in court. As Kurt Krolop's detailed case study

86 See Hannelore Burger, *Sprachenrecht und Sprachgerechtigkeit im österreichischen Unterrichtswesen 1867–1918* (Language Law and Language Justice in the Austrian School System). Vienna: Verlag der Österreichischen Akademie der Wissenschaften 1995, p. 65, 153; Robert Luft, Sind die böhmischen Deutschen Deutsche? Oder: Die Nationalität und das weiße Pferd! (Are Bohemian Germans Germans?). *Bohemia* 35 (1994), 403–409; Hartmut Binder, Paul Eisners dreifaches Ghetto (Paul Eisner's triple ghetto). In: Michel Reffet (ed.), *Le monde de Franz Werfel et la morale des nations. / Die Welt Franz Werfels und die Moral der Völker.* Berlin et al.: Peter Lang 2000, pp. 17–137, here p. 110, Tara Zarah, Bilingualism and the Nationalist 'Kampf um Kinder' in the Bohemian Lands, 1900–1938. In: Marek Nekula, Ingrid Fleischmann, Albrecht Greule (eds), *Franz Kafka im sprachnationalen Kontext seiner Zeit. Sprache und nationale Identität in öffentlichen Institutionen der böhmischen Länder* (Franz Kafka in the National Context of His Time. Language and National Identity in the Public Institutions of the Bohemian Crown Lands). Weimar: Böhlau 2007, pp. 229–244.

of the Feigl family shows, the information people supplied in the census could be far from authentic and may have been influenced by the ethnic setting in Prague, which at the time was dominated by Czechs.[87] Nevertheless, the number of Jews in Bohemia who declared Czech as their common language grew from one third in 1880 to 50% in 1890. Conversely, the number of Jews in Prague who claimed to be German-speakers fell from 74% in 1890 to 45% in 1900. This shift in language loyalty can, but does not have to be understood in terms of perceptions of national identity. Such a massive statistical shift cannot be explained in terms of migration from the Czech and German areas in Bohemia alone.[88]

Let us return to Hermann Kafka's relations with the Czech-Jewish movement. In favour of his involvement, some have invoked the supposed Czech origins that they claim predestined him linguistically, as he 'spoke Czech better than German'.[89] But even that is disputable. Remember that Hermann Kafka corresponded with his bride-to-be in German, and that after their marriage in September 1882 he ensured German was the family's first language. As for his own knowledge of German, suffice it to say that in 1893 he worshipped in a synagogue where we know that the service, or part of it, was held in German. That is why I think we can dismiss Wagenbach's assumption that the presence of Czech in the Kafka family was also decisive in matters of religion.

ANTISEMITISM AND ZIONISM

In the 1890s and the period around the elections to the *Reichsrath*, the ongoing nationality dispute between Czechs and Germans was accompanied by a militant antisemitism.[90] The anti-Jewish riots in Kolín following the murder of a Christian girl in 1893,[91] the inflammatory campaign in the Czech and German press around the Dreyfus affair in 1895, the pogroms in Prague and in

87 More see Krolop, Zu den Erinnerungen Anna Lichtensterns an Franz Kafka, pp. 21–60.

88 For an interpretation of the statistical results see, inter alia, Christoph Stölz, *Kafkas böses Böhmen. Zur Sozialgeschichte eines Prager Juden* (Kafka's Villainous Bohemia: On Social History of Prague Jews). Munich: Text + Kritik 1975; Cohen, *The Politics of Ethnic Survival*; Kieval, *The Making of Czech Jewry*.

89 Wagenbach, *Franz Kafka. Eine Biographie seiner Jugend*, p. 19.

90 Michal Frankl argues, however, that antisemitism in Bohemia went deeper and should not be seen as a product of the Czech-German conflict. Michal Frankl, *„Emancipace od židů." Český antisemitismus na konci 19. století* ('Emancipation from Jews.' Czech Antisemitism at the end of 19th Century). Prague; Litomyšl: Paseka 2007; Michal Frankl, *„Prag ist nunmehr antisemitisch." Tschechischer Antisemitismus am Ende des 19. Jahrhunderts* ('Prague is henceforth antisemitic.' Czech Antisemitism at the end of the 19th Century). Berlin: Metropol, 2011.

91 One of Hermann Kafka's brothers and his family lived in Kolín. For more on Kafka's family, see Northey, *Kafkas Mischpoche*.

Czech and German provinces when the Badeni reforms were introduced (and then abolished) in 1897, the Hilsner affair in 1899 – these were milestones in a gradual advance of antisemitism in Bohemia that also found support in political parties. Some Young Czech politicians resurrected the idea of a national anti-Jewish conspiracy that had already found expression in, for instance, Jan Neruda's pamphlet 'For Fear of Jewry' (1870);[92] pursued a policy of economic boycott; and interpreted social conflicts in ethnic (anti-German, anti-Jewish) terms. This tendency was personified by Václav Březnovský (1843–1918) and Karel Baxa (1863–1938), the Prague counterparts of the anti-Czech and antisemitic Viennese politician Karl Lueger (1844–1910). Georg von Schönerer (1842–1921) with his Pan-German party was by no means the only one to play the anti-Jewish card.[93]

Against this background it is hardly surprising that between 1890 and 1910 the number of Jews in Bohemia and Moravia fell by 10% through identity management and emigration.[94] An alternative response was active Jewish nationalism and the creation of Zionist associations, through which assimilated Jews (albeit hesitantly at first) signed up to the ideas of Theodor Herzl, who in 1896 had published *The Jewish State: Proposal for a Modern Solution for the Jewish Question*, in 1897 organized the Zionist Congress where national Jewish associations joined forces in the World Zionist Organization, and whose *Old New Land* (1902) and diaries Kafka read.[95]

It was only gradually, however, that the idea of a secular Jewish national movement gained widespread support. Orthodox and assimilated Jews were opposed to Herzl's political Zionism, and a Zionist congress planned in Munich had to be moved to Basel at the last moment due to resistance from the Jewish community in Munich.[96] Brod, writing with hindsight, saw the tension between the assimilation and the re-ethnicization programs not only as a generational, but also as a polarizing social conflict between the grande bourgeoisie and the socialists,[97] though he failed to distinguish between the various strands of socialism. Apart from the political Zionists, for whom the solution of the Jewish question lay in the founding of an internationally

---

92 See Michal Frankl – Jindřich Toman (eds), *Jan Neruda a Židé. Texty a kontexty* (Jan Neruda and Jews: Texts and Contexts). Prague: Akropolis 2012.

93 See Robert Wistrich, Georg von Schönerer and the genesis of modern Austrian antisemitism. *Wiener Library Bulletin* 29 (1976), pp. 20–29.

94 Kieval gives the figure of 94,479 Jews for 1890 and 85,826 for 1910, while the number of Czechs in the same period rose sharply. See Kieval, *The Making of Czech Jewry*, p. 13.

95 C.f. Andreas B. Kilcher, Kafka und das Judentum (Kafka and Jewishness). In: Bettina von Jagow – Oliver Jahraus (eds), *Kafka-Handbuch: Leben – Werk – Wirkung* (A Kafka Manual: Life – Oeuvre – Impact). Göttingen: Vandenhoeck & Ruprecht 2008, pp. 194–211, here p. 200.

96 For more see e.g. Brenner, *Kleine jüdische Geschichte*, pp. 243–257.

97 See Max Brod, *Sozialismus im Zionismus* (Socialism and Zionism). Vienna, Berlin: R. Löwit Verlag 1920, p. 15. See also Nekula, Theodor Lessing und Max Brod, p. 118.

guaranteed and recognized secular Jewish state with its own territory and autonomous economy (Theodor Herzl), there were also the cultural Zionists (Ahad Ha'am, Martin Buber) who emphasized the spiritual, moral and cultural regeneration of the Jewish nation. In practice these two main blocks were sub-divided and modified into all manner of groupings, both political and cultural.

In this context Kilcher points to the distinct roles of Yiddish as the language of the Jewish diaspora in Eastern Europe, and Hebrew as the language of the Judaic tradition and revival.[98] It should not be overlooked that the language question, which particularly in the Habsburg monarchy was hotly debated, also played a key role in crystallizing modern Jewish identity. Hugo Bergmann, for instance, believed that 'a Zionist student who can't speak Hebrew is a contradiction in terms'[99] – a clear echo of Herder's idea of the language-nation, or the Czech revivalist Josef Jungmann's watchword 'a Czech is one who not only thinks in Czech but speaks it'.[100] Shumsky deals with the role of discourse on monolingualism and bilingualism in Bohemia for Jewish national conception for Palestine.[101]

Antisemitism and reactions to it also affected the universities. In Prague alone, the *Teutonia* student fraternity (or 'Burschenschaft') was formed in 1876, the *Ghibellinia* in 1880 and, at the German part of the already divided Prague University, the *Germania* (which barred Jews from membership) in 1891.[102] In 1899 Prague Jewish students set up their own league, *Bar Kochba*, named after the leader of the Jewish uprising against the Roman emperor Hadrian. *Bar Kochba*, which grew out of the *Makabäa* society founded in 1893, was led in 1903–04 by Kafka's schoolmate and friend Hugo Bergmann (1883–1975), who visited Palestine in 1910 and later became the founder the Jewish National and University Library in Jerusalem and rector of the Hebrew University (1936–38). Bergmann left for Palestine in 1920, and in 1923 we find him trying to persuade Kafka to settle there too.[103] But Bergmann's brand of cultural

---

98 See Andreas Kilcher, Kafka, Scholem und die Politik der jüdischen Sprachen (Kafka, Scholem and the politics of Jewish languages). In: Christoph Miething (ed.), *Politik und Religion im Judentum* (Politics and Religion in Judaism). Tübingen: Niemeyer 1999, pp. 79–115.

99 Quoted in Kieval, *The Making of Czech Jewry*, p. 101. See also Pawel, *The Nightmare of Reason*, p. 38.

100 Josef Jungmann, O jazyku českém rozmlouvání první (The first dialogue on the Czech language). In: J.J., *Vybrané spisy původní a přeložené* (Selected Writings: Original and Translations). Ed. by Karel Hikl. Prague: Vojtěch Hrách [1806] 1918, pp. 39–45.

101 See Dimitry Shumsky, *Zweisprachigkeit und binationale Idee: Der Prager Zionismus 1900–1930* (Bilingualismus and the Idea of Binationalism: Prague Zionism 1900–1930). Göttingen: Vandenhoeck & Ruprecht 2012.

102 Pawel, *The Nightmare of Reason*, p. 35.

103 Hartmut Binder, Kafkas Hebräischstudien. Ein biographisch-interpretatorischer Versuch (Kafka's study of Hebrew: A biographically interpretative approach). *Jahrbuch der deutschen Schillergesellschaft* 11 (1967), pp. 527–556, p. 546 f.

Zionism, which embraced the ideas of both Martin Buber and Ahad Ha'am and strove for a balanced relationship with Czechs and Germans alike,[104] was too conciliatory for many students. Dissatisfied, a group led by Robert Neubauer, Jakob Fraenkl, Julius Löwy and Ernst Gütig founded *Barissia* with the aim of defending Jewish interests more militantly.[105] In 1907, at a time of heightened nationalist tensions before the first general parliamentary elections, Franz Steiner launched the weekly *Selbstwehr* (Self-Defence) which, under the editorship of Leo Herrmann, had through his person close links with *Bar Kochba*. From 1913 its editor-in-chief was Siegmund Kaznelson (1893–1959), from 1917 (briefly) Nelly Thoeringer, and from 1919 until 1938 the paper was run by Kafka's friend Felix Weltsch (1884–1964). During and after the First World War, Kafka – thanks to Brod and Weltsch – regularly read *Selbstwehr*.[106] That and publications such as the *Jüdische Rundschau* (Jewish Review),[107] along with his correspondence and conversations with both Brod and Weltsch, were Kafka's main but by no means only sources of information about the Zionist movement of his day.[108] He read books and articles by Martin Buber, Ahad Ha'am and other authors – in German, Yiddish and Hebrew.

Many members of *Bar Kochba* were pupils at Czech grammar schools or students at Czech universities and colleges, and some were at first closely involved in the Czech-Jewish movement.[109] In 1909 a group of Czech-speaking students established the Zionist *Spolek židovských akademiků Theodor Herzl* (Theodor Herzl Association of Jewish Academics). Tellingly, it was intended for 'Jewish academics of Zionist orientation' rather than 'Czech academics of Jewish origin' (as an equivalent organization had been named in 1876), reflecting the formation of a new Jewish intellectual community of the time.

---

104 For more see Shumsky, *Zweisprachigkeit und binationale Idee.*

105 See Čapková, *Czechs, Germans, Jews?* p. 178.

106 See e.g. Brod – Kafka, *Eine Freundschaft*, p. 193, 212, 274, 317, 358. See also Friedrich Thieberger, Kafka und die Thiebergers (Kafka and the Thiebergers). In: Hans-Gerd Koch (ed.), *„Als Kafka mir entgegen kam..." Erinnerungen an Franz Kafka* ('As Kafka approached me.' Recollections of Franz Kafka). Berlin: Wagenbach 1995, pp. 121–127, p. 124.

107 See e.g. Brod – Kafka, *Eine Freundschaft*, p. 189, 193, 200, 206.

108 See Hartmut Binder, Franz Kafka und die Wochenzeitschrift *Selbstwehr* (Franz Kafka and the weekly *Selbstwehr*). *Deutsche Vierteljahrsschrift für Literaturwissenschaft und Geistesgeschichte* 41 (1967), Vol. 2 (May), pp. 283–304; Ritchie Robertson, *Kafka, Judaism, Politics, and Literature.* Oxford: Clarendon Press 1985; Mark Gelber, Kafka und zionistische Deutungen (Kafka and Zionist interpretations). In: Bettina von Jagow – Oliver Jahraus (eds), *Kafka-Handbuch: Leben – Werk – Wirkung* (A Kafka Manual: Life – Oeuvre – Impact). Göttingen: Vandenhoeck & Ruprecht 2008, pp. 293–303; Carsten Schmidt, *Kafkas fast unbekannter Freund: Leben und Werk von Felix Weltsch. Philosoph, Journalist und Zionist* (Kafka's Nearly Unknown Friend: The Life and Work of Felix Weltsch. Philosopher, Journalist and Zionist). Würzburg: Königshausen u. Neumann 2010.

109 See Binder, Paul Eisners dreifaches Ghetto, p. 112.

The formation of the Zionist movement had been discussed in Masaryk and Herben's *Čas* (Time) as early as in 1898. Masaryk was sympathetic to Zionism and as president he even visited a Jewish settlement in Palestine.[110] It was also thanks to him that Jews in democratic Czechoslovakia received proper recognition and were granted full rights as a national minority in the 1920 constitution.[111] Equally, the new democratic values were respected by the Zionists, who felt that the program of linguistic, cultural and political assimilation represented by the Czech-Jewish movement was outdated and campaigned against it.[112]

But declared equality before the law is one thing; antisemitic prejudice in reality is quite another. And that showed little sign of disappearing, either in Prague or in other parts of Czechoslovakia. In 1918 and 1920 there were a number of anti-Jewish demonstrations.[113] In 1920 Kafka mentions reading about anti-Jewish protests in *Venkov*, and in a letter to Milena Jesenská (17–19 November 1920) he reports hearing a derogatory Czech phrase in the street: 'I recently heard someone call the Jews a '*prašivé plemeno*' (mangy breed)'.[114] And even after Kafka moved to Berlin he still came across antisemitic reactions.[115]

FRANZ KAFKA AND YIDDISH

Kafka went to see the Yiddish folk theatre from Lvov on 1 and 4 May 1910, but it was the profound impression made by Yitzchak Löwy's 'Original Jewish Company', which Kafka first saw on 5 October 1911, that inspired and initiated his 'Jewish rebirth'.[116]

> I love the Yiddish theatre; last year I may have gone to twenty of their performances, and possibly not once to the German theatre.[117]

One factor was undoubtedly the personality of Löwy himself, who had left his family home in Warsaw to pursue his artistic career. Kafka even goes

110 See Kieval, *The Making of Czech Jewry*, p. 109. See also Ernst Rychnovsky (ed.), *Masaryk und das Judentum* (Masaryk and Jews). Prague: Marsverlagsgesellschaft 1931.

111 See Pawel, *The Nightmare of Reason*, p. 39. See also Rychnovsky, *Masaryk und das Judentum*.

112 See Brod – Kafka, *Eine Freundschaft*, p. 305.

113 Explicitly referred to by Kafka, e.g. in a letter to Ottla, 11 November 1918. – See Kafka, *Briefe an Ottla und die Familie*, p. 59.

114 See Franz Kafka, *Briefe an Milena* (Letters to Milena). Extended new edition. Ed. by Jürgen Born and Michael Müller. Frankfurt am Main: S. Fischer 1998, p. 291 and 288.

115 Franz Kafka to Josef David, 3 October 1923. – See Kafka, *Briefe an Ottla und die Familie*, p. 135.

116 See Robertson, *Kafka, Judaism, Politics, and Literature*.

117 Franz Kafka, *Letters to Felice*. Translated by James Stern and Elizabeth Duckworth. New York: Schocken 1967; London: Vintage 1999, p. 38.

so far as to say that he would gladly prostrate himself 'in the dust' before him in admiration.[118] Through Löwy (Kafka's mother's namesake), he gained an insight into the spiritual world of the Eastern Jews, the Kabbalah and – as we see in his 'Character sketch of small literatures' – modern Jewish literature,[119] which was to influence his own writing. Thus Binder sees a link between Goldfaden's Yiddish novel *Two Bold Lads* and the two 'helpers' in Kafka's *Trial* and *Castle*.[120] Of course Kafka read the Jewish press, too: in 1912 he took out subscriptions to *Palästina* and *Jüdische Rundschau* (Jewish Review), and he was a regular reader of the Jewish monthly *Ost und West* (East and West). He also familiarized himself with Hasidic literature: Wolf Pascheles (*Sippurim*), Martin Buber, Micha Berdyczewski (better known as Bin Gorion), Alexander Elisaberg, Fritz Mordechai Kaufmann and others.[121] For his 'Introductory speech on Jargon [Yiddish] ' (see below) Kafka read Meyr Isser Pines' *Histoire de la Littreture judéo-allemande* (1911).[122]

During this period Kafka believed that in the traditional Yiddish folk theatre he could find Jews who still had their 'own' language and cultural identity and still lived in a natural ethno-national community. In contrast, the Jewish environment he lived in had become largely assimilated, in terms of both language and religion. Nonetheless, it is clear from his diary that he doubted to what extent a Jew can ever comprehend his world through a 'foreign' language:

> Yesterday it occurred to me that I did not always love my mother as she deserved and as I could, only because the German language prevented it. The Jewish mother is no 'Mutter', to call her 'Mutter' makes her a little comic (not to herself, because we are in Germany), we give a Jewish woman the name of a German mother, but forget the contradiction that sinks into the emotions so much more the heavily, 'Mutter' is peculiarly German for the Jew, it unconsciously contains, together with the Christian splendour Christian coldness also, the Jewish woman who is called 'Mutter' therefore becomes not only comic but strange. Mama would be a better name if only one didn't imagine 'Mutter' behind it. I believe that it is only the memories of the ghetto that still preserve the Jewish family, for the word 'Vater' too is far from meaning the Jewish father.[123]

118 Kafka, *Tagebücher*, p. 81.

119 For a full bibliography, see Kieval, *The Making of Czech Jewry*, p. 140. For relevant books in Kafka's library, see Born, *Kafkas Bibliothek*.

120 See Hartmut Binder, *Kafka-Kommentar zu den Romanen, Rezensionen, Aphorismen und zum Brief an den Vater* (Commentaries on Kafka' Novels, Reviews, Aphorisms and Letter to Father). Munich: Winkler Verlag 1976, p. 388.

121 See Kilcher, Kafka und das Judentum, p. 199 f.

122 See Hartmut Binder, *Kafka's Welt: Eine Lebenschronik in Bildern* (Kafka's World: Chronicle of His Life in Pictures). Reinbek bei Hamburg: Rowohl 2008, p. 263.

123 Franz Kafka, *The Diaries of Franz Kafka 1910–1913*. Edited by Max Brod and translated by Joseph Kresh. New York: Schocken 1948, p. 111.

While the Jew is losing his own, old language (Hebrew) just as he has lost his own homeland, in the new language (German) – an idiom shaped by the Christian world-view – he can find no new home. The German *Mutter* and German *Vater* are not the same as the Jewish mother and the Jewish father. These are better reflected in the appropriated 'hybrid' Yiddish *mûter* and *fóter* (colloquially, *mame* and *tate*) which neutralize 'the Christian splendour and coldness'. The German *Familie* is not the Yiddish *mišpoche*, although the similarity between *Mutter* and *mûter* and *Vater* and *fóter* tells us they are closely related. This is connected with a cultural relativization of German, the language Kafka and his friends had been hearing all their lives from their 'un-German mothers'.[124] Although German is his 'mother tongue' or 'natural language',[125] Kafka considers himself 'half-German'[126] and he cannot fully grasp his world with it. German is his mother tongue, yet still he feels its foreignness when he tries to name his mother in it; he is at home in German, yet still – whether he is on the inside looking out or on the outside looking in – he feels a stranger in it, as we will see in the chapter on 'mauscheln' or 'mumbling', as Yiddish and the Jews' distinctive way of speaking German were dismissively referred to by German speakers.

Yiddish, which as the 'hybrid' language of the diaspora signals the loss of Hebrew, may nevertheless be a way of overcoming that loss, as it is the language of a living ethno-national community. Kafka's fascination with Yiddish – evidenced by his 'Introductory speech on Jargon [Yiddish]' given at an evening organized by Yitzchak Löwy on 18 February 1912[127] – is aesthetically motivated. He speaks of the astonishing sense of estrangement from what is close to you, from what you know and own: You can't understand a word and yet – if you know German – you can understand it all. This tension between the alien and the familiar, the distant and the near, which makes Yiddish untranslatable into German, is what intrigues Kafka and sets him off on an 'ethnographic' study of Yiddish:

---

124 See Kafka, *Briefe 1914–1917*, p. 342; Kafka, *Letters to Friends, Family and Editors*, p. 152.

125 Franz Kafka to Milena Jesenská, 12 May 1920. – See Franz Kafka, *Briefe 1918–1920* (Letters 1918–1920). Ed. by Hans-Gerd Koch. Frankfurt am Main: S. Fischer 2013, p. 134; Franz Kafka, *Letters to Milena*. Edited by Willi Haas. Translated by Tania and James Stern. New York: Schocken Books [1953] 1965, p. 30.

126 Franz Kafka to Ottla, 21 February 1919. – See Kafka, *Briefe 1918–1920*, p. 72. See also Franz Kafka, *Letters to Ottla and Family*. Translated by Richard and Clara Winston. New York: Schocken Books 1982, p. 35.

127 For the background to this event see also Binder, *Kafka-Kommentar*, p. 387 ff., Evelyn Torton Beck, *Kafka and the Yiddish Theater. Its Impact on His Work*. Madison: University of Wisconsin Press 1971. There is a lot of scholarship on Kafka and Yiddish theatre. For more details see Guido Massimo, *Franz Kafka, Jicchak Löwy und das jiddische Theater. 'Dieses nicht niederzudrückende Feuer des Löwy'* (Franz Kafka, Yitzchak Löwy and Yiddish Theatre. 'This Irrepressible Fire of Löwy's'). Frankfurt am Main: Stromfeld & Nexus 2007.

> Because you can't translate Jargon into German. The connections between Jargon and German are so delicate and meaningful that they would rupture completely if you tried to translate Jargon back into German, that is, you wouldn't be translating Jargon, but something non-existent. Translating into French, for example, you can convey Jargon to the French; translating it into German you destroy it. 'Toit', for example, is certainly not 'tot', and 'Blüt' is in no way 'Blut'.[128]

Objectively, of course, 'toit' does mean 'tot' ('dead'), and 'blüt' or 'blut' does mean 'Blut' ('blood'). But the Yiddish words have – like 'múter' and 'fóter' – different associations and a different aesthetic value, besides their emotional one, which gain depth and breadth when set against the German. Their foreign sound – the 'Hasidic melody' of Yiddish – renders familiar words unfamiliar to the Central European listener brought up in a non-Yiddish setting, placing them, with new connotative value, in a different spiritual and social context of which it becomes an important part, if not the very precondition and (textual) objective for the reception of original Yiddish folk theatre and, as Buber saw it, the source of its creative power.

It is no accident that Kafka in his 'Character sketch of small literatures', in which he notates the findings of his 'ethnographic research', also touches on Czech. For the Czechs, too, at that time still a people without a state, it was equally true that a nation's backbone and instrument of self-definition is its literature, written in its own language. Giving Czech 'a voice' and an ethnographic canon was a project that satisfied both the aesthetic needs of the time and the nationalist agenda. We find something similar with Yiddish, which is seen as a 'folk' language ('*Volkssprache*') whose 'vitality' becomes an aesthetic value in itself and thus a substitute for a political program – as was the case with Czech.

Thus Kafka's fascination with 'jargon' goes beyond the merely aesthetic: for him Yiddish is the embodiment of 'unity', 'strength' and 'self-confidence':

> But once Jargon has you in its grip – and Jargon is everything: word, Hasidic melody and the essence of the Eastern Jewish actor himself – then you can forget about your former peace. Then you will get to feel the true *unity* of Jargon, so *strongly* that you will be afraid – not of the Jargon but of yourself. You wouldn't be able to bear this fear alone, if the Jargon didn't also fill you with *self-confidence*, which withstands the fear and is even stronger than it.[129]

---

128 Franz Kafka, *Beschreibung eines Kampfes und andere Schriften aus dem Nachlaß in der Fassung der Handschrift* (Description of a Struggle and other Literary Remains based on the handwritten manuscripts). Ed. by Hans-Gerd Koch. Frankfurt am Main: S. Fischer 1994, p. 152.

129 Kafka, *Beschreibung eines Kampfes*, p. 153. My emphases.

For Kafka, the vital 'unity', 'strength' and 'self-confidence' are rarely to be found outside the context of Yiddish:

> The second poem is by Frug and is called Sand and Stars. / It's a bitter interpretation of a biblical promise. It says we shall be as the sand on the seashore and the stars in the heavens. Well, we've already been trampled on like sand. When will the bit about the stars come true?[130]

For Kafka Yiddish is also a counterweight to the loss of cultural and social bonds. Its strength lies in the fact that the Eastern Jews live in unity with each other; they neither deny nor doubt their identity but actively espouse it. Max Brod, too, felt the 'life' in Yitzchak Löwy's folk theatre, whereas in the *Bar Kochba* academic society he saw only 'theory'.[131] For Hebrew-oriented Zionists, however, and for assimilated Prague Jews, any identification with Eastern Judaism and Yiddish might – in all but a few cases[132] – be taken as a provocation.[133] The first regarded Yiddish as a language of diaspora; the second saw its use as a mark of cultural reorientation and regression to a German 'jargon'.

In truth not even Kafka's parents – especially his father – had much understanding for their son's enthusiasm. They certainly did not attend a recital evening that he organized in the Jewish Town Hall, where he gave an introductory lecture.[134] The objective of the event was to raise money for Löwy's troupe, but in this it failed owing to a lack of interest among the Prague Jewish community it had aimed to address and convert. Kafka's support of Löwy could be seen as a demarcation line separating him from the world of his father or, more exactly, from the culture of assimilation. Kafka even writes of a 'lack of any kind of solid Jewish ground under [his] feet'.[135]

> Rather than psychology I prefer in this case the realization that this father complex, from which so many derive intellectual nourishment, concerns not the innocent father but the father's Judaism. Most people who started writing German wanted to get away from Judaism, mostly with their father's vague consent (it was this vagueness that was so offensive); they wanted to but, with their hind feet still stuck in father's Judaism, their front feet could find no new ground. The resulting desperation was their inspiration.[136]

130 Kafka, *Beschreibung eines Kampfes*, p. 151.
131 Max Brod, *Streitbares Leben. Autobiographie* (Disputatious Life: An Autobiography). Munich: Kindler 1960, p. 215.
132 Franz Kafka was supported by Max Brod's parents, at least, who bought tickets for the evening. – See Brod – Kafka, *Eine Freundschaft*, p. 470.
133 See Kilcher, Kafka, Scholem und die Politik der jüdischen Sprachen, p. 93.
134 Diary, 25 February 1912. – See Kafka, *Tagebücher*, p. 379.
135 Brod – Kafka, *Eine Freundschaft*, p. 402.
136 Brod – Kafka, *Eine Freundschaft*, p. 360.

Löwy and his company were the embodiment of values that Kafka and some of his friends found lacking in their fathers. Yiddish seemed to offer an alternative way of being Jewish in everyday life. Jiří (Georg) Mordechai Langer, a friend of Franz Kafka, to whom we shall return in the chapter 'Kafka's Czech reading in context', went to an Eastern *yeshiva* to learn more about Judaism and live his Jewish dream.[137] They, the sons, rejected assimilation and attempts at advancement in bourgeois society by those Jewish families that had 'gone cold'.[138] He later wrote to his father:

> Later, as a young man, I could not understand how, with the insignificant scrap of Judaism you yourself possessed, you could reproach me for not making an effort [...] to cling to a similar, insignificant scrap. It was indeed, so far as I could see, a mere nothing, a joke – not even a joke. Four days a year you went to the synagogue, where you were, to say the least, closer to the indifferent than to those who took it seriously [...][139]

This could explain his commitment to the 'zealous', 'lived' Jewishness that arrived in Prague in the person of Yitzchak Löwy and his theatre company, who put across their message in a 'Jewish' language used throughout a large ethno-national community: Yiddish.[140] But the assimilated Jews of Prague saw Löwy and his troupe, with their outlandish seeming language and customs, more as provocateurs than as models to be emulated. And provocative is clearly what the alienating otherness of Yiddish was meant to be, jolting the community out of its daily cultural certitudes. How else are we to understand Kafka's formulation in his lecture: 'you will be afraid – not of the jargon but of yourself'?[141]

This was not the only issue that drove a wedge between father and son. The son might lose patience with the father's caution in matters of language, criticising not only his assimilation in terms of language and religion, but also his passive involvement in the Czech-German language struggle by declaring himself and his family as Czech in a city which at the time was dominated by Czechs – although such caution was quite understandable given the intensity of the language war. So it is not surprising that Kafka's authorial subject expresses the 'The wish to be a Red Indian' (1912), to remove himself from

---

137 More in Walter Koschmal, *Der Dichternomade: Jiří Mordechai Langer ein tschechisch-jüdischer Autor* (A Nomad Poet: Jiří Mordechai Langer – a Czech-Jewish Author). Cologne, Weimar, Vienna: Böhlau 2010.

138 For more on conversions in the Kafka family see Northey, *Kafkas Mischpoche*.

139 Franz Kafka, *Dearest Father. Stories and Other Writings*. Translated by Ernst Kaiser and Eithne Wilkins. New York: Schocken 1954, p. 172.

140 See Brod – Kafka, *Eine Freundschaft*, p. 171.

141 Kafka, *Beschreibung eines Kampfes*, p. 153.

the public sphere,[142] to ride only one horse, not try and straddle two, he stops short, but does not become really an active Zionist like Max Brod.[143] Indeed, Kafka described the 11th Zionist Congress, which he briefly attended on 8 September 1913 while on a business trip to Vienna, as 'an entirely alien event'.[144] But, as the irony in the following passage makes clear, this was very far from the lack of involvement that characterized his father, or one Prague Jew

> who until the overthrow [1918] was (in secret) a member of both the German Club Deutsches Haus and the Czech Club Měšťanská beseda, who has only now succeeded, through various connections, in getting himself dismissed from the German Club (his name was deleted) and had his son transferred to the Czech Realschule [secondary school], [where] 'he will learn neither German nor Czech, only how to bark'. Naturally, his choice was governed 'by his faith'.[145]

Yet not even Yiddish provided lasting certainty: the language of diaspora was not the rock on which a renewed Jewish culture and Jewish spirit could be founded. Kafka became aware of this in the language of Yitzchak Löwy, whose 'language veers between Yiddish and German, inclining more to German'.[146]

FRANZ KAFKA AND HEBREW

In time Kafka's enthusiasm for Yiddish waned. In 1916 and 1917, the year in which Kafka wrote 'A page from an old manuscript', the Prague Jewish community was struggling to cope with a large influx of Eastern Jews fleeing from the front in Galicia.[147] Partly on account of this synchronicity, Binder sees the story as an allegorical portrayal of the Eastern Jews: without a language of their own, or rather without any language at all (the 'nomads' communicate like 'jackdaws' – *kavka* [kafka] in Czech – maybe a reference to the fact that the Jew *Kafka* also had no Jewish language), without culture (they feed on raw meat), and without a plan (they are drawn to the imperial palace but, unable or unwilling to attack it, stop at its gates). Before them are the massive walls of the palace. The inability of the nomads to penetrate the pal-

142 See Hartmut Binder, *Kafka-Kommentar zu sämtlichen Erzählungen* (Commentaries on Kafka's Complete Stories). Reprint of the 3. edition from 1982. Munich: Winkler 1986, p. 115.

143 See Brod – Kafka, *Eine Freundschaft*, p. 313.

144 See Brod – Kafka, *Eine Freundschaft*, p. 473.

145 Franz Kafka to Max Brod, March 1920. – See Brod – Kafka, *Eine Freundschaft*, p. 272.

146 Brod – Kafka, *Eine Freundschaft*, p. 171.

147 For details see Hartmut Binder, *Kafka-Handbuch in zwei Bänden* (A Kafka Manual in two Volumes). Stuttgart: Kröner 1979, p. 374. See also Jiří Kuděla: Galician and East European Refugees in the Historic Lands: 1914–16. *Review for the History of Czechoslovak Jews* 4 (1991–92), pp. 15–32.

ace, which can be equated with the Jewish temple and thus with the halacha and Hebrew, may be taken as Kafka's reorientation from Yiddish to Hebrew. Yiddish as the language of the Eastern Jews is now associated – for Kafka too, apparently – with adaptability, assimilation, diaspora.[148] Describing a meeting with an Eastern rabbi from Belz, he speaks of a 'strange mixture of enthusiasm, curiosity, scepticism, approval and irony'.[149] Brod dismisses Western apologists of 'Judaism' as 'Western lutenists', while Kafka eventually rejects Buber, calling his books 'disgusting'.[150] On the evidence of 'An old manuscript' it would seem that by 1917, or perhaps early 1918, Kafka's 'Yiddish phase' had come to an end,[151] although the story also admits of other interpretations as we shall see in the chapter 'Kafka's organic language'. It also raises the question as to which 'side' is shown in a more critical light: the nomads who, with no grammar, no culture and no agenda, come pouring pell-mell into the empire; or the local population who, like the narrator himself, have no means of resisting the intruders and despite their cultural 'superiority' can only respond with words – by recounting the horrific story of how a live ox was brutally hacked to pieces before their eyes. For Kilcher this suggests Kafka was still on the side of 'yiddishism'.[152]

Yet we do have other evidence of Kafka's shift from Yiddish to Hebrew at that time, at least in a linguistic sense. In May 1917 – possibly 'inspired' by Gershom Scholem[153] – Kafka began taking a more active interest in Hebrew, which as recently as 1913–14 had become the dominant language in Palestine.[154] And although he soon discontinued his Hebrew lessons for health and personal reasons, he resumed them the following year. His teacher was a young woman named Puah Ben-Tovim, who came to Prague 'on Hugo Bergmann's advice'[155] in 1922 and became an object of general awe as she belonged to the first generation brought up in Jerusalem with Hebrew as their native language:

> The news that she wishes to sing spreads immediately, and soon they come streaming in.[156]

---

148 See Kilcher, Kafka, Scholem und die Politik der jüdischen Sprachen, pp. 82 ff.

149 See Brod – Kafka, *Eine Freundschaft*, p. 150 ff., also 154. – See also Robertson, *Kafka, Judaism, Politics, and Literature*, pp. 176 ff., as well as Kilcher, Kafka und das Judentum, p. 204.

150 Brod – Kafka, *Eine Freundschaft*, p. 201, 228.

151 See Brod – Kafka, *Eine Freundschaft*, p. 226 f.

152 See Kilcher, Kafka und das Judentum, p. 203.

153 See Kilcher, Kafka, Scholem und die Politik der jüdischen Sprachen, p. 84.

154 See Kilcher, Kafka, Scholem und die Politik der jüdischen Sprachen, p. 91.

155 See Puah Menzel-Ben-Tovim, Ich war Kafkas Hebräischlehrerin (I was Kafka's Hebrew teacher). In: Hans-Gerd Koch (ed.), *„Als Kafka mir entgegen kam…" Erinnerungen an Franz Kafka* ('As Kafka approached me.' Recollections of Franz Kafka). Berlin: Wagenbach 1995, pp. 165–167, p. 165.

156 Franz Kafka, Josephine the singer, or The mouse people. In: *Franz Kafka, Stories 1904–1924*, translated by J.A. Underwood, with a foreword by Jorge Luis Borges. London: Abacus 1995, p. 257.

Kafka, who was never free of 'the not unjustified fear of disturbances',[157] was fascinated by the sense of conviction that emanated from Puah and her language.[158] In the dainty person of Puah – the 'only' one in Prague who speaks and lives 'proper' Hebrew, and whom Kafka's mother asked to teach her son[159] – we may discern the prototype of little, 'dainty'[160] Josephine, the central figure in the short story 'Josephine the Singer, or The mouse people' (March 1924),[161] who like Puah has an extraordinary way of 'singing':

> Anyone who has not heard her does not know the power of song. There is no one her singing does not enthral, which, given that as a species we are not fond of music, is saying a great deal.[162]

Kafka is not only talking about the teaching of Hebrew, with its emphases on singing and song; he is also criticizing the assimilationists of that time, who are in their 'being', as we read a few lines later, 'not fond of' singing. Yet Hebrew ('singing'), which by Kafka's day the average Central European Jew had stopped using or forgotten, apart from the few fragments he heard in the synagogue, is a fundamental attribute of 'The [...] People' – even if it is only 'squeaking' in Jargon:

> So is it in fact singing at all? We may be unmusical but we have our traditions of song; singing was not unknown to our people in the olden days; it is mentioned in legend, and there are even songs that have come down to us, though of course no one can sing them anymore. [...] We all squeak, though of course nobody thinks of passing it off as art; we squeak without paying any attention to the fact, indeed without being aware of it, and there are many among us who do not even realize that squeaking is one of our distinguishing characteristics.[163]

The narrator may tell us that the transition from singing to squeaking is barely discernible, yet still the two are construed as opposites, Josephine's singing (the Hebrew of Puah the 'new Jewess') being contrasted with the squeaking of 'the mouse people', whereby the 'people' in the discourse of the day – and thus also for Kafka – was associated with Yiddish: 'Anyway, the fact is that she denies any connection between her art and squeaking'.[164]

---

157 See Brod – Kafka, *Eine Freundschaft*, p. 385.
158 See Menzel-Ben-Tovim, Ich war Kafkas Hebräischlehrerin, p. 166.
159 See Menzel-Ben-Tovim, Ich war Kafkas Hebräischlehrerin, p. 165.
160 See Kafka, *Ein Landarzt*, p. 276.
161 For the mouse motif see Brod – Kafka, *Eine Freundschaft*, p. 198, 200, 202.
162 Kafka, Josephine the Singer, p. 253.
163 Kafka, Josephine the Singer, p. 254.
164 Kafka, Josephine the Singer, p. 255.

This is more than a matter of music or language. For even though the difference between squeaking (Yiddish) and singing (Hebrew) is very slight, if discernible at all, for the mouse people Josephine's singing means salvation:

> In a grave political and economic situation her singing supposedly constitutes nothing less than our salvation; if it does not banish misfortune, at least it gives us the strength to bear it. She does not say so, either directly or indirectly, she does not talk much at all, she is silent compared with us chatterboxes, but it flashes from her eyes, and on her closed lips [...] Whenever there is bad news [...] she immediately stands up, whereas most of the time she spends lying tiredly on the floor, she stand up and cranes her neck and tries to embrace her whole flock with her gaze as the shepherd does before the storm.[165]

The question remains whether in learning Hebrew Kafka was necessarily embracing 'hebraism'. In *Josefine*, singing – like Hebrew in the discourse of the day – does indeed represent more than a new quality of language and – in as far as it replaces Yiddish 'squeaking' – of Judaism itself, which sees in Hebrew a renewal of its age-old 'being' and collective self-awareness; on the other hand, there is the word 'supposedly' and the distancing which that implies. Nonetheless, in Kafka's study of Hebrew, in his life with Dora with her conservative Hasidic family background where both Yiddish and Hebrew were spoken,[166] and in his attendance at courses and lectures at the Institute for Jewish Studies[167] we can see a search for the 'being' mentioned at the start of this chapter, and a continual reaching out to the land he 'yearned for'.[168]

---

165 Kafka, Josephine the Singer, p. 259–60.

166 See Menzel-Ben-Tovim, Ich war Kafkas Hebräischlehrerin, p. 167.

167 See Max Brod, *Franz Kafka. Eine Biographie* (Franz Kafka: A Biography). Frankfurt am Main: S. Fischer 1963, p. 176; Kilcher, Kafka, Scholem und die Politik der jüdischen Sprachen, p. 103.

168 See Miriam Singer, Hebräischstunden mit Kafka. In: Hans-Gerd Koch (ed.), *„Als Kafka mir entgegen kam..." Erinnerungen an Franz Kafka* ('As Kafka approached me.' Recollections of Franz Kafka). Berlin: Wagenbach 1995, pp. 140–143, p. 143.

FRANZ KAFKA'S LANGUAGES

In this chapter I shall discuss the languages that Franz Kafka used in his everyday life and learned in school or in other contexts. Here I shall not be considering the place of languages in his fictional texts, for example the confused Babylonian languages in the story 'The city coat of arms', the language(s) used in the 'Building of the Great Wall of China', the jackdaw language of nomads in the story 'A page from an old manuscript', the language of jackals in the story 'Jackals and Arabs', the monkeyspeak in the story 'A report to an Academy', or the singing of Josephine and 'squeaking' of the mouse people in the story 'Josefine, the Singer, or The mouse people'. Admittedly, these linguistically hybrid inventions – including Odradek – are interesting with regard to Kafka's bilingualism and his and his family's position between linguistically defined cultures, but in this chapter I aim to reconstruct Kafka's language biography on the basis of his diaries, correspondence, school reports and other sources. I try to trace his acquisition and his family use of different languages in different everyday domains, as well as to identify the changing relevance of these languages in his life and the production of meaning associated with them. I also want to consider the relationship between Kafka's use and view of them and their status in the Prague of the late Habsburg monarchy and the newly founded Czechoslovakia.

Given the role of German as Kafka's first and lifelong dominant and literary language, this chapter may well seem to do it less than justice in terms of coverage: German is the last language I discuss in this chapter and I say more about Yiddish and Czech. On the other hand, I discuss Yiddish and Czech in their relationship to German – both from the point of view of language contact and from the point of view of bilingualism. This approach is intended to supplement and complement my treatment of these themes in my earlier monograph on Franz Kafka's languages.

With respect to German, I argued in the relevant chapter of my monograph[1] that it is wrong to see Kafka's German as the 'poor', 'sterilized' 'ghetto

1 Marek Nekula, *„...v jednom poschodí vnitřní babylonské věže..." Jazyky Franze Kafky* ('...on one Floor of the Inner Tower of Babel...' Franz Kafka's Languages). Prague: Nakladatelství Franze Kafky 2003, pp. 124–186, as well as Marek Nekula, *Franz Kafkas Sprachen „...in einem Stockwerk des*

German' of a Prague Jewish society isolated socially and in dialect[2] and I tried to shift the perspective from 'Sprachinselforschung' (research on isolated languages) to 'Stadtsprachenforschung' (research on urban languages). I have also followed this line in other publications and in my project mentioned in the foreword.[3] I argued that the doubts and deprecation expressed by Kafka and his contemporaries, as well as later essayists and German philologists, on the character of their German, had more to do with the tradition of fin-de-siècle scepticism about language in general than with Prague linguistic realities. Until 1918, when Kafka turned thirty-five, Prague was the centre of a bilingual, German-dominated Bohemia inside the Habsburg monarchy. This meant that Prague was the seat of Bohemian provincial institutions that were responsible also for the predominantly German-speaking 'province' and had used only German as the official language until 1880. This is reflected partly in Kafka's professional agenda at the insurance company, involving frequent business trips to predominantly German-speaking regions outside Prague.[4] Prague had its own German schooling system including the German university employing German staff, some of them from outside Prague and Bohemia, and drawing students from further afield than the German 'province' of Bohemia. Furthermore, Prague was a magnet for migration not only of Czechs from primarily Czech areas but for many years also for people

---

innern babylonischen Turmes…" (Franz Kafka's Languages. '… on one Floor of the Inner Tower of Babel…'). Tübingen: Niemeyer 2003, pp. 81–126.

2 See Pavel Eisner, Německá literatura na půdě ČSR. Od r. 1848 do našich dnů (German Literature in Czechoslovakia: from 1848 to the present). In: *Československá vlastivěda* (Encyclopaedic information on Czechoslovakia). Vol. VII: *Písemnictví* (Literature). Prague: Sfinx, 1933, pp. 325–377; Heinz Politzer, Problematik und Probleme der Kafka-Forschung (Themes and problems in Kafka research). *Monatshefte für deutschen Unterricht, deutsche Sprache und Literatur* 42 (1950), pp. 273–280; Klaus Wagenbach, *Franz Kafka.* Reinbek b. Hamburg: Rowohlt 1964: 55 f. etc. For a critical view see e.g. Pavel Trost, Das späte Prager Deutsch. Pozdní pražská němčina (Late Prague German). *Germanistica Pragensia* 1 (1962), pp. 31–39, here p. 37, Pavel Trost, Franz Kafka und das Prager Deutsch. Franz Kafka a tzv. pražská němčina (Franz Kafka and so-called 'Prague German'). *Germanistica Pragensia* 2 (1964), pp. 29–37; Hartmut Binder, Entlarvung einer Chimäre: Die deutsche Sprachinsel Prag (Unmasking a chimera: Isolated German in Prague). In: Maurice Godé – Jacques Le Rider – Françoise Mayer (eds), *Allemands, Juifs et Tchèques à Prague de 1890 1924. / Deutsche, Juden und Tschechen in Prag 1890–1924.* Montpellier: Bibliothèque d'Études Germaniques et Centre-Européennes, 1994, pp. 183–209; Hartmut Binder, Paul Eisners dreifaches Ghetto (Paul Eisner's triple ghetto). In: Michel Reffet (ed.), *Le monde de Franz Werfel et la morale des nations. / Die Welt Franz Werfels und die Moral der Völker.* Berlin et al.: Peter Lang, 2000, pp. 17–137.

3 See also Marek Nekula – Verena Bauer – Albrecht Greule (eds), *Deutsch in multilingualen Stadtzentren Mittel- und Osteuropas. Um die Jahrhundertwende vom 19. zum 20. Jahrhundert* (German in Multinational Cities in Central and East Europe. Around the Fin de Siècle from the 19th to the 20th Century). Vienna: Praesens 2008.

4 Franz Kafka, *Amtliche Schriften* (Office Writings). Ed. by Klaus Hermsdorf. Berlin: Akademie-Verlag 1984, as well as Franz Kafka, *Amtliche Schriften* (Office Writings). Ed. by Klaus Hermsdorf and Benno Wagner. Frankfurt am Main 2004. See also Nekula, *Jazyky Franze Kafky*, pp. 220–266, and Nekula: *Franz Kafkas Sprachen*, pp. 153–182.

from the German 'province', and even after 1918 from other German-speaking countries. Prague had close and intensive cultural connections with Vienna, Berlin, Munich and Leipzig, including not only guest theatre productions but also frequent readings and lectures. Prague cafés were full of German newspapers and journals; the newspaper *Prager Tagblatt* (Prague Daily News) was read further afield than Prague and its contributors were often drawn from German-speaking lands other than Bohemia. Last but not least, the second 'Sommerfrische' (summer resort) of the Kafka family was not far from Prague – 38 km by train. The fact is that German Prague was not linguistically or culturally isolated at all; on the contrary, it was a major and well-connected centre for German cultural and linguistic events.

In this context it is unrealistic to suppose that there was only one exclusive, unified and stable urban variety of 'Prager Deutsch' (Prague German), even though Kafka himself occasionally spoke of his German as 'Prager Deutsch' and some features of pronunciation and syntactic patterns typical for spoken German in Prague appear in his texts. The 'Prague German' of the time is better understood as a shorthand concept for a loose amalgam of several varieties of German used by various social and ethnic groups in different parts of the Prague agglomeration. As regards the standard of spoken and written German, Vienna was the primary model, although educated Germans in Prague also took note of the varieties of German written and spoken in other German cities such as Leipzig or Berlin. My approach in my earlier monograph was to emphasize Prague's intensive contacts with and exposure to texts and people from the other German-speaking territories, but I nevertheless tried to point out elements, forms and structures specific to Kafka's German, from the contemporary point of view, that correspond to the orthographic, morphological, syntactic and lexical idiosyncrasies of German in his territory and time. At the end of this chapter I shall briefly come back to these special features. They have already been and will be discussed in more detail in publications associated with the already mentioned project.[5]

5 The project *Language and Identity: Franz Kafka in a Central European Linguistic and Cultural Context* was realized through theses by Verena Bauer, Boris Blahak, Simona Švingrová and Ingrid Stöhr (Fleischmann). Nekula, *Jazyky Franze Kafky*; Verena Bauer, Regionalismen in Franz Kafkas Deutsch (Amtliche Schriften, Tagebücher, Briefe). Ein Projektbericht (Regionalisms in Franz Kafka's German (Office writings, diaries, letters). Project report). In: *brücken. Germanistisches Jahrbuch Tschechien – Slowakei.* NF. 14 (2006), pp. 341–372; Verena Bauer, Regionalismen in Franz Kafkas Deutsch – reflektiert vor dem Hintergrund des städtischen Kontextes Prags (Regionalisms in Franz Kafka's German – Against the background of the urban Prague context). In: Marek Nekula – Verena Bauer – Albrecht Greule (eds), *Deutsch in multilingualen Stadtzentren Mittel- und Osteuropas: Um die Jahrhundertwende vom 19. zum 20. Jahrhundert* (German in Multinational Cities in Central and East Europe. Around the Fin de siècle from the 19th to the 20th Century). Vienna: Praesens 2008, pp. 45–78; Verena Bauer, 'Schwimmen zwischen Sprachen' – Franz Kafka und Prag. Sprachliche Variabilität im Kontext städtisch geprägter Identitätsangebote und institutioneller Zwänge ('Swimming between languages' – Franz

German was then the 'mother tongue' of Franz Kafka,[6] but which other languages are in play in the case of Franz Kafka? From the outside and at a distance, the answer seems simple enough: Czech and, to some extent, Hebrew. These are the languages that Kafka read and wrote and that left their mark on Kafka's texts; these are also the languages that are usually discussed in regard to Kafka's origin and faith. If we consider only the languages that Kafka learned from an early age, the list contains just German and Czech.

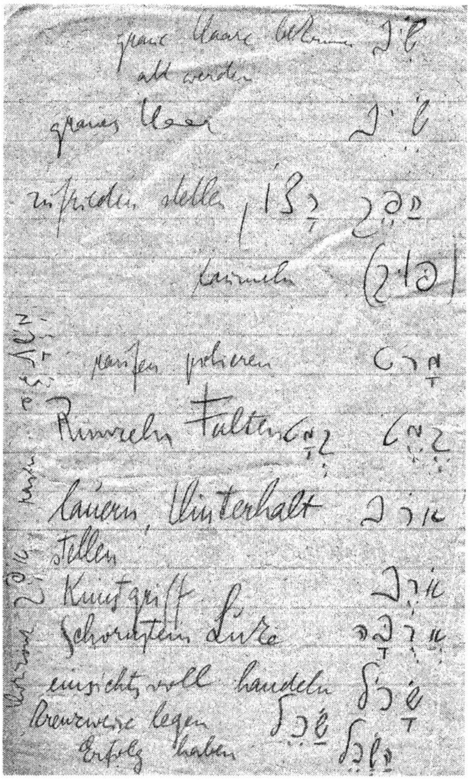

Learning Hebrew through German. Franz Kafka's vocabulary.
Archiv Kritische Kafka-Ausgabe.

Kafka and Prague. Language variability in the context of urban identities and institutional pressures). In: Katarzyna Lasatowicz (ed.), *Städtische Räume als kulturelle Identitätsstrukturen: Schlesien und andere Vergleichsregionen* (Urban Spaces as Cultural Identity Structures: Silesia and other Comparative Regions). Berlin: trafo 2007, pp. 155–172; Boris Blahak, *Franz Kafkas Literatursprache: Deutsch im Kontext des Prager Multilingualismus* (Franz Kafka's Literary Language: German in Context of Prague Multilingualism). Cologne, Weimar, Wien: Böhlau 2015.

6 Franz Kafka to Milena Jesenská, 12 May 1920. – See Franz Kafka, *Briefe 1918–1920* (Letters 1918–1920). Ed. by Hans-Gerd Koch. Frankfurt am Main: S. Fischer 2013, p. 134; Franz Kafka, *Letters to Milena*. Edited by Willi Haas. Translated by Tania and James Stern. New York: Schocken Books [1953] 1965, p. 30.

The list of languages grows, however, if we take a closer look and consider not just the languages that Kafka encountered at home, but those that he acquired at school and those to which he was exposed even if he did not use them actively. These evidently include English, which he mentioned in a job application form, and also Yiddish. At school Kafka came into contact with Latin, Greek, classical Hebrew and French in addition to Czech and German.

LATIN & GREEK

Latin and Greek, the languages of the 'Bildungsbürgertum' (educated middle to upper class), and German, were compulsory subjects in academic schooling, and were emphasized to a degree that today might seem excessive. Kafka took Latin throughout grammar school, for eight years altogether, with five to eight lessons a week. When he completed school, Kafka received a C for his final translation from Latin into German and a B for his translation from German into Latin. He also studied Greek for six years, from the third year of grammar school onwards, with four or five classes a week. Even though he earned a C in his final examination at the end of grammar school, he had sometimes been awarded with Bs.[7] If we leave aside the history of Roman law that he studied at the Faculty of Law, or Rzach's classes on the 'Interpretation of Cicero's speech Pro archia poeta' and on legal terminology,[8] Latin and Greek did not play a significant role in Kafka's subsequent life. Nevertheless, it is hardly possible to read Kafka's work adequately without knowing ancient mythology, as is evident from his short stories such as 'The silence of the Sirens', 'Poseidon' or 'Prometheus', as well as from the character's name Momos in his novel *The Castle* and many other references.

FRENCH

In contrast to the 'dead' languages, French was required only from the fifth year of grammar school onwards, for a total of four years (with two lessons a week). Kafka regularly earned Cs in French, but he also encountered French after finishing his school lessons,[9] both at home, thanks to Céline (Josephine)

---

7 See School catalogues of Kafka's schools from Archiv Hl. města Prahy; 22.–29. *Jahresbericht über das Deutsche Staats-Gymnasium mit deutscher Unterrichtssprache in Prag-Altstadt für das Schuljahr...* (Yearly School Reports on German State Grammar school with German as Instruction Language in Old Prague...) Prag 1894–1901: K.u.k. Hofbuchdruckerei A. Haase, and Nekula, *Jazyky Franze Kafky*, pp. 188–206.

8 See Nekula, *Jazyky Franze Kafky*, p. 302.

9 See School catalogues. Yearly school reports, and see Nekula, *Jazyky Franze Kafky*, pp. 188–206.

Bailly, a Belgian who worked there as a governess for the Kafkas in 1902,[10] and when reading books by Gustave Flaubert and other French authors together with Max Brod[11] as well as with Hedwig Weiler:

> Please, come; just before your letter arrived I thought how lovely it would be for us to meet on Sunday morning and read that French book I am in the midst of reading (I have so little time at present) which is written in a chilling, yet tattered French, the way I love it...[12]

It is difficult to say if Kafka's notes in German and Czech in the margins of Coursier's French reference book on Conversation in French and German[13] were made at this time, and to what extent Kafka used this book to extend his knowledge of French. After all, Kafka's reference to the poverty of his French could have resulted from other – let us say lover's – worries:

> If he speaks exquisite French, then that is a significant difference between the two of us, and the fact he can see you a lot is a damned difference.[14]

In any event, Kafka claimed to have mastered French in his letter to the Workers' Accident Insurance Company in Prague on 30 June 1908:

> The applicant is proficient in German and Czech, both in spoken and written form, and has a command of French and to a certain extent of English.[15]

Kafka seems to have had little chance to use French and English actively at this time. Two years before, when he filled in a form from another insurance company, Assicurazioni Generali, containing questions such as 'Do you know any other languages besides your native language? To what degree do you know them? Is your understanding of these languages merely passive, or are you able to use them while speaking or writing translations and articles?'

---

10 See Nekula, *Jazyky Franze Kafky*, p. 94.

11 See Max Brod – Franz Kafka, *Eine Freundschaft. Briefwechsel* (A Friendship: Correspondence). Ed. by Malcolm Pasley. Vol 2. Frankfurt am Main: S. Fischer 1989, p. 52. On Flaubert's books owned by Kafka see Jürgen Born, *Kafkas Bibliothek. Ein beschreibendes Verzeichnis* (Kafka's Library: A Descriptive Index). Frankfurt am Main: S. Fischer 1990, pp. 35–36. See Herbert Blank, *V Kafkově knihovně* (In Kafka's Library). Prague: Nakladatelství Franze Kafky 2004, pp. 60–61.

12 Franz Kafka, *Letters to Friends, Family, and Editors*. Translated by Richard and Clara Winston. New York: Schocken Books 1977, p. 33. The chronological data are based on the German edition.

13 See *Handbuch der französischen und deutschen Konversations-Sprache* (Handbook of French and German Conversation Language), for more see Nekula, *Jazyky Franze Kafky*, pp. 379–381.

14 Franz Kafka to Hedwig Weiler, 9 October 1907. – See Franz Kafka, *Briefe 1900–1912* (Letters 1900–1912). Ed. by Hans-Gerd Koch. Frankfurt am Main: S. Fischer 1999, p. 73.

15 Kafka, *Briefe 1900–1912*, p. 85.

he wrote: 'Czech, in addition to French and English, although I lack practice in the last two.'[16]

He did have some practice, however, for we know that Kafka, Max Brod and Willy Nowak attended French classes given by an unknown 'Frenchwoman' in the summer of 1910.[17] Kafka also travelled to France with Max Brod in October 1910 and again in September 1911. Max's brother, Otto, accompanied them on the first trip.

According to Max Brod's records, Kafka also spoke Czech on one of these trips, but it sounded more like 'Chinese' to Parisians:

> I know Hannovre street number 4, we first go to number 7. A woman in mourning dress invites us to come in. We first ask for information, and we begin to fall completely into a Prague way of behaving. She is more polite, delicate, witty and funny than the old ladies back home, who are almost stiff in their frustration, seemingly placed around such doors just to make the darkness thicker. In reply to the question, originally meant as a means of escape, as whether the ladies upstairs speak Czech as well, she begins to stutter in a humorous way: We don't speak Cz-Cz-Cz-Czech – but we do like checks! – She starts listing the prices we have to pay upstairs and apologizes at the same time: 'I am telling you quite openly.' – She doesn't understand 'derangement', a term with which we were familiar. We apologize by reference to the Brussels customs.[18]

His stay in France no doubt improved Kafka's knowledge of French, which was based on his firm knowledge of Latin. French literature and written texts thus became a common topic in Kafka's correspondence:

> Please, Max, if you should see any French papers in Germany, buy them at my expense and bring them back for me.[19]
>
> And one more request, it goes on forever but this is the last: I read here almost only in Czech and French, and nothing but autobiographies or correspondence, naturally in fairly good print.[20]
>
> I most want to read books that are originally Czech or French, not translations.[21]

---

16 2 October 1907. – See Josef Čermák, Franz Kafkas Sorgen mit der tschechischen Sprache (Franz Kafka's concerns with Czech). In: Kurt Krolop – Hans Dieter Zimmermann (eds), *Kafka und Prag* (Kafka and Prague). Berlin, New York: de Gruyter 1994, pp. 59–66.

17 Brod – Kafka, *Eine Freundschaft*, p. 464, 78.

18 Franz Kafka, *Reisetagebücher in der Fassung der Handschrift* (Travel Diaries Based on the Handwritten Manuscripts). Ed. by Hans-Gerd Koch. Frankfurt am Main: S. Fischer 1994, p. 180.

19 Franz Kafka to Max Brod, spring 1915, March at the latest. Kafka, *Letters to Friends, Family, and Editors*, p. 111.

20 Franz Kafka to Felix Weltsch, 23 September 1917. – See Kafka, *Letters to Friends, Family, and Editors*, p. 145.

21 Franz Kafka to Felix Weltsch, Siřem/Zürau. Probably 11 October 1917. – See Kafka, *Letters to Friends, Family, and Editors*, p. 154. On French newspapers and books see also Brod – Kafka, *Eine Freundschaft*, p. 141, 169.

Like Latin and Greek, French was very much a foreign language for Kafka. It had no special place in Kafka's life: his contact with French was restricted to his time at grammar school, to private lessons and to irregular vacations in France. Subsequent intensive reading strengthened his passive knowledge of standard French, just as his active knowledge was strengthened for some time by regular conversation with the governess mentioned above.

ITALIAN

Another of Kafka's foreign languages was Italian, which he learned in the autumn of 1907, when he was working in the insurance company Assicurazioni Generali, which had its headquarters in Trieste:

> I am learning Italian because I will probably go to Trieste first.[22]

His motivation for learning Italian diminished as soon as Kafka left the insurance company on 15 July 1908, although he was to use the basics of the language later, when travelling to Italian-speaking regions in 1909, 1911, 1913, and 1920. It is most probable that he took up Italian again even before those travels, although not much of his Italian had remained from the autumn of 1907:

> Today I was in Malcesine where Goethe had the adventure you would know about if you had read the *Italian Journey*, which you ought to do soon. The castellan showed me the place where Goethe did his drawing; but this spot did not correspond with the journal and so we could not agree about that, any more than we could in Italian.[23]

Kafka's self-irony concerning his ability to speak Italian was apparent even as he made travel arrangements:

> Please look out for a place for summer or autumn where I could live in vegetarian style, stay healthy, where I could be alone without feeling forlorn, where even a blockhead can learn Italian etc.[24]

---

22 Franz Kafka to Hedwig Weiler, after 9 October 1907. – See Kafka, *Briefe 1900–1912*, p. 73.

23 Franz Kafka, *Letters to Ottla and the Family*. Translated by Richard and Clara Winston. New York: Schocken Books 1982, p. 7.

24 Franz Kafka to Mr and Mrs Brod, 4 February 1913. – See Kafka, *Letters to Friends, Family, and Editors*, p. 94.

The use and knowledge of Italian seems to have slowly disappeared from Kafka's life and private texts, but it remains a presence in his writings – at least in 'The aeroplanes in Brescia' or in the novel *The Trial*.[25]

ENGLISH & SPANISH

At various times Kafka also mentioned two other languages, English and Spanish:

> [...] if my prospects don't improve by October, I shall take the advanced course at the Business Academy and learn Spanish, in addition to my French and English. If you want to join me, it would be nice. I would make up for the edge you have over me at studying impatiently; my uncle would have to find a position for us in Spain, or else we could go to South America or to the Azores, to Madeira.[26]

In regard to English Kafka confessed on the form from Assicurazioni Generali that he 'lacks practice'.[27] He seems not to have used the English that he probably also picked up during his studies at the Business Academy, where he was improving his practical qualifications before starting his career, to obtain information about America for his 'American novel'.[28] For this he used Czech, among other resources. Kafka's plan to learn Spanish, which arose from his insecurity about earning a living at the very beginning of his career, evidently came to nothing after he got the job at Assicurazioni Generali. However, evidence of some residual knowledge of Spanish emerged later in connection with Alfred Löwy, an uncle on his mother's side, and in 'Memoirs of the Kalda railway'.[29]

HEBREW

By contrast, Kafka's encounter with the basics of biblical Hebrew was closely connected to his education at grammar school, where he was introduced

25 See e.g. Boris Blahak, „...wo die Menschen schreien, als brenne der Boden". Italienbilder bei Franz Kafka („...where the people cry, as if the Earth were burning". Images of Italy in Franz Kafka). *Halbjahresschrift für südosteuropäische Geschichte, Literatur und Politik* 19 (2007), pp. 84–97.

26 Franz Kafka to Max Brod, middle of August 1907. – See Kafka, *Letters to Friends, Family, and Editors*, p. 25.

27 Even though Mathesius was designated an Associate in English from a Czech university no earlier than 1911, knowledge of English was already quite widespread especially in technical intellectual circles by that time. For example, a distant relative of Max Brod, Emil Weis (1854?–1922), made a living by teaching English. Josef David, Kafka's brother-in-law, had experience with English as well.

28 See Nekula, *Jazyky Franze Kafky*, p. 310.

29 See Anthony Northey, *Kafkas Mischpoche* (Kafka's Mishpoche). Berlin: Wagenbach 1988, chapter 4.

to Hebrew in his religious classes. Apart from the study of translations, an annual report from the grammar school mentions reading the Bible in the 'original' and describes the study of the original text in detail, mentioning the books of the Prophets, the 2nd, 3rd and 5th books of Moses (Exodus, Leviticus, Deuteronomy) and the Psalms.[30] Hebrew naturally had a specific symbolic value for Kafka and his family, but outside the synagogue, Kafka had contact with Hebrew only at grammar school. In this period, as later, he learned Hebrew through German.

David Suchoff has set Kafka's interest in Jewish languages in a broader literary context.[31] Here I concentrate on Kafka's acquisition of the language itself. Kafka began to take more of an interest in studying Hebrew again after 1917, when Modern Hebrew was recognized together with English as an administrative language of the Jewish regions in the British protectorate of Palestine. Biblical Hebrew was not the only variety that Kafka set himself to master. Although Friedrich Thieberger, the oldest son of a rabbi in Prague, who gave Kafka lessons starting in autumn of 1918, based them – in his own words – on biblical Hebrew, Kafka also began learning Hebrew from the German textbook of the Hebrew language by Moses Rath,[32] which – at least according to Max Brod – contained material on some 'everyday' situations such as cooking and school. In addition to German and Hebrew textbooks and Hebrew grammar books, Kafka's library contained a second edition of Rath's textbook of 1917.[33] Contradicting Brod's testimony, Bodenheimer argues that the textbook did not contain Modem Hebrew,[34] and indeed, with its method of using modified Bible texts, Rath's textbook is far from taking a communicative approach. All the same, Kafka studied Hebrew mainly because he wanted to be able to communicate in it. In that sense, Brod's testimony is correct.

In 1917, Kafka immersed himself in Hebrew to a greater extent than he admitted to his friends. In a diary entry of 10 September 1917, Brod notes that Kafka confided that he had been learning Hebrew. He had covered 45 lessons and hadn't said a word to Brod about it when he surreptitiously tested Brod's knowledge by asking about numbers and pronunciation.[35] At this time Kafka

30 See Yearly school reports and Nekula, *Jazyky Franze Kafky*, pp. 188–206.

31 See David Suchoff: *Kafka's Jewish Languages: The Hidden Openness of Tradition.* Philadelphia: University of Pennsylvania Press 2012.

32 See Friedrich Thieberger, Kafka und die Thiebergers (Kafka and the Thiebergers). In: Hans-Gerd Koch (ed.), *„Als Kafka mir entgegen kam..." Erinnerungen an Franz Kafka* ('As Kafka approached me.' Recollections of Franz Kafka). Berlin: Wagenbach 2005, pp. 128–134, here p. 132 f.

33 See Born, *Kafkas Bibliothek*, p. 155.

34 See Alfred Bodenheimer, A Sign of Sickness and a Symbol of Health: Kafka's Hebrew Notebooks. In: Mark Gelber (ed.), *Kafka, Zionism, and Beyond.* Tübingen: Niemeyer 2004, pp. 259–270, p. 263.

35 See Franz Kafka, *Dopisy přátelům* (Letters to Friends). Translated by Věra Koubová. Ed. by Hans-Gerd Koch, Věra Koubová, Michaela Jacobsenová and Marek Nekula. Prague: Nakladatelství F. Kafky 2007, p. 938.

tried to use Hebrew intensively, for example in an excuse for an rare failure to do homework.[36] Despite his self-deprecating remarks he learned enough Hebrew to communicate in it during his stay in Meran.

> One of the guests, for example, was a Turkish-Jewish rug dealer, with whom I exchanged my scanty words of Hebrew […][37]

Reading Hebrew texts such as newspapers printed in Hebrew letters or Kabbalah became a regular activity.[38]

Kafka studied Hebrew not only with Thieberger, but also with Max Brod and Jiří Mordechai Langer and then with Irma (Miriam) Singer and Felix Weltsch in the following years. In a letter in German to his fiancée Julie Wohryzek, he wrote a greeting phrase in Hebrew letters: מנוחה נעימה (pleasantly peace).[39] According to Brod's memoirs, Kafka studied Hebrew together with him and Jiří Langer and was ahead of Brod, as is clear from Kafka's letters of 1918:

> Dear Max, Thank you for the letter and your caution. Your Hebrew is not bad; there are a few mistakes at the beginning, but once you get in, you make no errors. I learn nothing, seek only to hold on to what I know nor would I have it otherwise. I spend the whole day in the garden.[40]
>
> Once I am in Schelesen I may send you a list of questions on Hebrew matters. It will not mean much work for you, the questions are such as can be answered with a word or shake of the head and we will have a correspondence in Hebrew.[41]

According to Miriam Singer, Kafka took private lessons in Hebrew with her and Felix Weltsch.[42] A retrospective claim by Langer that Kafka was able to communicate with him in Hebrew fluently[43] does not, however, seem credible in view of the circumstances: it is not likely that tram passengers

---

36 See Thieberger, Kafka und die Thiebergers, p. 133.

37 Franz Kafka to Max Brod, 6–8 April 1920. – See Kafka, *Letters to Friends, Family, and Editors*, p. 232.

38 Max Brod to Franz Kafka, 8 February 1918. – See Brod – Kafka, *Eine Freundschaft*, p. 235. To the Kabbalah see Franz Kafka to Max Brod, beginning of February 1921. – See Brod – Kafka, *Eine Freundschaft*, p. 316.

39 Kafka, *Briefe 1918–1920*, p. 82.

40 Franz Kafka to Max Brod, 21 September 1918. – See Kafka, *Letters to Friends, Family, and Editors*, p. 205.

41 Franz Kafka to Max Brod, 29 October 1918. – See Kafka, *Letters to Friends, Family, and Editors*, p. 209.

42 See Miriam Singer, Hebräischstunden mit Kafka (Hebrew lessons with Kafka). In: Hans-Gerd Koch (ed.), *„Als Kafka mir entgegen kam…" Erinnerungen an Franz Kafka* ('As Kafka approached me.' Recollections of Franz Kafka). Berlin: Wagenbach 1995, pp. 139–141, here p. 140.

43 See Jiří Langer, Vzpomínka na Kafku (A memoir of Kafka). In: Jiří Langer, *Studie, recenze, články, dopisy* (Papers, Reviews, Articles, Letters). Prague: Sefer 1995, p. 140. (Hebrew original in the magazine *Hege*, 23.2.1941, resp. 27. ševat 5701).

would understand and look on with admiration as two people spoke about so complex a topic as aviation in Hebrew. In view of the revived antisemitism in Prague after World War I, it is improbable that the two would have used Hebrew openly. In private, Kafka played with Hebrew even in Czech, as is apparent from a Czech note to Ottla and Josef David:

> I'm looking forward to Věra [= at this time 10 weeks old], she is surely very talented, after all she already speaks Hebrew, as you write. Haam then is Hebrew and means 'the people'. However, she doesn't pronounce the word quite correctly; it should be 'haám' not 'háam'.[44] Please correct her; if she gets habituated to this mistake in her youth it might stick.[45]

Kafka's Hebrew notes – Bodenheimer mentions hundreds of pages – contain mostly common words.[46] Although Kafka stopped taking Hebrew lessons in 1922 for health and personal reasons, he started again in 1923 and learned Modern Hebrew from Puah Ben-Tovim, as mentioned in the previous chapter. At that time Kafka was receiving Hebrew letters and himself wrote in Hebrew to Puah Ben-Tovim in the spring and summer of 1923.[47] An English excerpt from the draft of one of his Hebrew letters demonstrates that Kafka's knowledge of the language was sufficient for more than just trivial conversation:

> I don't understand your troubles with your parents' disapproval of your study. I took it for granted that you would stay a year and half in Europe (don't laugh), isn't that certain yet? Are they settling the matter right now? By the way, it's impossible that you've already received from your parents the letter with the results of Hugo's discussion with them. His wife, who I talked to today, has also not yet received a letter from her husband, who is in Jerusalem. But I well understand the chaos one often feels when waiting for a decisive letter that is lost somewhere. I have felt the same anxiety many times in my life. It's a wonder that nobody turns to ash earlier than they actually do. I'm sorry that you are suffering so much, poor, dear Puah, meanwhile the letter has come and everything is all right now.

---

44 The meaning 'nation' or 'people' can be expressed in Hebrew by 'AM' – an allusion to Ascher Ginsberg (1856–1927) alias Ahad Ha'am ('one of the people'), a proponent of cultural and spiritual Zionism.

45 Kafka, *Letters to Ottla and the Family*, p. 75.

46 Bodenheimer, A Sign of Sickness and a Symbol of Health, p. 269.

47 Franz Kafka to Robert Klopstock, before 18 April 1923. – See Hugo Wetscherek (ed.), *Kafkas letzter Freund: Der Nachlaß Robert Klopstock (1899–1972). Mit kommentierter Erstveröffentlichung von 38 teils ungedruckten Briefen Franz Kafkas* (Kafka's Last Friend: The Literary Remains of Robert Klopstock. With the First Edition of 38 Partially Unpublished Letters Including Commentary). In collaboration with Ch. Frey and M. Peche. Vienna: Inlibris Verlag 2003, p. 54. See also Franz Kafka to Hugo Bergmann, June or beginning of August 1923. – See Kafka, *Dopisy přátelům*, p. 701.

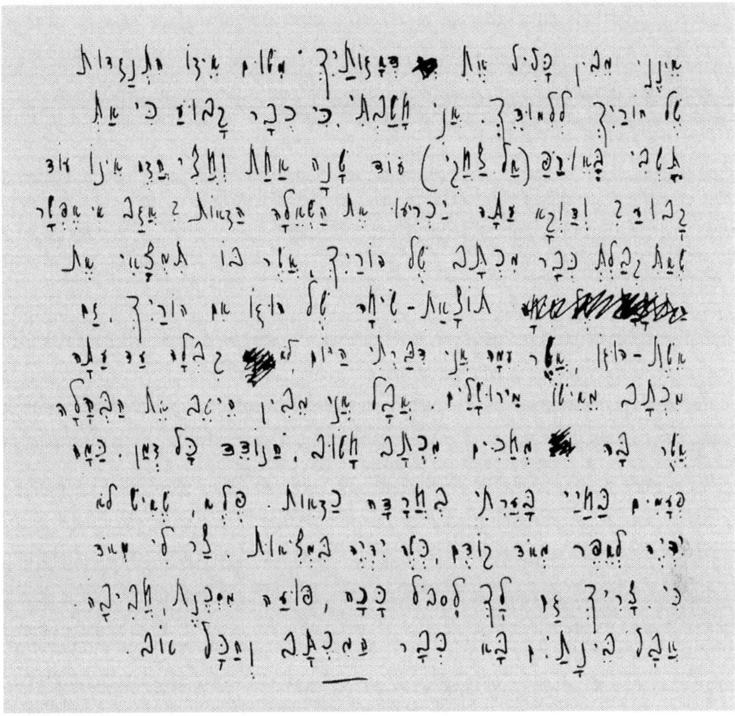

Draft of a letter in Hebrew to Puah Ben-Tovim, spring / summer 1923.
Archiv Kritische Kafka-Ausgabe.

In May/June 1923 Kafka checked a Hebrew text and translated Hebrew business texts for Oskar Baum.[48] Kafka did not quit learning Hebrew in July 1923 even in Müritz, where he was confronted with 'lots of Hebrew-speaking, healthy, happy children'.[49] He read Hebrew together with Dora Diamant, whom he met there,[50] and received Hebrew letters from young participants in a camp organized by a Jewish youth centre in Berlin:

> Please give my regards to all my friends at the Home, especially to Bine, to whom I would have written long time ago if I did not cherish the ambition to thank her for her fine Hebrew with Hebrew on my part, although not so fine. In my present state of restlessness, I have not found the composure to make such an effort in Hebrew.[51]

48 Franz Kafka to Oscar Baum, 12 June 1923. – See Kafka, *Dopisy přátelům*, p. 690, 1046. See also (Samuel) Hugo Bergmann, Schulzeit und Studium (School and student years). In: Hans-Gerd Koch (ed.), *„Als Kafka mir entgegen kam…" Erinnerungen an Franz Kafka* ('As Kafka approached me.' Recollections of Franz Kafka). Berlin: Wagenbach 1995, pp. 13–24, here p. 23.

49 Franz Kafka to Robert Klopstock, 13 July 1923. – See Kafka, *Dopisy přátelům*, p. 694.

50 Franz Kafka to Tile Rössler, 3 August 1923. – See Kafka, *Dopisy přátelům*, p. 697 f.

51 Franz Kafka to Tile Rössler, 3 August 1923. – See Kafka, *Letters to Friends, Family, and Editors*, p. 376.

Hebrew also had its place at the 'Institute for Jewish Studies' that Kafka attended after moving to Berlin in 1923; this was his main point of contact with the outside world.

Hebrew even played a role *in* Kafka's reading: 'Otherwise I *have been* reading little, and only in Hebrew.'[52] He was probably referring to Josef Chajim Brenner's Hebrew novel *Infertility and Failure*.[53] Kafka mentioned this title, in Hebrew, in a letter to Robert Klopstock and attempted to analyze the meaning of the two title words:

> **שְׁכֹל וְכִשָּׁלוֹן** are two words, nouns which I also don't understand completely, but which in any case seem to try to convey the notion of misfortune. **שְׁכֹל** literally means childlessness, maybe fruitlessness, unfruitfulness, senseless effort as well and **כִּשָּׁלוֹן** literally means: to stumble, to fall.[54]

Here he also mentioned the pace of his own reading: 'Now I've been here for a month and I have read thirty-two pages.'[55] The slow pace was a result of the fact that Kafka was not enthused by Brenner's novel and had some problems understanding it.

Moreover, it seems possible that Hebrew was relevant in Kafka's home and private life in this time. Based on everything that is known about Kafka and Dora Diamant, he read in Hebrew from the beginning of their relationship. Diamant mentioned that Kafka had planned to go to Palestine with her, and she repeatedly refers to her inadequate competence in German in her letters to Brod and Klopstock.[56] Diamant, daughter of an ultra-conservative East European Chassidic family, could speak and read both Hebrew and Yiddish without difficulty, and so she may also have done so with Kafka.[57] Kafka himself, however, was quite self-deprecating about his own Hebrew:

> I realized that if I wanted to go on living somehow I would have to do something altogether radical and wanted to go to Palestine. I certainly would not have been up to it,

---

52 Franz Kafka to Robert Klopstock, 17 November 1923. – See Wetscherek, *Kafkas letzter Freund*, p. 60. See also Kafka, *Letters to Friends, Family, and Editors*, p. 394.

53 Franz Kafka to Max Brod, 22, 23 and 24 October 1923. – See Brod – Kafka, *Eine Freundschaft*, p. 436, 513.

54 Wetscherek, *Kafkas letzter Freund*, p. 61.

55 Franz Kafka to Robert Klopstock, 25 October 1923. – See Kafka, *Letters to Friends, Family, and Editors*, p. 390.

56 See for example Dora's part in a letter from Franz Kafka to Max Brod, 14 January 1924. Brod – Kafka, *Eine Freundschaft*, p. 452–453.

57 According to Alfred Bodenheimer, Kafka's pronunciation in certain cases approximated to Ashkenazic (Western Yiddish) pronunciation (this was also characteristic for Freud's pronunciation), but Bodenheimer's examples are from the time before Kafka met Dora. See Bodenheimer, A Sign of Sickness and a Symbol of Health, p. 266.

> I am also fairly unprepared in Hebrew and in other aspects; but I had to give myself something to hope for.[58]

Kafka even saw Berlin as a 'transit station' on the way to Palestine.[59] There is no doubt that Kafka connected Hebrew with health, freedom and life, and that 'he yearned for' Palestine.[60] His daily contact with Hebrew embodied and fulfilled this desire. This is evident from his insertion of Hebrew phrases into his German when he lived with Dora Diamant:

> Those few days I lived on you (I would almost say, based maybe on a Hebrew idiom: on your fat); the paper I am writing on comes from you, the pen comes from you, etc.[61]

Hebrew – unlike the classical languages he learned at grammar school or the foreign languages he studied at the beginning of his career (French, English, or Italian) – acquired a special position in his life. Kafka learned Hebrew more or less on his own or under professional guidance for several years; he could read and partially write it; he was able to communicate in Hebrew, and it is possible that, at least to some extent, he associated Hebrew with his private domain, which may explain the linguistic interference in German mentioned above. Nevertheless, Bodenheimer has reservations about his faculties in Hebrew, claiming that Kafka 'had steady contact with religious Hebrew expressions and writings' and 'that he was quite eager to grasp classical figures of speech, but he lacked any knowledge of the sources of references to the Bible and the prayer book. Hebrew was a foreign language to him in every sense of the word.'[62]

YIDDISH

Kafka's 'Jewish revival' in 1911–12, was related not to Hebrew but to Yiddish, or rather to performances given in Prague by an East European theater company, starting on 5 October 1911.[63] On 18 February 1912, Kafka organized a poetry evening for Yitzchak Löwy. Kafka also introduced him in a speech now known under the title 'Introductory speech on Jargon'. The speech con-

58 Franz Kafka to Ottla David, née Kafka, before 28 October 1923. – See Franz Kafka, *Briefe an Ottla und die Familie* (Letters to Ottla and Family). Ed. by Hartmut Binder and Klaus Wagenbach. Frankfurt am Main: S. Fischer 1974, p. 146.

59 Kafka, *Briefe an Ottla und die Familie*, p. 146.

60 See Singer, Hebräischstunden mit Kafka, p. 143.

61 Franz Kafka to Ottla David, née Kafka, mid-December 1923. – See Kafka, *Briefe an Ottla und die Familie*, p. 148.

62 Bodenheimer, A Sign of Sickness and a Symbol of Health, p. 267.

63 See Ritchie Robertson, *Kafka, Judaism, Politics, and Literature*. Oxford: Clarendon Press 1985.

cerned Eastern Yiddish, which Kafka was enthusiastic about but did not always understand fully. In his diary, for example, he translated the Eastern Jewish word *Belfer* as 'Hilfslehrer' (assistant teacher) or *Schmatten* as 'Hadern' (rags) in brackets.[64] Elsewhere, his literal translation of the phrase 'toire is[...] die beste schoire [shoire]' as 'Thora ist die beste Ware'[65] or 'Torah is the best commodity' might be interpreted as ironic, but could be the result of unfamiliarity with the phrasematic meaning 'knowledge is the best kind of investment'. Certainly it is no coincidence that Kafka only quoted single words in Yiddish, whereas he was able to reproduce whole Czech sentences that he had heard without mistakes in grammar and orthography, and could therefore write letters in Czech. This may be considered an indication that Kafka's familiarity with Yiddish was passive and limited.

Given that Kafka was 'the Westernmost of Western Jews', as he characterized himself in a letter to Milena, not only Eastern Yiddish but also Western Yiddish, which Kafka's grandparents may still have spoken in their youth, should also be taken into account. During the 19th century Western Yiddish disappeared from the Bohemian lands as a result of Jewish emancipation and assimilation. A halfway stage of this process was the Jewish-German ethnolect also called 'Mauscheldeutsch' or 'Schwundstufen-Jiddisch',[66] used by the generation of speakers who were born in the ghetto or its remnant and aimed to establish themselves in a society dominated by German. This ethnically-marked version of German was lampooned, for example, by Štěpánek's plays from the first half of the 19th century, and by Kafka himself in a description of *mauscheln* discussed in the next chapter.

The parodies of Štěpánek highlight the low prestige of this variety, and of Yiddish in general, in the Bohemian lands; this was why the ethnolect vanished during the second half of the 19th century, just as Western Yiddish itself had disappeared as a result of self-regulatory efforts by Jewish speakers in favour of the German 'standard', or more accurately in favour of the variety of German that the speakers in Bohemia viewed as standard. It was because of the common sources of Yiddish and German that traces of Yiddish could survive in the German of those speakers into the second half of the 19th century. Yiddish was originally based on a Southern variety of German,[67] and this complicated the identification of substrate interferences e.g. in pronunciation

64 Diary, 25 December 1911, and 24 November 1914. – See Franz Kafka, *Tagebücher* (Diaries). Ed. by Hans-Gerd Koch, Michael Müller and Malcolm Pasley. Vol. 1. Frankfurt am Main: S. Fischer 1990, p. 316, 699.

65 Diary, 5 December 1917. – See Kafka, *Tagebücher*, p. 282. See also Bauer, Regionalismen, p. 355.

66 See Peter Demetz, Spekulationen über Prager Jiddisch (Speculations on Prague Yiddish). In: Peter Demetz, *Böhmen böhmisch. Essays* (Bohemian Bohemia: Essays). Vienna: Zsolnay 2006, pp. 9–27, here p. 19.

67 See Eckhard Eggers, Zur Rolle Regensburgs bei der Entstehung des Jiddischen (On a role of Regensburg in the origin of Yiddish). In: Susanne Nässl (ed.), *Regensburger Deutsch. Zwölfhundertjahre Deutschsprachigkeit in Regensburg* (German in Regensburg: More than twelve Hundred Years of Germanness in Regensburg). Frankfurt am Main et al.: Lang 2002, pp. 127–137.

or syntax for speakers who had shifted from Yiddish to German. It also complicates the identification of Yiddish semantic substrate for us,[68] but we see Yiddish fragments still appearing in Kafka's parents' letters, or perhaps more accurately, we can see that the language of these texts might be interpreted as influenced by Yiddish or variants of South German dialects. In the very same cases Czech might also be regarded as an influence, and so we could be dealing with multiple models for the contact replicas.

One possible echo of Western Yiddish in Hermann Kafka's German is the form *mechst* (instead of *möchtest*), which – in the sentence *u*[nd] *Du erst Donerstag mein Brief erhalten* ***mechst*** – functions as an auxiliary verb referring to the future, and thus performs a function similar to the Eastern Yiddish *veln* ('wollen' with the meaning 'will' instead of 'want').[69] This hypothesis would have to be tested against other examples of the German used by the Prague Jewish community, especially since there is no support for it in the standard literature such as Lockwood.[70] The example *ich habe* [?gegen?] *meiner Princip geschrieben* could represent a sediment of the Yiddish substrate forms *mayner, mayne, mains* instead of *mein, meine, mein;*[71] the preposition *gegen* is combined in Bavarian German with the dative. Other phenomena that might be reminiscent of Yiddish include the following: the regular infinitive *schmeichelen* and *versicheren* instead of *schmeicheln* and *versichern,*[72] lack of discrimination between the dative and accusative of the article, word order of pronouns in the dative-accusative instead of the accusative-dative in *und werde Dir es* instead of 'und werde es Dir',[73] absence of frame construction in *Daß wird werden ein freudiges Wiedersehen* instead of 'Das wird ein freudiges Wiedersehen werden',[74] relative *was* like in *zwei Tage,* ***was*** *ich von Dir Abschied genommen habe,*[75] etc. The problem is – for the speaker as well as for us – that these phenomena also have parallels in the non-native German of Czechs, as well as in spoken German and South German dialects. A good example is the

68 Here I follow the reconstruction of Yiddish in Salomo A. Birnbaum, *Grammatik der jiddischen Sprache* (Yiddish Grammar). Hamburg: Buske 1988; Ronald Lötzsch, *Jiddisches Wörterbuch* (Yiddish Dictionary). Mannheim, Leipzig, Vienna, Zürich: Dudenverlag 1992; William Burley Lockwood, *Lehrbuch der modernen jiddischen Sprache* (Textbook of Yiddish). Hamburg: Buske 1995, or Werner Weinberg, *Die Reste des Jüdischdeutschen* (The Remains of Modern Yiddish). Stuttgart: Kohlhammer 1969, pp. 11–15. For more see the new book by Boris Blahak, *Franz Kafkas Literatursprache: Deutsch im Kontext des Prager Multilingualismus* (Franz Kafka's Literary Language: German in Context of Prague Multilingualism). Cologne, Weimar, Wien: Böhlau 2015.

69 Hermann Kafka to Julie Löwy, 11 July 1882. Bodleian Library Oxford.

70 See also Bauer, Regionalismen, p. 350. Lockwood, *Lehrbuch*, p: 72–98.

71 Hermann Kafka to Julie Löwy, 11 July 1882. Bodleian Library Oxford.

72 Hermann Kafka to Julie Löwy, 9 June 1882, and 11 July 1882. Bodleian Library Oxford.

73 Hermann Kafka to Julie Löwy, 29 July 1882. Bodleian Library Oxford. – For Yiddish see Lockwood, *Lehrbuch*, p. 133; possible also in Czech and Bavarian German.

74 Hermann Kafka to Julie Löwy, 1 August 1882. Bodleian Library Oxford. – For Yiddish see Lockwood, *Lehrbuch*, p. 135; possible also on spoken German.

75 Hermann Kafka to Julie Löwy, 11 July 1882. Bodleian Library Oxford.

delabialization *mechst* instead of *möchtest* (Hermann Kafka sometimes used the 'correct' form as well), which could be explained with reference to Yiddish or Czech non-native varieties of German, as well as with reference to the South German dialects or language spoken in the South.

Similar phenomena can be identified in the language of Kafka's mother, Julie Kafka, *née* Löwy. Blahak points out that her father was a Jewish hop merchant and this group was said to have used Yiddish as its working language until the 20th century.[76] Other non-lexical phenomena, which appear sporadically, like the absence of *-n* in the dative plural in *Von meinen lieben Eltern und Geschwister*[n] and *von Vater und Kinder*[n],[77] the imperatives *gebe* instead of *gib* or *vergesse* instead of *vergiss*,[78] and word order forms such as *Die frühere Adresse habe ich vom Onkel angegeben* etc.,[79] are hardly strong proof of a Yiddish substrate because they are also present in non-standard German varieties. The Yiddish vocabulary, like *Mischpoche* or *Mišpoche* (mischpóche) etc.,[80] is very restricted in Julie Kafka's German texts, as is usual in a substrate situation as well as in a situation of language shift, but it is nonetheless present, suggesting that the Yiddish heritage had been transferred from the grandparents' generation to the parents' generation in this case.

Some non-lexical phenomena in Kafka's German could also relate to a Yiddish substrate: the pronunciation *Vorworf*,[81] or perhaps *frägen*,[82] the apocope in *Brück, Diel, Tasch*,[83] plural *8 Tag, die Haar*[e], or *Körpers*,[84] as well as lack of distinction made between dative and accusative of pronouns and articles, the gender and case indifference of the indefinite article, or the plural of de-adjectival substantives without *-n*,[85] features also present in Bavarian German.

---

76 See Boris Blahak, 'Deutsch, das wir von unsern undeutschen Müttern noch im Ohre haben'. Sedimente des Westjiddischen in Franz Kafkas Literatursprache' ('German that we have in our ears from our un-German mothers': West-Yiddish Sediments in Franz Kafka's Literary Language). In: *brücken. Germanistisches Jahrbuch Tschechien – Slowakei* NF 18 (2010), pp. 293–321, p. 299.

77 Julie Löwy to Hermann Kafka, 18 June 1882, and Julie Kafka to Ottla and Franz Kafka, 6 April 1918. Bodleian Library Oxford. – For Yiddish see Lockwood, *Lehrbuch*, p. 161.

78 Julie and Hermann Kafka to Ottla Kafka, 12 July 1925, and Julie and Hermann Kafka to Felix Hermann, 12 December 1925. Bodleian Library Oxford. – For Yiddish see Lockwood, *Lehrbuch*, p. 84.

79 Julie Kafka to Elli and Karl Hermann, 14 March 1926. Bodleian Library Oxford.

80 Julie and Hermann Kafka to Ottla David, née Kafka, 12 July 1925, and Julie Kafka to Ottla David, née Kafka, unknown, from Pürstein near Karlsbad. Bodleian Library Oxford.

81 Kafka, *Tagebücher*, p. 127 (apparatus volume) and p. 19 (text volume). See *worf* in Lötsch, *Jiddisches Wörterbuch*, p. 181.

82 Kafka, *Tagebücher*, p. 127 (apparatus volume) and p. 9 (text volume). See Yiddish *fregn*.

83 Kafka, *Tagebücher*, p. 127 (apparatus volume) and 26 (text volume), p. 148 (apparatus volume) and p. 934 (text volume), p. 131 (apparatus volume) and p. 177 (text volume). See *brik* and *tasch* in Lötsch, *Jiddisches Wörterbuch*, p. 52 and 168.

84 Kafka, *Tagebücher*, p. 150 (apparatus volume) and 986 (text volume), p. 127 (apparatus volume) and p. 9 (text volume), p. 129 (apparatus volume) and p. 94 (text volume). For Yiddish see Lötsch, *Jiddisches Wörterbuch*, p. 170 (*tag* – pl. *teg*) and 168 (*hor*), and Lockwood, *Lehrbuch*, p. 21 (*kerper* – pl. *kerpers*).

85 See Nekula, *Jazyky Franze Kafky*, p. 149 ff.

Another marked feature is the high frequency of diminutives (Yiddish, like Czech and other Slavonic languages, even has two levels of diminutives),[86] or – according to Krolop – the greater frequency of the construction *vergessen auf* etc.[87] Blahak even thinks that the manuscripts of Kafka's literary texts reflect the West Yiddish pronunciation in Bohemia, as in the cases of *Zache* corrected by Kafka to *Sache* and the hypercorrect *suständig* corrected to *zuständig*, or *Vort* corrected to *Wort* and *fas* corrected to *was*.[88] Yet these pieces of evidence are hardly strong proof of a Yiddish substrate in Franz Kafka's German because even these examples can be explained as writing errors, analogies (*Dunkel der Fauteuils und Körpers*) or dialectal South German phenomena (lack of sonority in lenis consonants). We must add that these phenomena are not consistent but appear – with the exception of Blahak's examples concerning pronunciation of *s*/*z* and *f*/*v* – only in isolated instances, as in the case of the German of Franz Kafka's mother.

On the other hand, these pieces of evidence – especially the apocopes in *Brück, Diel, Tasch* or the orthography of compositions like *Dorf-Winterarbeit*[89] – have a higher frequency during the years 1911–1912, which was the time of Kafka's 'Jewish rebirth'. This could support the theory that Kafka – at least to some degree – consciously evoked Yiddish in his German texts during this time. He at least is conscious of these forms. Later he comments, for example, on Tile Rössler's misspelling of *Schale* as *Schaale* by pointing to the Yiddish spelling of *fraage* instead of the German *Frage:*

> It is charming the way you write *Schaale* with a double *a*, the way *Frage* is written in Yiddish, I think. Yes, the *Schale* (bowl) is also intended to be a *Frage* (question) addressed to you, the question: 'Say, Tile, when will you get around to smashing me?'[90]

Kafka also noticed and commented on the possible translation of Yiddish phrases in Karl Kraus' German, as presented in the next chapter, and in Max Brod's German translation of Leoš Janáček's *Její pastorkyňa* (Jenůfa), in which Brod tried to find equivalents to convey the special flavour of an opera originally written in Czech dialect. In a letter to Brod written on 6 October 1917, Kafka quoted some phrases and sentences from the translation that seemed to him similar to the German 'that we have learned from the lips of our un-Ger-

---

86 See Nekula, *Jazyky Franze Kafky*, p. 164 ff.

87 Kurt Krolop, Sprachprobleme bei der Lektüre des ‚Prozesses' (Language problems in reading of 'The Trial'). *Wissenschaftliche Zeitschrift der Martin-Luther-Universität Halle-Wittenberg* 41 (1992), vol. 1, pp. 49–57, here p. 54.

88 Blahak, 'Deutsch, das wir von unsern undeutschen Müttern noch im Ohre haben', p. 304 ff.

89 See Nekula, *Jazyky Franze Kafky*, p. 162 f., For Yiddish see Lockwood, *Lehrbuch*, p. 11.

90 Franz Kafka to Tile Rössler, 3 August 1923. – See Kafka, *Letters to Friends, Family, and Editors*, p. 376.

man mothers'.[91] He also hears these (Yiddish) 'sounds from the ground' in the German speech of his father, as in *ich zerreisse dich wie einen Fisch*,[92] as well as in the Yiddish substrate patterns in Prague German:

> I don't know whether 'nur' is 'jen' here, you see this 'nur' is a Prague-Jewish *nur*, signifying a request, like 'ihr könnt es ruhig machen' (go ahead and do it).[93]

As usual in a substrate situation combined with a language shift, the Yiddish loanwords in German are very rare, but nevertheless they are present in Kafka's private texts as well, for example in references to Kafka's father calling Max Brod *meschuggener ritoch*.[94] Kafka also used the term *Moule*,[95] that is *Moule/moul/moül*, which is a widespread form of the Hebrew *Mohel* (circumciser) in Western Yiddish.[96]

This evidence still does not support any claim that Kafka was an active speaker of Western or Eastern Yiddish. Circumstances suggest otherwise. It is more likely a matter of the Yiddish substrate in the German spoken by assimilated German Jews, a substrate that also survived because Yiddish and German share some common origins, so that Yiddish or bilingual Yiddish and German speakers of the grandparents' generation who preferred or were shifting to German could not control the Yiddish substrate in their German. The next generation, learning the German of its parents, could not identify these specific forms as distinctive at least before going through school, if at all. Hermann Kafka's school career was, of course, very short, while as regards his wife, female schooling did not extend to the secondary level until the second half of the 19th century.

Kafka also used some semantic loans from Western Yiddish unconsciously. The term *Winkel* in the meaning 'Ecke' (corner) in the sentence *Ich habe kaum etwas mit mir gemeinsam und sollte mich ganz still, zufrieden damit daß ich atmen kann in einen* ***Winkel*** *stellen*,[97] used by Kafka, is precisely this kind of substrate interference from Westem Yiddish. Kafka's exclusive use

91 Franz Kafka to Max Brod, 7 or 8 October 1917. – See Kafka, *Briefe April 1914–1917* (Letters April 1914–1917). Ed. by Hans-Gerd Koch. Frankfurt am Main: S. Fischer 2005, p. 342. See also Franz Kafka, *Letters to Friends, Family and Editors*, p. 152.

92 Kafka, *Tagebücher*, p. 214.

93 Franz Kafka to Milena Jesenská, September 1920. – See: Franz Kafka, *Letters to Milena*. Translated and with an introduction by Philip Boehm. New York: Schocken Books 1990, p. 207.

94 Kafka, *Tagebücher* p. 214.

95 See Kafka, *Tagebücher*, p. 311.

96 See Franz J. Beranek, *Atlas der sudetendeutschen Umgangssprache* (Atlas of German Common Language in Sudetian Area). Vol. I. Marburg: Elwert 1970, p. 120, carte 58, as well as Bauer, Regionalismen, p. 355; Bauer, 'Regionalismen in Franz Kafkas Deutsch – reflektiert vor dem Hintergrund des städtischen Kontextes Prags', p. 68.

97 Diary, 8 January 1914. – See Kafka, *Tagebücher*, p. 622. See Siegmund A. Wolf, *Jiddisches Wörterbuch: Wortschatz des deutschen Grundbestands der jiddischen Sprache mit Leseprobe* (Yiddish Dic-

of the term *Junge* (boy) instead of the usual South German *Bub*, common in Prague, can be explained either by the North Bohemian *Junge* or by the lexeme *Junge/jingel* that is common in Western Yiddish.[98]

In describing Yitzchak Löwy, Kafka characterized the situation of bilingual speakers of two closely related languages living in Bohemia at the start of the emancipation process: 'Their language fluctuates between Yiddish and German, inclining more to German'.[99] In Kafka's case, because he himself belonged to the second generation without Yiddish, or without German and Yiddish bilingualism, we cannot talk of individual interferences, but rather of collectively used forms that can be understood as substrate traces of Western Yiddish in German spoken by Bohemian (and Moravian) Jews. Kafka acquired them as a part of German in his social context, a context that he is aware of, and can manage, although some substrate pattern replications and semantic loans from Jargon to German were out of his control. In reaction to two opposing reviews, one seeing 'Metamorphosis' as 'ur-German' and the other considering it 'the most Jewish document of our time', Kafka asked himself if he was 'a circus rider on 2 horses', in danger of falling.[100] In regard to German his seat on the horse was firm.

GERMAN & CZECH

It is clear that standard German was not the first variety of German that Kafka acquired and used. It was at school that Kafka went on to learn standard German – not so firmly stabilized or fully established at this time – as was and is usual. German, as well as Czech, was the language Kafka acquired in primary socialization at his parents' home as a first language. Acquired through the Czech staff in the household of his father and mother, Franz Kafka's knowledge of Czech in addition to German could be characterized as early bilingualism, and it was probably at this time that the foundations of his later ability to switch between German and Czech were laid. This ability was developed in secondary socialization at school and later in his private and professional life. Yet there is a clear difference between the status, use and knowledge of the two languages for Kafka.

---

tionary: Vocabulary of the German Basis in Yiddish with a Reading Example). 2nd ed. Hamburg: Buske 1993, p. 191. See also Bauer, 'Schwimmen zwischen Sprachen'.

98 See Alfred Klepsch, *Westjiddisches Wörterbuch. Auf der Basis dialektologischer Erhebungen in Mittelfranken* (West Yiddish Dictionary: Based on Dialectological Research in Middle Franconia). Tübingen: Niemeyer 2004, p. 746. See also Bauer, 'Schwimmen zwischen Sprachen'.

99 Franz Kafka to Max Brod, 29 September 1917. – See Brod – Kafka, *Eine Freundschaft*, p. 171.

100 Franz Kafka to Felice Bauer, 7 October 1916. – See Franz Kafka, *Briefe 1914–1917* (Letters 1914–1917). Ed. by Hans-Gerd Koch. Frankfurt am Main: S. Fischer 2005, p. 250.

The difference was not so distinct in his pre-school years, when Kafka was surrounded by domestic staff who spoke Czech. Hermann Kafka's household employed Czech staff, as I showed in the previous chapter, for various reasons including the fact that knowledge of both German and Czech was a prerequisite for the success of the future heir of a Prague dealer in fancy and dry goods. It was also a question of economy; Czech staff were not as expensive as German. Whatever the balance of reasons, Czechs were at this early time an integral part of Kafka's everyday life and one might even speculate that Kafka's 'stammering' when speaking to his father resulted from the cognitive pressure that can be part of bilingualism when a speaker acquires two languages without identifying them with distinct speakers:

> What I got from you [...] was a *hesitant, stammering mode of speech,* and even that was still too much for you, and finally I kept silent, at first perhaps out of defiance and then because I could neither think nor speak in your presence.[101]
>
> I remember going for a walk one evening with you and Mother, it was on Josephsplatz near where the Länderbank is today, and I began talking about these interesting things, in a stupidly boastful, superior, proud, detached (that was lying), cold (that was genuine), and *stammering manner; as indeed I usually talked to you,* reproaching the two of you for the fact that I had been left uninstructed, that I had been close to great dangers [...]; but finally I hinted that now [...] everything was all right.[102]

There may well have been other reasons for this problem, such as sheer fear of his father, but it cannot be ruled out that Kafka had difficulties separating Czech and German because the languages were not connected distinctively with different speakers or speaker groups: German with parents and Czech with the staff. His parents were bilingual in the spoken language and could switch between the two languages especially when talking to domestic staff, many of whom could not understand or speak German effectively, as well as when talking on domestic topics. We can thus assume that there were situations in which code-switching took place in the presence of little Franz, the first child in the family. This would not necessarily imply that Kafka acquired Czech first and better than German through the domestic staff responsible for him. His mother, of course, was present at home not just during her confinements for the births of her sons Georg and Heinrich, although she helped her husband in the store and with accounts.

That there was language switching in the immediate family is also suggested by evidence that Czech played a certain role in the language of Julie Kafka and the way that she addressed her children. According to Kafka's letter

---

101 Letter to his Father; Kafka, *Zur Frage der Gesetze*, p. 54. My emphases.
102 Letter to his Father. Kafka, *Zur Frage der Gesetze*, p. 54. My emphases.

to Felice Bauer of 3 November 1912, she had 'constantly addressed [Felix] 'good boy' or 'little boy' in Czech'.[103] Julie's use of Czech in this way was probably not limited to her grandson Felix, the son of the predominantly German-speaking couple Valerie and Karl Hermann. Even after her daughters had grown up, she addressed them in German letters using the diminutive forms of Czech vocatives *Ottilko, Ellinko* etc. as mentioned in the previous chapter. Czech was thus the language of emotion, and the play with code switching and hybridity of speech was probably a part of everyday culture in the family, including songs like 'Wir sind die tapferen Idioten / mit den zerrissenen *Kalhot*en ...',[104] where the Czech word *kalhoty* (pants) is inserted in the German texts and acquires a German ending.

Yet it is also clear in this hybrid word and song that German was the first language for all the Kafkas, not only the parents. Julie Kafka's words about herself and her husband shed light on this:

> I, as father is too, am fond of him [= Josef David, Ottla's future Czech husband]. If only he were willing to speak a little bit of German; but he doesn't speak a single word and although we speak Bohemian quite well, it is nevertheless a strain to be forced to speak Czech for a whole evening. Perhaps you could point this out to him.[105]

Code-switching can be assumed to have taken place among staff as well, for at least a rudimentary knowledge of German was a prerequisite for employment in middle-class, German-speaking families. Little Franz may therefore have had problems with the fact that Czech and German were not strictly connected with particular speakers and situations – staff or parents – in Hermann Kafka's household. This may have been exacerbated by the fact that Franz had no natural partner for conversation until 1889, when his sister Elli was born (his brothers Georg and Heinrich died before they were able to speak) and Franz was beginning elementary school. It certainly took a while before Elli started speaking, but after her birth and the births of other sisters (Valli in 1890 and Ottla in 1892), German became the primary language of Franz's conversation in Hermann Kafka's household in terms of relative time spent speaking in it as well as its status. It was the dominant language of the 'nuclear' family when staff were not present, even though the Czechs Františka Nedvědová, Marie Zemanová (nanny) and Anna Čuchalová (wet nurse) were working in the household at that time (around 1890). The family could afford a German baby-sitter, Elvira Sterk, only in later years

103 See Kafka, *Briefe 1900–1912*, p. 207.

104 Based on an interview with Věra Saudková, October 1999.

105 Quoted in Hartmut Binder, Kafkas Briefscherze (Kafka's letter jokes). In: *Jahrbuch der deutschen Schillergesellschaft* 13 (1969), pp. 536–559, here p. 537.

(the growing prosperity of the family was also reflected in the move to a new apartment). Elvira worked there until 1902 and was succeeded by the Czech Anna Pouzarová.[106]

With such a background, it is no wonder that little Franz (or his parents) listed both German and Czech in answer to the question about his 'common language' when he enrolled in the 1st grade of the German public school in 1889. German was not only the language of instruction there; from the 1st to 4th grade, students also studied the German language in classes on reading, handwriting, spelling, and writing style. Czech classes started in the 3rd grade with fewer hours. During grammar school, the asymmetry in the status of German and Czech in Bohemia and in Kafka's school daily life became more marked. In comparison with German (the language of instruction) Czech was only an optional subject at German grammar schools, with less homework and fewer hours of instruction. It was here, in the 3rd and 4th grade of primary school and during eight years of grammar school (with the exception of one half-year of stenography instead of Czech), that Kafka significantly enlarged his vocabulary, acquired the written form of the Czech language, and learned how to spell in Czech correctly (with only minor mistakes in diacritics). In the chapter on Franz Kafka at school I will sketch Kafka's education in Czech and in Czech literature in more detail.

The often mentioned declaration of Czech alongside German in school records for Kafka's first two years of primary school refers, incidentally, not to Kafka's 'mother tongue' but to his 'common language', a category referring to knowledge of language for ordinary communication and not identical with the category of nationality. Indeed, although little Franz may well have picked up on discussions about the national implications of such information at home, e.g. in connection with the impending 1890 census, we can hardly consider the information given by a six- or seven-year old boy to be an avowal of an internalized linguistic, national identity. Furthermore, the school lists are a record of structured interviews with the children's parents or guardians, which means that the data about 'common' language may be of limited value given the sensitive nature of the language issues and the formality of the interview situation.[107] Nevertheless, despite the fact that a national interpretation of this data was inadmissible according to Austrian legislation and legal practice at the time, this inference continues to

---

106 See Nekula, *Jazyky Franze Kafky*, pp. 91–95, 269–273.

107 See also Ingrid Fleischmann (= Stöhr), Sprachen an deutschen Prager Volksschulen (Languages in primary schools in Prague). In: Marek Nekula, Ingrid Fleischmann, Albrecht Greule (eds), *Franz Kafka im sprachnationalen Kontext seiner Zeit. Sprache und nationale Identität in öffentlichen Institutionen der böhmischen Länder* (Franz Kafka in the National Context of His Time. Language and National Identity in the Public Institutions of the Bohemian Crown Lands). Cologne, Weimar: Böhlau 2007, pp. 183–212.

be made. Incidentally, in records from Kafka's fourth school year onwards, we simply find his language defined as 'German'.[108] It was also the language of instruction at school and university and of Kafka's legal jobs as well as the language of his literary activities. This is in no way at odds with the fact that Kafka voluntarily took Czech lessons at the German grammar school for years in order to learn to write in Czech in expectation of the future importance of Czech in the business of his father or as a lawyer in a state institution or a corporate company in socially bilingual Bohemia.

CZECH

The mode of acquisition of Czech in the Kafka family has been described above. As regards his tutored acquisition of Czech I shall say more in the chapter on Franz Kafka at school. The Czech classes were also important for Kafka's reading competence in Czech, as discussed in the chapter on Franz Kafka's Czech reading. In the present section I would like simply to give a brief sketch of situations in which he used Czech and to present the characteristic features of Czech texts authentically drafted by Franz Kafka.

During his studies at the German University in Prague, Kafka encountered Czech only in informal situations. It is no wonder that – despite continued contact with his Czech teacher from grammar school[109] – Kafka lost the knack of actively using the 'classic' forms.[110] On 30 June 1908, he applied for a position in the Workers' Accident Insurance Company for the Kingdom of Bohemia using a dual-language German and Czech application form. In this application he mentioned his knowledge of German and Czech in spoken and written form and signed the German version as *Franz Kafka* and the Czech version as *František Kafka*.[111] Before 1918, however, he only occasionally used German and Czech in bilingual correspondence with the board of the insurance company, but could use Czech in conversation with some employees in the company, with officials in the state and municipal administration as well as with civil servants.

His lack of practice in written Czech became evident after 1918, as Czech became the main official language and the preferred language on the board

108 See Marek Nekula, Franz Kafka ve škole. Výuka a znalosti češtiny. (Franz Kafka at school. His Czech lessons and knowledge of Czech). In: *Kafkova zpráva o světě. Sborník ze semináře Společnosti Franze Kafky 20.–21. října 1999* (Kafka's Report on the World. Proceedings from the Franz-Kafka-Society seminar, 20–21 October 1999). Prague: Nakladatelství Franze Kafky 2000, pp. 59–78.

109 Franz Kafka to Max Brod, 6 July 1910. – See Brod – Kafka, *Eine Freundschaft*, p. 77.

110 Franz Kafka to Ottla, 27 January 1921. – See Kafka, *Briefe an Ottla und die Familie*, p. 101 f.

111 Kafka, *Briefe 1900–1912*, p. 85 f.

of the insurance company.[112] Kafka switched to Czech in correspondence addressed to the board on 12 January 1919 and more than twenty official Czech letters apparently from Kafka to the board of the company have survived. But only two of them – written on 4 May 1920 in Meran and on 16 March 1921 in Matliary – are definitely authentic in the sense of his own unaided draft, while another three – written on 1 March 1919, 14 November 1919, and 6 May 1921 – may possibly have been drafted by Kafka himself. The others are translations or were checked by Josef David, Kafka's Czech brother-in-law, or by Kafka's sister Ottla, specifically the letters written to the insurance company on 27 January 1921, 18 August 1921, 20 December 1923, or 8 January 1924.[113] The shift to Czech is also evident in the form of address on envelopes of letters sent to the family in Prague.

Czech was nonetheless a part of Kafka's everyday life both before and after 1918, although with a greater intensity after 1918. Thus, Kafka spoke Czech to the domestic staff and to employees in the household and store of his parents, as described above. Kafka also communicated in Czech with workers in his family's asbestos factory in Prague Žižkov as well as with his landlords (Michls, Hniličkas) and staff at the Schönborn Palace in Prague or Zürau/Siřem. In a letter to Milena written around 5 May 1920, Kafka quoted a maid from the Schönborn Palace who had commented on his spitting blood: 'Pane doktore, s Vámi to dlouho nepotrvá.' (You won't be around for long, Mr Kafka.)[114] After 1918 these Czech allusions multiplied. To a certain extent this also applied to his circle of friends. He communicated in Czech not only with Milena Jesenská, but in certain situations with his friend Max Brod (outside of Bohemia),[115] the Czech dramatist František Langer, Czech poet Fráňa Šrámek and translator Rudolf Fuchs. I document these literary and/or culturally relevant contacts in the chapter on Kafka's Czech reading.

Kafka also used Czech in conversation with employees and patients in sanatoria in Bohemia and Slovakia. In his leisure activities (swimming, rowing, gardening), and in fact whenever he was out and about in Prague (on the streets, in restaurants, at the *Selbstwehr* editorial office), Kafka was not

---

112 See Marek Nekula, Franz Kafka als Beamter der Arbeiter-Unfall-Versicherungs-Anstalt für Böhmen in Prag (Franz Kafka as an official in the Worker's Accident Insurance Company for Bohemia in Prague). *Brünner Beiträge zur Germanistik und Nordistik* 15 (2001), pp. 113–140. Documented in Kafka, *Amtliche Schriften*, and in more detail in the dissertation by Simona Švingrová: *Tschechisch oder Deutsch? Auf dem Weg von Konkurrenz zu Dominanz. Zum Einsatz von innerer und äußerer Amtssprache in der Arbeiter-Unfall-Versicherungs-Anstalt im Prag der Kafka-Zet (1908–1922)* (Czech or German? On the Way from Rivality to Dominance. On Use of the Internal and External Official Language in the Worker's Accident Insurance Company in Prague of Kafka's Time, 1908–1922). Prague: Charles University 2010.

113 For more detail see Nekula, *Jazyky Franze Kafky*, pp. 363–373.

114 See Kafka, *Briefe 1918–1920*, p. 130.

115 See Franz Kafka. *Reisetagebücher der Fassung der Handschrift* (Travel Diaries Based on the Handwritten Manuscripts). Ed. by Hans-Gerd Koch. Frankfurt am Main: S. Fischer 1994, 171.

only confronted with Czech, but could respond in Czech without difficulty, as well as remember and write down Czech words and whole sentences without a single mistake.[116] This is worth noting given the contrast with Kafka's use of Yiddish, which he heard from the group of East European actors and from Löwy, and which was limited to isolated words at most.

Nevertheless, Kafka's written Czech shows the influence of German. The fact that Kafka wrote only a limited number of Czech texts as well as the range and character of domains within which Kafka functioned in German or Czech, and last but not least his choice of German as literary language, reveal that Kafka's bilingualism was functional, but with respect to written Czech not completely structural.

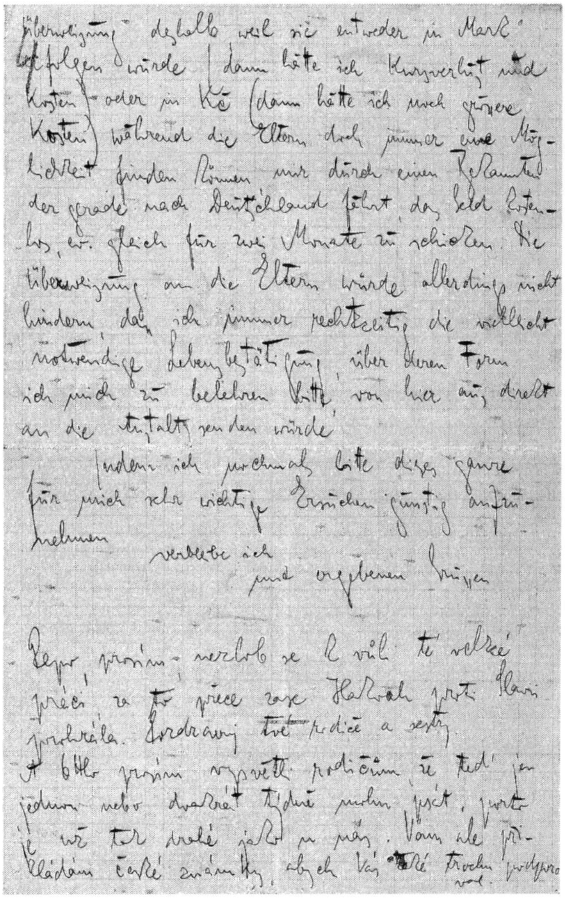

Franz Kafka to Josef David, in a letter to Ottla Davidová, née Kafka, mid-December 1923.
Archiv Kritische Kafka-Ausgabe.

116 See Nekula, *Jazyky Franze Kafky*, pp. 267–300.

The form of his Czech can be demonstrated using all these written texts. Some were authentically drafted by Kafka: two or five official texts to the insurance company, six short texts to Josef David (4th week of January 1921; 4 March 1921; June 1921; 22–23 August 1921; 3 October 1923; mid-December 1923) and some text fragments in letters to Ottla, further quotations in diaries and letters to Max Brod and Milena Jesenská as well as one text to Marie Wernerová (16–19 January 1924) and another to Růžena Hejná (1 October 1917), a draft for Olga Stüdl (Franz Kafka to Otlla, end of March 1919) and the draft of a tax declaration for 1920.[117]

It is not a large corpus but it enables us to say a great deal. The diacritical orthography and typeface of Kafka's texts were essentially correct but Kafka seems to have had a problem with vocal quantity. He used not only *vúbec* instead of *vůbec*, but also short vowels for long – especially at the end of words, such as *nepotřebuji* (3.ps.pl.), *dělaji* (3.ps.pl.), *hezky* (adj.) or (*oprav*) *ji* (*to*), which is possible in non-Standard Czech pronunciation, particularly in Prague. He also used a hypercorrect lengthening in *děkují* instead of *děkuji* (1.ps.sg.), as well as a lengthening in *totíž* instead of *totiž*, *cený* instead of *ceny*, and possibly also *hebrejský* instead of *hebrejsky* (adverb). Further, he used long instead of short vowels in the first syllable, stressed in Czech, such as *náděje*, *Jířiček*, *dívadlo*, *sními*, *láhvička*, *nábidka* etc. The last feature is a clear interference from German where all long vowels are stressed, and the lengthening of the first stressed syllable gives the impression that he was a speaker of Czech with a German accent. The influence of German is also present in the German-like spellings *Horáz* instead of *Horác*, *kommunisté* instead of *komunisté*, *o Berlinském eventu* instead of *o berlínském eventu* etc.

His declension of nouns and adjectives is on the whole correct, including correct inflection of words with genus that are different in Czech and German: *horečka* (f.) vs. 'Fieber' (n.), *na přátelské noze* (f.) vs. 'Fuß' (m.) / 'Bein' (n.), *čas* (m.) vs. 'Zeit' (f.), as well as use of allomorphs and suppletive forms: *na přátelské noze* (loc. sg.) vs. 'noha' (nom. sg.), *na druhé stránce* (loc. sg.) vs. 'stránka' (nom. sg.), *dobrý* – *lepší* (good – better). There are only a few special features in Kafka's declension of Czech. He used progressive, more colloquial substantive forms: *vojáků*, *vůdců*, *papírů*, *řádků*, *vkladů*, *závodů*, *dnů* (gen. pl.) instead of 'vojákův, vůdcův, papírův, řádkův, vkladův, závodův, dnův' (standard at this time). He also employed non-standard substantive, pronominal and verbal forms: *slinama*, *s těma kalhotama* instead of 'slinami, s těmi kalhotami' (instrumental fem.), *celé noce* instead of 'celé noci' or *nehet pravého malíčka* instead of 'nehet pravého malíčku', *nepotřebuji*, *dělaji* instead

117 See Nekula, *Jazyky Franze Kafky*, pp. 503–521, as well as Kafka, *Briefe an Ottla und die Familie*, p. 117 f., 122, 128, 130 f., 139, 151 (J. David); Kafka, *Briefe 1914–1917*, p. 341 (R. Hejná); Kafka, *Briefe 1918–1920*, p. 885 (for O. Stüdl).

of 'nepotřebují, dělají', *zatrh jsem si* instead of 'zatrhl jsem si', and agrammatism (non-declension) of some proper names and toponyms: *čtu v 'Selbstwehr'* instead of 'čtu v 'Selbstwehru'', *mohl koupit 'Kid'* instead of 'mohl koupit 'Kida'' and *u Waldek & Wagner* instead of 'u Waldeka & Wagnera', *je tu Tatra* instead of 'jsou tu Tatry'. Similarly, we find female and other special forms of names given without marking as e.g. female through derivation: *Hálka* instead of 'Hálková', *Bugsch* instead of 'Bugschová' and *rodina Gross* instead of rodina 'Grossova' or 'Grossovi'. In the address of letters to Ottla he used the simple 'German' form *Kafka*,[118] whereas in the address of letters to Ottla David he used the derived form *Davidová*, but preferred the form *David*.[119] The use of non-standard forms shows that his Czech was based primarily on conversation, and the last listed feature reveals the indirect influence of standard German usage as acquired in the formal acquisition of language.

Concerning the verbal aspect, Kafka sometimes had problems with it, as demonstrated in the first chapter. He used most verbs correctly, but his grasp of aspect could be shaky: *buď bude třeba abych se dále léčil totiž bude náděje že bych se mohl* ***ještě dále vyléčit*** instead of 'buď bude třeba abych se dále léčil totiž bude náděje že bych se mohl **vyléčit**', *že bych snad z Vašeho dvora mléko pravidélně* ***dostati*** *mohla* instead of 'že bych snad z Vašeho dvora mléko pravidelně mohla **dostávati** mohla', *Písemně Vám ale* ***děkovat*** *nemůže* instead of 'Písemně Vám ale **poděkovat** nemůže' and 'Na Křivanu jsem se dal **vyfotografovat** jak to na druhé stránce vidíš' rather than *Na Křivanu jsem se dal* ***fotografovat*** *jak to na druhé stránce vidíš*, or 'znáte tu uzávěrku, že? Ta se vždy časem **rozpadne**' rather than *znáte tu uzávěrku, že? Ta se vždy časem* ***rozpadá***.

This specific use has more to do with aspect semantics in specific contexts and situations than with purely formal inflection but still indicates that his grasp of Czech aspect – effectively acquired by native speakers in pre-school years and fixed later – was "influenced" indirectly by German as a dominant language that makes more elaborate differentiations in school language teaching of grammar than Czech does. A similar case is the hypercorrect use of adjective *mluví* [...] *hebrejský* (she speaks Hebrew) instead of the adverb 'mluví [...] hebrejsky'. This suggests Kafka's uncertainty about the differentiation and may be explained by the fact that German does not differentiate between adverbs in adverbial phrases and adjectives in the predicative (both in the context of verbal phrase), whereas Czech does.

---

118 Envelopes of letters from Franz Kafka to Ottla Kafka, 27 February 1919, November 1919, 13 November 1919, 6 April 1920, 17 April 1920, 8 May 1920, 21 May 1920, 11 June 1920; 28 June 1920. Bodleian Library, Oxford.

119 Envelopes of letters from Franz Kafka to Ottla Davidová / David, 28 July 1921, 8 August 1921, 14–15 August 1920 vs. 25 July 1920, 21 May 1921, 26 September 1923, 26 Septeber 1923, 2 October 1923, 13 October 1923, 14 October 1923, 16 October 1923, 17 November 1923. Bodleian Library, Oxford.

On the syntactic level we can point out that Kafka's Czech sentences are grammatically correct and mostly well formed including congruence in the sentence as well as in specific nominal phrases with numerals; Kafka correctly combines the numeral 'five' with the genitive numerative: *pět slov* (five words). Otherwise syntax provides the best examples of the dominance of German in Kafka's use of language in his everyday life. In contrast to Czech with its 'free' word order governed by differentiation of topic and focus, Kafka tends in Czech to keep to the grammatically bound second position of finite verbs in a independent clause like *neboť já* ***zacházím*** *už s tím ústavem, jako dítě s rodiči by se zacházeti neodvážilo* instead of 'neboť já už s tím ústavem **zacházím**, jako dítě s rodiči by se zacházeti neodvážilo' (because I already treat my company in a way that no child would dare to treat its parents) etc. as well as to placing a finite verb last in a subordinate clause as in German: *...že bych snad z Vašeho dvora mléko pravidelně* ***dostati mohla*** instead of '...že bych snad z Vašeho dvora **mohla** pravidelně **dostávat** mléko' (so that I might be able to obtain milk regularly from your farm), *...u kterého Vaše slečna sestra* ***byla zaměstnána*** instead of '...u kterého **byla zaměstnána** Vaše slečna sestra' (with whom your sister was employed) etc.

We also find many phrases and sentences in his Czech texts based on and formed according to German models: correct Czech 'mít strach **z** Berlína' or 'strašit Berlínem' × Kafka's *dělat strach* ***před*** *Berlinem* (instrumental) ↔ 'Angst **vor** Berlin haben / machen' (have / make fear **for** Berlin), 'Hakoah prohrála **se** Slavií' × *Hakoah* ***proti*** *Slavii prohrála* ↔ 'Hakoah verlor **gegen** Slavia' (Hakoah lost **to** Slavia), '(být) mimo domov (accusative)' × *(být) mimo domov****a*** (genitive) ↔ 'außerhalb + genitive (sein)' ((be) outside of), 'psaní řediteli' × *psaní* ***na*** *ředitele* (accusative) ↔ 'Schreiben **an** den Direktor' (letter **to** the director), although the Czech models already looked different at the beginning of the 20th century.

We now move on to vocabulary. In the chapter on Franz Kafka at school I point out that the school provided good conditions for the intensive acquisition of rich vocabulary. Comparison of Kafka's use of lexical units with a dictionary of frequencies shows that more than 40% of the words that he used came from outside the set of 2000 basic words.[120] Though he certainly had an excellent vocabulary, the codeswitching in *To je tak jako* ***Eulen nach Athen tragen*** (It is like carrying coals to Newcastle), *těch dvacet korun předal jsem jednomu* ***Kinderhort****u* (I gave those twenty crowns to a kindergarten) or *referát o Berlinském* ***event****u* (report about the event in Berlin) reveals that it was not without gaps. There are also some semantic interferences, such as use of *přijít* instead of 'přijet', reflecting the situation in German which lacks the Czech differentiation between *přijít / kommen* (come) and *přijet /*

120 See Nekula, *Jazyky Franze Kafky*, p. 421 f. and pp. 440–502.

kommen (come by car, train etc.) etc. While he used some phrasemes, like *na druhé stránce* (stránka) instead of 'na druhé straně' (strana; on the other hand) incorrectly, he was otherwise able to identify the phraseme *na přátelské noze stojí* used by his father as a germanism replicating a German phrase 'auf freundschaftlichem Fuße stehen' (to be on good terms).[121]

Last but not least, Kafka was able to use different Czech registers, as can be seen from the official style of his letters to the head of the insurance company and the informal style of his private letters. The informal style of the private letters also explains some of his colloquial forms. Furthermore, Kafka is obviously able to differentiate stylistically within a single text. In a letter to Josef David of January 1921 he changed the topic from a formal thanks for help to a description of an informal annoying situation in which he employed colloquial forms like *točejí, křičejí* instead of the standard 'točí, křičí' (they run around in circles shouting) to characterize the speech of the protagonists. Moreover in the same text he switched from standard to non-standard and back to standard as marked by the switch from formal infinitive form *-ti* to the informal form *-t* and later back again to *-ti*. The *-t* form is characteristic of spoken language in informal situations. This can be expected from him who subscribed to the Czech linguistic journal *Naše řeč* (Our Speech), oriented to language culture, from 1919–1922.[122]

But despite codeswitching and some semantic, syntactic and possibly also phonetic interference from German, his texts show very clearly that Kafka was fully in control of his communication in Czech. All the same, he tried to avoid using Czech, e.g., in his letters to Milena where he said: 'don't force me to write you Czech'.[123] Elsewhere he reflects on his formal correspondence with the insurance company in a self-deprecating style. He describes himself as a 'poor boy' and his strategy as a 'lie about my excellent Czech, a lie which I set in the world and which probably nobody believes'.[124] The self-irony is followed by a request for translations of two other letters to help him maintain face. Yet for Kafka Czech was also the language of affection. In a letter to Milena at the beginning of their relationship he writes that Czech would have been 'much more affectionate' for him than German.[125]

---

121 Franz Kafka to Ottla, 20 January 1919. – See Kafka, *Briefe an Ottla und die Familie*, p. 67.

122 See Hartmut Binder, *Kafka's Welt: Eine Lebenschronik in Bildern* (Kafka's World: Chronicle of His Life in Pictures). Reinbek bei Hamburg: Rowohl 2008, p. 604.

123 Franz Kafka to Milena, 13 June 1920. – See Kafka, *Briefe 1918–1920*, p. 183.

124 Franz Kafka to Ottla, 3–4 January 1924. – See Kafka, *Briefe an Ottla und die Familie*, p. 153.

125 Franz Kafka to Milena Jesenská, 12 May 1920. – See Kafka, *Letters to Milena*, p. 30.

GERMAN

In contrast to Czech, Kafka characterizes German as his 'mother tongue' and 'natural' for him even though he had not lived 'among German people'.[126] Commenting on his sister Ottla's German, which supposedly contained 'translations from Czech' he elsewhere ironically called himself 'half-German'.[127] In the next chapter I shall explain the way in which this pragmatic, addressee-oriented self-deprecation can be understood as a bitter irony concerning the German of Jewish German-speakers. Of course, Kafka wrote to Max Brod about the German of their 'un-German mothers' as discussed above,[128] but it is notable that although he was a self-aware language user and also very critical of his German in terms of the supposed norm, Kafka did not go as far in his diagnosis of the situation as Fritz Mauthner, for example. Mauthner refers to a 'dead body of three languages' within him and as a Jew feels the absence of a 'true mother tongue'[129]. In fact the fin de siècle trends of stylization and literary skepsis with regard to language were a more important factor than the shape of language itself.

At the beginning of this chapter I argued against the notion of a 'poor ghetto German'. Here I would like to summarize Kafka's acquisition and use of German as well as comment on its locally specific shape. Franz Kafka acquired German naturally, untutored, in the later mainly German-speaking household of his parents, and continued and extended the acquisition of his first language at elementary and grammar school. German was not only the language of instruction there, but was the subject of special German classes. At elementary school Kafka had four years of special classes in reading, writing, grammar and spoken expression orientated primarily to pupils with German as mother tongue. He achieved As and Bs there. At grammar school German was also the language of instruction and the compulsory classes in German were more frequent and intensive than the optional classes in Czech. He had to write a class test in German every 8–10 days. His usual mark was B, but in some cases he was given an A or C. After grammar school he studied at Prague's Charles University and then found employment in insurance companies, eventually finding a post at the Worker's Accident Insurance Company for

126 Franz Kafka to Milena Jesenská, 12 May 1920. – See Kafka, *Letters to Milena*, p. 30.

127 Franz Kafka to Ottla, 20 February 1919. – See Kafka, *Briefe 1918–1920*, p. 72. See also Franz Kafka, *Letters to Ottla and Family*. Translated by Richard and Clara Winston. New York: Schocken Books 1982, p. 35.

128 Franz Kafka to Max Brod, 7 or 8 October 1917. – See Franz Kafka, *Briefe April 1914–1917*, p. 342. See also see Franz Kafka: *Letters to Friends, Family and Editors*. Translated by Richard and Clara Winston. New York: Schocken Books 1958, p. 152.

129 Fritz Mauthner, *Prager Jugendjahre: Erinnerungen* (Youth in Prague: Memoirs). München: Müller 1918, p. 51 ff. See also Blahak, 'Deutsch, das wir von unsern undeutschen Müttern noch im Ohre haben', p. 298.

the Kingdom of Bohemia in Prague, which was dominated by German until 1918. In this position Kafka was responsible primarily for German-speaking territories and agenda. German also determined other domains of communication in his life. Even though he had friends and peers who were not German native speakers, most of these still spoke German, and, of course, as a literary writer, Kafka used only German.

Still, Kafka observed that his spoken idiom was recognizable as 'Prager Deutsch': 'a landlady, the merry wife of the booksellers Taussig with very red and fat cheeks, recognizes my Prague German immediately'.[130] Brod recalled that his friend checked and changed some expressions in his literary texts using Grimm's dictionary to prepare them for publication in Leipzig, and supposed that this involved erasing 'Prague-isms' like *paar* instead of 'ein paar' as well as idiosyncrasies based on Czech syntax.[131] This memory, however, suggests Kafka's awareness of the difference between language norms in Leipzig and Prague, or in the 'Reich' and Austria, rather than his conviction in the poverty, insufficiency or deficiency of his language.

Krolop has analyzed Kafka's German with respect to the comprehensibility of his literary texts for readers outside Austrian territory and has pointed out some lexical 'austrianisms', also used to some extent in South Germany, that might have caused difficulties for other German readers. These include *Auslage* for 'Schaufenster' (store window), *dafürstehen* for 'sich lohnen' (be worth it), *Gasse* for 'Straße' (street), *Hausfrau* for 'Vermieterin' (landlord), *Haustor* for 'Haustür' (front door), *Kamin* for 'Schornstein' (chimney), *Kasten* for 'Schrank' (dresser), *laufen* for 'gehen' (walk), *Plafond* for '(Zimmer-) Decke' (ceiling), *in erster Reihe* for 'in erster Linie' (in the front row), *Sessel* for 'Stuhl' (chair), *springen* for 'laufen' (run), *sperren* for 'schließen' (close), *Tasse* for 'Tablett' (tray), *Stiege* for 'Treppe' (staircase), *überwälzen* for 'abwälzen' (unload), *Verkühlung* for 'Erkältung' (cold), *Vorzimmer* for 'Diele' (hallway) etc., that might potentially complicate the understanding of Kafka's literary texts.[132]

The local shape of Kafka's texts is also revealed in his non-literary texts. It affects the vocabulary of food and drink (*Jause* for 'Frühstück' (breakfast) as well as *jausen*, *Nachtmahl* for 'Abendessen' (dinner) as well as *nachtmahlen*, *Vogerlsalat* for 'Feldsalat' (salad), *Schlagobers* for 'Sahne' (cream) etc.), houses and buildings (*Kaffeehaus* for 'Café' (cafe), *Haustor* for 'Haustür' (front door), *Kanzlei* for 'Büro' (office), *Vorzimmer* for 'Diele' (hallway), *Stiege* for 'Treppe' (staircase), *Durchhaus*, *Pawlatsche* etc.), pieces of furniture (*Kanapee* and *Fau-*

130 Franz Kafka to Ottla, 5 April 1920. – See Kafka, *Briefe 1918–1920*, p. 115.

131 Max Brod, *Franz Kafka: Eine Biographie* (Franz Kafka: A Biography). Frankfurt am Main: S. Fischer Verlag 1954, p. 300 f.

132 Krolop, Sprachprobleme bei der Lektüre des ‚Prozesses'.

teuil for 'Sofa' (coach), *Kasten* for 'Schrank' (dresser), *Sessel* for 'Stuhl' (chair), *Kredenz* for 'Küchenschrank' (cupboard), *Leintuch* for 'Betttuch' or 'Laken' (sheet), *Waschkasten* for 'Waschtisch' (washstand) etc.), time expressions (*Jänner* for 'Januar' (January), *Feber* for 'Februar' (February), *öfters* for 'öfter' (more often) etc.), and personal names (*Drecksorsch, Hausfrau* for 'Vermieterin' (landlord), *Junge* vs. Bavarian *Bub* (lad), Germ./Bohemian *Klempfner* vs. Bavarian 'Spengler' (plumber), *Zimmerherr* for 'Vermieter' etc.) as well as vocabulary in other areas, such as *Matura* for 'Abitur' (final exam), *Gendarm* for 'Polizist' (policeman), together with *Polizeimann*, and *Gendarmerie* for 'Polizeistation' (police station).[133] In the context of his work at the insurance company he used professional Austrian terminology, such as *Ausfolgung* for 'Auszahlung' (paying out), *Beiziehung* for 'Heranziehung' (attraction), *Drucksorten* for 'Drucksachen' (printed matter), *Einreihung* for 'Einstufung' (classification), *Exekution* for 'Pfändung' (seizure), *Cassa* for 'Kasse' (cash register), *Petent* for 'Antragsteller' (applicant), *Rekurswerber, Urgenz* for 'Mahnung' (reminder), *Versicherungskataster* (insurance register) etc.[134]

The lexical items also have a specific orthography matching the orthographical rules of Kafka's time and space as well as pronunciation. A change in the orthography around 1902 is reflected – with a delay in Kafka's texts, such as the shifts from *Muth, nöthig, Theil, Thier*... to *Mut, nötig, Teil, Tier*...; from *Corridor, Rangclasse, Tuberculose, Publicum*... to *Korridor, Rangklasse, Tuberkulose, Publikum*...; from *Proceß* (Kafka), *Mediciner*... to *Prozeß, Mediziner*... (Brod); from *Litteratur* (Kafka) to *Literatur* (Brod), or in doublets such as *Theater/Teater*, etc. The regional standard orthography is evident in *gleichgiltig/gleichgültig, endgiltig/endgültig, villeicht/vielleicht, verleumden/verläumden* etc. The (local) pronunciation is reflected in some instances of spelling of *Tier* for 'Tür' (Kafka also used *Tür*), *Tringgeld* for 'Trinkgeld', *können* for 'gönnen', *kennen* for 'können', *Ausprache/Aussprache, Auschlag/Ausschlag, Austellung/Ausstellung, Hauschuhe/Hausschuhe, Winterock/Winterrock, Vorderad/Vorderrad, Haupteil/Hauptteil, gefühlos/gefühllos, freudschaftlich/freundschaftlich*, as well as in *Augenblich/Augenblick, wirchlich/wirklich, Klempfner/Klempner, wen/wenn, Nachtmal/Nachtmahl*, or in *Wohnungsuchen* for 'Wohnungssuche'.[135]

Regional variants can also be identified in the grammatical gender and case markers of substantives and/or other nouns, such as *der Gehalt* for 'das Gehalt' (salary), *der Polster* for 'das Polster, *der Pacht* for 'die Pacht' (lease), *der Pult* for 'das Pult' (desk), *der Akt* for 'die Akte' (file), *die Gedränge* for 'das

133 Nekula, *Jazyky Franze Kafky*, pp. 176–181, Bauer, Regionalismen, p. 358 f.

134 Nekula, *Jazyky Franze Kafky*, pp. 176–181, Bauer, Regionalismen, p. 359.

135 Nekula, *Jazyky Franze Kafky*, pp. 140–149, Bauer, Regionalismen, p. 359, as well as Blahak, *Franz Kafkas Literatursprache*.

Gedränge' (crowd), das/die *Erklärung* (explanation), das/die *Einladung* (invitation), die/der *Vorteil* (advantage), der/die *Brust* (chest), der/die *Tür* (door), *die Mädchen* instead of *das Mädchen* (girl), *die Weg* instead of *der Weg* (path) etc., and the plural forms *Pölster* for 'Polster' (cushions), *Bogen* for 'Bögen' (arcs), *Balkone* for 'Balkons' (balconies), *Lampione* for 'Lampions' (lampions) etc. The substantives often lack *-n* in dative plural, as discussed above, while in this period the dative singular masculine and neuter still took the ending *-e*, as in *im Dienste, zum Ausdrucke* etc. One very distinctive area is that of the declension of articles, pronouns (*ein/eine, ein/einen, ihn/ihm, ihn/ihnen, den/dem, niemanden/niemandem, jemanden/jemandem*) and adjectives (*mit ihn / lauten Lachen, um ihm / einem Prozeß, vor ihn / den Tor* etc.) with apocope and/or without a difference made between *-n* and *-m* as well as the area of congruence in the nominal phrase (see below on syntax) with repetition of a gender marker (*von eine**m** fest zugeknöpfte**m** Rock* etc.) or with other local idiosyncrasies (*keine eigentliche*[n] *Betten* etc.).[136]

Verbs have regional forms, too, as in *er lauft/läuft, er ladet ein, er fahrt* for 'er läuft / lädt ein / fährt' (he is running / he is inviting / he is driving), as well as *er erschreckt* for 'er erschrickt' (he is scared), *(er) ist gesessen / gestanden / gelegen*, for '(er) hat gesessen / gestanden / gelegen' (he was sitting / standing / laying), *ich kauf* for 'ich kaufe' (I am buying). The subordinate clause without an auxiliary, as in *Karl der schon nahe daran gewesen* [war] (Karl who had already been nearby),[137] is usual in the written texts of this time as were the archaic but usual forms *gieng(e), fieng, hieng* for 'ging, fing, hing' (he walked / caught / hung) or *giebt* for 'gibt' (he gives). Southern German variants are also manifest in the derivation used in Kafka's texts, such as *Kontrollor* for 'Kontrolleur' (inspector), probably also *verständig* for 'verständlich' (understandable), *unaufschieblich* for 'unaufschiebbar' (urgent), *vorsichtlich* for 'vorsichtig' (careful), *gemeinschaftlich* for 'gemeinsam' (together), and also in composition, such as *Schweinsbraten* for 'Schweinebraten' (pork roast) or *-färbig/-farbig* (coloured), as well as in idiosyncratic forms such as *Werkstag* for 'Werktag' (workday), *Zugsverbindung* for 'Zugverbindung' (train connection), *Fabrikschef* of 'Fabrikchef' (factory director), *Fensternrand* for 'Fensterrand' (window frame) etc. [138]

Last but not least, there are many specific syntactic forms, mentioned above in connection with congruence, and specific prepositional and verb patterns, such as *auf einen Augenblick* for 'für einen Augenblick' (for a moment), *nahe dem Ausgang* for 'nahe am Ausgang' (close to the exit), *Freude von solchen*

136 Nekula, *Jazyky Franze Kafky*, pp. 149–160, Bauer, Regionalismen, p. 359.

137 On the afinite construction see e.g. Jaromír Zeman: 'Neue' Entwicklungstendenzen in der deutschen Syntax (New tendencies in the development of German syntax). *Brünner Beiträge zur Germanistik und Nordistik* 21 (2007), R 12, pp. 46–49.

138 Nekula, *Jazyky Franze Kafky*, pp. 160–166, Bauer, Regionalismen, p. 359.

Erfolgen for 'Freude an solchen Erfolgen' (joy at such success), *in Franz stoßen* for 'an Franz stoßen' (encounter Franz), *auf jemanden vergessen* for '(an) jemanden vergessen' (forget someone), *es steht nicht dafür* for 'es lohnt sich nicht' (it is not worth it) etc.[139] The area of syntax is still wide open for further exploration. This includes analysis, with an eye to Prague, Bavarian and Austrian varieties of German from the perspective of orality and language contact, of Kafka's use of specific prepositional and verbal patterns, congruence within nominal phrase and sentence, word order, sentences without explicit subject (pro-subject) and the reflexive *sich*, as well as his use of definite and indefinite articles and articles following prepositions.

It is true that there are instances where Kafka's German seems shaky in orthography, genus, derivation and syntax, but that was typical of a period in which standard German was not yet stabilized. It is also undeniable that his official and literary texts contain variants typical for Austria or South Germany, but this is hardly surprising. An analysis of Kafka's German and comparison with his German-speaking contemporaries in Austria, Bohemia and Prague does not in fact reveal any significant differences. Both lexical and non-lexical Austrianisms in the official language and elsewhere reflect the linguistic and political situation of his time, when Austrian German was becoming established as the standard used in the territory of the Habsburg monarchy. It is self-evident that these Austrianisms are not an indication of inadequate, but only of different German. Moreover, Kafka's writings show elements of dialect (article indifference, weakened declension, agreement in attribute...) both in official texts and in the manuscripts of his literary texts. The frequency of some phenomena, such as compounds with and without an interfix *-s/Ø* etc.,[140] needs further evaluation. On the basis of earlier analyses as well as the present account, we can say that Kafka was proficient in his German: he used 'standard' forms in official and 'non-standard' forms in private letters, and he could correctly navigate between different varieties. The linguistic sobriety of his literary texts, sometimes explained in terms of the supposed isolation of the Prague idiom as a matter of poverty and inadequacy, was actually a conscious semantic gesture on Kafka's part.[141]

---

139 Nekula, *Jazyky Franze Kafky*, pp. 166–176, Bauer, Regionalismen, p. 359, as well as Blahak, *Franz Kafkas Literatursprache*.

140 See also Nekula, *Jazyky Franze Kafky*, pp. 124–186.

141 See Milan Kundera, *Kastrující stín svatého Garty* (The Castrating Shadow of Saint Garta). Brno: Atlantis 2006, pp. 46–52.

KAFKA'S 'ORGANIC' LANGUAGE: LANGUAGE AS A WEAPON

MAUSCHELN

This chapter considers Kafka's discourse of language as a discourse of conflict, drawing on his First World War texts and focusing mainly on the story 'A page from an manuscript'. I would like to begin my deliberations with a quotation taken from a letter in which Kafka discusses the word *mauscheln*, a word which by this time had become a part of the verbal ammunition of anti-semitism:[1]

> The wit principally consists of Yiddish-German-mauscheln – no one can mauscheln like Kraus, although in this German-Jewish world hardly anyone can do anything else. This mauscheln – taken in a wider sense, and that is the only way it should be taken – consists in a bumptious, tacit, or self-pitying appropriation of someone else's property, something not earned, but stolen by means of a relatively casual gesture. Yet it remains someone else's property, even though there is no evidence of a single solecism. That does not matter, for in this realm, the whispering voice of conscience confesses the whole crime in a penitent hour. This is not to say anything against mauscheln – in itself it is fine. It is an organic compound of bookish German and pantomime. (How expressive this is: 'So he's got talent? Who says?' Or this, jerking the arm out or its socket and tossing up the chin. *You think so?* Or this, scarping the knees together: 'He writes? Who about?') What we have here is the product of a sensitive feeling for language which has recognized that in German only the dialects are really alive, and aside from them, only the most individual High German, while all the rest, the linguistic middle ground, is nothing but embers which can only be brought to a semblance of life when excessively lively Jewish hands rummage through them. That is a fact, funny or terrible as you like.
>
> But why should the Jews be so irresistibly drawn to this language? German literature existed before the emancipation of the Jews and attained great glory. After all, that literature was, as far as I can see, in no way less varied than today – in fact, today there may be less variety. And there is a relationship between all this and Jewishness, or more precisely between young Jews and their Jewishness, with the frightful inner

1 Hans Peter Althaus, *Mauscheln. Ein Wort als Waffe* (Mauscheln: A Word as Weapon). Berlin, New York: de Gruyter 2002, p. 92.

predicament of these generations. This is something Kraus especially recognized, or more precisely, this was something that came to light by being contrasted with him.[2]

Kafka is referring here to the feud between Karl Kraus and Franz Werfel who in their polemic about the word *dorten* (= dort = there) had accused each other of *mauscheln*. Upon Werfel's charge that Kraus had inadvertently used a Yiddish word in his parody *Literatur oder Man wird doch da sehn* (1921, Literature, or We will see), Kraus had triumphantly pointed out that Werfel only knew the word as a Yiddish one, whilst in fact it was also used in German. Although there was a very specific and concrete reason for Kafka to make a general remark about *mauscheln* in his letter to Max Brod, his use of the polysemous word *mauscheln* – '*mauscheln* in its broadest sense' – must be understood as a comment on the language use of linguistically assimilated German Jews in general. Through Kafka's use of *mauscheln* the difficulties of Jewish assimilation, and his refusal to take these on, are thrown into sharp relief.

The Yiddish word *mauscheln* was said to have meant 'to speak like a Jew, i.e. Yiddish';[3] it initially stood for Western Yiddish before being used later to refer to the Yiddish spoken by Eastern Jews. It was used by non-Jews to describe the incomprehensibility of the language used by Jewish traders as their working language.[4] In time, their 'secret language' came to be viewed negatively by outsiders, and it was not long before this negative view made its way into dictionaries of the period. As early as 1809 we see *mauscheln* being defined in Campes' dictionary as 'to try and cheat someone in a more or less sly and underhanded way'.[5] Assimilating Jews believed that they could counter the negative view of the use of Yiddish, which resonates in the word *mauscheln*, by, for instance, abandoning Yiddish for German and suppressing any traces of Yiddish when they spoke German. The meaning of *mauscheln*, however, was simply broadened to refer to the 'impure' Jewish ethnolect of German which apparently still bore audible traces of Yiddish even if the speaker had switched to German:

---

2 Franz Kafka to Max Brod, June 1921. – See Franz Kafka, *Letters to Friends, Family and Editors*. New York: Schocken Books 1977, p. 288.

3 Althaus, *Mauscheln*, p. 10.

4 In Czech the word for *Mauscheln* is *mumlání* (incomprehensible murmuring, secretive talking). See Jindřich Toman, Mumlání, špatná čeština a nedostatek poetického citu. Židé v kontextu českého nacionalismu, 30. a 40. léta 19. století (Mauscheln, poor Czech and the lack of poetic sensibility: Jews in the context of Czech nationalism, 1830s and 1840s). In: Zdeněk Hojda – Marta Ottlová – Roman Prahl (eds), *Slovanství a česká kultura 19. století* (Slavonic World and Czech Culture in the 19th Century). Prague: KLP 2006, pp. 352–360.

5 Quoted in Althaus, *Mauscheln*, p. 33.

> My father, who in his own way fought for an exemplary use of the German language, [...] despised and fought mercilessly against the slightest trace of [...] 'Mauscheldeutsch' [Yiddish] and endeavoured, with the insufficient means he had at his disposal, to teach us a pure, exaggeratedly purist standard German.[6]

The abandonment of Yiddish for German thus goes hand in hand with assimilating Jews' doubts about the German language they had adopted, which was also passed on to future generations. This echoes in Kafka's own misgivings about the German 'that we have learned from the lips of our non-German mothers'.[7] The use of *mauscheln* in the sense of a Jewish ethnolect of German ultimately resulted in speakers themselves worrying about being guilty of *mauscheln* or in their being reproached by others for doing so even when their speech contained no traces of Yiddish, that even when is their language was 'pure'. It was enough to be Jewish for the fear or accusation of *mauscheln* to arise. For, as many people saw it, whoever was not joined to the land and did not have roots in the territorial dialect – and this was said of the Jews – could 'not be in possession of a true mother tongue'.[8] This is also reflected in Kafka's remark that one is only 'really' alive in language when using dialects or the 'most individual' High German.[9]

Thus, in Kafka's times, the word *mauscheln* was regarded as part of the verbal ammunition of antisemitism which was bound up with the linguistic ostracism of 'the impure'. The sound of 'the Jewish accent' in one's ear (see quotation below) became, at a time when sound and the spoken *Volkssprache* was believed to have an organic connection with meaning and the *Volksgeist*, proof also of their foreign spirit and foreign attitudes. This was also suspected on occasions when 'not a single language error could be proven'.[10] People could be suspected or accused of *mauscheln* on the basis of a Jewish name or appearance, as Kafka illustrated in another letter to Max Brod of 10 April 1920:

> After the first few words it came out that I was from Prague. Both of them — the general, who sat opposite me, and the colonel — were acquainted with Prague. Was I Czech? No. So now explain to those true German military eyes what you really are. Someone else suggested "German-Bohemian," someone else "Little Quarter." Then the subject

6 Fritz Mauthner, *Prager Jugendjahre: Erinnerungen* (Youth in Prague: Memoirs). München: Müller [1918, p. 33] 1969, p. 30.

7 Franz Kafka to Max Brod, 7–8 October 1917. – See Kafka, *Letters to Friends, Family and Editors*, p. 152.

8 Mauthner, *Prager Jugendjahre*, p. 49.

9 Franz Kafka to Max Brod, June 1921. – See Kafka, *Letters to Friends, Family and Editors*, p. 286.

10 Max Brod – Franz Kafka, *Eine Freundschaft: Briefwechsel* (A Friendship: A Correspondence). Ed. by Malcolm Pasley. Vol. 2. Frankfurt am Main: S. Fischer 1989, p. 359.

> was dropped and people went on eating, but the general, with his sharp ears linguistically schooled in the Austrian army, was not satisfied. After we had eaten, he once more began to wonder about the sound of my German, perhaps more bothered by what he saw than by what he heard. At this point I tried to explain that by my being Jewish. At this his scientific curiosity, to be sure, was satisfied, but not his human feelings.[11]

The reproach and self-reproach of *mauscheln* as well as the linguistic exclusion of Jews are thus based on several assumptions. The first of these (widely held since Romanticism) saw the spoken language of the people (*Volkssprache*) as essentially bound up with the *Volksgeist*, that is to say its sound bound up with the meaning materialised in the sound. A second assumption claimed that mind is so closely bound up with spoken language that it cannot be conceived without it – this is reflected in the common German metaphor that a person whom we can hear but cannot understand, or whom we cannot understand because of his pronunciation, is 'un*verständ*lich' (incomprehensible; literally 'without' [rational] mind). Thirdly, it is assumed that an individual's spirit, like the *Volksseele* or *Volksgeist*, is an organ of the body, or of the national body. In this way – viewed from a different perspective and exaggerated somewhat – a person was deemed incapable of acquiring the *Volkssprache* if he did not possess the corresponding *Volksgeist*, an organ of the national body.

This organic understanding of *Volkssprache* is ironically invoked by Kafka in the above quotation through the characterisation of *mauscheln* as an 'organic compound of bookish German and pantomime'[12]. Whilst Romantic language philosophy and linguistics saw an organic connection between the spoken *Volkssprache* and *Volksgeist*, that is, between sound (phonetic image) and meaning, Kafka highlights the organic linkage between gestures and writing. It is precisely these alternative channels of communication of the 'deaf and dumb' which served as an argument for the empiricist Anton Marty, professor at Charles University in Prague, that 'sound is not the "essential and necessary expression of the spirit" ', in the way it is claimed by the 'nativists'.[13] As Kafka's allusion to Marty goes deeper than the actual context of his

11 Kafka, *Letters to Friends, Family and Editors*, p. 233. My emphases.

12 Kafka, *Letters to Friends, Family and Editors*, p. 288.

13 Anton Marty, *Über den Ursprung der Sprache* (On the Origin of Language). Würzburg: A. Stuber 1875, p. 15. On the distinction between 'nativists' and 'empiricists', see Marty himself; see also Emanuel Kovář, *O původě lidské mluvy* (On the Origin of Human Speech). Prague: Bursík a Kohout 1898. Even in his later work, Marty insistently rejected the idea that 'expressions could be in their inner linguistic form abbreviations of the meaning', and tried to present 'all so-called "organic" word components as synsemantic or autosemantic'; see Anton Marty, *Untersuchungen zur Grundlegung der allgemeinen Grammatik und Sprachphilosophie* (Investigations into the Foundation of General Grammar and Language Philosophy). Halle: M. Niemeyer 1908, vol. 1, here p. 163 and p. 212.

comments initially suggest, I want in the following section to look briefly at the language discourse of the nineteenth century.

LANGUAGE DISCOURSE OF THE NINETEENTH CENTURY

In his engaging analysis of Kafka's story 'A report to an Academy' (April 1917) Axel Gellhaus demonstrates that the story can be read as a poetic reflection on language which parodistically alludes to Johann Gottfried Herder's *Treatise on the Origin of Language* (1770/72).[14] In that work Herder considers opposing views of the origin of language: on the one hand the 'organic' view that stressed instinct and reflex and the organic union of sound and sense through imitation; on the other the 'social' view, where language was seen as a set of associations anchored in convention, that is, a social contract between men, or between man and God.[15] Herder believes he avoids the paradox that 'primal screams', like the 'primal words' of a primal language, could neither occur spontaneously to man with no concept of language, nor be connected to one another. He does so by claiming that the capacity for language is inscribed in man's 'nature' through 'deliberateness' ('Besonnenheit'), i.e. it is inherent. These primal words, according to Herder, emerged from the concrete context of a 'natural reaction' to man's environment through the audible imitation of what man heard. As this brief account of his theory shows, Herder stands firmly in the camp of the organic understanding of language. In 'A report to an Academy' about his acquisition of language and his transformation into a human being, the speaking ape Rotpeter endorses Herder's arguments on reason (he must have been a human being from the beginning to be able to speak and thus become a human being). Yet, at the same time he brings this very reasoning into question by allowing the audience to recognise that following this logic, man has never really stopped being an uncivilised ape: 'Your apedom, gentlemen, to the extent that you have something of the sort behind you, cannot be more remote from you than mine is from me'.[16] This is Herder's theory in the words of Kafka's Rotpeter.[17]

---

14 Axel Gellhaus, 'Das Schweigen der Sirenen'. Poetische Sprachreflexion in der Prosa Franz Kafkas ('The silence of the Sirens': Poetic language reflections in Franz Kafka's stories). In: Axel Gellhaus, Horst Sitta (eds), *Reflexionen über Sprache aus literatur- und sprachwissenschaftlicher Sicht* (Reflections of Language from the Point of View of Linguistics and the Theory of Literature). Tübingen: Niemeyer 2000, pp. 13–39.

15 See also Marty, *Über den Ursprung der Sprache*, p. 2.

16 Franz Kafka, *Selected Stories*. Translated and edited by Stanley Corngold. New York, London: J. J. Norton 2005, p. 77.

17 Such talking animals, or animal-like humans who cannot speak, are a frequent feature of Kafka's work; examples include the investigating dog, the singing mouse, the talking jackals, the talking vulture and mole or the nomads who screech like jackdaws, the mute insect Gregor Sam-

Herder's organic theory with its emphases on sound and the spoken *Volkssprache* was taken up by the German Romantics,[18] with further impulses coming from historical linguistics and psychology.[19] As a rule, language was not just explained using organic metaphors; it was also conceived as an organism and bound up with the *völkisch* organism, that is, the national body and later on even race.[20] Alongside Knobloch, the psychologists Chajim Heymann Steinthal (1823–1899) and Moritz Lazarus (1824–1903) were among the most influential pioneers of the organic discourse on language in the second half of the nineteenth century. In his work, Lazarus advocated the argument that the *Volkssprache* was an expression and benchmark of the *Volksgeist*, in the same way that the language of an individual was expression and benchmark of his own 'spirit'.[21] Lazarus and Steinthal defended an organic understanding of language down to the finest details: the expressions for objects, facts and events were said to have developed from the 'material' which had emerged as a physiological reflex to all kinds of sensory stimuli and which was *inscribed* into man's body via acoustic, tactile, optical and other stimuli. These stimuli did not just make their way into the brain, but also impressed themselves via shared or entangled nerve tracts on the speech organs which were simultaneously activated by any form of sensory stimulus. The mind would then fall back on this 'material' when it looked for the proto-word

---

sa etc. However, only the story of the imitating ape explicitly addresses the contentious debate on the origin of language.

18 On the influence of Johann Gottlieb Fichte's *Reden an die deutsche Nation* (Speeches to the German Nation) in Martin Buber's, Hugo Bergmann's and Robert Weltsch's oeuvre see, for example, Manfred Voigt's *„Wir sollen alle kleine Fichtes werden!" Johann Gottlieb Fichte als Prophet der Kultur-Zionisten* ('We all should become like Fichte!' Johann Gottlieb Fichte as Prophet of Cultural Zionism). Berlin, Vienna: Philo Verlag 2003.

19 See Clemens Knobloch, *Geschichte der psychologischen Sprachauffassung in Deutschland von 1850 bis 1920* (History of Psychological Conceptions of Language in Germany from 1850 until 1920). Tübingen: Niemeyer 1988, p. 182.

20 See Knobloch, *Geschichte*. For example, Humboldt's 'energeia' connected language to man's sexual drive, and according to Jakob Grimm, the roots of words 'couple' like organisms. In Schelling's theory, people are understood as cells of a national body whose soul is revealed in language. Charles Darwin (1809–1882), in *The Descent of Man*, also contributed to the organic, genetic understanding of language. See Charles Darwin, *The Descent of Man and Selection in Relation to Sex*. London: D. Appleton 1872. August Schleicher (1821–1868), who was in Prague from 1849–1856/7, based his phylogenetic tree model of languages (*Die ersten Spaltungen des indogermanischen Urvolkes*, 1853) on genetics and in doing so also presented his case for an organic understanding of languages. Languages were understood to obey similar laws of evolution to those expounded by the natural sciences. For this reason, Schleicher regarded linguistics as a discipline belonging to the natural sciences and connected it with Darwin's theory of the origin of species; see Charles Darwin, *On the Origin of Species by Means of Natural Selection*. London: J. Murray [1859] 1861, and August Schleicher, *Die Darwinsche Theorie und die Sprachwissenschaft – offenes Sendschreiben an Herrn Dr. Ernst Haeckel* (Darwin's Theory and Linguistics – An Open Letter to Dr. Ernst Haeckel). Weimar: H. Böhlau 1863.

21 See Moritz Lazarus, *Geist und Sprache. Eine psychologische Monographie* (Mind and Language: A Psychological Monograph). Berlin: F. Fümmler 1884 [1st ed. 1856/7], p. 400.

('Ur-Wort'). In this way, according to Lazarus and Steinthal, an organic, non-arbitrary connection was formed between the object as subject, state of affairs or event (sense) on the one hand, and the body, mind and sound on the other. In Steinthal's view, the difference between different national languages was explained by the geographically and physiologically determined '*bodily* influences on the soul' which cause 'certain qualities in the mind', 'namely in the same way in all individuals, which is why they all share the same *Volksgeist*'. 'This *Volksgeist* at first manifests itself in language, and then in a people's customs'.[22] The *Volkssprache* is, according to this theory, essentially connected with the national body through the *Volksgeist*, the organ of the national body. This connection between *Volkssprache* and *Volksgeist* manifests itself in every member of the nation and this in turn ensures his belonging to the national body *(Volkskörper)*.

It seems likely that Kafka would have been familiar with at least the fundamentals of the theories of Lazarus and Steinthal; they were, after all, prominent figures in the organic discourse on language which was also taken up by authors whom Kafka certainly knew. For example, Fritz Mauthner in his book *Language* (1907) discusses both authors.[23] Lazarus and Steinthal's claim that the registering of language in the mind (in the sense of reason) through its registration in the body may well have been taken up by Kafka's 'poetic shorthand' in the metaphor of the writing apparatus in the story 'In the penal colony' (1914).[24] In the story, the judgment is 'carved' into the body by the unusual writing apparatus and it is only in this way that the victim's

---

22 See Heymann Steinthal, *Grammatik, Logik und Psychologie, ihre Prinzipien und ihr Verhältnis zueinander* (Grammar, Logic and Psychology, their Principles and their Relation to each Other). Berlin: F. Dümmler 1855, p. 390 f. (my emphases).

23 Fritz Mauthner, *Die Sprache* (Language). Frankfurt am Main 1907. There is, however, no evidence that Kafka knew this book by Mauthner. As is known, his library only held Mauthner's memoir *Prager Jugendjahre* (1918, A Youth in Prague) which contains the above-mentioned comment on *mauscheln*. See Herbert Blank, *V Kafkově knihovně / In Kafkas Bibliothek* (In Kafkas's Library). Prague: Nakladatelství Franze Kafky 2004, p. 165.

24 On the illuminating metaphor of the 'poetic shorthand' through which Kafka 'records' contemporary discourses in his work, see Benno Wagner, 'Sprechen kann man mit den Nomaden nicht'. Sprache, Gesetz und Verwaltung bei Otto Bauer und Franz Kafka ('You cannot talk to the nomads.' Language, law and administration). In: Marek Nekula, Ingrid Fleischmann, Albrecht Greule (eds), *Franz Kafka im sprachnationalen Kontext seiner Zeit. Sprache und nationale Identität in öffentlichen Institutionen der böhmischen Länder* (Franz Kafka in the National Context of his time. Language and National Identity in the Public Institutions of the Bohemian Crown Lands). Cologne, Weimar, Vienna: Böhlau 2007, pp. 109–128. According to Alt, Kafka was inspired by a parlograph, a kind of dictaphone, which Kafka's fiancée Felice was responsible for selling in her job at Lindström AG. Alternatively, he may have been inspired by the phonograph with vibrating metal disc and needle invented by Thomas Alva Edison; on this see Peter-André Alt, *Franz Kafka. Der ewige Sohn. Eine Biographie* (Franz Kafka. The Eternal Son. A Biography). Munich: Beck 2005. Gellhaus sees in this metaphor the pantograph which was used in the Bohemian glass industry to decorate glass by drawing patterns on it using a template; see Gellhaus, 'Das Schweigen der Sirenen', p. 13.

mind is able to fully comprehend it. It also evokes Friedrich Nietzsche's 'violent inscription' of moral in the human body in his *Zur Genealogie der Moral* (Towards a Genealogy of Morals, 1887; part 2,3).

The most likely place that Kafka might have encountered the organic, nativist language theory of Lazarus and Steinthal will have been the three-hour course on descriptive psychology taught by Anton Marty (1847–1914), which he attended at Prague University in his second semester (1902).[25] Marty was an established expert on and opponent of Lazarus and Steinthal's ideas. Even in his first publication *On the Origin of Language* (1875), he unequivocally rejected their organic, physiological explanation of the origin of language. Marty is likely to have shared his empiricist arguments against the nativist school of thought in the context of the philosophical Brentano circle in which, as is well known, Kafka participated for some time. The empiricists argued that the necessity of coordinating oneself and communicating is anthropologically universal and not anchored in biology; language, moreover, is arbitrary and to be understood as a result of the social contract.[26] Even if Kafka did not sit an exam related to Marty's lecture,[27] he takes up the idea of 'sign language' in his characterisation of *mauscheln* in the letter to Brod.

Furthermore, in his image of the nomads in his story 'A page from an old document' (1917) he refers to the 'screech',[28] which also plays a central role in Marty's discussion of the origin of languages. Marty rejects Moreau de Maupertuis' account (which Kafka may well have challenged in his story 'A page from an old manuscript'), that 'in the very beginning, certain gestures and inarticulate high-pitched sounds, which were natural signs of inner states, served to enable elementary communication between humans' and that people 'accordingly also occasionally used gestures and cries with arbitrary meaning'.[29] The reference to 'deaf mutes' who communicate with one another through gestures (and which we recognise in Kafka's nomads and his remark about the 'organic compound of bookish German and panto-

---

25 See the transcript of records of seminars which Kafka attended. Facsimile in this book on p. 153 f. The course is described as 'descriptive and genetic psychology' in Ekkehard W. Haring, Leben und Persönlichkeit (Biography and personality). In: Manfred Engel – Bernd Auerochs (eds), *Kafka-Handbuch. Leben – Werk – Wirkung* (A Kafka Manual: Biography – Oeuvre – Impact). Stuttgart, Weimar: Metzler 2010, pp. 1–27, here p. 6.

26 Wilhelm Wundt in his *Völkerpsychologie* (1900–20; Psychology of Nations) was one of several psychologists who later opposed the organic, biological understanding of language. In this work, he spoke of an 'unsubstantial common soul' and emphasesed the role of culture over organic causes.

27 Hartmut Binder, *Kafka-Handbuch in zwei Bänden* (A Kafka Manual in two Volumes). vol I: *Der Mensch und seine Zeit* (Man and his Time). Stuttgart: Kröner 1979, p. 75. See also Blank, *V Kafkově knihovně*, p. 165, Haring, Leben und Persönlichkeit, p. 6.

28 Kafka, *Selected Stories*, p. 66.

29 Marty, *Über den Ursprung der Sprache*, p. 6.

mime') is used by Marty in order to refute the nativist approach, according to which 'the language sense compels the articulated sound from the body's organs'.[30] Even though Kafka was also critical of such an understanding of language, his 'Introductory speech on Jargon (1912) still resonates with an organic understanding of language:

> You are already very close to Yiddish when you bear in mind the fact that at work within you is not only knowledge but also forces and connections between forces which enable you to understand Yiddish through feeling.[31]

Kafka's everyday life and his views were influenced by this nativist, organic understanding of language, which forges an essential 'organic linkage' between sound and sense, i.e. between *Volkssprache* and *Volksgeist*, and which was intrinsic to the period's language-based, nationalist ideology and its commitment to primordialism, nativism and monolingualism. Such ideology determined his contemporaries' attitudes to mother tongues (in the Jewish context, as well, 'nation' was understood as an 'inherited language community'),[32] as well as their approach to bilingualism, which in the Bohemian context and Prague was prominently connected with Jews. To a certain extent, there was, and continues to be, some justification for this.[33] Thus,

---

30 Marty, *Über den Ursprung der Sprache*, p. 14 f., who here paraphrases Humboldt.

31 Franz Kafka, *Nachgelassene Schriften und Fragmente* (Literary Remains and Fragments). Ed. by Malcolm Pasley. Vol. 1. Frankfurt am Main: S. Fischer 1993, p. 193.

32 See e.g. Heinrich Loewe, Der Nationalismus (Nationalism). *Zion. Monatsschrift für die nationalen Interessen des Judentums* 2 (1895), pp. 33–41, here p. 33; cited in Andreas Kilcher, Kafka, Scholem und die Politik der jüdischen Sprachen (Kafka, Scholem and the politics of Jewish languages). In: Christoph Miething (ed.), *Politik und Religion im Judentum* (Politics and Religion in Judaism). Tübingen: Niemeyer 1999, pp. 79–115, here p. 68 f. This genetic, organic understanding of the 'language nation' is also clear in the Czech ethno-terminology of 'národ' (people, nation), the etymology of which can be traced back to 'narodit' (to give birth). As a result, the Czech 'národ', which from the middle of the nineteenth century onwards defined itself first and foremost through the Czech language, was at the same time also understood to refer to a people related also through blood (i.e. an ethnic group).

33 The period's outwardly imposed judgment differs significantly from today's attitudes. Alongside the more or less explicitly antisemitic view of bilingualism at the time, there is also evidence of more tolerant attitudes to (Jewish) bilingualism, as is suggested by terms such as 'Utraquisten' (Utraquists), 'Böhmische Maranen' (Bohemian Marranos) or 'Neobohemisten' (neo-Bohemians). For more on this, as well as for an analysis of bilingualism in connection with Prague Jews, see Kilcher, Kafka, Scholem und die Politik der jüdischen Sprachen, p. 78 f.; Robert Luft, Sprache und Nationalität an Prager Gymnasien um 1900 (Language and nationality at Prague grammar schools around 1900). In: Klaas-Hinrich Ehlers et al. (eds), *Brücken nach Prag. Deutschsprachige Literatur im kulturellen Kontext der Donaumonarchie und der Tschechoslowakei* (Bridges to Prague: German-written Literature in the Cultural Context of the Habsburg Monarchy and Czechoslovakia). Frankfurt am Main: P. Lang 2000, pp. 105–122; Ingrid Stöhr, *Zweisprachigkeit in Böhmen. Deutsche Volksschulen und Gymnasien im Prag der Kafka-Zeit* (Bilingualism in Bohemia: German Elementary and Grammar Schools in the Prague of Kafka's Time). Cologne, Weimar, Vienna: Böhlau 2010.

in the contemporary context a relationship was formed between mother tongue and national spirit; bilingualism was denigrated as a 'loosening of the spiritual community of monolingual countrymen' and as a 'weakening of the feel for language':

> A waste of time and energy at the expense of other work, a weakening of linguistic sensitivity due to the interaction of two languages, inappropriate word choice, language diffusion, an impoverishment of active vocabulary, the loosening of intellectual unity with monolingual speakers, i.e. with the majority of fellow countrymen.[34]

As a result, in spite of their linguistic assimilation, the linguistically flexible Jews were excluded from the 'true' language community. This prompted Max Brod to laud the story 'A report to an Academy' as the 'most brilliant satire of assimilation'.[35] In the following section, I want therefore to look briefly at Kafka's own language biography from this perspective.

KAFKA'S LANGUAGES

From a biographical perspective, several languages played a role in Kafka's life. Alongside German, the main languages were Czech and Hebrew. In addition to the languages he learned at school he was also exposed to Yiddish. Substrate traces of Yiddish were most likely to have been heard in Hermann and Julie Kafka's German, and even his own as discussed in the previous chapter. Yet the attribute 'organic', also used by Kafka himself, would only really be applicable to German and Czech or Hebrew and Yiddish. This attribute, according to the ideology of language-based nationalism, would encompass the 'inheritance of the *Volksgeist*' and 'natural language acquisition' within the family (as of course is suggested by the term used for one's first language, 'mother tongue').

In Kafka's case, however, his 'naturally' acquired language(s) – from the perspective of the monolingual nationalist ideology – was not necessarily also handed down 'organically'. For even if German (and Czech) were his naturally,

34 Eduard Blocher, Zweisprachigkeit: Vorteile und Nachteile (Bilingualism: Advantages and disadvantages). In: Wilhelm Rein (ed.), *Encyklopädisches Handbuch der Pädagogik* (Encyclopaedic Handbook of Pedagogy). Vol. 10. Langensalza: Beyer & Söhne [1909] 1910, second edition, pp. 665–670, here p. 669.

35 Max Brod, Literarischer Abend des Klubs jüdischer Frauen und Mädchen (A literary evening in the Club for Jewish Women and Girls). *Selbstwehr* 12 (1918) [4. January], p. 4 f.; quoted in Hans-Gerd Koch, Ein Bericht für eine Akademie (A report to an Academy). In: Michael Müller (ed.), *Franz Kafka. Romane und Erzählungen* (Franz Kafka: Novels and Stories). Stuttgart: Reclam 1994, pp. 173–196.

i.e. untutored, acquired languages,[36] his parents, according to the proponents of linguistic nationalism, could hardly be regarded as part of the German or Czech national 'body'. Further, as Jews they were incapable of 'properly' handing down German or Czech to Kafka in the way it was understood by the ideology of language-based nationalism. In other words, they were capable of handing down the language to him, but not the *Volksgeist* inherent within it and an organ of the nation's body. Thus, they were also unable, according to language-based, nationalist ideology, to pass down the *Volkssprache* 'properly' or – in an essentialist sense – 'truly'. This is an idea which we see explored in the ape Rotpeter as well as by Kafka himself when he talks about *mauscheln* or problematizes the German 'of our un-German mothers'.[37]

On the other hand, according to that same ideology of language-based nationalism, Kafka's parents would have been in a very good position to pass down the Jewish *Volksgeist*. Yet because Bohemian Jews, including the Kafka family, had lost their Jewish languages (both Hebrew and Yiddish) in the course of their linguistic assimilation, Hebrew, for example, could only be acquired 'unnaturally', i.e. actively tutored, and thus could not become a 'natural', 'proper', 'organic language'. As we know, Kafka learned Hebrew in theology lessons or, after 1919, in private language lessons. Kafka identified this rift between the acquired possibilities of expressing himself in German and the nevertheless felt, but non-communicable, *Volksgeist* in the diary entry of 24 October 1911, which has been discussed in the chapter on Kafka's Jewish context.

This dovetails with his understanding of Yiddish in the 'Introductory speech on Jargon' (1912), which was quoted from above, and in which the idea of 'active forces' resounds with an organic understanding of language. The contemporary organic understanding of language which sees the *Volkssprache* and the *Volksgeist* as connected in an organic, nativist way, is alluded to, and indeed treated critically even in these years, in Kafka's stories 'A report to an Academy' (1917) or 'In the penal colony' (1914). Equally, these ideas are to be found in his private comments, such as the above remarks on *mauscheln*, the German of 'our un-German mothers', or the self-ironic description of himself as a 'half-German',[38] etc.

Of course, we should not be misled by such remarks into doubting Julie or Franz Kafka's German skills, as some scholars have been. In an early letter to the Czech Milena Jesenská, in which he is referring merely to his ability to

---

36 Franz Kafka to Milena Jesenská, 12 May 1920. – See Franz Kafka, *Briefe 1918–1920* (Letters 1918–1920). Ed. by Hans-Gerd Koch. Frankfurt am Main: S. Fischer 2013, p. 134; Franz Kafka, *Letters to Milena*. Edited by Willi Haas. Translated by Tania and James Stern. New York: Schocken Books [1953] 1965, p. 30.

37 Franz Kafka to Max Brod, October 1917. – See Kafka, *Letters to Friends, Family and Editors*, p. 152.

38 Franz Kafka to Ottla, 20 February 1919. – See Kafka, *Briefe 1918–1920*, p. 72.

communicate in German and Czech, Kafka rightly identifies German as his 'mother tongue', albeit with the significant relativisation that 'I have never lived among Germans'.[39] The case for German being Kafka's mother tongue is also made by the contexts in which he learned and used German. Therefore, his use of categories such as 'half-German' or 'un-German mothers' is about something else, namely the organic, nativist connection between the *Volkssprache* and *Volksgeist*, the essentialist conception of linguistic identity, derived from one's belonging to the national body from which those who *mauscheln* are excluded.

The linguistic chauvinism coupled with this was commented upon by Kafka and Max Brod in their travel diaries in August 1911 as they made their way though Switzerland en route to a holiday in France. Their comments are heavy with irony; since their perspective has been sharpened by the situation in Bohemia, Brod's remarks can also be understood as a statement on this:

> Lucerne is like a German city that has been taken over by the French. It seems that Germanness is no less in decline here than it is in Bohemia. Is this perhaps a quality inherent to Germanness? – Even the word 'Kursaal' sounds French here. It is, after all, one of the few foreign words that the French have acquired from us. So for the sake of the French the kurhaus here is called the kursaal. – Matins wherever you look, French books.[40]

> In the men's bathhouse. Very crowded. There are signs in an unusually large number of languages – *the Swiss solution to the language question*. Everything is made confusing so that even a chauvinist doesn't know what's going on. First he finds German to the left, then to the right, German in connection with French or Italian or both or even with English, and German sometimes is missing completely. In Flüelen, it was prohibited in German-Italian to go on the train tracks. The slow passing of cars was in German-French. – Switzerland is certainly a school for statesmen![41]

Kafka replies like an echo:

> Where is the German population that warrants the German signs?[42]

---

39 Franz Kafka to Milena Jesenská, 12 May 1920. – See Kafka, *Briefe 1918–1920*, p. 134; Kafka, *Letters to Milena*, p. 30; See Kafka, *Letters to Milena*. Translated by Philip Boehm. New York: Schocken 1990, p. 14.

40 Brod quoted in Kafka, *Reisetagebücher in der Fassung der Handschrift* (Travel Diaries based on the Handwritten Manuscripts). Ed. by Hans-Gerd Koch. Frankfurt am Main: S. Fischer 1994, p. 125.

41 Brod quoted in Franz Kafka, *Reisetagebücher*, p. 123

42 Travel diary entry from Lucerne, around August 1911. – See Kafka, *Reisetagebücher*, p. 436.

> Max: Confusion of Tongues – the solution to national problems. The chauvinist doesn't know what is going on anymore.[43]

Even before the First World War, the competition between German and Czech in the public sphere of Bohemia and Prague can be described as a language conflict. This became more acute during the First World War, developing into an 'internal war' which continued to be fought out even after the end of World War One, for example, in connection with the Constitution and the Language Act of 1920. Kafka was directly confronted with this raging German-Czech language conflict during the First World War, notably at the Worker's Accident Insurance Company which in around 1917 some attempted to divide up along the two fronts of linguistic nationalism. Especially during this time, Kafka continued to use as his professional signature 'DrFKafka' instead of 'Franz Kafka' and/or 'František Kafka', which allowed him to avoid being pigeon-holed according to his nationality. This contrasts with his earlier usual signatures containing his first name, 'Franz Kafka' or 'František Kafka', which could be interpreted as an avowal of a specific linguistic, national identity. The identification of people on the basis of their professional signatures was actually practiced retroactively at the Company after 1918[44] and it involved the civil servant Václav Krofta and Herr Otto Přibram/Przibram, the president of the Workers' Accident Insurance Company, at the beginning of 1919.[45] Switching of this kind 'Franz Kafka' and 'František Kafka' was common practice before 1918 but not after, and not only at the Workers' Accident Insurance Company. After 1918 people had to be consistent in the language they used to sign their name, which at that time virtually meant committing loyalty to a nation defined by language. Kafka denied this through his ambiguous signature.

Elsewhere, Kafka experienced the vehement public rejection of the 'renaming' of Bohemian Jews by Czech names. This rejection, motivated by language-driven nationalist and apparently racist sentiments, was voiced in Czech newspapers around the time of the founding of Czechoslovakia. In October 1918, Kafka sent his friend Max Brod, accompanied by his own comments, the bi-monthly magazines *Česká stráž* (Czech Guard) and *Česká svoboda* (Czech Freedom) which both contained articles distancing themselves from this Czech rendering of surnames which Bohemian Jews with German

---

43 Travel diary entry, around August 1911. – See Kafka, *Reisetagebücher*, p. 435.

44 More on this in Nekula, *Jazyky Franze Kafky*, pp. 220–268.

45 Václav K. Krofta, Im Amt mit Franz Kafka (In the Office with Franz Kafka). In: Hans-Gerd Koch (ed.), „Als Kafka mir entgegen kam…" Erinnerungen an Franz Kafka ('As Kafka approached me.' Recollections of Franz Kafka). Berlin: Wagenbach 1995, pp. 92–94, here p 92. Otto Przibram was at the time 'general manager' of the insurance institute. See Krofta, Im Amt mit Franz Kafka, p. 94.

surnames had acquiesced in.[46] The 'expulsion' of Jews from the 'national language body' would acquire disturbing forms in the 1930s and 1940s.

It is fairly obvious that the language discourse found its way into the literary texts which Kafka wrote during World War One as a discourse of conflict. At the beginning of the story 'The householder's concern' (written before August 1916), the central theme of which is domestic peace, a similar struggle over the German or Slavonic meaning of the name Odradek is addressed. This is also true of other texts in which war and defence are dealt with alongside the language question, such as the stories 'A page from an old document' (second half of March 1917), 'Jackals and Arabs' (early February 1917) from the volume *A Country Doctor* or the fragments 'Building of the Great Wall of China' (March 1917), 'The city coat of arms' (1920) etc. In the following section, I want to focus specifically on the story 'A page from an old document' and read it alongside the language discourse of the time.

LANGUAGE DISCOURSE AS A DISCOURSE OF CONFLICT IN KAFKA'S TEXTS: 'A PAGE FROM AN OLD DOCUMENT'

In the light of research done by the Constance School of Reception Aesthetics, it is surely no longer necessary to explain or justify the view that one single text has several possible interpretations and that one explanation does not exclude any other.[47] After all, literary texts are not written for philologists to exert their own monopoly of interpretation over; nor are they written for historians who use them as a source for contemporary reflections about the world. They are not – partly nonreflective – accounts of the everyday, but literary texts with an aesthetic function and impact.[48] At the same time, from the perspective of New Historicism there is little point in reading a text outside of its contemporary discursive worlds, both as far as medium, genre and form are concerned, as well as the concepts it deals with. Literary texts, too, are rooted in the discourse of a given time (Michel Foucault), which of course is not the same as a crude imitation of reality.[49] In this way, Kafka, too, may well have referred to the contemporary language discourse in his texts as a discourse of conflict.

---

46 See Brod – Kafka, *Eine Freundschaft: Briefwechsel*, p. 252.

47 See Hans Robert Jauss, *Literaturgeschichte als Provokation der Literaturwissenschaft* (Historiography of Literature as a Provocation of the Theory of Literature) Constance: Universitätsverlag 1967 and Wolfgang Iser, *Der Akt des Lesens* (The Act of Reading). Munich: Fink 1976.

48 Walter Bulst, Bedenken eines Philologen (Concerns of a philologist). *Studium generale* 7 (1954), pp. 321–323.

49 See Moritz Baßler (ed.), *New Historicism*. Tübingen: Francke 2001; Jonathan Bolton (ed.), *New Historicism*. Brno: Host 2007.

For instance, the language conflict, a conflict (which was also a literal/literary conflict), is referred to in Theodor Herzl's article 'Die Juden Prags zwischen den Nationen' (The Prague Jews between the nations). Still of great relevance for us today, it was first published in 1897 and was re-published in 1917 because of its topicality in the collected volume *Das jüdische Prag* (Jewish Prague), which was edited by the Prague-based Jewish weekly newspaper *Selbstwehr* (Self-Defence) and read by Kafka. In that article, Herzl takes a Jewish perspective on the German-Czech language conflict of 1897 and on the riots in which, following the Badeni crisis, the Jews of Prague and Bohemia had become scapegoats of the Bohemian language conflict. Similarly, Kafka's short story 'The householder's concern' (1917) alludes to the German-Czech language conflict; in his other stories, however, the battle lines of the language discourse as a discourse of conflict are much more universal.

By undertaking a 'wide reading' of Kafka's 'A page from an old document' whilst at the same time reading it within the context of the contemporary language discourse, I do not mean to exclude other interpretations. It should by now be the general consensus that Kafka's works are to be read with full regard to this polyphony (and partly also inconsistency) of interpretation, also taking into account the other materials of the period to which we have access.[50] Let us therefore briefly remind ourselves of the fact that this story, written in March 1917, was perhaps read by Binder too literally as a partly autobiographical literary response to the wave of Jewish refugees fleeing Galicia in World War One. The fully assimilated Prague Jews are said to have been appalled by the behaviour and appearance of the Eastern Jewish refugees arriving in Prague.[51] Kilcher regards the story as a narrative participation in the discourse within Zionism on the future orientation of the Jewish movement (i.e. Yiddishism vs. Hebraism), while I point out the links to the discourses of German-Czech emancipation and anti-emancipation. Kremer's psychoanalytic reading sees references to autoerotic practices in the phrases 'often a rider lies next to his horse while both feed off the same piece of meat, one at each end'.[52]

---

50 See, e. g., Benno Wagner, Karl Kraus, Franz Kafka und das Schreiben gegen den Krieg (Karl Kraus, Franz Kafka and writing against the war). In: Manfred Engel – Ritchie Robertson (eds), *Kafka, Prag und der Erste Weltkrieg. Kafka, Prague, and the First World War*. Würzburg: Königshausen & Neumann 2012, pp. 257–272.

51 Binder, *Kafka-Handbuch*, p. 374.

52 Kilcher, Kafka, Scholem und die Politik der jüdischen Sprachen; Nekula, *Jazyky Franze* Kafky; Detlef Kremer, Ein *Landarzt* (A Country Doctor). In: Michael Müller (ed.), *Interpretationen. Franz Kafka. Romane und Erzählungen* (Interpretations. Franz Kafka. Novels and Short Stories). Stuttgart: Reclam 1994, pp. 197–214, here p. 198, as well as Kafka, *Selected Stories*, p. 67.

If we disregard the fact that the story was initially entitled 'A page from an old document from China' in Kafka's Octavo Notebook C[53] and that the fragment 'Building of the Great Wall of China' was written almost immediately before it, then such Eurocentric interpretations might be allowed to stand. Perhaps, however, in the light of such explicitly orientalist references, we might regard the line of battle in the story between the aggressive, cultureless and parasitic nomads/barbarians and the defensive guardians of cultural accomplishments not as one between Eastern Jews and assimilated Western Jews, or cultural Zionists and political Zionists, or Czechs and Germans, but between Jews and non-Jews. In the shoemaker's story, the affected demarcation between language and non-language thus goes hand in hand with the demarcations between mind and non-mind, or reason and non-reason, man and animal, culture and non-culture, which can also be found in 'A report to an Academy' and in the discourse of antisemitism.

This becomes even more apparent upon a closer reading of the text. In the 'war reporting' of the shoemaker narrator, who belongs to the people 'under attack' in the story 'A page from an old document', the offensive nomads from the north are regarded as underdeveloped at best. They are denied any culture in their very categorisation as 'nomads'.[54] Furthermore, there are differences in their 'way of life' and language; the nomads are even likened to their 'wild horses' who also are 'meat eaters', and to 'jackdaws' whose 'screeching' resembles no real human language.[55] Such comparisons place them on the same level as animals. The conflict between those who possess their own language and reason and by virtue of these are human beings, and those who through a denial of their own (national) language and reason are turned into animals, seems to me to be of central importance to the story. The physical conflict is projected onto the linguistic conflict, in which the struggle is offset through the discourse of language as a discourse of conflict, in which the nomads are discursively defeated.

Herein lies the function of the jackdaws' screech which is ascribed to the conquering nomads by the narrator, a member of the conquered, as soon as he claims to have noticed that they do not know 'our language' and that 'they hardly have one of their own'.[56] The 'screech of jackdaws' thus does not replace human language, but merely underscores the nomads' lack of language who, accordingly, appear like animals. The narrator observes that the nomads 'are also ill-disposed to any sort of sign language' and that 'You can dislocate your jaws and twist your hands out of joint, but they have not understood you, and

53 See Franz Kafka, *Nachgelassene Schriften und Fragmente* (Literary Remains and Fragments). Vol. I. Edited by Malcolm Pasley. Frankfurt am Main: S. Fischer 1993, p. 303.

54 Kafka, *Selected Stories*, p. 66.

55 Kafka, *Selected Stories*, p. 66 f.

56 Kafka, *Selected Stories*, p. 66 f.

they will never understand you', whilst they communicate with their grimaces like animals – 'their eyes roll up in their heads and foam flows out of their mouths, but these are not meant either to convey anything or to frighten people;[57] they do it because that is how they are'.[58] These descriptions mark the absolute absence of human language, for even the non-verbal gestures and grimaces are incomprehensible: 'they do it because that is how they are'.[59]

It seems paradoxical that human beings, even if they were nomads, would have no human language, or not even use or understand a sign language comprehensible to humans. For along with 'screeching sounds', non-verbal sign-language is meant to have been the earliest and most elementary form of human communication and coordination.[60] Whether the nomads (who anyway are busy 'whetting their swords, sharpening their arrows, with manoeuvres on horseback', using 'whips',[61] are 'attracted' by the Imperial Palace and take over the imperial city)[62] in reality do have their own language, we are never told. In any case, they are denied one by the shoemaker narrator and are degraded through their ignorance of 'our language',[63] the supposed lack of their own language, and their inability to at least communicate through sign language. As a result, they are degraded as subhumans who are mute, or screech like jackdaws, and are likened to animals. The good citizens set themselves apart from these creatures through their own language and their own cultured way of life.[64]

How is this paradox, which rests on the assumption that human beings become human through language, in order also to coordinate their actions with others, to be resolved? And can it be resolved at all (as is occasionally questioned in relation to Kafka's paradoxes)? If we take Kafka at his word – and, as far as Kafka is concerned, this is always the best solution[65] – then the starting point would be the 'screech of jackdaws' which the nomads emit.[66] As we know, 'Dohle' ['jackdaw'] is the equivalent of *Kafka/kavka* (pronounced *kafka*) – a pun which was no doubt deliberate on Kafka's part. We encounter

---

57 According to Marty's thoughts on the precursors to language, man's grimaces have an 'arbitrary meaning'. Marty, *Über den Ursprung der Sprache*, p. 6.

58 Kafka, *Selected Stories*, p. 66 f.

59 Kafka, *Selected Stories*, p. 66.

60 Marty, *Über den Ursprung der Sprache*, p. 6.

61 Kafka, *Selected Stories*, p. 66.

62 Kafka, *Selected Stories*, p. 67.

63 Kafka, *Selected Stories*, p. 66.

64 Kafka, *Selected Stories*, p. 66 f.

65 See Aage A. Hansen-Löve, Vor dem Gesetz (Before the law). In: Michael Müller, (ed.), *Interpretationen. Franz Kafka. Romane und Erzählungen* (Interpretations. Franz Kafka. Novels and Short Stories). Stuttgart: Reclam 1994, pp. 146–157.

66 Kafka, *Selected Stories*, p. 66 f.

the phrase 'screech of jackdaws' in a diary entry of 19 June 1910;[67] a similar pun is also to be found in the fragment 'The hunter Gracchus' (Dec. 1916 to April 1917), in which the name 'Gracchus' can be explained as the Italian equivalent of jackdaw (*Kafka / kavka*).

Thus we might read into the 'languagelessness' of the nomads who screech like jackdaws the 'languagelessness' of Kafka and in general of the Western Jews who, through their existence in the Galuth and their linguistic assimilation over the course of this, have become languageless, that is, lacking a specific Jewish language. Through the reference to *mauscheln* they are denied any language and with regard to the so-called *Volksgeist* in the period's antisemitic discourse they are reproached precisely for their 'wildness', 'uncleanliness', 'rootlessness', 'landlessness', 'living parasitically off their host people', 'monstrosities in the slaughter of animals' etc.[68] These are qualities with which the 'nomads' of the story are also characterised, and, of course, 'uncleanliness', 'rootlessness' or 'living parasitically' are also connected with characteristics of *Mauscheln* in contemporary discourse. In this way, we might recognise in the 'screech of jackdaws' an allusion to *Mauscheln* which becomes a non-language by the mere virtue of the fact that its speakers' ignorance of 'our language'[69] is identified in tandem with the absence of 'our' *Volksgeist* – 'they do it because that is how they are'),[70] is how it is put in Kafka's story.[71] At the same time, in the story's discourse on foreigners, which is not dissimilar to antisemitic discourse, the speakers of the 'jackdaw language' are also quickly denied any humanity and any language 'of their own' through the narrator's recourse to animal comparisons and animal metaphors,[72] even if the reference to their language of signs and gestures quickly puts paid to this notion. For it is precisely this exaggeration that makes Kafka's irony tangible, even to the average reader – and it is here, at the very

67 Franz Kafka, *Tagebücher* (Diaries). Ed. by Hans-Gerd Koch, Michael Müller, Malcolm Pasley. Frankfurt am Main: S. Fischer 1990, p. 19 f.

68 On the context, see Christoph Stölzl, *Kafkas böses Böhmen: Zur Sozialgeschichte eines Prager Juden* (Kafka's Villainous Bohemia: on Social History of Prague Jews). Munich: Text + Kritik 1975; Miloš Pojar (ed.), *Hilsnerova aféra a česká společnost 1899–1999* (The Hilsner Affair and Czech Society 1899–1999). Prague: Židovské muzeum 1999. On 'landlessness' vs. 'language focussedness' see Kilcher, Kafka, Scholem und die Politik der jüdischen Sprachen, p. 66 f., who refers to, amongst others, Moritz Steinschneider, *Die hebräischen Übersetzungen des Mittelalters und die Juden als Dolmetscher: Ein Beitrag zur Literaturgeschichte des Mittelalters* (Hebrew Translations in the Middle Age and Jews as Translators: A Contribution to the History of Middle Age Literature). Berlin 1893.

69 Kafka, *Selected Stories*, p. 66.

70 Kafka, *Selected Stories*, p. 67.

71 Here Kafka uses the Herderian term 'Lebensweise' (way of life), which, through the use of 'our', he transforms into the phrase often used in discourses about foreigners 'our way of life'. Kafka, *Selected Stories*, p. 67.

72 Kafka, *Selected Stories*, p. 66.

latest, that the deconstruction of the shoemaker's narrative by the critical reader should begin.

The story contains further paradoxes which one could follow up in connection with this: the 'new' linguistic antisemitism is dealt with in an 'old document'; the story within the story is told by one of the conquered, who controls the discourse of the conquest through his war reporting and portrays the conquered as conquerors in his narrative, at least in a cultural and linguistic sense, etc. The parallels between 'A page from an old document' and 'Jackals and Arabs' (beginning of February 1917) can also hardly be overlooked. These include, for example, the ironic treatment of the organic connection between the 'wailing tone' ('Klageton'), the 'natural voice' and the jackals' 'nature',[73] Kafka's ironic treatment of the antisemitic discourse in his carving out of the opposition between the life forms of a parasitic collective and those of its host or master people, which has been read as an allegory for the oppositions of (West-)Jews and non-Jews,[74] Germans and Czechs, and finally also Arabs and Jews (or Jews and Arabs).[75] For now, however, I am simply concerned with highlighting the discursive parallels between the treatment of *Mauscheln* and the narrative construction of the 'screech of jackdaws', which also include the parallel between 'pantomime' and grimaces.

WRITING AND *MAUSCHELN*: IN PLACE OF A CONCLUSION

In the first section of this chapter it was established that Yiddish (and later also the 'impure' Jewish varieties of German) was denigrated as *mauscheln*.

---

73 Kafka, *Selected Stories*, p. 70.

74 William C. Rubinstein, Kafka's *Jackals and Arabs. Monatshefte* 1 (1967), pp. 13–18; Jens Tismar, Kafkas *Schakale und Araber* im zionistischen Kontext betrachtet (Kafka's *Jackals and Arabs* from Zionist point of view). In: *Jahrbuch der deutschen Schillergesellschaft* 19 (1975), pp. 311–313; Mark H. Gelber, Kafka und zionistische Deutungen (Kafka and Zionist interpretations). In: Bettina von Jagow – Oliver Jahraus (eds), *Kafka Handbuch. Leben – Werk – Wirkung* (A Kafka Manual: Biography – Oeuvre – Reception). Göttingen: Vandenhoeck & Ruprecht 2008, pp. 293–302; Reiner Stach, *Kafka. Die Jahre der Erkenntnis* (Kafka: Years of Insight). Frankfurt am Main: S. Fischer. 2008, p. 198 f.

75 Scott Spector, *Prague Territories. National Conflict and Cultural Innovation in Franz Kafka's Fin de Siècle*. Berkely, Los Angeles, London: University of California Press 2000; Alef Botros, *Kafka. Ein jüdischer Schriftsteller aus arabischer Sicht* (Kafka. A Jewish Author from the Arabic Point of View). Wiesbaden: Reichert 2009; Dimitry Shumsky, Czechs, Germans, Arabs, Jews. Franz Kafka's *Jackals and Arabs* between Bohemia and Palestine. *Association for Jewish Studies Review* 33 (2009) 1, pp. 71–100; see also the discussion on this subject in Kateřina Čapková, 'Ich akzeptiere den Komplex, der ich bin'. Zionisten um Franz Kafka ('I accept the complex which I am.' Zionists around Franz Kafka). In: Peter Becher – Steffen Höhne – Marek Nekula (eds), *Kafka und Prag* (Kafka and Prague). Weimar, Cologne, Vienna: Böhlau 2012, pp. 79–95. An interpretation from a gender perspective is no doubt also possible; on the suppression and condemnation of impure sexuality, or on jackals (connected with the feminine symbol of 'scissors') as 'female' see Alt, *Franz Kafka*, p. 520 f.

Those charged with *mauscheln* were accused of lacking the German *Volksgeist*, i.e. that which could turn *mauscheln* into German, into a language. If we accept the 'screech of jackdaws' as a metaphor for *mauscheln*, then in the shoemaker's narrative of 'A page from an old document' it is represented as a non-language in every respect. In this way, in the quotation at the beginning of this chapter, by characterising *Mauscheln* as an 'organic compound of bookish German and pantomime', Kafka does not only form a connection between *mauscheln* and the writing process, but also between *mauscheln* and literary writing. Using insect imagery, he follows up his remarks on *mauscheln* with observations on the role of the young Jewish generation of German writers and discusses the role of literature for members of the young Jewish generation, 'who began to write German', and who

> with their posterior legs [they] were still glued to their father's Jewishness and with their waving anterior legs they found no new ground. The ensuing despair became their inspiration. [...] the product of their despair could not be German literature, though outwardly it seemed to be so. They existed among three impossibilities, which I just happen to call linguistic impossibilities. It is simplest to call them that. But they might also be called something entirely different. These are: The impossibility of not writing, the impossibility of writing German, the impossibility of writing differently. One might also add a fourth impossibility, the impossibility of writing [...]. Thus what resulted was a literature impossible in all respects, a gypsy literature which had *stolen* the German child out of its cradle and in great haste put it through some kind of training, for someone has to dance on the tightrope. (But it wasn't even a German child, it was nothing; people merely said that somebody was dancing).[76]

Instead of the inspiration of a young writer who painstakingly records in his diary his daily contact with his pen,[77] who experiences the word as his body's flesh[78] and who celebrated the day after putting 'The judgment' (1912) to paper as a union of body and soul, or the moment when body and mind became an organic whole,[79] the above quotation reveals the desperation of being unable to write in German, or in a different language, or even at all. Thus, against the background of contemporary language discourse, the reference to language, through which he characterises the state of the young generation of assimilated German Jews, touches upon something fun-

76 Franz Kafka to Max Brod, June 1921. – See Kafka, *Letters to Friends, Family and Editors*, p. 289. My emphases.

77 See e.g. Diary, 18–19 May 1910. – See Kafka, *Tagebücher*, p. 16f. and p. 25 f.

78 See Diary, 3 October 1911. – See Kafka, *Tagebücher*, p. 54

79 'It is only in this context that writing can be done, only with this kind of coherence, with such a complete unfolding of the body and the soul'. Franz Kafka, Diary, 23 September 1912. – See Kafka, *Selected Stories*, p. 197.

damental which goes beyond language and writing. A connection is forged between writing, like *mauscheln*, and the discourse of antisemitism through the image of 'stealing'. This image was used to characterise Jews as having a merely reproductive, mechanical mind and, following Richard Wagner's essay 'Jewishness in Music' (1850; authorised 1869), denied them any creative spirit. This categoric dismissal – also in the area of artistic creativity – equally accounts for Jewish hopelessness and self-doubt in relation to language and literature.

The condition of having no solid, Jewish ground under one's feet is also addressed in a letter to Max Brod of 30 July 1922 in which a clear connection is made with antisemitism. In connection with Friedrich von der Leyen's monograph *German Literature* Kafka remarks:[80]

> I had only a minute to look into it. It would be interesting to read it more carefully. It seems to be accompanying music to the *Secessio Judaica* and it is astonishing how within a minute a reader, to be sure a well-disposed one, can organize things with the help of the book, how *the crowd of half-familiar, surely honest creative writers who turn up in a chapter entitled 'Our Land' are classified by landscapes: German property not to be annexed by any Jews*. And even if Wassermann should rise at four in the morning day after day and his whole life long plow up the Nuremberg region from end to end, the land would still not respond to him and he would have to take pretty whisperings in the air for its response. There is no index in the book, so that I found only one mention of you in the text, a not unfriendly one; I think it was a comparison between a novel of Löns and your Tycho. *Tycho was found, in all due respect, suspiciously dialectic*.[81]

Here Kafka does not only paraphrase the title of Hans Blüher's work *Secessio Judaica*,[82] but also alludes to the apparent characteristics (rootlessness and nomadism) which were ascribed to Jews in antisemitic discourse also in connection with language, or rather *mauscheln*, and which were also meant to justify – as in the book under discussion – their ostracisation. If we choose to read the words 'suspiciously dialectic' (semantic polyvalent) as 'suspiciously dialectical', then this also exposes the implicit reproach of *mauscheln* by Friedrich von der Leyen. In doing so he must have focused more on the name than the language of the author Max Brod, whose German he accuses of being unnatural by remarking on its lack of linguistic rootedness, then the 'dialectical' is 'suspiciously' excessive. But due to its polyphony, to

---

80 Friedrich von der Leyen, *Deutsche Dichtung* (German Literature). Jena: Diederichs 1922.

81 Letter to Max Brod, end of July 1922. – See Kafka, *Letters to family, friends and editors*, p. 346 f. My emphases.

82 Hans Blüher, *Secessio Judaica. Philosophische Grundlegung der historischen Situation des Judentums und der antisemitischen Bewegung* (Secessio Judaica. Philosophical Foundation of the Historical Situation of Judaism and the antisemitic Movement). Berlin: Der Weiße Ritter-Verlag 1922.

use Mikhail Bahtin's terminology, the 'dialectic' is already 'suspicious' for von der Leyen. Kafka's three or four impossibilities for Jewish writers are also attested to from the outside: the impossibility of writing in German, or another language, or even at all, is not only felt from the inside, but – through the organic understanding of language and the denial of a creative spirit – is also claimed in antisemitic discourse. Kafka explicitly reflects on this impossibility regarding language and writing in the letters to Max Brod. Yet they had already been dealt with in Kafka's 'poetic shorthand' in the language-related paradoxes of, for example, the stories 'A report to an Academy' or 'A page from an old document'. Here the national struggle between languages is alluded to as a cultural struggle with an antisemitic dimension.

FRANZ KAFKA AT SCHOOL
KAFKA'S EDUCATION IN CZECH LANGUAGE AND LITERATURE

As I pointed out in the chapter 'Franz Kafka's languages', Franz Kafka learned Czech in his parental home before he started going to school. That does not mean he learned Czech through communication with his parents, with whom, even though they knew and used Czech, he and his sisters spoke – and later exchanged letters – in German.[1] Kafka probably learned Czech primarily through communicating with his parents' servants and with his peers. There are certain indications that his Czech was influenced by these speakers, for example in his use of the word *noc* (night) in the non-standard form *noce* (nominative plural) generally used in central, western and northern regions of Bohemia, whereas in the dialect of South Bohemia, where his father grew up, the common form is *noci*.[2] The following analysis, however, is confined to Kafka's tutored acquisition of standard Czech, the main basis of his ability to read official, literary and academic texts in Czech and use the Czech language actively – with certain limitations – in writing.

THE 'VOLKSSCHULE'

The assertion that Kafka learnt his Czech at school may at first sight seem misleading, if not confusing. Although Kafka scholarship 'from the Prague perspective' tends to see Hermann Kafka as a Czech Jew, young Franz was enrolled at the 'Deutsche Volks- und Bürgerschule für Prag 1' (German Elementary and Lower Secondary School in Prague I), founded in the 1870s, which he attended from 1889 to 1893. There German was not only the language of instruction from the 1st to 4th grade; pupils also studied the German language in classes on reading, handwriting, spelling, and writing style. Czech classes, by contrast, started in the 3rd grade and with fewer hours. This

---

1 For the status of Czech in the household of Hermann Kafka and the extent to which Franz Kafka used the language, see also Anna Pouzarová, Als Erzieherin in der Familie Kafka (Governess in the Kafka family). In: Hans-Gerd Koch (ed.), *„Als Kafka mir entgegen kam..." Erinnerungen an Franz Kafka* ('As Kafka approached me.' Recollections of Franz Kafka). Berlin: Wagenbach 1995, pp. 55–65, here p. 62.

2 For more on Czech dialects see Jan Balhar et al., *Český jazykový atlas* (Atlas of the Czech Language). Vol. 4. Prague: Academia 2002, p. 182, 185.

clearly shows the different status of Czech and German in the German school system, which affected Kafka's acquisition of both languages.

But we are also particularly interested in the linguistic composition of the classes Kafka attended. As Tables I and II and the following diagram make clear, until 1882, when Prague University was split into a German and a Czech section, around 30% of the pupils at the school were linguistically of Czech origin – that is, they declared Czech as their mother tongue. This can be seen from the abbreviations against their names in the school registers and lists. Pupils' native languages are usually recorded as either *b.* / *č.* (*böhmisch* / *čeština*, i.e. Czech) or *d.* (*deutsch*, i.e. German), or a combination of these (*d.-b.*, *d.u.b.*, *d-b*, i.e. German and Czech). Only rarely do other languages appear (*chorv.*, i.e. Croatian). In 1883 the proportion of Czech pupils at Kafka's German school fell to 20%. By 1889, the year when Franz Kafka enrolled, that figure – based on data from his own and parallel classes – had shrunk to 10%. The reduction in Czech pupils was accompanied by an increase in the number of Jewish children, from 30% in 1877 to 82.6% in 1889 – figures similarly derived from school registers, which include entries such as *mosaisch* / *jüdisch* (*m.*, *i.*, i.e. Jewish), *katholisch* (*k.*, i.e. Catholic), and occasionally *evangelisch* (*e.*, i.e. Protestant). The entry 'ohne Bekenntnis' ('without confession') was extremely rare. Private pupils are generally listed without information as to their faith or mother tongue. Among those whose stated mother tongue is Czech, the majority were Catholic. This is the context in which the young Kafka grew up. It shows that the Czech minority in his school was already very small by that time and that in the school context Czech was a language that was studied rather than spoken in the schoolyard.

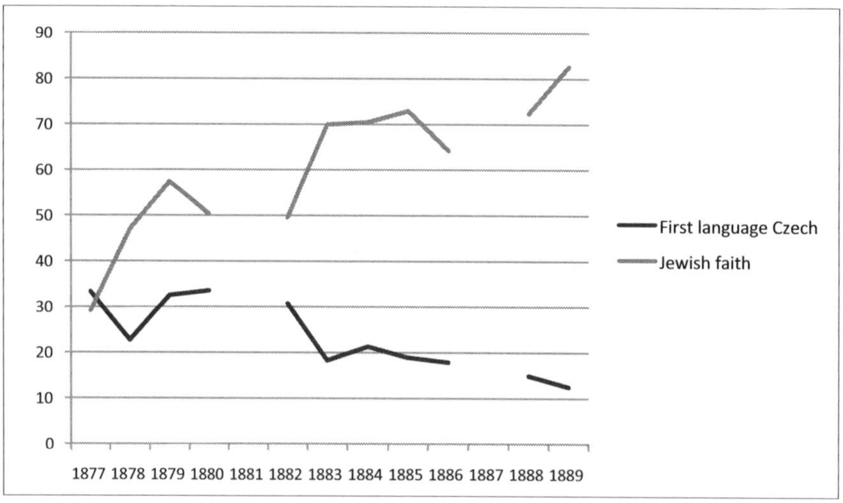

Diagram based on data in tables I and II

Arriving at these figures was somewhat problematic. Despite a ministerial decree of 6 March 1880 requiring schools to keep a record of pupils' mother tongues,[3] this only started happening at Kafka's school in 1884–85. The situation prior to that date has therefore been reconstructed using the class registers of previous (i.e. higher) years at the Elementary and Lower Secondary School, an approach justified on the assumption that most pupils registered at the lower secondary school ('Bürgerschule') would also have attended the elementary school ('Volksschule') rather than its Czech equivalent, and vice-versa. While there were doubtless some exceptions, the figures as presented are probably an adequate reflection of the situation in the period in question.[4] That is why in Table I presented bellow the year (cohort) and year of its first enrolment are listed side by side, whereas the diagram shows only the year of enrolment. This table is based on the schools records for academic year 1884–85. For the Lower Secondary (Municipal) School I have evaluated data from two First Classes, one Second and one Third. The data I had available for the Volksschule was for Class 4a (with no record of mother tongue or confession), 3a, 3b, 2b and 1a. For the following years in Table II, I used data for pupils from the corresponding first years, as I had no access to data from school year 1887–88. The tendency evident in the table and diagram for the years 1885–1889 is confirmed by the data for pupils of the preceding years, who later attended the lower secondary school, contained in the corresponding registers of that school. I also checked my results against data from the registers of other cohorts. These statistics have also been the subject of a broader and more detailed study by Ingrid Stöhr, who analysed the records of all classes in Kafka's school and other comparable German and Czech schools in Prague.[5] She points out the same tendency in the proportion of Jewish and Catholic pupils in both public schools for Prague I (for girls and boys), where the figures are quite different from those in elementary and grammar schools in other parts of the city.[6]

The linguistic and religious composition of the German Volksschule in Prague 1 attended by Kafka, outlined briefly above, can nevertheless be seen

---

3 See Emil Brix, *Die Umgangssprachen in Altösterreich zwischen Agitation und Assimilation: Die Sprachenstatistik in den zisleithanischen Volkszählungen 1880 bis 1910* (Common Languages in Old Austria between Agitation and Assimilation: Language Statistics in the Austrian Censuses, 1880–1910). Vienna, Cologne, Graz: Böhlau 1982.

4 Cohen states that whereas in 1890 about 40% of pupils at German Volksschulen were native Czech speakers, by 1910 the figure had fallen to around 17%. See Gary B. Cohen: *The Politics of Ethnic Survival: Germans in Prague 1861–1914*. Princeton: Princeton University Press 1981, p. 132. The data from the 'Jewish' school in Prague Old Town show that in comparison with other German schools the 'escape' of Czech Christian pupils was more dynamic.

5 Ingrid Stöhr, *Zweisprachigkeit in Böhmen – Deutsche Volksschulen und Gymnasien in Prag der Kafka-Zeit* (Bilingualism in Bohemia: German Elementary and Grammar Schools in the Prague of Kafka's Time). Weimar: Böhlau 2010.

6 Stöhr, *Zweisprachigkeit in Böhmen*, 377 f.

Table I

Elementary and Lower Secondary School for Prague I		First language Czech	Jewish faith
3rd Municipal	1877	33.33%	29.166%
2nd Municipal	1878	22.72%	46.970%
1st Municipal	1879	32.54%	57.356%
5th Class	1880	33.57%	50.365%
4th Class	1881		
3rd Class	1882	30.76%	49.573%
2nd Class	1883	18.33%	70.000%
1st Class	1884	21.31%	70.492%

Table II

Elementary School for Prague I		First language Czech	Jewish faith
1st Class	1885	18.91%	72.973%
1st Class	1886	17.85%	64.286%
	1887		
1st Class	1888	14.94%	72.414%
1st Class	1889	12.50%	82.60%

as a reflection of social processes that had a wider import. We see a clear and continuous increase in the proportion of German-speaking Jews attending the German schools in Prague, while especially Czech 'Christian' families began avoiding them. The trend of leaving schools with German as the language of instruction by Czechs is more pronounced in 'Jewish' schools. Nationalist agitation and latent antisemitism thus came to affect public institutions.

These 'discrepancies' can be seen in a broader Prague and Bohemian context. Binder and Stöhr have drawn attention to the social structure of the schools to show that most of the fathers of the German-speaking Jewish children in the Prague schools were merchants, while those of Czech-speaking Christians were generally tradesmen or worked in the service sector.[7] Binder has also drawn attention to the – by today's standards intolerable – conditions

7 See Hartmut Binder, Kindheit in Prag. Kafkas Volksschuljahre (Childhood in Prague: Kafka's years at Volksschule). In: Harry Järv (ed.), *Humanismen*. Stockholm: Atlantis 1987, pp. 63–115, here p. 85 ff. In a later work, however, Binder modifies his view: 'whereas a quarter of the Prague population who identified themselves as German belonged to lower-income groups, at least half of them being labourers and tradesmen'. See Hartmut Binder, Paul Eisners dreifaches Ghetto (Paul Eisner's triple ghetto). In: Michel Reffet (ed.), *Le monde de Franz Werfel et la morale des*

in the public elementary schools, with class sizes ranging from 55 to 90. In first grade Kafka was in a class of 86 pupils;[8] in second grade 90; in third 55 and in fourth 61. In Prague this situation stemmed from the reluctance of the City Council, which was dominated by Czechs, to support German Volksschulen.[9] In parts of the country where ethnic Germans controlled local councils, Czech pupils had to put up with similar conditions.[10] In Budweis, for example, due to official resistance to the idea of parallel classes in the public Czech boys' school, 99 pupils were registered in one class and in another as many as 133, so that only 60 of them had a proper place to sit with the others standing between desks, by the blackboard or next to the stove.[11] In the predominantly German Bohemian towns such as Reichenberg, Leitmeritz, Neuern, Trautenau, Theresienstadt, Brux, Teplitz and Saaz, the Czech-speaking population numbered over 20,000 in the 1870s, yet no one thought of opening any Czech-language schools or even classes.[12] And although the number of schools (elementary and secondary) grew in Bohemia from 2073 German and 2286 Czech in 1881 to 2355 German and 3206 Czech in 1900, there were almost twice as many Czech pupils as German.[13] The situation for Czech pupils in Prague was quite different as they could switch to Czech schools.

---

nations. / Die Welt Franz Werfels und die Moral der Völker. Berlin et al.: Peter Lang 2000, pp. 17–137, here p. 53. More recently see Stöhr, *Zweisprachigkeit in Böhmen.*

8 Of those 69 were Jewish and 17 Christian. Four of the private pupils gave Czech as their native language, six said they spoke Czech better than German, while seven stated the opposite. Data is from records of the German National School in Prague 1, Prague City Archive. A similar situation applied in the Prague 1 Bürgerschule. See also Marek Nekula, Franz Kafka ve škole. Výuka a znalosti češtiny (Franz Kafka at school. His Czech lessons and knowledge of Czech). In: *Kafkova zpráva o světě. Sborník ze semináře Společnosti Franze Kafky 20.–21. října 1999* (Kafka's Report on the World. Proceedings from the Franz Kafka Society seminar, 20–21 October 1999). Prague: Nakladatelství Franze Kafky 2000, pp. 59–78. Binder's figures are inconsistent. See Binder, Paul Eisners dreifaches Ghetto, p. 68 and 113.

9 See Gustav Strakosch-Grassmann, *Geschichte des österreichischen Unterrichtswesens* (History of the Austrian School System). Vienna: Pichler 1905; Binder, Kindheit in Prag, p. 89 ff.; Hannelore Burger, *Sprachenrecht und Sprachgerechtigkeit im österreichischen Unterrichtswesen 1867–1918* (Language Law and Language Justice in the Austrian School System 1867–1918). Vienna: Verlag der Österreichischen Akademie der Wissenschaften 1995, p. 169.

10 See Jiří Kořalka, Das Nationalitätenproblem in den böhmischen Ländern 1848–1918 (The Nationality Problem in the Bohemian Lands 1848–1918). *Österreichische Osthefte* 5 (1991), pp. 1–11, here p. 9.

11 See Burger, *Sprachenrecht und Sprachgerechtigkeit*, p. 104 f.

12 See Burger, *Sprachenrecht und Sprachgerechtigkeit*, p. 92.

13 Kořalka states that according to the 1900 census 62.67% of the population of Bohemia were Czechs. See Jiří Kořalka, *Tschechen im Habsburgerreich und in Europa 1815–1914* (Czechs in the Habsburg Empire and in Europe 1815–1914). Vienna, Munich: Oldenbourg 1991, p. 128. Burger cites the number of pupils attending Czech elementary and secondary schools as 604,122, and those at German Volks- and Bürgerschulen as 360,409. Burger, *Sprachenrecht und Sprachgerechtigkeit*, p. 173. See also the table in Burger, ibid., pp. 246 ff. This means the ratio of Czech schools to German schools was 57.65% to 42.35%, while that of Czech pupils to German pupils was 62.63% to 37.37%.

Among other reforms introduced by the 'Reichsschulgesetz' of 1869, attendance at elementary schools was extended to eight years and class sizes were limited to a maximum of eighty. New, separate local and regional councils were also set up along ethno-national lines. And in the early 1870s school fees were abolished. Certain aspects of the law were problematic from a language parity point of view. Municipalities were obliged (Para. 62) to set up a school if the number of children resident within one hour's journey of the town or village exceeded 40 over a five-year period (Para. 59), and if within a radius of four kilometres no school was available offering tuition in the national language determined by their parents. Burger sees this as a positive change in that it led to a denser network of schools in Bohemia and Moravia and thus to a higher level of education in the Bohemian lands.[14]

In the years that followed, the status of the country's second language as a medium of instruction in elementary schools in Bohemia and Moravia became a topic of heated debate both in the courts and in parliament. This was because the decision as to whether Czech (for example) should be a compulsory or non-compulsory school subject in Prague German schools – or whether it should be taught at all – depended not on the law-makers but on the wishes of often competing local councils and of the parents themselves. And acting upon these wishes was not seen as a breach of the ban on 'majorization', as the overruling by language majority was known.[15]

It was against this background that Franz Kafka's parents decided to send him to the German boys' school in Prague 1, even though in the late 19th century such a course was considered (albeit not officially) as an act of ethno-national identification. This helps explain why at that time boys of Czech origin at the Prague 1 German School became a small minority. Yet the data on Kafka's mother tongue contained in the 'Katalog über den Schulbesuch und Fortgang' ('Catalogue of school attendance and progress') is contradictory. In the first class the entry *d.u.b.* ('deutsch und böhmisch' – German and Czech) can be found against his name, which could refer either to his mother tongue or to his common language. In view of the fact that this entry does not appear immediately below the name, as is the case with 'Religion', but in the 'Anmerkung' ('Remarks') column, and that the same entry can be found against all pupils who in the following years consistently have the simple entry *d.* (such as Richard Hrudka), it may be assumed that in this case *d.u.b.* refers to the boys' ability to understand both languages – which, in the first class, was clearly not without importance.[16] Be that as it may, in the school

---

14 See Burger, *Sprachenrecht und Sprachgerechtigkeit*, p. 45 f.

15 See esp. Burger, *Sprachenrecht und Sprachgerechtigkeit*, pp. 111–114.

16 The class teacher could also leave the 'language' field blank, as was the case in Class 4a at Kafka's school in 1884–85.

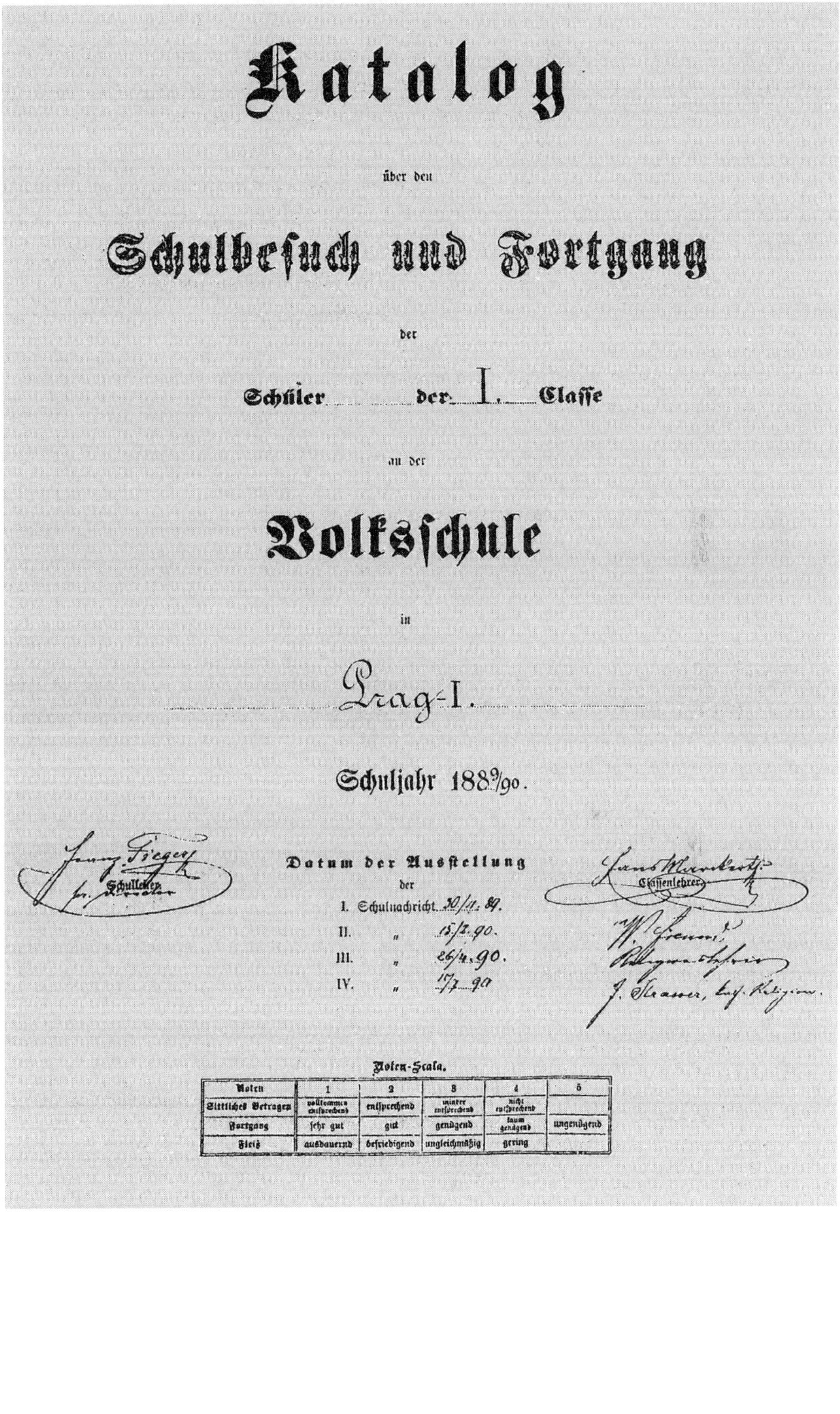

Katalog

über den

Schulbesuch und Fortgang

der

Schüler der I. Classe

an der

Volksschule

in

Prag-I.

Schuljahr 1889/90.

Schulleiter

Datum der Ausstellung

der

I. Schulnachricht 30/11. 89.

II. „ 15/2. 90.

III. „ 26/4. 90.

IV. „ 17/7 90

Classenlehrer

Noten-Scala.

Noten	1	2	3	4	5
Sittliches Betragen	vollkommen entsprechend	entsprechend	minder entsprechend	nicht entsprechend	
Fortgang	sehr gut	gut	genügend	kaum genügend	ungenügend
Fleiß	ausdauernd	befriedigend	ungleichmäßig	gering	

Catalogue for 1890–91, Kafka's second year, we once again find, now next to the record of his religion (*m.*, i.e. 'mosaisch' for Jewish), the letters *d.u.b.* – German and Czech. In the Class Three records there is no entry opposite Kafka's name; and in Class Four we find the single letter *d.* – i.e. 'deutsch' for German. Henceforth, at Grammar school and later at the German university of Prague, Kafka always declares himself a German speaker. The note *d.u.b.* (German and Czech) in the first two years of elementary school certainly need not be taken as a statement of ethnic (or 'national') identity. Rather, it can be seen as meaning that in Franz's preschool years both German and Czech were spoken in the Kafka household.

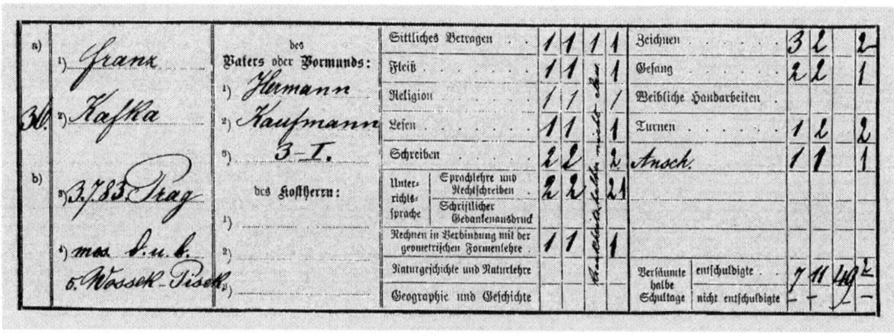

But do these data tell us anything about the language situation in Kafka's school? Even though it is clear from the records that 10% of his schoolmates spoke Czech, that does not necessarily mean that after school or during break the Czech speakers would go into a huddle together, or that Kafka would join them. On the other hand we also know that Kafka's knowledge of Czech was much influenced by his Czech classes at school, suggesting that it was very much a second language for him. At the Volksschule Czech was taught from Third Year and Kafka's quarterly school reports in Classes 3 and 4 all give him a grade of 1 (Excellent) in the subject. As for German, the language of instruction, his results were as follows in Table III.

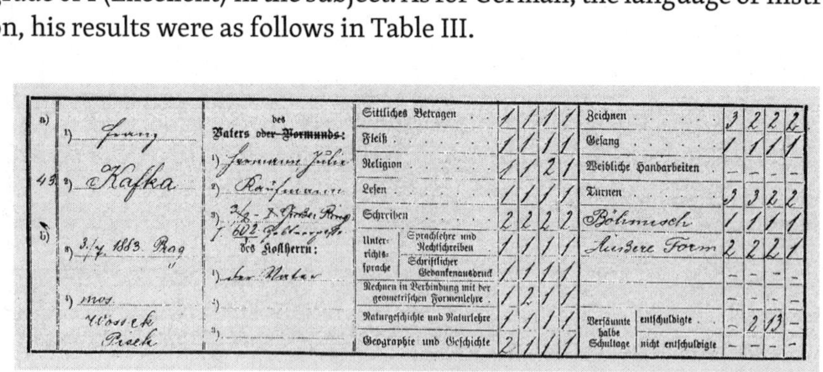

Entry for Franz Kafka in the Catalogue of school attendance and progress
Prague Municipal Archive

Table III

F. Kafka		German				Czech
		Reading	Writing	Grammar & Orthography	Writen Expression	
1st Class	1889/90	2-2-1-1[17]	2-2-1-1			
2nd Class	1890/91	1-1-X-1	2-2-X-2	2-2-X-2/1[18]		
3rd Class	1891/92	1-1-1-1	2-2-2-2	1-1-1-1	1-1-1-1	1-1-1-1
4th Class	1892/93	1-1-1-1	2-2-2-2	1-1-1-1	1-1-1-1	1-1-1-1

Kafka's results in Czech compare very favourably with those of other pupils, even of those whose declared native language is Czech. Given this, and the remarks about Kafka's knowledge of Czech and German in the Classes 1 and 2, it seems unlikely that Kafka's Czech was so poor that he had to take extra lessons from František X. Bašík, a young man two years Franz's senior who worked for Hermann Kafka as a trainee from 15 September 1892 to 31 January 1895. This may be Bašík's retrospective literary self-construction.[19] But we can also see Bašík's testimony from another point of view – as evidence that Kafka spoke Czech regularly with his peers and that his family considered it important to know the language well.

Yet as Table III shows, Kafka's results in Czech were similar to those he achieved in German. The status of Czech and German in the Prague 1 German Boys' School were not comparable. German was taught at Kafka's school for four years as a compulsory subject and was assessed using four different criteria, whereas Czech was taught less intensively, and only for two years. In this respect, however, Prague seems to have been the exception since, as Cohen points out, between 80 and 90 percent of the German pupils in Prague studied Czech in the primary school.[20] This is well illustrated by the data for

17 Each grade is for one academic quarter.

18 In the third quarter Kafka did not receive a grade owing to a 5-day absence.

19 František X. Bašík (1881–1961), whose memoirs, written under the name František Bártík in 1940–43, were published by his great-grandson J. J. K. Nebeský, claims not to have known that Franz Kafka, whom he gave extra Czech lessons to, later became a writer. See František X. Bašík, *Vyučil jsem se u Kafků: Praha a Mladá Boleslav na konci 19. století očima dospívajícího muže* (I was an Apprentice in the Kafka Store: Prague and Mladá Boleslav at the end of 19th Century through the Eyes of an Adolescent). Prague: Prostor 2003. Extracts from his memoirs were published in Jiří J. K. Nebeský, Nové obrázky z Kafkova dětství (New images of Kafka's childhood). *Host* 17 (2001), No. 7, 64–68. See also Marek Nekula, Ad Nové obrázky z Kafkova dětství (Ad New images of Kafka's childhood). *Host* 10 (2001), No. 8, p. 74.

20 See Cohen, *The Politics of Ethnic Survival*, p. 133; also Binder, Paul Eisners dreifaches Ghetto, p. 115, and Robert Luft, Sprache und Nationalität an Prager Gymnasien um 1900 (Language and nationality at Prague grammar schools around 1900). In: Klaas-Hinrich Ehlers at al. (eds), *Brücken*

whole country: whereas German was taught as a compulsory subject in 1071 Czech elementary schools and 29 Czech secondary schools and as an optional subject at 1000 Czech elementary schools and 511 Czech secondary schools, Czech was compulsory in only 41 German elementary schools (2%) and 1 German secondary school and optionally in 205 German elementary schools (10%) and 107 German secondary schools – including those in Prague.[21] In terms of absolute numbers, there were as more Czech than German elementary and secondary schools.

GRAMMAR SCHOOL

In 1893 Kafka entered the 'Deutsches Staatsgymnasium zu Prag-Altstadt' (German State Grammar School in Prague Old Town),[22] where he remained until his school-leaving examination in 1901. There were 41 pupils in his first year class, of whom 34 (83%) declared themselves as Jews and only five (12%) as native Czech speakers (from 1894–95 on, the word *böhmisch* 'Czech' is replaced with *čechoslawisch* – 'Czechoslav'). Against Kafka's name we consistently find the entry *d* (German). The Czech speakers in his class do not usually stay for long, mainly because of their poor grades in German, and in Class Six

Table IV

Kafka's class, by year		**Pupils with Czech as mother tongue**	**Pupils in class**	**Pupils enrolled in Czech class**	**Pupils enrolled in French class**
1st Class	1893/94	5 Czechs	41 (A–K)	20	
2nd Class	1895/95	4 Czechoslavs	36	20	
3rd Class	1895/96	3 Czechoslavs	32	13	
4th Class	1896/97	3 Czechoslavs	22	5	
5th Class	1897/98	2 Czechoslavs	29 (A–Z)	14	14
6th Class	1898/99		23	10	12
7th Class	1899/00		22	8	7
8th Class	1900/01	2 Czechoslavs	24	9	1

nach Prag. Deutschsprachige Literatur im kulturellen Kontext der Donaumonarchie und der Tschechoslowakei (Bridges to Prague: German-written Literature in the Cultural Context of the Habsburg Monarchy and Czechoslovakia). Frankfurt am Main: P. Lang 2000, pp. 105–122.

21 For figures for all kingdoms and countries of the Empire, see Burger, *Sprachenrecht und Sprachgerechtigkeit*, p. 248.

22 Binder points out that Kafka's teacher Mathias Beck recommended he first complete fifth year before moving on to grammar school. See Franz Kafka: *Tagebücher 1914–1923 in der Fassung der Handschrift* (Diaries 1914–1923 Based on the Handwritten Manuscripts). Ed. by Hans-Gerd Koch. Frankfurt am Main: S. Fischer 1994, pp. 172 f., and Binder, Kindheit in Prag, p. 104.

and Seven the number of Czech pupils is zero. In eighth year two new Czech speakers join the class, but they have trouble with their final exams, again because of their inadequate German. One, Zdenko Vaněk, actually failed the exam.

Given that the Czech pupils attended the grammar school primarily in order to improve their German and prepare for their future careers, it is unlikely that the Czech language was much used at the school – say, among the boys during break. We must therefore assume that any formative influence on Kafka's Czech in the school was derived from his Czech lessons, which in his first year were attended by half his class. By fourth year the proportion had fallen to a quarter, a drop no doubt caused by the need to prepare for the coming division between those who would continue to the lower secondary school and those who would leave school at the end of the year. In years five and six the number of boys enrolled in the 'relatively obligatory' Czech class again rises to half the total class, while in years seven and eight it falls off. By and large, the core group remains the same: sons of merchants, doctors and to a lesser degree civil servants (albeit from the lower echelons), that is to say of people for whom a knowledge of Czech was a vital necessity.

The composition of the group that studied Czech would suggest that the course was of a fairly high standard. Most were what might be called high achievers, while those who fared less well either had difficulties in other subjects, too, or simply gave up. Despite the high level of Czech among most of the group, the lessons were designed more as a foreign language than a second language course, with the result that only some of those whose mother tongue was Czech enrolled. Zdenko Vaněk, for example, attended; Leopold Bergmann did not.

Table V

In the columns German, Czech and French, the class average is given; in the columns next to these are Kafka's own grades – one mid-year, the other end-of-year.

Class	German	Kafka	Czech	Kafka	French	Kafka	Kafka Latin	Kafka Greek
1	2.975	2–2	3.342	2–2	–	–	2–3	–
2	2.819	2–2	3.5	3–2	–	–	3–2	–
3	2.984	2–1	3.416	2–3	–	–	2–2	2–2
4	3.069	2–3	2.6	2–2	–	Stenogr.	2–3	3–3
5	2.315	2–2	2.92	X–2	3.074	3–3	3–3	3–3
6	2.5	2–2	3.00	2–2	2.782	3–3	2–2	3–3
7	2.977	2–3	2.687	2–2	2.727	3–2	2–2	3–2
8	3.145	3–3	2.529	2–3	3.00	–	2–3	2–2

Kafka attended Czech classes during all his eight years at Grammar school, except for the first half of his fifth year when he was doing a course in stenography. Missing half a year of teaching had no negative effect on his grades in the following term, suggesting that Kafka's Czech was very good. This is further borne out by a comparison of his grades with the class average. The reason Kafka studied stenography for the first term instead of Czech could have been the high intake of weaker pupils in the Czech course following the merging of classes and a consequent dip in the standard, or simply the desire to acquire a practical skill of some kind.[23] Or it could have been Václav Rosický, Kafka's Czech teacher, who besides being an outstanding pedagogue was also an enthusiastic proponent of stenography in Bohemia and Moravia – an enthusiasm he was able to impart to his pupils. This is probably why after leaving school Kafka kept in touch with Rosický, whom we assume is referred to in a letter to Max Brod written in July 1910: 'I'd like to read a few poems, although my Czech teacher is waiting for me'.[24]

CZECH TEACHING AT THE GERMAN STATE GRAMMAR SCHOOL OF PRAGUE OLD TOWN

The annual reports issued by the German State Grammar school of Prague Old Town tell us quite a lot about what was taught in Czech, as they include among other things lists of the textbooks used.

During the time Kafka was there Czech was a 'relatively obligatory' subject. The syllabus was divided into six sections, as was the class itself. From 1893 to 1897 the Czech teachers were Josef Quaiser, Dr. Wenzel (or Václav) Rosický and, in the school year 1895–96, Dr. Adolf Lindner, with each teaching the various parts of the course in rotation. From 1897 Rosický was the sole Czech teacher.

Two periods a week were devoted to Czech, and in sections II–IV pupils were required to write class tests every four weeks. The time commitment was thus similar to that for other 'relatively obligatory' and optional subjects such as French, though French was only taught in years 5–8 (for 2–3 hours a week) and, as far as we can tell from the syllabus and the number of set books, did not place such heavy demands on the pupils as did Czech.[25]

---

23 See also the memoirs of Kafka's classmate H. Bergmann. Hugo Bergmann, Schulzeit und Studium (School and student years). In: Hans-Gerd Koch (ed.), *„Als Kafka mir entgegen kam…" Erinnerungen an Franz Kafka* ('As Kafka approached me.' Recollections of Franz Kafka). Berlin: Wagenbach 1995, pp. 13–24, here p. 17.

24 Max Brod – Franz Kafka, *Eine Freundschaft. Briefwechsel* (A Friendship: Correspondence). Ed. by Malcolm Pasley. Vol. 2. Frankfurt am Main: S. Fischer 1989, p. 77.

25 For more about French see the chapter on Franz Kafka's languages.

Even compared with the number of hours devoted to the core curriculum, Czech did not fare badly. German was taught four hours a week (and from fourth year only three), Latin eight (from third year six, from seventh year five), and Greek, starting in third year, five (four in years four and seven); two hours were devoted to religion, three each to history and geography, three to mathematics (in fifth year, four), two to biology, two to physics (only in years three and seven; in fourth year, three), and to philosophy (only in seventh year) two. The interesting comparison is with German, which despite being the language of instruction was allotted only slightly more time than Czech. And those hours included, apart from rhetoric, German literary history and the reading associated with it (The Nibelungenlied, Walther von der Vogelweide, Wieland, Klopstock, Lessing, Herder, Schiller, Kleist, Goethe, Grillparzer…) plus the fundamentals of poetics. Admittedly, more was expected of the pupils, with class tests in German every 8–10 days.

However, we should not overstate the emphases placed on Czech at Kafka's grammar school, nor indeed at any of the German grammar schools in Bohemia and Moravia. A brief comparison with the status of German in Czech grammar schools will suffice. In the 1892–93 annual report of the Czech Senior Grammar School in Truhlářská Street in Prague New Town, for example, we see that German, a compulsory subject,[26] was taught four hours a week from first year to fourth year (three hours from fifth to eighth year), while only three hours a week were spent on Czech, and in fourth year only two. In other words German accounted in the Czech grammar school for more classroom hours than Czech, which was not only a core subject but also the language of instruction. Pupils started doing written tests in German as early as in fifth year (the same as in Czech), as well as exercises in rhetoric based on themes taken partly from their German reading: 'Erzherzog Karl als Vertheidiger des Vaterlandes' (Archduke Charles as defender of the fatherland), 'Rudolf II. als Förderer der Künste und Wissenschaften in Prag' (Rudolph II as a patron of the arts and sciences in Prague), 'Die Fabel der Götheschen Iphigenie' (The fable of Goethe's Iphigenie), 'Inhaltsangabe und Erklärung des Gedichtes Die Kreuzschau von Chamisso' (Summary and interpretation of Chamisso's poem 'Die Kreuzschau'), to name only a few.[27] Moreover, the number of prescribed texts as well as the frequency of written tests is markedly lower for Czech courses at German schools than for German courses at Czech schools. Nor should we forget that in the Czech grammar school German was an obligatory subject in the school-leaving examination.[28] Pupils at the Ger-

26 The formulation used in the report is 'obligatory subjects and German language'. See *Výroční zpráva cís. král. vyššího gymnasia českého na Novém Městě v Praze* (Annual Report of the Imperial and Royal Czech High Grammar School in Prague New Town). 1896–97, p. 30.

27 See *Výroční zpráva*, pp. 38–39.

28 See *Výroční zpráva cís. král. vyššího gymnasia českého na Novém Městě v Praze*. 1892–93, p. 48.

man grammar school did not progress nearly as far in their Czech classes. This glaring discrepancy between the way Czech was taught at German grammar schools – primarily as a foreign language and optional, 'relatively obligatory' subject meriting only two hours per week – and the importance attached to German at Czech grammar schools – four hours a week, as a compulsory and 'maturita' subject (at least in Prague at the time) – indicates the underlying unidirectionality of Czech-German bilingualism.

SYLLABUS

The annual report of the German State Grammar school in Prague 1 also gives us a very good idea of the material content and organization of the various sections:[29]

Section 1: introduction to correct reading and writing, tenses and modality of the verb *být i* (to be), declension of nouns and hard adjectives, personal and possessive pronouns, present tense of (regular) verbs[30]

Section 2: *pluralia tantum*, vestiges of duality, soft adjectives, comparison of adjectives and adverbs, cardinal and ordinal numerals, types of verb, formation of the passive, imperative and subjunctive[31]

Section 3: pronouns and quantifiers[32]

Section 4: extension of conjugation of verbs in the present, formation of perfect and future tenses (perfective and imperfective), prepositions with names[33]

Section 5: conjoining sentences, indirect speech, use of conjunctions, use of synonyms[34]

Section 6: revision of grammar, translation from German into Czech, idioms with constant regard to their equivalents in Czech, German and Latin, history of modern literature with reading of selected extracts from contemporary literature[35]

---

29 22.–29. *Jahresbericht über das Deutsche Staats-Gymnasium mit deutscher Unterrichtssprache in Prag--Altstadt für das Schuljahr...* (Annual Report of German State Grammar School with German as Language of Instruction in Prague Old Town). 1894–1901: Prague: K.u.k. Hofbuchdruckerei A. Hase.

30 Also, from 1896–97, Past Tense ('Vergangenheit').

31 Also, from 1895–96, exceptions to regular declension.

32 Also, from 1895–96, the conjugation of verbs; and from 1896–97, perfective and imperfective verbs and the imperative.

33 Also, from 1897–98, the subjunctive, the passive, participles and irregular verbs.

34 Also, from 1894–95, the use of participles, the infinitive and the imperative; also case. From 1895–96 and 1893–94 syntax and précis; in 1896–97 declension (case); in 1897–98 and 1898–99 case again, and translation from German into Czech; in 1899–1900 idioms and translation from German into Czech; in 1900–01 case and translation from German into Czech.

35 In 1897–98 and 1898–99 there is no mention of grammar revision.

From this it is clear that in German grammar schools Czech was taught as if it were a foreign language – unlike the approach to German in these schools. Starting with the most elementary sentence types with the verb 'to be' (i.e. copular sentences) and a gradual, verb-based exposition of grammar that assumed minimal previous knowledge, the method was quite different from that found in German textbooks for native speakers of Czech in the Czech schools, which systematically worked through the parts of speech, starting with nouns and adjectives. The Czech syllabus at the German State Grammar school for Prague 1 was thus designed in theory for beginners; this is particularly evident in the introduction to reading and writing in Czech and to the use of diacritics. In practice, however, lessons were probably geared to the core group in the class who attended Czech lessons all through secondary school. A further indication is that in this group the grades for Czech were adjusted against those awarded to Czech native speakers, and that newcomers to the course regularly dropped out. The quality of the core group is also reflected in the Czech syllabus: in the academic year 1897–98, German-Czech translation was moved from section 6 to section 5, grammar revision for the higher groups was scrapped, while participles were moved from section 5 to section 4.

TEXTBOOKS

The method and scope of Czech teaching outlined above is also reflected in the textbooks used, as listed in the school's annual reports. These can be divided into two broad categories: (1) language textbooks in the strict sense of the word that extend and reinforce the pupils' active use of the Czech language system; and (2) books that foster a passive understanding of the language while at the same time providing a grounding in Czech culture, especially literature.

The first category includes *Methodisches Elementarbuch der böhmischen Sprache* (Methodic Book of Basic Czech) by Augustin Ritschel and Matthias Rypl (up till 1896–97), *Böhmische Schulgrammatik* (Czech Grammar for Schools) by Josef Masařík (5th revised edition, also until 1896–97), and the three-volume *Lehrgang der böhmischen Sprache* (Course of Czech Grammar) by Karel Charvát and Eduard Ouředníček (from 1896–97).

The first two, from the point of view of the language and terminology they use and their overall approach, are decidedly 'German'. This is apparent not only in their analysis of verb forms, where they talk of the 'conjunctive' rather than the conditional, but also and chiefly in their treatment of aspect, in which they avoid the terms 'perfective' and 'imperfective' (although they were in common use at the time, as we saw above in the annual reports), referring instead to the 'mode of action' (*Aktionsart*). Thus Ritschel and Rypl (1891) distinguish between durative, finitive (perfective), punctual, punctual-finitive (perfective) and iterative verbs as well as between the iterative and the frequentative of punctual verbs, while Masařík differentiates between durative, iterative, frequentative and inchoative.[36] Charvát and Ouředníček refer to imperfective and perfective verbs as 'continuous and single-time verbs'[37] and point out the specific formation of the future tense for particular verb types ('single-time', 'punctual', 'verba singularia').[38] But in its terminology, its telegraphic descriptions of the phenomena under discussion and its failure to distinguish between verbal aspect and mode of action, their analysis is far from satisfactory. This is hardly surprising, as the first substantial work on aspect in Czech, by František Trávníček, in which aspect was defined as a function of grammar and mode of action as a function of semantics, was not to appear until 1923. Interestingly, aspect was one of the few areas of grammar that Kafka never mastered with absolute confidence – evidence that after all Czech was only his second language, as documented in the first and third chapters.

But the fact that both the Ritschel and Rypl and the Masařík grammars were replaced in 1896–97 by Charvát and Ouředníček's textbook tells us a lot about Czech teaching at the German State Grammar school of Prague Old Town.[39] As a Czech grammar it is superior; it also assumes, at a relatively early stage, at least a passive (and very soon an active) knowledge of Czech that would be unimaginable if the pupils had no contact with the language outside school.

Moreover, the first part of the textbook, used in sections 1 and 2 of the course, contains virtually no tables or overviews and looks more like a book of exercises for the purpose of reinforcing existing knowledge of a second language which – in terms of grammar – was perfectly adequate for everyday communication. These include copular sentences with *být* (to be), negation, declension of nouns, 'soft', 'hard' and possessive adjectives, present and past tenses of verbs and the comparative. This, plus the fact that verb conjugation

---

36 Based on Josef Masařík, *Böhmische Schulgrammatik. Für deutsche Mittelschulen und Lehrer-Bildungsanstalten bearbeitet* (Czech Grammar for Schools: Prepared for German Secondary Schools and Teacher Training Institutes). 6th revised edition. Prague: F. Tempsky 1894.

37 Karel Charvát – Edvard Ouředníček, *Lehrgang der böhmischen Sprache für deutsche Mittelschulen* (Course in Czech Language for German Secondary Schools). Vol. 2. Olomouc: Ed. Hölzel 1893, p. 24.

38 Ibid. 25.

39 The following analysis is based on the first volume of the 2nd, revised edition of Charvát's book published in 1897, and on Vols. II and III of Charvát and Ouředníček, which were used at Kafka's grammar school and to which I had access. See Karel Charvát – Edvard Ouředníček: *Lehrgang der böhmischen Sprache für deutsche Mittelschulen* (Course in Czech Language for German Secondary Schools). Vol. 1. Olomouc: Ed. Hölzel 1891; Vol. 2, 1893; Vol. 3, 1895.

(past tense) was moved from section 4 to section 1 (!), German-Czech translation from section 6 to section 5 and the transgressive from section 5 to section 4, etc., suggests that the course advanced quite rapidly and that the teaching of Czech – initially conceived as the teaching of a foreign language – responded to pupils' actual knowledge, whether acquired at home or at school, and transformed itself into the teaching of a second language.[40]

Charvát and Ouředníček – unlike the authors they superseded – also introduce Czech grammatical terms in their German text in the first part of their textbook; and already in the second part, where the grammar is explained in Czech, there are texts for translation from German into Czech that improve active knowledge of Czech as well as translation from Czech into German, supporting a passive knowledge of Czech. From Part Three on, the practice texts tend to focus exclusively on Czech history and culture. We thus find the stories of Čech (or Czech, legendary ancestor of the nation), Krok and his daughters, and the Maidens' War, as well as texts on education in 10th–12th century Bohemia, George of Poděbrady and, in some detail, the Unity of the Brethren, the Thirty Years' War, etc.,[41] chiefly by outstanding Czech cultural figures such as Josef Dobrovský, Josef Jungmann, Jan Kollár, F. L. Čelakovský, Božena Němcová and Svatopluk Čech,[42] including extracts from works of literature. Besides Jan Kollár and Svatopluk Čech, there are extensive passages from Božena Němcová's *Babička* (The Grandmother),[43] a book of special importance to Kafka as we shall see in the chapter on his reading in Czech.

While pupils in sections 1 and 2 were expected to manage everyday communication with a minimum of grammatical mistakes, boys in the third and higher sections had to understand abstract Czech texts and even translate quite challenging German texts into Czech. A vocabulary list appended to the textbook shows that together the three volumes provided in a German-Czech lexicon an active vocabulary of four thousand lemmas (lexical items) and in a Czech-German lexicon a passive knowledge of over seven thousand – enough to handle all normal communicative situations. We may assume Franz Kafka's Czech vocabulary was at least as large.[44]

---

40 Grammar school pupils would also have had Czech classes at elementary school.

41 See Karel Charvát – Edvard Ouředníček, *Lehrgang der böhmischen Sprache für deutsche Mittelschulen* (Course in Czech Language for German Secondary Schools). Vol. 3. Olomouc: Ed. Hölzel 1895, pp. 16, 27, 49, 78, 37, 83 ff., 80 f.

42 See Charvát – Ouředníček, *Lehrgang der böhmischen Sprache für deutsche Mittelschulen*, pp. 87–89, 92–94, 95–99, 100–102, 104–105, 106–107.

43 See Charvát – Ouředníček *Lehrgang der böhmischen Sprache für deutsche Mittelschulen*, pp. 112–142.

44 Each of the three volumes contains a vocabulary appendix. Vol. I has a list of words from the Czech texts (1510 lexical items) and an alphabetical Czech-German glossary (1208 lexical items). In Vol. II there is one vocabulary list for the German texts (710 lexical items), one for the Czech texts (3828 lexical items) and an alphabetical Czech-German glossary (1505 lexical items).

These language textbooks show that despite the original approach to teaching Czech as if it were a foreign language, the Prague Old Town German Grammar school did take the boys' knowledge of Czech (however it was acquired) into account, developing and deepening it in a way more akin to the methods of second language acquisition. The textbooks not only gave them a solid grasp of grammar and vocabulary; they also fostered an active command of written Czech (translation into Czech) and a passive ability to make subtle stylistic distinctions in written Czech. It appears that no active distinction was made between the spoken and written forms of the language (dialogue is rendered in the standard 'written' form) – a fact that may account for the colloquialisms occasionally found in Kafka's written Czech.

Among the titles in the second category of textbooks – those that promoted a deeper understanding of both the Czech language and Czech culture – we should mention the two-volume *Böhmisches Lesebuch für Deutsche insbesondere für Schüler an deutschen Mittelschulen* (A Czech Reader for Germans, Especially for Pupils at German Secondary Schools) by Karl Tieftrunk.[45] The annual school reports also list *Malá Slovesnosť* (Short Poetics), compiled 'as a textbook and reader for the higher classes of secondary schools' by Jan Kosina and František Bartoš and replaced in 1896–97 by a fifth edition with the additional authorship of Leandr Čech.[46] By the following year, however, it was no longer in use as, among other reasons, its sections on genre duplicated material covered in the German and Latin syllabi.

Despite its German title, the Tieftrunk reader, which was in use at the German Grammar school when Kafka attended Czech classes there, contains

---

Vol. III has one vocabulary list for the German texts (628), another for the Czech texts (1906) and an alphabetical glossary of 1383 lexical items. That makes a total of 7244 lexical items in the Czech word lists (passive vocabulary) and 4096 in the bilingual glossaries (active vocabulary). In all the lists some words occur more than once, whereas many lexical items that do appear in the texts are not listed as it is assumed they are already known. This means that these data regarding the probable extent of Kafka's Czech vocabulary can be no more than approximate.

45 In the academic years 1893–94 and 1894–95 the 6th edition of Vol. I was used and the 3rd revised edition of Vol. II; in 1895–96, the same edition of Vol. I and the 4th revised edition of Vol. II; and in 1896–97 the 7th edition of Vol. I. In 1897–98 Tieftrunk's book was superseded by Truhlář's reader (see below). See Karl Tieftrunk, *Böhmisches Lesebuch für Deutsche insbesondere für Schüler an deutschen Mittelschulen. Česká čítanka, zvláště pro žáky na gymnasiích a realních školách* (Czech Reader for Germans, especially for Pupils on German Secondary Schools). Vol. 1. Prague: F. L. Kober ^{4}1881, ^{5}1886, ^{6}1889, ^{7}1896; vol. 2. Prague: F. L. Kober ^{3}1884, ^{4}1893.

46 See Jan Evangelista Kosina – František Bartoš, *Malá Slovesnosť, kterou za knihu učebnou a čitací pro vyšší třídy škol středních* (Short Poetics, which Can be Used as Textbook and Reader for Higher Secondary Schools). Brno: Karl Winker 1876; 3th edition, 1883; 4th edition, 1893. In the academic years 1893–94 and 1894–95 the 3rd edition was used; in 1895–96 the 4th edition. The textbook covers the fundamentals of Czech scansion, an introduction to poetics, i.e. the main literary genres (fairy tales, myths, epics, epic lyric verse, ballads, romances, short stories, novels, novellas, dramas and didactic literature), and the rudiments of stylistics (but excluding spoken Czech). It also contains extracts from the works of Božena Němcová, Karel Jaromír Erben, František Ladislav Čelakovský, Jan Neruda and others.

mostly fairly simple Czech texts abridged or adapted for teaching purposes. In Volume I we find ancient Czech legends such as Libuše and Přemysl or Horymír's Leap, as well as the lives of important figures in Czech history such as King Ladislav, John Jiskra (in Václav Hanka's version), Maria Theresa and Joseph II. There are also literary texts such as Puchmajer's fable 'Vrána a liška' (The crow and the fox), Erben's 'Polednice' (The noon witch) and his fairy tale 'Tak svět odplácí' (Thus the world repays), poems by Čelakovský and two texts by Božena Němcová, 'Dvě rady' (Two counsels) and 'Silný Ctibor' (Strong Ctibor). The volume is completed with model letters to parents, fellow-pupils and sponsors, as well as sample texts of a practical nature (invoices, certificates, etc.) and formalised conversations between pupils on subjects such as tidiness and school holidays which, while lending the collection a degree of stylistic variety, still fail to make a clear distinction between the standard and colloquial forms of Czech. The appended Czech-German vocabulary contains around 6300 lexical items.

Volume II contains poems by Václav Hanka, the poems 'Znělka' (Sonnet) and 'Štěstí' (Happiness) by Jan Kollár, Karel Hynek Mácha's 'Vorlík' (Vorlík pond), 'Toman a lesní panna' (Toman and the wood nymph) and other poems by František Ladislav Čelakovský, 'Poklad' (The treasure) and other fairy tales by Karel Jaromír Erben, and Josef Jungmann's 'Příběh satirický' (A satirical tale). There are also more abstract and demanding texts such as Comenius' 'Mravní naučení' (Moral teachings), Palacký's geographical treatise 'Země česká' (The land of Bohemia), as well as his historical biography of Cyril and Methodius and his edited excerpts from Šafařík's *Slovanské starožitnosti* (Slavonic Antiquities) about the Slavs' early settlement of Bohemia and Moravia. Other history-related pieces are extracts from the Green Mountain and Queen's Court manuscripts – *Kytice* (A Bouquet) and *Jaroslav, vítěz nad Tatary* (Jaroslav, Vanquisher of the Tartars) – as well as texts about the Czech nation and its history such as 'Boleslav', 'Vítězství nad Tatary' (Victory over the Tartars), 'Výprava proti Milánu' (The Milan campaign), *Karel IV.* (Charles IV), 'Albrecht II.', 'Laudon', 'Hrad Karlštejn' (Karlstein castle), 'Královský hrad v Praze' (The royal castle in Prague) and 'Jeskyně Sloupská' (The cave of Sloup). There is also a section on business correspondence. The appended Czech-German glossary contains approx. 5600 lexical items that only marginally duplicate the word lists in Volume I. In view of the fact that the vocabulary listed in Volume I contains basic items such as *a – und* (a – and) and *babička – Großmutter, Großmütterchen* (*babička* – Grandmother, Granny), we can assume that the word lists contained in the whole textbook covered all the vocabulary required at the start of section six of the course. If we omit duplicated items we arrive at a figure of approximately 10,000 lexical items – certainly an adequate vocabulary even for more demanding communicative situations.

The contents of these textbooks merit closer consideration. What they tell us (and what Kafka scholarship has hitherto failed to notice) is that the study of Czech at German grammar schools was more than a social and communicative necessity for the sons of Prague German merchants: the books also attempted to provide them with an insight into Czech literature and culture and contribute to a better understanding between the two ethno-linguistic communities. This can be seen even more clearly in a book by Antonín Truhlář, who taught Czech at the Academic Grammar school of Prague Old Town. Truhlář's book was introduced in 1897–98,[47] replacing Tieftrunk's reader. Since Czech texts were read mainly by pupils in the highest section – where Kafka was in that academic year – it is likely that this book in particular shaped his view of 18th and 19th century Czech literature.

The book is also worth a closer look because while it was used in German grammar schools it was in fact written for pupils in Czech grammar schools. This means that German-speaking boys who were interested in Czech literature were taught it in a comparable fashion (at least as far as the teaching materials were concerned) to that employed with Czech speakers in Czech schools.[48] So although Franz Kafka attended a German grammar school, he probably knew as much about Czech literature as the average pupil at an equivalent Czech school.

If this was indeed the reader that Kafka learned from at school (and we can only presume it was, then given how knowledgeable his teacher Václav Rosický was about Czech culture, and how positive his pupil felt towards him), Kafka's own knowledge must have been far from superficial. For in that book we find an extremely detailed chronological exposition of the Czech National Revival in its various phases, consisting of explanatory texts as well as extracts from the literature of each period. The only omissions are controversial writers such as Karel Havlíček Borovský, who is not even mentioned in the general overview.

Truhlář divides the National Revival into two main periods, 'Resurrection' (1774–1820) and 'Renewal' (1820–1850), with an additional section including works from 'most recent times'. From the 'resurrection' period Truhlář mentions the grammars, apologies for the Czech language, the awareness-rais-

---

47 In that school year and in 1898–99 the second edition was used. In 1899–1900 it was replaced by the third edition, on which the following analysis is based. Antonín Truhlář, *Výbor z literatury české. Doba nová* (Anthology of Czech Literature: Modern Period). 3 vol. Prague: Bursík & Kohout 1886, ²1892, ³1898.

48 According to the annual report of the Czech grammar school in Prague New Town, Truhlář's reader was used there for teaching modern Czech literature (*Výroční zpráva cís. král. vyššího gymnasia českého na Novém Městě v Praze*. 1896/97, p. 46), as well as Kosina and Bartoš's *Malá slovesnosť* (Short Poetics; see above). A comparison of the annual reports of the Czech Senior Grammar school in Prague New Town with those of the German State Grammar school in Prague Old Town suggests that Truhlář's reader was introduced at roughly the same time in the two schools.

ing and publishing work of Václav Matěj Kramerius and František Martin Pelcl/Pelzel, the publications of František Faustin Procházka, Antonín Jaroslav Puchmajer and his circle of poets and the group centred on Josef Jungmann, as well as the work of Jan Nepomuk Hromádko at Vienna University (1813–1817). Among the literary excerpts Truhlář includes are passages from Václav Matěj Kramerius, Antonín Jaroslav Puchmajer, Šebestián Hněvkovský, Milota Zdirad Polák, Václav Hanka, Juraj Palkovič and translations by Josef Jungmann. Factual literature is represented with a text by František Martin Pelcl/Pelzel about the founding of Stará Boleslav by St Wenceslaus' brother, and a piece about Václav (Wenceslaus) II's efforts to introduce higher education in Bohemia. There is also an essay by František Faustin Procházka about Dalimil, the early 14th century chronicler; Dobrovský's 'Čech nebo Čechové, odkud tak slují' (Where does the word, Czech, come from?); and Jungmann's 'Obohacování jazyka českého' (The enrichment of the Czech language) and 'O postavení a úloze českého spisovatelstva' (On the position and purpose of Czech literature). In short, the book contained everything of any importance relating to the first period of the National Revival.

In the second, 'renewal' phase Truhlář stresses the founding of the Patriotic Museum and the revivalist publishing house *Matice česká* (Czech Foundation); the importance of newly established periodicals; the publication of the Green Mountain and Queen's Court manuscripts (presented as authentic rather than the forgeries they later proved to be); the nation-building endeavours of Jungmann and his associates; and the support provided by powerful aristocratic families (Chotek, Kolovrat, Kinský). He divides the writers of the period into two groups – the 'chieftains' (*náčelníky*) of Czech literature, and the rest – both of which include Slovak writers, who are regarded as a part of the Czechoslovak national body. Among the 'chieftains', whose texts Truhlář prefaces with brief biographies and appreciations, we find Jan Svatopluk Presl, Jan Kollár and his sonnets, Pavel Josef Šafařík and his study *Slovanské starožitnosti* (Slavonic Antiquities), František Palacký and his writings on Czech history and Hussitism, František Ladislav Čelakovský with his ballads, songs, sonnets and essay 'Osudy slovanské bohoslužby v Čechách' (The story of Slavonic liturgy in Bohemia), Jan Erazim Vocel, and Karel Jaromír Erben with his 'Kytice' (Bouquet) and 'Zlatý Kolovrat' (The golden spinning wheel). Other writers are grouped by genre. In the epic section there are works by Ján Hollý, J. J. Marek, Josef Kajetán Tyl, Samo Chalupka, František Pravda, Karel Hynek Mácha's *Máj* (May), and extracts from 'Pohorská vesnice' (Mountain village) and 'Štědrý večer na zámku' (Christmas Eve at the castle) by Božena Němcová. Under lyric verse we find Josef Krasoslav Chmelenský, Karel Alois Vinařický, František Sušil and many more, while Josef Jaroslav Langer, František Jaromír Rubeš and Jan Pravoslav Koubek come under the heading 'Various'. Drama is represented by Václav Kliment Klicpera, František Turinský a Karel Simeon

Macháček, and the academic writing of the period by Jan Evangelista Purkyně (natural sciences), Antonín Rybička (philosophy) a Václav Vladivoj Tomek (history).

Truhlář's textbook also addresses the 'most recent' period, though his introductory text is rather scant. But he does at least refer to a number of new cultural institutions, among them the National Theatre, the Bohemian Academy of Sciences and Arts. In fact he mentions virtually all the important writers of the second half of the 19th century, apart from those who emerged in its last two decades. Thus we find the poets Vítězslav Hálek, Jan Neruda, Adolf Heyduk, Julius Zeyer, Josef Václav Sládek, Svatopluk Čech, Eliška Krásnohorská and Jaroslav Vrchlický, the prose writers Karolina Světlá, Alois Vojtěch Šmilovský, Václav Kosmák, Václav Beneš Třebízský and Alois Jirásek (extracts from his historical novels *Psohlavci* and *F. L. Věk*), and the non-fiction and academic writers Václav Vladivoj Tomek (history of Prague), Hermenegild Jireček (military history), Václav Zelený (biography of Jungmann), Vincenc Brandl (biography of Dobrovský), Josef Durdík (aesthetics), Jan E. Kosina (Homer), František Bartoš (an essay on the Czech national 'spirit') and Jan Gebauer (the evolution of the Czech language). Truhlář's choice of factual texts, in particular, tells us how keen he was to familiarize his students with Czech theoretical writing, foster their understanding of such texts and help them distinguish different styles of written Czech.

Without going into a detailed analysis of these writers and writings, it is safe to say that Kafka's schooling provided him with a sound basic knowledge of the 19th century Czech National Revival and the cultural and political forces it unleashed. Despite its omission of certain authors such as Karel Havlíček Borovský, Truhlář's textbook enabled Kafka to get to know 18th and 19th century Czech literature – a literature that placed the national aspirations of the time above aesthetic considerations. This view of culture as defined by language, and the resulting artistic canon in which aesthetic values were subservient to ethno-national values, remained widespread among the Czech public, though it was denounced by the younger generation in the 1895 *Manifest moderny* (Manifesto of the Modern Age). Franz Kafka, too, who later in life was more drawn to modern Czech writing than to older literature, consistently judged Czech culture by aesthetic criteria alone. But this does not mean that in his schooldays he did not know and appreciate the works of 18th and 19th century and even earlier Czech writers. In fact his textbooks gave him a fairly nuanced picture of Czech literature and culture – a culture that was in many respects the embodiment of a national political program rather than a literature, as he noted in his 'Character sketch of small literatures'. Indeed, that essay well reflects the broad scope of Kafka's Czech cultural receptivity based also on his school reading, which laid down the markers for his future reading, whether of fiction or non-fiction.

KAFKA'S CZECH READING IN CONTEXT

The aim of this chapter, which will consider Kafka's awareness of Czech literature and culture and, indirectly, his passive knowledge of the Czech language, is not to create the impression that Kafka spent his spare time immersed in Czech literature or literature translated into Czech. His correspondence with Max Brod and a cursory look at his library show that this was certainly not the case. In his letters to Brod he mentions not only 'classics' and contemporary writers such as Goethe, Kleist, Thomas Mann, Stefan George, Robert Walser, Rudolf Kassner, Paul Ernst and Karl Kraus; he also refers to his reading in the 'history of literature',[1] undertaken partly as preparation for the lectures by August Sauer he attended.[2]

The vast majority of the volumes in his library are German or printed in German. In addition to books written, translated or published by people he knew personally such as Oskar Baum, Max Brod, Rudolf Fuchs, Ernst Hardt, Gottfried Kölwel, Otto Pick, Melchior Vischer, Ernst Weiß and Franz Werfel, we also find such authors as Peter Altenberg, Karl Brand, Adelbert von Chamisso, Theodor Däubler, Stefan George, Johann Wolfgang Goethe, Gottfried Keller, Conrad Ferdinand Meyer, Eduard Mörike, Arthur Schnitzler, Carl Sternheim, Adalbert Stifter, Theodor Storm, Karl Hans Strobl, Frank Wedekind, Christoph Martin Wieland and Stefan Zweig.[3] However, we should not assume that a single mention of a writer such as Strobl in the correspondence, or the presence of his work on Kafka's bookshelves, implies

1 See Max Brod – Franz Kafka, *Eine Freundschaft. Briefwechsel* (A Friendship: Correspondence). Ed. by Malcolm Pasley. Vol. 2. Frankfurt am Main: S. Fischer 1989, pp. 13, 18, 44, 50, 89, 104, 121, 358, 394, and the list Kafka enclosed in a letter to Brod before he started attending Sauer's lectures. For the scope of Kafka's general reading see Jürgen Born, *Kafkas Bibliothek. Ein beschreibendes Verzeichnis* (Kafka's Library: A Descriptive Index). Frankfurt am Main: S. Fischer 1990; Hartmut Binder, *Kafka-Handbuch in zwei Bänden* (A Kafka Manual in two Volumes). Stuttgart: Kröner 1979; Manfred Engel, Dieter Lamping (eds), *Franz Kafka und die Weltliteratur* (Franz Kafka and World Literature). Göttingen: Vandenhoeck & Ruprecht 2006; Monika Schmitz-Emans, *Poetiken der Verwandlung* (Poetics of Metamorphosis). Innsbruck, Vienna, Bozen: Studienverlag 2008.

2 See list of classes Kafka attended at university on p. 153 f. For more on Sauer see Steffen Höhne (ed.), *August Sauer (1855–1926) – ein Intellektueller in Prag im Spannungsfeld von Kultur- und Wissenschaftspolitik* (August Sauer: An Intellectual in Prague between Cultural and Scholarly Politics). Cologne, Weimar, Vienna: Böhlau 2011.

3 For a more complete study see Herbert Blank, *V Kafkově knihovně / In Kafkas Bibliothek* (In Kafka's Library). Prague: Nakladatelství Franze Kafky 2004.

any special significance. There is no doubting the importance of Goethe, Kleist, Stifter, Walser, Kraus and Wedekind for Prague German literature and for Kafka in particular; with Kölwel, Hardt and some others the case is not so clear.[4] The same distinction applies to Czech writers, who will be discussed below.

As a reader of fiction, magazines and periodicals such as *Die Aktion* (Action), *Die Fackel* (The Torch), *Vom jüngsten Tag* (Judgment Day), *Prager Tagblatt* (Prague Daily News), *Der Artist* (The Artist), *Der Anbruch* (Dawn), *Donau* (Danube) and *Das junge Deutschland* (Young Germany)[5], Kafka should thus be seen primarily in a 'German' intellectual context,[6] although some of what German scholars claim as German literature (on the basis of the language it is written in) is not necessarily regarded as such by Kafka himself – his own work not excepted.[7] In his visits to the cinema or cabaret he quite clearly preferred programs in German.[8] Yet his interests were by no means confined to German literature and culture. His familiarity with Yiddish and Hebrew literature extended well beyond the Yiddish theatre, and his reading of periodicals such as *Selbstwehr* (Self-Defence), *Jüdische Rundschau* (Jewish Review), and *Der Jude* (The Jew),[9] as well as more academic works on the art, history and religion of Judaism (which were also to be found in his library), oblige

---

4 For Kölwel and Hardt see Franz Kafka, *Briefe an Felice und andere Korrespondenz aus der Verlobungszeit* (Letters to Felice and other Correspondence from the Time of Engagement). Ed. by E. Heller and Jürgen Born. Frankfurt am Main: S. Fischer 1967, p. 748 and p. 573.

5 We know that in 1917–18 Max Brod sent Kafka copies of *Die Aktion*. See Brod – Kafka, *Eine Freundschaft*, pp. 181, 185, 193, 206, 211, 221, 230, 233, 237, 490, 512 f. For *Die Fackel* see Kurt Krolop, Prager Autoren im Lichte der ‚Fackel' (Prague Writers in the light of 'Die Fackel'). In: *Prager deutschsprachige Literatur zur Zeit Kafkas* (Prague German-written Literature in Kafka's Time). Ed. by Österreichische Franz-Kafka-Gesellschaft Wien-Klosterneuburg. Vienna: Braunmüller 1989, 92–117; for *Der Artist*, *Der Anbruch*, *Donau* and *Das junge Deutschland* see especially Brod – Kafka, *Eine Freundschaft*, pp. 487, 206, 219.

6 See reprint of Born's article 'Kafka als Leser' (Kafka as reader) in Jürgen Born, *„Daß zwei in mir kämpfen..." und andere Aufsätze zu Franz Kafka* ('Two combatants at war within me ...' and Other Papers on Franz Kafka). Furth im Wald, Prague: Vitalis 2000, p. 147ff. See also Bert Nagel, *Kafka und die Weltliteratur. Zusammenhänge und Wechselwirkungen* (Kafka and World Literature: Contexts and Impacts). Munich: Winkler 1983.

7 See Brod – Kafka, *Eine Freundschaft*, p. 360.

8 See Hanns Zischler, *Kafka geht ins Kino* (Kafka Goes to the Cinema). Reinbek b. Hamburg: rowohlt 1996; Hartmut Binder, *Wo Kafka und seine Freunde zu Gast waren. Prager Kaffeehäuser und Vergnügungsstätten in historischen Bilddokumenten* (Where Kafka and his Friends met: Prague Cafés and Etablissements in Historical Pictorial Documents). Prague, Furth im Wald: Vitalis 2000. Měšťan mentions Kafka's visits to the Czech cabaret in the Lucerna theatre, his apparent enthusiasm for the film *Daddy Long Legs*, which he saw in its Czech version *Táta dlouhán*, and his liking for Czech operetta. Kafka was certainly familiar with the Pištěk Theatre in Vinohrady. See Antonín Měšťan, Slované u Franze Kafky (Slavs in Franz Kafka's oeuvre). In: Antonín Měšťan, *Česká literatura mezi Němci a Slovany* (Czech Literature between Germans and Slavs). Prague: Academia 2002, pp. 38–67, p. 50.

9 See correspondence with Max Brod and Felice Bauer. See Brod – Kafka, *Eine Freundschaft*, p. 189 et al., Kafka, *Briefe an Felice* et al. Also see Born, *Kafkas Bibliothek*.

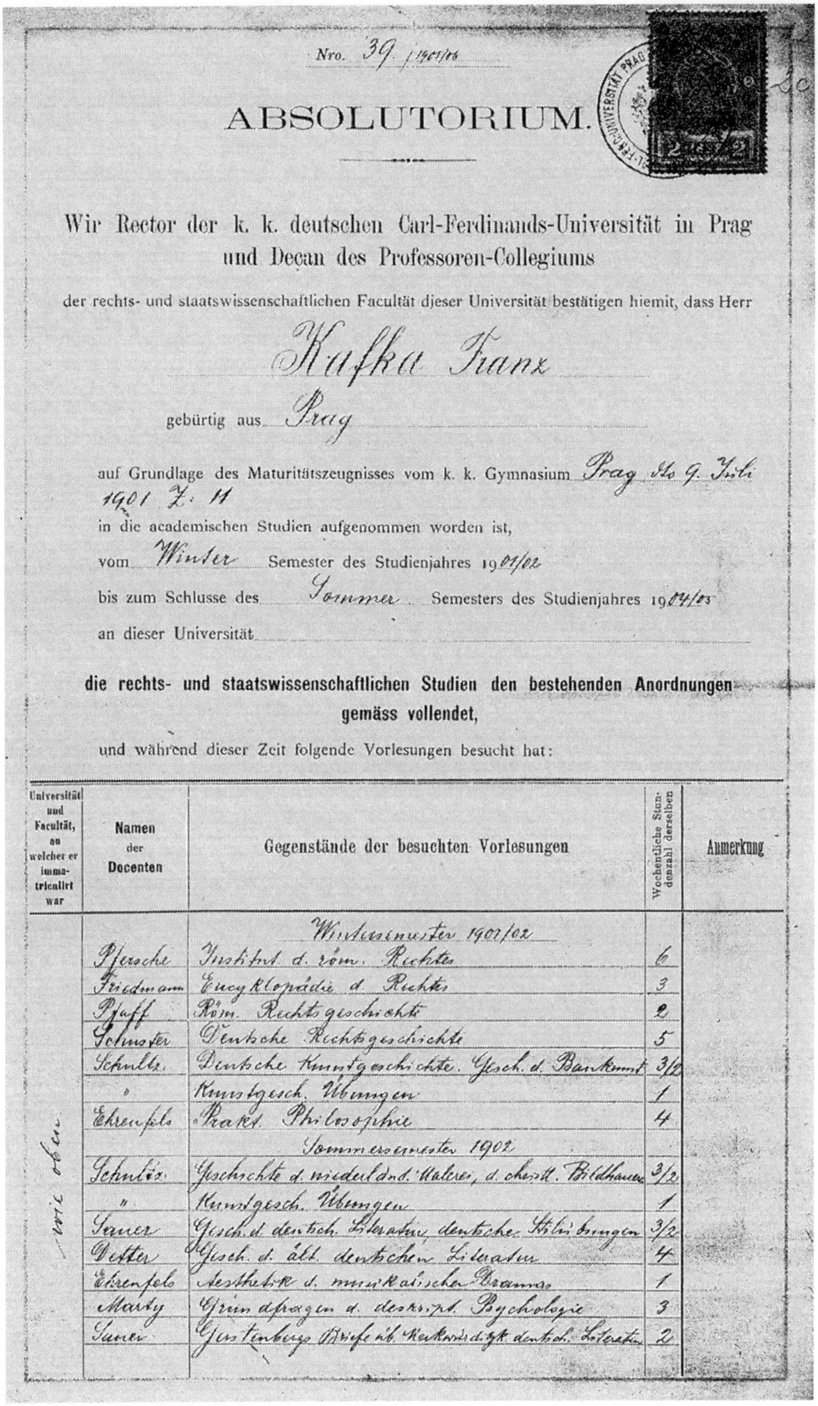

Nro. 39 / 1901/06

ABSOLUTORIUM.

Wir Rector der k. k. deutschen Carl-Ferdinands-Universität in Prag und Decan des Professoren-Collegiums

der rechts- und staatswissenschaftlichen Facultät dieser Universität bestätigen hiemit, dass Herr

Kafka Franz

gebürtig aus Prag

auf Grundlage des Maturitätszeugnisses vom k. k. Gymnasium Prag Ido 9. Juli 1901 Z. 11

in die academischen Studien aufgenommen worden ist,

vom Winter Semester des Studienjahres 1901/02

bis zum Schlusse des Sommer Semesters des Studienjahres 1904/05

an dieser Universität

die rechts- und staatswissenschaftlichen Studien den bestehenden Anordnungen gemäss vollendet,

und während dieser Zeit folgende Vorlesungen besucht hat:

Universität und Facultät, an welcher er immatriculirt war	Namen der Docenten	Gegenstände der besuchten Vorlesungen	Wochentliche Stundenzahl derselben	Anmerkung
		Wintersemester 1901/02		
	Pfersche	Institut. d. röm. Rechtes	6	
	Friedmann	Encyklopädie d. Rechtes	3	
	Pfaff	Röm. Rechtsgeschichte	2	
	Schuster	Deutsche Rechtsgeschichte	5	
	Schultz	Deutsche Kunstgeschichte. Gesch. d. Baukunst	3/2	
	"	Kunstgesch. Übungen	1	
	Ehrenfels	Prakt. Philosophie	4	
wie oben		Sommersemester 1902		
	Schultz	Geschichte d. niederländ. Malerei, d. christl. Bildhauer	3/2	
	"	Kunstgesch. Übungen	1	
	Sauer	Gesch. d. deutsch. Literatur, deutsche Stilübungen	3/2	
	Detter	Gesch. d. ält. deutschen Literatur	4	
	Ehrenfels	Aesthetik d. musikalischen Dramas	1	
	Marty	Grundfragen d. deskript. Psychologie	3	
	Sauer	Gerstenbergs Briefe üb. Merkwürdigk. deutsch. Literatur	2	

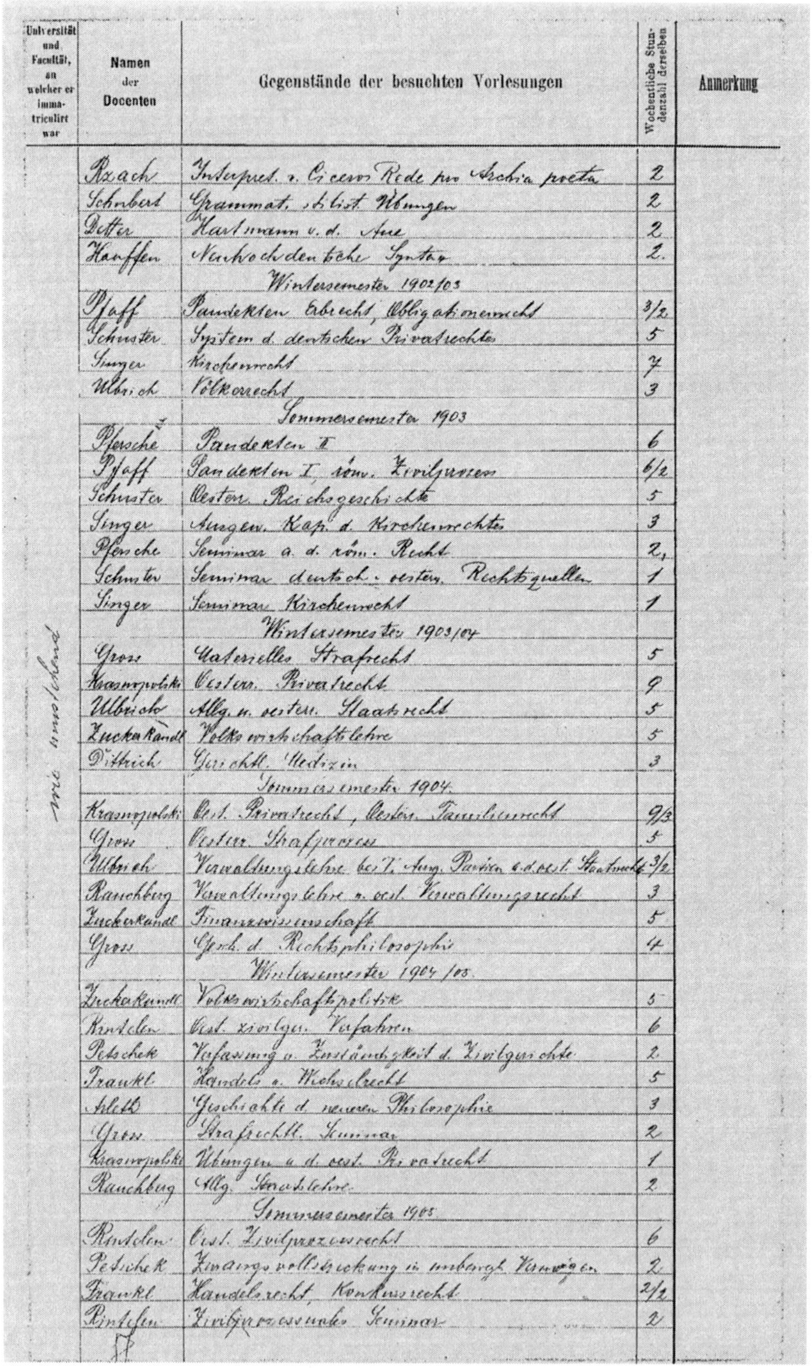

Universität und Facultät, an welcher er immatriculirt war	Namen der Docenten	Gegenstände der besuchten Vorlesungen	Wochentliche Stundenzahl derselben	Anmerkung
wie umstehend	Rzach	Interpret. v. Ciceros Rede pro Archia poeta	2	
	Schubert	Grammat. stilist. Übungen	2	
	Detter	Hartmann v. d. Aue	2	
	Hauffen	Neuhochdeutsche Syntax	2.	
		Wintersemester 1902/03		
	Pfaff	Pandekten, Erbrecht, Obligationenrecht	3/2	
	Schuster	System d. deutschen Privatrechtes	5	
	Singer	Kirchenrecht	7	
	Ulbrich	Völkerrecht	3	
		Sommersemester 1903		
	Pfersche	Pandekten II	6	
	Pfaff	Pandekten I, röm. Zivilprozess	6/2	
	Schuster	Oesterr. Reichsgeschichte	5	
	Singer	Ausgew. Kap. d. Kirchenrechtes	3	
	Pfersche	Seminar a. d. röm. Recht	2,	
	Schuster	Seminar deutsch.-oesterr. Rechtsquellen	1	
	Singer	Seminar Kirchenrecht	1	
		Wintersemester 1903/04		
	Gross	Materielles Strafrecht	5	
	Krasnopolski	Oesterr. Privatrecht	9	
	Ulbrich	Allg. u. oesterr. Staatsrecht	5	
	Zuckerkandl	Volkswirtschaftslehre	5	
	Dittrich	Gerichtl. Medizin	3	
		Sommersemester 1904		
	Krasnopolski	Oest. Privatrecht, Oester. Familienrecht	9/3	
	Gross	Oesterr. Strafprozess	5	
	Ulbrich	Verwaltungslehre bez. T. Ausg. Partien a. d. oest. Staatsrecht	3/2	
	Rauchberg	Verwaltungslehre u. oest. Verwaltungsrecht	3	
	Zuckerkandl	Finanzwissenschaft	5	
	Gross	Gesch. d. Rechtsphilosophie	4	
		Wintersemester 1904/05		
	Zuckerkandl	Volkswirtschaftspolitik	5	
	Rintelen	Oest. Zivilger. Verfahren	6	
	Petschek	Verfassung u. Zuständigkeit d. Zivilgerichte	2	
	Frankl	Handels- u. Wechselrecht	5	
	Arleth	Geschichte d. neueren Philosophie	3	
	Gross	Strafrechtl. Seminar	2	
	Krasnopolski	Übungen a. d. oest. Privatrecht	1	
	Rauchberg	Allg. Staatslehre	2	
		Sommersemester 1905		
	Rintelen	Oest. Zivilprozessrecht	6	
	Petschek	Zwangsvollstreckung in unbewegl. Vermögen	2	
	Frankl	Handelsrecht, Konkursrecht	2/2	
	Rintelen	Zivilprozessualer Seminar	2	

Franz Kafka's absolutorium sheet
Literární archiv Památníku národního písemnictví
(Literary Archive of Museum of Czech Literature)

us to see him equally in a 'Jewish' intellectual context.[10] We should also consider Czech literature as a part of Kafka's literary field,[11] including the Czech periodicals that published translations of his short stories (many in his own lifetime), and not be surprised to find resonances from and parallels with both classic and modern Czech literature in his own texts.

Kafka's knowledge of Czech literature and culture was surprisingly comprehensive. He had his first encounter with Czech culture in Czech lessons at school. Without that thorough grounding, which doubtless also encouraged him in his later reading for both work and pleasure, it is hard to imagine how in the post-war years he could have fared so well in his job at the Workers' Accident Insurance Company, where Czech was the working language not only officially but partially also in everyday practice. Indeed, one part of his school subjects had been also the study of Czech abstract texts. And this contact with written Czech and Czech intellectual life continued after he left school in 1901, so that years later we find him reading Czech newspapers and periodicals and apparently knowing all about the most recherché writers and literary groupings of the day.

Kafka's knowledge of Czech literature and culture has been documented by Jürgen Born on the basis of the diaries, the correspondence and the books contained in his estate,[12] though the author provides no commentary. František Kautman, who went into the subject in some depth in the 1960s, concluded that mentions of Czech literature in the diaries and other sources were quite random titles that don't tell us much about Kafka's interest in Czech culture'.[13] This observation, however, applies equally to German authors and books which, while occurring far more frequently in the same sources, provide us with little insight into Kafka's mental world without an accompanying commentary. Here too – as with the references to Czech literature and culture – the data requires further interpretation.[14]

---

10 Born, *Kafkas Bibliothek*, p. 109ff. In this context we could also mention Kafka's reading of Abraham Grünberg. See Brod – Kafka, *Eine Freundschaft*, 172, p. 480 et al.

11 See Pierre Bourdieu, *Rules of Art: Genesis and Structure of the Literary Field*. Stanford University Press 1996.

12 Kafka's library was not officially included in his estate. For documentation of the estate see Martin Svatoš, *Písemná pozůstalost. Franz Kafka (1883–1924)* (Written Remains: Franz Kafka). Prague: Literární archiv Památníku národního písemnictví 1984; Martin Svatoš, Pozůstalostní spis Franze Kafky (Documentation of remains of Franz Kafka). *Documenta Pragensia* 15 (1997), pp. 301–338.

13 František Kautman, Franz Kafka und die tschechische Literatur (Franz Kafka and Czech literature). In: Eduard Goldstücker – František Kautman – Paul Reimann (eds), *Franz Kafka aus Prager Sicht* 1963 (Franz Kafka from the Prague Perspective). Prague: ČSAV 1965, 44–77, here p. 49.

14 See also Peter Zusi, Kafka and Czech literature. In: Caroline Duttlinger (ed.), *Kafka in Context*. Cambridge UP, in print.

CZECH AS A MEDIUM LANGUAGE

Kafka's active knowledge of spoken and written Czech was considerable. Although his use of the language was not error-free, he was able to meet all his communicative needs in a wide range of communicative areas. In view of the range of authors in his library and the references to them in his letters and diaries, it is clear that Czech – like German – provided Kafka with a means of access to the literatures of other languages, and above all to works by Slavonic writers, to whom the Czech intellectuals of the day paid particular attention. Thus as well as reading Dostoyevsky in German[15], Kafka also read his political writings in Czech translation.[16] Tolstoy, too, he knew through Czech translations,[17] as was probably also the case with Gorki's 'Reminiscences of Tolstoy'.[18] But his interest was not confined to Russian culture. A diary entry for 20 October 1911 reads: 'with Löwy in the National Theatre for the "Dubrovnická trilogie" (Dubrovnik Trilogy)',[19] a work dating from 1903 with elements of both symbolism and naturalism by the Croatian playwright Ivo Vojnović (1857–1929). Here, too, Czech was Kafka's bridge to the Slavonic world.

There can thus be no arguing with Bert Nagel's assertion that Kafka felt a strong affinity with Russian writers.[20] In those years Tolstoy and especially Dostoyevsky, both of whom were well represented in Kafka's library, were – each for a different reason – key authors not only for Kafka but for a host of Prague intellectuals, both Czech and German: Tolstoy for (among other things) his ideas on social reform, Dostoyevsky for the way he saw beyond external appearances, which – as illustrated in Filla's 1907 painting *Reader of Dostoyevsky* – resonated with Kafka's 'psychoanalytical generation'. What is less understandable, however, is why Nagel's book excludes any mention of Czech writers – including figures of unquestionable international stature such as Otakar Březina – despite Kafka's familiarity with them and despite the importance of Czech for him as a gateway to other literatures and cultures. This applies not only to the Slavonic world, but to a certain extent also to Hebrew, Classical, French and American culture.[21]

---

15 See Born, *Kafkas Bibliothek*, p. 30 ff., 326.

16 Felix Weltsch to Franz Kafka, 5 October 1917. – See Franz Kafka, *Briefe April 1914–1917* (Letters April 1914–1917). Ed. by Hans-Gerd Koch. Frankfurt am Main: S. Fischer 2005, p. 756.

17 See Franz Kafka, *Briefe an Milena* (Letters to Milena). Extended new edition. Ed. by Jürgen Born and Michael Müller. Frankfurt am Main: S. Fischer 1998, p. 277ff.

18 According to Gustav Janouch, *Gespräche mit Kafka. Aufzeichnungen und Erinnerungen* (Conversations with Kafka. Notes and Memoirs). Frankfurt am Main: S. Fischer [1968] 1981, p. 111.

19 Franz Kafka, *Tagebücher* (Diaries). Ed. by Hans-Gerd Koch, Michael Müller, Malcolm Pasley. Vol. 1. Frankfurt am Main: S. Fischer 1990, p. 93.

20 See Nagel, *Kafka und die Weltliteratur*, p. 328.

21 Felix Weltsch to Franz Kafka, 5 October 1917. – See Kafka, *Briefe April 1914–1917*, p. 756. See also Milena Jesenská's translation of Claudel.

Thus in Kafka's library we find the volume *Židovské besídky* (A Jewish Miscellany),[22] published in Roudnice nad Labem in 1912 by the rabbi Richard Feder. Among its authors and translators, besides Feder himself, were Alfred Fuchs, Otakar Smrčka and O. L. Šťastný. Aimed mainly at the younger reader, its contents are quite heterogeneous. Alongside translations of Shakespeare, Lessing and Byron by Josef Václav Sládek and Jaroslav Vrchlický we find texts by and relating to Judah Ha-Levi and L. A. Frankl, as well as Jewish anecdotes and texts on the Hanukkah and rules of conduct from the Talmudic period.

The book was praised (as the cover informs us) by Josef Sedláček, professor of theology at Charles University in Prague. His book *Základové hebrejského jazyka biblického* (A Primer in Biblical Hebrew), published in 1892 by Stýblo in Prague, was also in Kafka's possession.[23] The Hebrew vocabulary notebooks kept by Kafka, which can be inspected at the Bodleian Library in Oxford, suggest that he learnt Hebrew through German. Nonetheless, the existence of Sedláček's textbook in his library proves he was able to read lengthy theoretical texts in Czech and could use Czech as a possible medium for acquiring a new language – or, at the very least (if he received it as a gift), that other people thought he could do so. The fact that the book looks 'used' (although it contains no notes or underlinings), might argue – albeit with little certainty – that Kafka made use of it when studying Hebrew. The German-language Hebrew textbooks he owned also have a used look about them, but they too are without notes or markings, save the occasional 'underlining' in the margin.[24]

The assumption that Kafka was able to read substantial Czech texts on specialised subjects as a result of his thorough schooling is supported by the existence of other theoretical and philosophical works in Czech that he is known to have read, among them Jaroslav Goll's *Chelčický a Jednota bratrská v XV. století* (Chelčický and the Unity of Brethren in the 15th Century), Vlastimil Kybal's *Svatý František z Assisi* (St Francis of Assisi), and Tomáš G. Masaryk's *Sebevražda hromadným jevem* (Suicide as a Mass Phenomenon).[25] Although the Goll and Masaryk titles first appeared in German,[26] Kafka seems to have read them in Czech.

---

22 See Born, *Kafkas Bibliothek*, p. 93.

23 Also mentioned in Born, *Kafkas Bibliothek*, p. 155.

24 For a list of sources contained in the University Library, Wuppertal, see Born, *Kafkas Bibliothek*.

25 See Born, *Kafkas Bibliothek*, p. 9. For Goll, see also Franz Kafka to Ottla, 1 February 1919. – See Kafka, *Briefe: April 1914–1917*, p. 66.

26 German titles: Jaroslav Goll, *Quellen und Untersuchungen zur Geschichte der Böhmischen Brüder* (Sources and Studies on the History of the Bohemian Brethren). Vol. 1: *Der Verkehr der Brüder mit den Waldensern. – Wahl und Weihe der ersten Priester* (The Brethren's Contacts with the Waldensians – Election and Consecration of the First Priests). Prague 1878. Vol. 2: *Peter Chelčický und seine Lehre* (Peter Chelčický and his Doctrine). Prague 1882. [Reprint: Hildesheim/New York 1977.] –

As regards Classics, which had a prominent place in the grammar school curriculum, we know Kafka had a copy of Plato's *Phaedo* in Greek 'for use in schools',[27] which had an introduction in Czech. It even contains handwritten notes in Czech, though they are unlikely to be Kafka's. If we compare the handwriting with that of Kafka's manuscripts from the 1920s we find the same sloping script, but while the letter *z* appears similar, the *k*, *t* and other letters are noticeably different. It is the same with his copy of E. Coursier's *Handbuch der französischen und deutschen Konversations-Sprache* (Manual of French and German Conversation), which contains notes in both German and Czech. Again, Kafka's authorship is highly unlikely.

More helpful is a passage in a Czech letter to his brother-in-law Josef David concerning their joint reading of Horace:

> Why a poem, Pepa; don't put yourself to such trouble, why a new poem? Horace has already written many beautiful poems and we have read only one and a half of them. Besides, I already have a poem of yours. Near here there is a small military infirmary and all evening there is marching along the road and it's always 'Panthers' and 'turning round and round' [reference to Czech popular songs].[28]

Binder explains this apparent shared reading of Horace thus:[29] Josef David, inspired by Kafka's idea of taking off for the remote forests of the High Tatras, adapted Horace's Latin ode in praise of the Sabine Hills and subsequently translated it into Czech.[30] In his letter Kafka draws an ironic parallel between literature (Horace) and reality (the loudly singing soldiers).

Czech was certainly a means of getting to know North American culture: witness for example the lecture Kafka attended by František Soukup, *Amerika a její úřednictvo* (America and its Public Administration)[31], or his reading of Benjamin Franklin's autobiography, which he recommended to his father[32] and which may have provided certain ideas or motifs for the unfinished novel

---

T. G. Masaryk, *Der Selbstmord als sociale Massenerscheinung der modernen Civilisation* (Suicide as Social Mass Phenomenon in Modern Civilization). Vienna 1881.

27 See also Born, *Kafkas Bibliothek*, p. 153.

28 Kafka to Josef David, last week of January 1921. – See Franz Kafka, *Letters to Friends, Family, and Editors*. New York: Schocken 1977, p. 258.

29 See Kafka, *Briefe an Ottla und die Familie* (Letters to Ottla and Family). Ed. by Hartmut Binder and Klaus Wagenbach. Frankfurt am Main: S. Fischer 1974, p. 102.

30 See Hartmut Binder, Kafkas Briefscherze (Kafka's epistolary jokes). In: *Jahrbuch der deutschen Schillergesellschaft* 13 (1969), pp. 536–559, here p. 541.

31 See Kafka, *Tagebücher*, p. 424.

32 See Franz Kafka, *Zur Frage der Gesetze und andere Schriften aus dem Nachlaß in der Fassung der Handschrift* (On the Question of Laws and other Literary Remains based on the Handwritten Manuscripts). Ed. by Hans-Gerd Koch. Frankfurt am Main: S. Fischer 1994, p. 45; Born, *Kafkas Bibliothek*, p. 169, and Friedrich Thieberger, Kafka und die Thiebergers (Kafka and the Thiebergers). In: Hans-Gerd Koch (ed.), *„Als Kafka mir entgegen kam…" Erinnerungen an Franz Kafka* ('As

Der Verschollene (The Man Who Disappeared), also known by the title chosen by Max Brod, *Amerika*. The book's genesis, however, was far from straightforward.[33]

Kafka also had lighter Czech reading-matter sent to him. During his rustic retreat in Siřem (Zürau) in autumn 1917, he received a letter from Felix Weltsch (written 5 October 1917) outlining the likely contents of his next book parcel:

> About the books: we don't have the Stekel. I can do nothing about that. Memoirs: I found one Cz. edition series that deals exclusively in those kinds of autobiographies as well as Cz. translations from French; they would be all together. They're quite small books, easy to transport; print is so-so; but maybe in the country there is more light than in the town.
> I have ready for you:
> Paměti (Memoirs) of Countess Potocka
> „ M. de Marbot
> „ again
> Zpověď (Confessions) of Prince Rakoczy
> Polit[.] úvahy (Polit. Writings) of Dostoyevsky
> more Marbot again (something else again)
> Rolandová, Paměti (Memoirs by Madame Roland)
> Hel. Rakowitza – On Lasalle
> Chamfort – Příhody (Anecdotes)
> Sir Malet – Život diplomatův (Sir Edward Malet – Life of a Diplomat)
> La Porte, Komoří Ludv. XIV – Paměti (Memoirs of Pierre de La Porte, Louis XIV's valet)
> Please send someone to pick up the books, or tell me which you would like.[34]

Kafka approached me.' Recollections of Franz Kafka). Berlin: Wagenbach 1995, pp. 121–127, here p. 125.

33 More see Manfred Engel – Bernd Auerochs (eds), *Kafka-Handbuch: Leben – Werk – Wirkung* (A Kafka Manual: Life – Oeuvre – Impact). Stuttgart, Weimar: Metzler 2010, pp. 175–191.

34 See Franz Kafka, *Briefe April 1914–1917.* (Leters April 1914–1917) Frankfurt am Main: S. Fischer 2005, p. 756. The Czech editions of the titles referred to are probably: *Paměti z let 1794–1820* by Anna Countess Potocká, translated from the French by Jiří Staněk, Prague: St. Sokol 1906; *Janov – Slavkov –Jena – Jílov: Paměti*, the memoirs of Marcellina de Marbot, translated from the French by Jiří Staněk, Prague: St. Sokol 1907; *Madrid – Wagram – Torrès – Védras: Paměti*, memoirs of Marcellina de Marbot, translated from the French by Jiří Staněk, Prague: St. Sokol 1908; *Berezina – Lipsko – Waterloo: Paměti*, memoirs of Marcellina de Marbot, translated from the French by Jiří Staněk, Prague: St. Sokol 1909; *Zpověď – vlastní životopis od Františka knížete Rakocsyho*, translated from the French by Adolf Gottwald, Prague: St. Sokol 1908; *Politické úvahy* by Fyodor Mikhailovich Dostoyevsky, translated from the Russian by J. Skružný, Prague: St. Sokol 1907; *Paměti* by Marie Roland, translated from the French by Maryša Šárecká, Prague: St. Sokol 1909; *Příhody a povahy* by Nicolas Chamfort, translated from the French by K. Kovář, Prague: St. Sokol 1910; *Život diplomatův: rozmanité obrazy z mé činnosti ve čtyřech dílech světa* by Edward Malet, translated from the French by J. Skružný, Prague: St. Sokol 1910; *Paměti pana de*

LANGUAGE AND VALUES

Alongside German, the Czech language and Czech culture formed the very air that Kafka breathed. By this I do not mean merely that Kafka enjoyed walking the streets of Prague, listening to Czech and admiring the city's architecture and monuments. Kafka was neither a compulsive urban pedestrian à la Apollinaire, nor a modern tourist, but a native of Prague with his roots firmly in Czech lands. As a little boy he apparently created a puppet show about George of Poděbrady[35] (his mother in fact hailed from Poděbrady), the 15th century Bohemian ruler who became a central figure in the national myth of the unique identity of the Czechs – a nation defined by language and devoted to freedom and democracy. These values were considered to be rooted in Hussitism and the Reformation, as mythologized by František Palacký (who also drew on Czech pre-history and the Libuše saga) in his *Dějiny národu českého v Čechách a v Moravě* (History of the Czech Nation in Bohemia and Moravia) and Tomáš G. Masaryk in *Česká otázka* (The Czech Question) – though the latter avoids any reference to the 'prehistorical' period. Post-1918 this myth became part of the state ideology. As we noted above, it was a subject that clearly occupied Kafka – to the extent that he even read specialized literature on it.

Hussitism and its iconography were highly visible in Prague. From 1915 on, Kafka's daily route across Old Town Square took him past the Art Nouveau monument to Jan Hus by Ladislav Šaloun (1870–1946), which was unveiled in that year to commemorate the martyr burnt at the stake in Constance in 1415.[36] He was also familiar with the allegorical monument to František Palacký (1798–1876), a work by Šaloun's contemporary Stanislav Sucharda (1866–1916) that had been unveiled on the banks of the Vltava three years earlier.[37] Much of Palacký's oeuvre can be seen as an interpretation of Hussitism – even Sucharda's monument alludes to the resurrection narrative. The Hussite theme is also evident in the sculpture of František Bílek (1872–1941), whose works include the (nationally non-specific) *Blind Man* (1902),[38] designs for national monuments to Jan Žižka and John Amos Comenius,[39] as well as the Hus memorial in Kolín,[40] which Kafka particularly admired:

La Porte, prvého komořího Ludvíka XIV., translated from the French by Adolf Gottwald, Prague: St. Sokol 1909.

35 According to Max Brod, *Franz Kafka. Eine Biographie* (Franz Kafka: A Biography). Frankfurt am Main: S. Fischer 1963, p. 19; see also Born, *Kafkas Bibliothek*, p. 19.

36 Kafka to Max Brod, 30 July 1922. – See Brod – Kafka, *Eine Freundschaft*, p. 395.

37 Kafka to Max Brod, 30 July 1922. – See Brod – Kafka, *Eine Freundschaft*, p. 395.

38 Kafka to Max Brod, 30 July 1922. – See Brod – Kafka, *Eine Freundschaft*, p. 395.

39 Franz Kafka to Max Brod, 7 August 1922. – See Brod – Kafka, *Eine Freundschaft*, p. 401. For contemporary accounts of the Žižka monument around 1911, see Marie Halířová – Hana Larvová (eds), *František Bílek (1872–1941)*. Prague: Národní galerie 2001, p. 212.

40 Franz Kafka to Max Brod, 20 July 1922, and Franz Kafka to Max Brod, 7 August 1922. – See Brod – Kafka, *Eine Freundschaft*, pp. 390, 401. The Hus monument in Kolín bears the inscrip-

> In saying this I keep thinking of the *Hus* at Kolín (not so much the statue in the Modern Gallery and the monument in Vyšehrad Cemetery and still less the mass of relatively inaccessible small pieces in wood and graphic which used to be shown and are growing dim in my memory). At Kolin you come out of the side street and see before you the big square with the small houses bordering it, and in the centre *Hus*. At all times, in snow and in summer, it has a breathtaking, incomprehensible, and thus seemingly arbitrary unity, which is nevertheless imposed anew at every moment by that powerful hand and even takes in the spectator himself. The Weimar Goethe House achieves something of the sort, perhaps largely through the blessing of time. But it would be rather difficult to campaign for the creator of that, and the door of his house is always closed.[41]

While Kafka enthused about Bílek's work, he rejected that of Šaloun and Sucharda:

> You also do not mention Bílek, though I wish you would take him in your arms. I have long been thinking of him with great admiration. Lately a remark in a *Tribuna* article dealing with other matters (I think it was by Chalupný) reminded me of him again. It is a wanton and senseless impoverishment of Prague and Bohemia that mediocre stuff like Šaloun's *Hus* or wretched stuff like Sucharda's Palacký are erected with all honours, while on the other hand sketches of Bílek's for a Žižka or Komenský monument, sketches of incomparable quality, remain unexecuted. If it were possible to rectify this disgrace, that would be doing a great deal, and a government organ would be the right place to begin.[42]

All three sculptors, however, draw for their themes on the Czech national myth of democratism (still very much alive at the time) personified by Hus, Žižka and Comenius as representatives of the Czech Reformation, which for Palacký was one of the high points of Czech history. Yet in Kafka's opinion only Bílek produced a masterpiece, suggesting that national considerations played no part in his artistic judgment, but only aesthetic criteria. It is certainly not by chance that Kafka mentions Bílek in his correspondence in 1922, at the time of his exhibition at the *Dům umělců* (House of Artists) – an exhibition introduced by Otokar Březina,[43] to whom we shall return later. By then, however, Kafka was already acquainted with the sculptor's work.

tion 'A tree struck by lightning, for all eternity burning'. See Halířová – Larvová, *František Bílek*, p. 103.

41 Kafka, *Letters to Friends, Family, and Editors*, p. 349.

42 Franz Kafka to Max Brod, 30 July 1922. – See Kafka, *Letters to Friends, Family, and Editors*, p. 347.

43 See Halířová – Larvová, *František Bílek*, p. 417. My assumption that Kafka saw this exhibition is based on the formulation of a reference to the 'Moderne Galerie' in his letter to Max Brod, 7 August 1922. – See Brod – Kafka, *Eine Freundschaft*, p. 401.

Czech visual art, existing as it did without the need of written language, appears to have had a special importance for Kafka. In a diary entry for 5 June 1922[44] he recorded as a momentous event the funeral of Josef Václav Myslbek (1848–1922), whose sculptural work was of primary importance for Czech culture and Czech national consciousness – witness his contribution to the decoration of the National Theatre (opened in 1881, reopened after fire in 1883), the figures from Czech pre-history and myth he created for Palacký Bridge, and the equestrian statue of St Wenceslas in Wenceslas Square in Prague, unveiled in 1912. An earlier diary entry of 12 September 1911 shows that Kafka was also familiar with Alfons Mucha (1860–1939),[45] whose works include the monumental cycle The Slav Epic (1910–1928), as well as with Mikuláš Aleš.[46] As we noted above, Kafka was no stranger to the National Theatre,[47] where besides Myslbek's sculptures he would also have seen Aleš's murals. He certainly also knew the writings of Alois Jirásek (1851–1930), whose historical novels are a romanticised and sentimentalised take on Palacký's *History*.[48] In 1916 Jirásek's *Husitský král* (The Hussite King), based on the life of George of Poděbrady, started to appear in instalments in the daily *Národní politika* (National Politics), of which Kafka was a reader, but after a few issues it was banned for political reasons.

One could continue, if not indefinitely then for a considerable time, cataloguing the many substantiated facts documenting Kafka's contacts with Czech literature, Czech visual arts, and generally Czech culture and its history. But that is not the point. These facts serve simply to show that on the basis of sometimes quite marginal allusions to Czech culture – a marginality perhaps ascribable to the fact that Kafka and his circle took such things for granted – we may assume he had a good overall knowledge of what was going on in Czech culture and society. It is surely no accident that is his 'Character sketch of small literatures' Kafka drew not only on Yiddish but equally on his knowledge of Czech literature.

---

44 Diary, 5 June 1922. – See Kafka, *Tagebücher*, p. 922.

45 See Kafka, *Tagebücher*, p. 245.

46 Franz Kafka to Milena Jesenská, mid-November 1920. – See Kafka, *Briefe an Milena*, p. 291. Mikoláš Aleš (1852– 1913) was one of many artists who contributed to the decoration of the National Theatre, which in the late 19th century represented not only the hub of Czech dramatic and musical culture but, with its depictions of real and imagined Czech history, a cultural and political symbol of Czech nationhood. Aleš also illustrated Jirásek's *Staré pověsti české* (Old Czech Legends, 1894).

47 See Diary, 16 October 1911, 17 December 1911, and 21 January 1922. – See Kafka, *Tagebücher*, p. 93, 397 f., 883.

48 Franz Kafka to Max Brod, 12 July 1922. – See Brod – Kafka, *Eine Freundschaft*, p. 385.

KAFKA'S 'CHARACTER SKETCH OF SMALL LITERATURES'

In 1911 Kafka twice wrote in his diary about his 'Character sketch of small literatures'. In this he was able to draw on his knowledge of Czech as well as of Yiddish literature, to which he had recently been introduced by the actor Yitzchak Löwy:

> 25 December [1911]. What I understand of contemporary Jewish literature in Warsaw through Löwy, and of contemporary Czech literature partly through my own insight, points to the fact that many of the benefits of literature – the stirring of minds, the coherence of national consciousness, often unrealized in public life and always tending to disintegrate, the pride which a nation gains from a literature of its own and the support it is afforded in the face of a hostile surrounding world, this keeping a diary by a nation which is something entirely different from historiography and results in a more rapid (and yet always closely scrutinized) development, the spiritualization of the broad area of public life, the assimilation of dissatisfied elements that are immediately put to use precisely in this sphere where only stagnation can do harm, the constant integration of a people with respect to its whole that the incessant bustle of the magazines creates, the narrowing down of the attention of a nation upon itself and the accepting of what is foreign only in reflection, the birth of a respect for those active in literature, the transitory awakening in the younger generation of higher aspirations, which nevertheless leaves its permanent mark, the acknowledgment of literary events as objects of political solicitude, the dignification of the antithesis between fathers and sons and the possibility of discussing this, the presentation of the national faults in a manner that is very painful, to be sure, but also liberating and deserving of forgiveness, the beginning of a lively and therefore self-respecting book trade and the eagerness for books – all these effects can be produced even by a literature whose development is not in actual fact unusually broad in scope, but seems to be, because it lacks outstanding talents. The liveliness of such a literature exceeds even that of one rich in talent, for, as it has no writer whose great gifts could silence at least the majority of cavillers, literary competition on the greatest scale has a real justification.
>
> A literature not penetrated by a great talent has no gap through which the irrelevant might force its way. Its claim to attention thereby becomes more compelling. The independence of the individual writer, naturally only within the national boundaries, is better preserved. The lack of irresistible national models keeps the completely untalented away from literature. But even mediocre talent would not suffice for a writer to be influenced by the unstriking qualities of the fashionable writers of the moment, or to imitate the foreign literature that has already been introduced; this is plain, for example, in a literature rich in great talents, such as the German is, where the worst writers limit their imitation to what they find at home. The creative and beneficent force exerted in these directions by a literature poor in its component parts proves

especially effective when it begins to create a literary history out of the records of its dead writers. These writers' undeniable influence, past and present, becomes so matter-of-fact that it can take the place of their writings. One speaks of the latter and means the former, indeed, one even reads the latter and sees only the former. But since that effect cannot be forgotten, and since the writings themselves do not act independently upon the memory, there is no forgetting and no remembering again. Literary history offers an unchangeable, dependable whole that is hardly affected by the taste of the day.
A small nation's memory is not smaller than the memory of a large one and so can to digest the existing material more thoroughly. There are, to be sure, fewer experts in literary history employed, but literature is less a concern of literary history than of the people, and thus, if not purely, it is at least reliably preserved. For the claim that the national consciousness of a small people makes on the individual is such that everyone must always be prepared to known that part of the literature which has come down to him, to support it, to defend it – to defend it even if he does not know it and support it.[49]

A character sketch of small literatures.
Good results in both cases.
Here the results in individual instances are even better.

1. Liveliness:
    a. Conflict.
    b. Schools.
    c. Newspapers.
2. Less constraint:
    a. Absence of principles.
    b. Minor themes.
    c. Easy formation of symbols.
    d. Throwing off of the untalented.
3. Popularity.
    a. Connection with politics.
    b. Literary history.
    c. Faith in literature, can make up their own laws.

It is difficult to readjust when one has felt this useful, happy life in all one's being. [...]
How weak this picture is. An incoherent assumption is thrust like a board between actual feeling and the metaphor of the description.[50]

49 Franz Kafka, *The Diaries of Franz Kafka 1910–1913*. Edited by Max Brod and translated by Joseph Kresh. New York: Schocken 1948, p. 191 ff.
50 Kafka, *The Diaries of Franz Kafka, 1910–1913*, p. 195, 201.

Although these texts do not contain the name of a single writer, we can surely agree with Kafka that he knew Czech literature from his 'own insight', and not only of 'contemporary' authors. His conclusions that 'literature is less a concern of literary history than a concern of the people', that in small literatures 'literary events' become objects of 'political solicitude', and that the nation takes pride and succour in a literature that acts as its 'journal', and reveres people engaged in literature – all this applies to the central role of language and literature in 19th century Czech national culture, defined as it was by language and therefore predominantly verbal, in which for a socially undeveloped ethnic community that defined itself primarily in terms of language, a consciously created and cultivated literature[51] became a substitute – at least initially – for political engagement, finding an outlet even in the National Theatre (along with the Czech press a key institution of Czech culture), which Kafka as a theatre-goer was well acquainted with.

This typically 19th century identification of literature with nation, confirmed here by Kafka, can also be clearly seen, in the context of Czech national 'resurrection' and 'renewal', in 19th century Czech school readers such as those used by Kafka in his Czech lessons at grammar school. Thus Antonín Truhlář writes:

> Among the Czech people, whose literary significance was minimal because of past misfortunes, the reforms contributed to an awakening and enlivening of national consciousness.[52]

A nation and its 'condition' is thus measured by the extent and importance of its literary output. Literature and its language are not simply one feature of a nation's culture; they are the principal emblem of that nation. This explains the key role played by writers, who are regarded as leaders or – to use Truhlář's word – 'chieftains' in the process of national revival.[53]

But if literature becomes identified with the nation, and the 'national character' is reinforced thanks to the 'applause of audiences' and 'more distant works [...] such as The Bartered Bride',[54] the values through which literature and writers are viewed and judged must be other than aesthetic. In

51 See esp. Vladimír Macura, *Znamení zrodu: české národní obrození jako kulturní typ* (Signs of Rebirth: Czech National Rebirth as Cultural Type). Jinočany: H & H 1995.

52 Antonín Truhlář, *Výbor z literatury české. Doba nová* (Anthology of Czech Literature: Modern Period). Vol. 1. Prague: Bursík and Kohout 1898, 3th edition, p. 2.

53 See Truhlář, *Výbor*, p. 3.

54 Kafka, *Tagebücher 1909–1912 in der Fassung der Handschrift* (Diaries 1909–1912 Based on Handwritten Manuscripts). Ed. by Hans-Gerd Koch. Frankfurt am Main: S. Fischer 1994, p. 56. Max Brod, too, repeatedly refers to Smetana's opera – for the first time in a review in 1913. For more see Barbora Šrámková, *Max Brod und seine tschechische Kultur* (Max Brod and his Czech Culture). Wuppertal: Arco 2009.

Truhlář and others we repeatedly find writers being evaluated not in terms of literary or aesthetic merit, but solely with regard to their national sentiment and their commitment to the language and the nation. This, of course, Kafka could scarcely fail to notice:

> These writers' undeniable influence, past and present, becomes so matter-of-fact that it can take the place of their writings.[55]

What is valued in this conception of literature is the fostering of love for one's own people, the raising of awareness of national concerns, and the strengthening of the foundations of national literature as the representative of the nation.[56] Kafka, too, discerns these traits in small literatures – albeit from a critical distance. As one who judges literature by aesthetic criteria, he is sceptical about literatures 'not penetrated by a great talent' that have 'no gap through which the irrelevant might force its way'. It is not that there are no talents; only that there are none gifted enough to break through the requirements of a nationally conceived literature and its canon of values, where what constitutes 'genius' is decided and judged by national rather than aesthetic criteria. That, of course, does not reflect terribly well on the Czech literary classics that Kafka has in mind. But Kafka knows what he's talking about.[57] He also knows that in a literature like that there is no place for him.

CZECH CLASSICAL LITERATURE

The lecture on small literatures that Kafka drafted but never delivered, made public mention of no specific writers, nonetheless shows that he was well acquainted with the issues surrounding Czech and Yiddish literature. He even tells us explicitly that he can judge contemporary Czech literature 'through my own insight'.[58] As we know from research on Kafka's study of Czech literature at school this is no exaggerated claim and applies as much to older Czech literature as to that of the 19th century. Zimmermann seeks

---

55 Kafka, *The Diaries of Franz Kafka, 1910–1913*, p. 193.

56 Truhlář, *Výbor*, p. 2, 3, 80.

57 'Small literatures' or 'literatures of small nations' is a subject also discussed by Max Brod, *Im Kampf um das Judentum. Politische Essays* (In the Struggle for Jewishness: Political Essays). Vienna, Berlin: R. Löwit 1920, 104–113. For 'small literatures' see also Klaus Hermsdorf, Werfels und Kafkas Verhältnis zur tschechischen Literatur (Werfel's and Kafka's relation to Czech literature). *Germanistica Pragensia* 2 (1964), pp. 39–47 as well as Gilles Deleuze – Félix Guattari: *Kafka: Pour une littérature minuere* (Kafka: Toward a Minor Literature). Paris: Les Édition de Minuit 1975, and reception of this approach.

58 See Kafka, *Tagebücher*, p. 312.

to draw a parallel between Comenius's *Labyrinth of the World and Paradise of the Heart* and *The Castle*. In his interpretation the name *Klamm*, for example, is an allusion to Comenius and his characters *Klam* and *Mam* which mean 'illusion' and 'deception'.[59] We have already mentioned Kafka's interest in the Unity of the Brethren, of which Comenius was the last bishop. Comenius exercised a dominant influence on Czech literature and culture, as well as on Prague German writers such as Franz Werfel, to whom we shall return later. Of course the name *Klamm* has other possible associations. It could refer to Count Clam-Gallas, the owner of Frýdlant Castle, depicted on a postcard to Max Brod dated 1/2 February 1911.[60] And naturally Kafka knew Clam-Gallas Palace, the family property in the heart of Prague Old Town.

Kafka's familiarity with the classics of Czech literature was based primarily on knowledge he acquired at school, but also on his frequent visits to the National Theatre. This familiarity is taken quite for granted by Kafka and his correspondents (such as Max Brod, or his sister Ottla), so that in the letters a simple mention of a writer's or artist's name generally suffices, without any explanatory comment. Or even less. When, referring to František Bílek, he talks about 'the tomb in Vyšehrad Cemetery'[61] – i.e. Bílek's sculpture *Grief* – he is indirectly alluding to the historical novelist Václav Beneš Třebízský (1849–1884) as well as to Slavín itself, the part of the cemetery reserved for the nation's great writers and artists. In those days, to walk among the tombs of Vyšehrad was to be given a comprehensive review of 19th century Czech literature and culture.[62]

When it comes to particular writers mentioned by Kafka, Božena Němcová has a special place. Extracts from her writings were included in his Czech school readers and were discussed in class. So it is no surprise to find Anna Pouzarová recalling[63] how he recommended Němcová's novel *Babička* (The Grandmother) to his sisters and even bought an illustrated Czech edition from which she has to read to them. And we know he returned to

---

59 See Hans Dieter Zimmermann, Das Labyrinth der Welt: Kafka und Comenius (The Labyrinth of the World: Kafka and Comenius). In: Klaas-Hinrich Ehlers et al. (eds), *Brücken nach Prag. Deutschsprachige Literatur im kulturellen Kontext der Donaumonarchie und der Tschechoslowakei* (Bridges to Prague: German-written Literature in the Cultural Context of the Habsburg Monarchy and Czechoslovakia). Frankfurt am Main: Peter Lang 2000, pp. 309–319. The philosopher Karel Kosík made a similar observation in a 1963 article. See Karel Kosík, *Století Markéty Samsové* (Century of Markéta Samsa). Prague: Český spisovatel 1993.

60 See Brod – Kafka, *Eine Freundschaft*, p. 89.

61 Franz Kafka to Max Brod, 7 August 1922. – See Brod – Kafka, *Eine Freundschaft*, p. 401.

62 For more on Slavín, see Marek Nekula, *Smrt a zmrtvýchvstání národa: Sen o Slavíně v české literatuře a kultuře* (Death and Resurrection of a Nation: The Dream of the Slavín Pantheon in Czech Literature and Culture). Prague: Karolinum 2016.

63 See Anna Pouzarová, Als Erzieherin in der Familie Kafka (Governess in the Kafka family). In: Hans-Gerd Koch (ed.), *„Als Kafka mir entgegen kam..." Erinnerungen an Franz Kafka* ('As Kafka approached me.' Recollections of Franz Kafka). Berlin: Wagenbach 1995, pp. 55–65, here p. 62.

Němcová later in life. In a letter to Felix Weltsch dated 22 September 1917 he told his friend how impressed he was with her letters,[64] which he had been reading in Siřem (Zürau). In a letter to Ottla dated 28 July 1921 he mentions how he used to think of Němcová when he was at Domažlice.[65] And elsewhere he wrote: 'In Czech I know of only one musical language – that of Božena Němcová.'[66]

It is therefore likely that Kafka had absorbed Němcová's *The Grandmother*, and that the impulse for the story in *The Castle* of Amalia and Sortini the official came from Christina's tale of harassment at the hands of the Italian manservant Piccolo in *The Grandmother*.[67] Němcová's story 'V zámku a podzámčí' (Castle and village) has a similar structure. But in one respect the two writers differ radically: while Němcová's *The Grandmother* ends, thanks to the princess, on a conciliatory note, the surveyor in Kafka's *The Castle* enters a world that no intercession can redeem – either on the part of Count Westwest or of his senior official. As Kautman rightly observes, Kafka's attitude to Božena Němcová can be characterized as 'attraction based on contrasts'.[68]

But Kafka could also be scathing of 'the classics'. Commenting on a stage production by Jaroslav Kvapil of Jaroslav Vrchlický (1853–1912), he criticised the playwright as much as the director:

> Day before yesterday *Hippodamie*. Bad play. A rambling about in Greek mythology without rhyme or reason. Kvapil's essay in the program which expresses between the lines the view apparent throughout the whole performance, that a good production (which here, however, was nothing but an imitation of Reinhardt) can make a bad play into a great theatrical work. All this must be sad for a Czech who knows even a little of the world.[69]

---

64 See Franz Kafka, *Briefe 1902–1924*. Ed. by Max Brod. Frankfurt am Main: S. Fischer 1958, p. 170. Probably the 3-volume 'scandalous' edition of Božena Němcová's *Correspondence*, published between 1912 and 1920 in her *Collected Works*, which contains some letters of a very intimate nature. See also Jaroslava Janáčková, Alena Macurová et al., *Řeč dopisů, řeč v dopisech Boženy Němcové* (Language of Letters, Language in Božena Němcová's Letters). Prague: ISV nakladatelství 2001.

65 See Kafka, *Briefe an Ottla*, p. 130.

66 Kafka to Milena Jesenská, 29 May 1920. – See Kafka, *Briefe an Milena*, p. 22; Franz Kafka, *Letters to Milena*. Edited by Willi Haas. Translated by Tania and James Stern. New York: Schocken Books [1953] 1965, p. 35.

67 See e.g. Max Brod, The Castle: Its genesis. In: Angel Flores – Homer Swander (eds), *Franz Kafka Today*. Madison: University of Wisconsin Press 1958, pp. 161–164; and Klaus Wagenbach, *Franz Kafka. Eine Biographie seiner Jugend 1883–1912* (Franz Kafka: A Biography of his Youth 1883–1912). Bern: Francke 1958, as well as Hans Dieter Zimmermann, Franz Kafka liest Božena Němcová (Franz Kafka reads Božena Němcová). In: *brücken – Germanistisches Jahrbuch* N.F. 15 (2007), 182–192.

68 Kautman, Franz Kafka, p. 61.

69 Franz Kafka, *The Diaries of Franz Kafka, 1910–1913*, p. 181.

This negative appraisal was no doubt influenced by Kafka's reluctance to spend the evening watching Vrchlický's drama, just when his thoughts were beginning to 'move more freely' and he felt he might be 'perhaps be capable of something'.[70] That may explain his later interest in Vrchlický's correspondence with Sofie Podlipská.[71] As writer of the epic *Bar Kochba* (1897) and the drama *Rabínská moudrost* (The Rabbi's Wisdom, 1886) with its clearly philosemitic stance, Vrchlický was highly thought of in the Czech Jewish movement.[72]

NEWSPAPERS, PERIODICALS AND OTHER MEDIA

Knowing the Czech language, being able to handle its more complex literary forms, and keeping abreast of Czech literature and culture are a far cry from actually identifying with that culture. Modern culture, in any case, operates along different lines. Still, we can safely say that Kafka had a very good grasp of its past and present problems, values and symbols. One fact alone may suffice to justify this assertion: Kafka's regular attendance at the pre-election meetings of Czech politicians. Brod mentions František Soukup, Václav Klofáč and Karel Kramář. Kautman thinks we should add Tomáš G. Masaryk, while Janouch mentions Alois Rašín. But on the evidence of Kafka's texts we can only be certain of an 'encounter' with Jan Herben and František Soukup, and with Masaryk's writings.[73] Moreover, we know that Kafka was a more or less regular reader of the Czech press (especially *Čas*, *Národní listy* and *Národní politika*),[74] which he subscribed to or had sent to him even after

70 Diary, 17 December 1911. – See Kafka, *Tagebücher*, p. 298; Kafka, *The Diaries of Franz Kafka, 1910–1913*, p. 180.

71 Kafka to Max Brod, 13 February 1918. – See Brod – Kafka, *Eine Freundschaft*, p. 236; Born, *Kafkas Bibliothek*, p. 221; J. Vrchlický, *Dopisy Jaroslava Vrchlického se Sofií Podlipskou z let 1875–1876* (Letters of Jaroslav Vrchlický and Sofie Podlipská) published by F. X. Šalda (Prague 1917). Gustav Janouch claims that Kafka read Vrchlický's translation of Walt Whitman. See Janouch, *Gespräche mit Kafka*, p. 185 f.

72 See e.g. Oskar Donath, *Židé a židovství v české literatuře 19. a 20. století* (Jews and Jewishness in the Czech Literature of the 19th and 20th century). 2 Vol. Brno: privately printed 1930.

73 See Brod, *Franz Kafka*, p. 91. Also Hartmut Binder, *Kafka. Ein Leben in Prag*. Munich: Mahnert-Lueg 1982, p. 119; Kautman, Franz Kafka, p. 51; Janouch, *Gespräche mit Kafka*, pp. 127, 151, and in particular Franz Kafka to Max Brod, 10 March 1910, and Diary, 19 September 1917. – See Brod – Kafka, *Eine Freundschaft*, p. 72, and Kafka, *Tagebücher*, p. 424.

74 The magazines and newspapers Kafka knew, or at any rate mentioned, are as varied as the reasons he must have read them for: *Cesta* (Kafka, *Briefe an Milena*, p. 135), *Čas* (Brod – Kafka, *Eine Freundschaft*, p. 73), *Červen* (Kafka, *Briefe an Milena*, p. 284), *Česká stráž* (Brod – Kafka, *Eine Freundschaft*, p. 252), *Česká svoboda* (Brod – Kafka, *Eine Freundschaft*, p. 252), *Kmen* (Kafka, *Briefe an Milena*, p. 8, 135, 228, 245, 277; Kafka, *Briefe an Ottla*, pp. 81, 87), *Lidové noviny* (Kafka, *Briefe an Ottla*, p. 118), *Lípa* (Kafka, *Briefe an Milena*, p. 135), *Národní listy* (Kafka, *Briefe an Milena*, p. 82, 305), *Naše řeč* (Kafka, *Briefe an Milena*, p. 78), *Tribuna* (Kafka, *Briefe an Ottla*, p. 102; Kafka, *Briefe an Milena*,

illness had somewhat reduced his financial circumstances,[75] and in which he may have found inspiration for his writing. Nuska, for example, sees a number of parallels between *The Trial* and the political scandal involving Karel Šviha, *Reichsabgeordneter* and chairman of the parliamentary fraction of the Czech National Socialist Party, who was alleged to have acted as an informant on his own party and other politicians. The story, which broke in *Národní listy* in March 1914 and culminated in May with Šviha's trial (at which the unconvincing public prosecutor was, ironically, widely regarded as a suspect), aroused considerable interest not only in Bohemia but in Vienna and Germany as well. The parallels Nuska reconstructs are sometimes very compelling, especially in some of the novel's secondary motifs and passages later excised by the author.[76] Another factor that could be cited in support of Nuska's interpretation is Kafka's proven interest in judicial proceedings: 'I arrive on Wednesday. We could think about whether we should go to the Kestranek trial.'[77]

Czech literature and culture also formed (even before Czechoslovak independence in 1918) an integral part of the cultural landscape of the 'Arconauts', as they were known – the habitués of the Arco coffee house in Hybernská Street. We know that Max Brod (1884–1968), Rudolf Fuchs (1890–1942) and Otto Pick (1887–1940), as well as Franz Werfel (1899–1945) and Ernst Pollak, with whom Kafka was in regular contact, had long championed Czech art and Czech artists both at home and abroad. Through Max Brod, for example, Kafka knew the composers Leoš Janáček[78] and Josef Suk,[79] as well as the Langer brothers. And it was probably because his friends had translated a number of Czech works that Kafka had in his possession German editions of Petr Bezruč, Fráňa Šrámek and, in all likelihood, Otokar Březina.

p. 135, 172, 189, 193, 206, 212, 227, 246, 277, 304 f.), *Večer* (Kafka, *Briefe an Ottla*, p. 84), *Venkov* (Kafka, *Briefe an Ottla*, p. 107).

75 Franz Kafka to Ottla, 1 May 1920, and 21 May 1920. – See Kafka, *Briefe an Ottla*, p. 84 and 89.

76 See Bohumil Nuska – Jiří Pernes, *Kafkův Proces a Švihova aféra* (Kafka's *The Trial* and the Šviha Affair). Prague: Barrister & Principal 2000.

77 See Brod – Kafka, *Eine Freundschaft*, p. 66.

78 Kafka read and corrected Brod's translation of the libretto of *Její pastorkyňa* (Jenufa), as is apparent from their correspondence. See Brod – Kafka, *Eine Freundschaft*, pp. 173, 174, 175, 177, 197, 201. Brod also forwarded to Kafka a letter from Janáček in Czech. For more on the role of Max Brod see Šrámková, *Max Brod und seine tschechische Kultur*.

79 Max Brod to Franz Kafka, 19 January 1921. – See Brod – Kafka, *Eine Freundschaft*, p. 305. Janouch also names Vítězslav Novák. – See Janouch, *Gespräche mit Kafka*, p. 155.

ANTHOLOGY

In his monograph on German translations of Czech poetry, Nezdařil notes the special position occupied by anthologies of modern Czech poetry to which Prague German writers had also contributed.[80] The most relevant of these with regard to Kafka is the first, published by Franz Pfemfert (1879–1954) in Berlin in 1916 under the title *Jüngste tschechische Lyrik. Eine Anthologie* (Recent Czech Poetry. An Anthology), which Pfemfert sees as 'a political act binding peoples together'. Besides works by Bezruč and Březina, who were of particular interest to the Cafe Arco group, the anthology also contained texts by Petr Křička,[81] Stanislav Kostka Neumann, Josef Kodíček, Ervín Taussig, Stanislav Hanuš and Richard Weiner. Among others represented in the volume were Karel Hlaváček, Jiří Karásek ze Lvovic, Otokar Fischer, Josef Svatopluk Machar, Antonín Sova and Fráňa Šrámek.

Included in this colourful company were vitalists (Křička, Šrámek), anarchists (Neumann, Šrámek, Karel Toman), and the writers of the *Moderní revue* circle (Hlaváček, Karásek, Theer), to whom we shall return later. There also appeared works in Czech by Jewish authors, such as Weiner, Taussig, Kodíček and Fischer. Classic Czech modernism was represented by Březina and Sova, as well as Machar and Bezruč. The translations were by Otto Pick, Rudolf Fuchs, Paul Eisner, Emil Saudek, Ernst Pollak and Jan V. Löwenbach.

Binder believes that Kafka not only knew this anthology,[82] but actually helped Rudolf Fuchs translate a number of the poets into German (Bezruč, Hlaváček, Dyk, Kodíček, Křička, Neumann, Sova, Taussig and Theer), an assertion supported among other things by Kafka's recommendation of Rudolf Fuchs to Martin Buber after they met in Vienna in 1917.[83] For Binder the clue is a note that Kafka posted to Fuchs on 18 August 1916,[84] in which he

80 Ladislav Nezdařil, *Česká poezie v německých překladech* (Czech Poetry in German Translations). Prague: Academia 1985.

81 Petr Křička (1884–1949), who was serving on the Russian front at the time, first attracted attention in 1916 with his collection *Šípkový keř* (The Dog-Rose Bush). Brod wrote about his brother, the composer Jaroslav Křička (1882–1969), in the *Prager Abendblatt*, 29 November 1923. – Franz Kafka to Max Brod, 17 December 1923. – See Brod – Kafka, *Eine Freundschaft*, p. 445.

82 See Hartmut Binder (ed.), *Prager Profile. Vergessene Autoren im Schatten Kafkas* (Prague Profiles. Forgotten Writers in the Shadow of Franz Kafka). Berlin: Gebr. Mann Verlag 1991, 21f.

83 See Kafka, *Letters to Friends, Family, and Editors*, p. 133, and Rudolf Fuchs, Erinnerungen an Franz Kafka (Recollections of Franz Kafka). In: Max Brod, *Franz Kafka: Eine Biographie* (Franz Kafka: A Biography). Frankfurt am Main: S. Fischer Verlag 1954, 327–330, here 329. For Binder's interpretation, see Binder, *Prager Profile*, p. 27.

84 Copy in the Literární archiv Památníku národního písemnictví (Literary Archive of Museum of Czech Literature). Quoted in Ilse Seehase, Drei Mitteilungen Kafkas und ihr Umfeld (Three messages from Kafka and their context). *Zeitschrift für Germanistik* 8 (1987), No. 2, pp. 178–183, here p. 180.

apologises for a delay in sending a manuscript to Otto Pick, who at the time was acting as co-ordinating editor for the anthology.

A few years later, in June 1921, Otto Pick (who had recently joined the editorial board of the state-run *Prager Presse*) published a volume entitled *Tschechische Erzähler* (Czech Storytellers)[85] that included among others Karel Čapek. He and his brother Josef, who was for a while a member of a group of artists known as the *Skupina výtvarných umělců* that cultivated dialogue with Prague German artists, had already established links with the Czech avant garde at the time of publication of the verse anthology.[86] But Otto Pick and his circle were not alone in their endeavours. As early as in 1917 Paul Eisner had published a *Tschechische Anthologie. Vrchlický – Sova – Březina* (Czech Anthology. Vrchlický – Sova – Březina) as the twenty-first volume in Hugo von Hofmannsthal's *Österreichische Bibliothek* (Austrian Library) series.[87]

There can be no doubt that Kafka knew the anthology *Jüngste tschechische Lyrik*, on which so many of his friends and acquaintances had worked. We will come across many of these names in connection with Kafka later, mostly in allusions that, the names being well-known to all concerned, required no further explanation.

OTOKAR BŘEZINA

In 1923 Kafka received a copy of *Musik der Quellen* by Otokar Březina (1868–1929) direct from its Leipzig publisher Kurt Wolff, as we know from a letter dated 18 October.[88] The title of the newly-published volume was taken from a collection of essays, *Hudba pramenů* (Music of the Springs). The German translator was Emil Saudek, on the basis of whose literal version Franz Werfel recreated the poems in verse. Yet Kafka must surely have encountered Březina's work long before that, at the very least in Pfemfert's *Die Aktion* or in the Prague press.[89]

---

85 *Prager Presse*, No. 96, 3 July 1921, p. 13.

86 See Rudolf Fuchs, *Die Prager Aposteluhr. Gedichte, Prosa, Briefe* (The Prague Astronomical Clock: Poems, Prose, Letters). Ed. by Ilse Seehase. Halle, Leipzig: Mitteldeutscher Verlag, 1985, pp. 340–349. See also Binder, *Prager Profile*, p. 20. Karel Čapek was in close contact with S. K. Neumann from around 1912. 22 October 1918, together with V. Dyk, O. Fischer, J. Herben, J. S. Machar, M. Rutt and K. Toman, he was on the staff of *Národní listy* (of which Kafka was a reader) until he left the paper in 1921. In 1920 Čapek's translations appeared in *Cesta* (The Way), a journal favoured by the Czech Left and also read by Kafka – on account of Milena Jesenská. For more on Karel Čapek see below.

87 See also Nezdařil, *Česká poezie*.

88 See Born, *Kafkas Bibliothek*, p. 186.

89 Theodor Lessing, a freelance contributor to the Prager Tagblatt, also knew Březina's work. See Marek Nekula, Theodor Lessing und seine Rezeption in der Tschechoslowakei (Theodor Lessing and his reception in Czechoslovakia). In: *brücken. Germanistisches Jahrbuch Tschechien – Slowakei.* NF 4 (1996), pp. 57–103.

In the almanac *Vom jüngsten Tag*,[90] published by Wolff in 1917, Kafka underlined in red a number of names – Max Brod, Carl Sternheim, Franz Werfel and others on the *Neue Bücher junger Dichter* (New Books by Young Poets) list – as well as Otokar Březina's *Hymnen* (Hymns), first brought out by Wolff in 1913 in a translation by his friend Otto Pick. On page 252 of the same almanac we find Březina's 1897 poem *Gebet für Feinde* (Prayer for Enemies) in a verse translation by Albert Ehrenstein. It is clear that Březina's works – as can be seen in Werfel's preface to the German edition of Bezruč's *Slezské písně* (Songs of Silesia),[91] or Hermann Bahr's foreword to the German edition of Šrámek's poems, which appeared under the title *Flammen* (Flames)[92] – formed a self-evident part of the cultural landscape not only for the 'Arconauts' (and thus for Franz Kafka), but also for the authors of Austrian and German modernism – witness the activities of Hugo von Hofmannsthal, Hermann Bahr and Franz Pfemfert.

This is because much of Otokar Březina's work was translated soon after its appearance. A bibliophile edition of his *Hände* (after the Czech title *Ruce* – Hands) had been produced by the Vienna publisher Moritz Frisch in 1908, in a translation by Emil Saudek (1876–1941), with 'book decoration' and four illustrations by František Bílek. After Březina's *Hymnen*, Kurt Wolff published, in Munich, *Baumeister am Tempel* (1920, The Temple Builders; in the Czech original *Stavitelé chrámu*) translated by Otto Pick, and in the same year, also in Munich, the collection *Winde von Mittag nach Mitternacht* (Winds from Noon to Midnight; original Czech title *Větry od pólů*, literally, 'Winds from the [N and S] Poles'), in translations by Emil Saudek and Franz Werfel.[93] In 1923 Wolff brought out *Musik der Quellen* (as we noted above), this time in Leipzig, also translated by Saudek and Werfel. Translations of Březina in Kafka's day were not hard to find: apart from the almanac *Vom jüngsten Tag* (From Judgment Day, 1917) and a number of newspapers and periodicals, they also appeared in Paul Eisner's *Tschechische Anthologie* (Czech Anthology, 1917), and could be heard, for example, at a literary evening held at the Mozarteum in Prague on 29 March 1920.[94] In view of his trip to Meran it is unlikely that Kafka attended that particular event; but over the years he had plenty of

90 See also Born, *Kafkas Bibliothek*, p. 158.

91 See Franz Werfel, Vorrede (Foreword). In: Petr Bezruč, *Die schlesischen Lieder* (The Silesian Songs). Leipzig: Kurt Wolff Verlag 1917, pp. 5–22, here p. 16 f.

92 See Hermann Bahr, Vorwort (Foreword). In: Fráňa Šrámek, *Flammen* (Flames). Leipzig: Ernst Rowohlt Verlag 1913, V-VIII, here VI, written in 1912. This foreword, with other texts, is reprinted in the correspondence of Hermann Bahr and Jaroslav Kvapil in an excellent edition by Kurt Ifkovits. See Hermann Bahr – Jaroslav Kvapil: *Briefe, Texte, Dokumente* (Letters, Texts, Documents). Ed by Kurt Ifkovits. Berlin et al.: Lang 2007.

93 Kafka presented one of these books as a gift to the poet Hans Klaus. See Binder, *Prager Profile*, p. 62.

94 *Prager Tagblatt* 45, No. 77, 13 March 1920, p. 4.

opportunities – some of them positively documented – to become acquainted with Březina's work.

FRÁŇA ŠRÁMEK

One of the books in Kafka's library was Otto Pick's German translation of Šrámek's *Flammen* (Flames, original title *Plameny*),[95] which we have already referred to. It was published in Leipzig in 1913 in the last days of the first Rowohlt Verlag, with a foreword by Hermann Bahr. In the same year there appeared *Erwachen* (Awakening / *Probuzení*); in 1920, *Der silberne Wind* (Silver Wind / *Stříbrný vítr*); and in 1921 *Sommer* (Summer / *Léto*) – all in translations by Pick. Kafka was probably also familiar with Šrámek's work from Pfemfert's anthology *Jüngste tschechische Lyrik* (1916). Here, too, the translator was Otto Pick, who in 1927, three years after Kafka's death, compiled his own collection called *Wanderer in den Frühling* (Strolling into Spring). It was published by František Khol (1877–1930), with whom Kafka was in contact – certainly in 1913–14.[96] Khol was chief librarian at the National Museum from 1904 to 1915, then dramaturg at the National Theatre until 1925. Kafka is likely to have also known Šrámek's texts in the Czech original – one identified by Born is *Splav* (The Floodgate).[97]

Kafka almost certainly knew Šrámek personally, either through their mutual friend Otto Pick or through Max Brod, as certain diary entries indicate: 'At Fr.'s with Max',[98] 'Yesterday Fráňa'.[99] This form of the name František is sufficiently unusual – added to the known fact of Šrámek's contacts with Prague's German writers – to justify the assumption that these meetings were indeed with the Czech poet.

For the German intellectuals Fráňa Šrámek embodied the general mood of anarchist, pacifist protest. Together with Stanislav Kostka Neumann, Antonín Sova and Karel Teige, he initiated the establishment of a 'socialist council of intellectual workers' on 6 July 1919,[100] and in a proclamation pub-

95 See Born, *Kafkas Bibliothek*, p. 44.

96 See Jan Wagner, Dopis Franze Kafky inž. Františku Kholovi v Literárním archivu (Franz Kafkas letter to Ing. František Khol in Literární archiv). In: *Sborník národního muzea v Praze. Acta Musei Nationalis Pragae* 8 (1963), Serie C, vol. 8, No. 2, p. 84, and Měšťan, Slované u Franze Kafky, p. 48.

97 See Born, *Kafkas Bibliothek*, p. 9.

98 Diary, 11 April 1922. – See Kafka, *Tagebücher*, p. 273.

99 Diary, 12 June 1922. – See Kafka, *Tagebücher*, p. 923.

100 F. Ulbrich Grochtmann, *Anarchosyndikalismus, Bolschewismus und Proletkult in der Tschechoslowakei 1918–1924. Der Dichter Stanislav Kostka Neumann als Publizist in der tschechoslowakischen Arbeiterbewegung* (Anarchosyndicalism, Bolshevism and Prolekult in the Czechoslovakia 1918–1924: The Poet Stanislav Kostka Neumann as Publicist in the Czechoslovak Proletarian Movement). Munich: Lerche 1979, 101f. See also Binder, *Prager Profile*.

lished in two languages in the periodical *Červen* (June, in Czech literally the 'Red Time'), they called on their German colleagues to join them. Some, such as Hugo Sonnenschein, Franz Werfel and Albert Ehrenstein, actually heeded the call. On 20 March 1920, at a socialist protest evening at the Mozarteum organised by Otto Pick, there were readings from Max Brod, Oskar Baum, H. G. Scholz, Otto Pick, Johannes Urzidil and Fráňa Šrámek.[101] Šrámek was also on the program at a second literary evening on 29 March 1920, when works by Bezruč, Březina, Dyk, Machar, Sova and Karel Čapek were also presented.[102] And on 28 May an 'Abend sozialer Lyrik' (An evening of social poetry) again included texts by Šrámek, as well as Weiß, Trakl, Werfel and Hasenclever.[103]

While Kafka's acquaintance with Šrámek, both literary and personal, is well documented for the latter years of his life, it is doubtful whether they met in the years around 1910 in the anarchist circles mentioned by Max Brod, which will be discussed below.[104]

PETR BEZRUČ

Another book in Kafka's library was the first volume of *Schlesische Lieder* (Songs of Silesia) by Petr Bezruč (1867–1958), published in 1917 in a translation by Rudolf Fuchs and with a foreword by Franz Werfel. (The second volume did not appear until 1926.) Eva Brod, in a letter to Kafka dated 20 December 1917,[105] mentions the book in a way that presupposes his prior knowledge of it,[106] as this particular German edition had enjoyed unexpected success. Fuchs's first translation of Bezruč had appeared in 1912 in *Herder-Blätter*, a Prague journal in which Kafka himself published.[107] We may assume that Kafka was also aware of other Czech writers working and publishing in the same environment, especially since their translators were people he knew well.

As the case of these three writers (Březina, Šrámek and Bezruč) shows, Kafka's acquaintance with Czech literature was by no means limited to a few

---

101 *Prager Tagblatt* 45, No. 59, 9 March 1920, p. 5.
102 *Prager Tagblatt* 45, No. 77, 31 March 1920, p. 4.
103 *Prager Tagblatt* 45, No. 122, 26 May 1920, p. 4.
104 See Brod, *Franz Kafka*, p. 91.
105 Kurt Wolff Verlag, Leipzig. Born dates the book 1917, though it bears no publication date. See Born, *Kafkas Bibliothek*, p. 60. Nezdařil dates the second volume 1926. See Nezdařil, *Česká poezie*, p. 226.
106 See Brod – Kafka, *Eine Freundschaft*, p. 215.
107 No. 3: *Erstes Kapitel des Buches 'Richard und Samuel"* [First chapter of the book 'Richard and Samuel' by Max Brod and Franz Kafka] – with M. Brod; No. 4/5: *Großer Lärm* (A Great Noise). It was also here, in the 'Neue tschechische Literatur' (New Czech literature) section (pp. 47–50); that the first translations of Bezruč appeared (p. 50), with the important introductory texts 'Tschechische Dichtkunst' (Czech poetry) by Otto Pick (pp. 47–49) and 'Petr Bezruč' by Hans Janowitz.

isolated modern authors viewed without context. Rather, his was a deeper, broader understanding, originating in his school years, then fostered and nurtured in the specific context of the Prague intellectual community.

In this Kafka was no exception. Werfel, for instance, the author of *Das Reich Gottes in Böhmen* (The Kingdom of God in Bohemia, 1930)[108], attempts in his foreword to the German edition of Bezruč's Songs of Silesia to invoke the 'creative tradition' of Czech culture by naming, in the same breath, Chelčický, Comenius and Březina:

> But compare the titles that the author of 'Orbis pictus' gave his books with those of Březina; 'The Centre of Safety', 'The Paradise of the Heart' and 'The Mournful' is what Comenius called three of his works; in another, in a strange and mystical architecture, he attempted to construct a 'Pansophia' based on the ground plan of the temple of Solomon. Now consider Březina's titles: 'The Temple Builder', 'Winds from both Poles'. Does one not feel in these chance features the deep, slow, full tolling of the same blood? – Again it must be stressed that Hussitism is not a negative; it is not a nationalistic revolt that sprang from a hatred of Germans: it is the holy urge of an entire nation towards return and rebirth.[109]

Whereas the Leipzig censors failed to pick up these words, their colleagues in wartime Prague and Vienna were sharper-eyed. For the reference to Herder, who saw in Jan Hus and Hussitism the spark that ignited the Reformation, could be seen as implying that the same spark had leapt to Masaryk's *Česká otázka* (The Czech Question) and thence might equally inflame his readers, so that the book was almost certain to be banned. Masaryk, it must be remembered, believed that the same spark had ignited not only the Reformation but the Czech national revival itself, helping to bring to an end the so-called Dark Age[110] and providing, so he thought (as had Palacký before him), a constant axis of meaning running through Czech history. It was this axis that he invoked in his proclamation 'Independent Bohemia', issued in 1915 on the anniversary of Hus's burning at the stake in Constance, at a time when he himself had been branded a war enemy and sentenced to death *in absentio* for high treason. This 'enemy' had won the trust of Werfel and the other 'Arconauts' before 1918.[111]

---

108 The Slav/Czech theme also appears in *Barbara oder Die Frömmigkeit* (Barbara or Piety, 1929; Czech edition *Barbara neboli zbožnost*, 1931). – See also Hartmut Binder, Paul Eisners dreifaches Ghetto (Paul Eisner's triple ghetto). In: Michel Reffet (ed.), *Le monde de Franz Werfel et la morale des nations. / Die Welt Franz Werfels und die Moral der Völker.* Berlin et al.: Peter Lang 2000, pp. 17–137, here p. 33.

109 Werfel, Vorrede, XVI–XVII.

110 Werfel says of this period: 'The Jesuit tossed a hundred thousand books into the flames, which almost devoured a language and its literature for ever'.

111 Brod writes of Masaryk's various activities (the Hilsner affair, the 'Manuscripts dispute') but also of his belief in the future president, which he owed to his Czech-educated friends who

THE LANGER BROTHERS

Kafka's contacts with Jiří (Georg) Mordechai Langer (1894–1943), who had attended the same grammar school as Alfred Fuchs and was on friendly terms with him, began in 1915 on Langer's return from Galicia: 'with Max and Langer on Saturday at the Wonder-rabbi's'.[112] Their acquaintance (it was Brod, Langer's cousin, who had brought them together) soon grew closer on account of their shared interest in religion. They studied and practised Hebrew together;[113] Kafka wrote in his diary about 'Langer's stories'.[114] This is echoed in Langer's Hebrew poem 'On the death of the poet Franz Kafka', most likely written in 1924, but at the latest in 1929.[115] Their exchanges probably covered a wide range of intellectual topics:

> With Langer: he will only be able to read Max's book thirteen days from now. He could have read it on Christmas Day – according to an old custom you are not allowed to read Torah at Christmas (one rabbi made a practice of cutting up his year's supply of toilet paper on that evening) but this year Christmas fell on Saturday.[116]

The last trace of Georg Langer, whom Brod (and Kafka) wished but were unable to help in his work,[117] is a diary entry on 20 October 1921: 'In the afternoon Langer, then Max, who read *Franzi* aloud'.[118] However, Langer's poem suggests that their friendship lasted until Kafka's death.

František Langer (1888–1965), George's brother, also appears to have been in regular contact with Kafka, who asked the Leipzig publisher Kurt Wolff to

---

went to Masaryk's lectures and talked about them afterwards. Brod also recounts a meeting with Masaryk, apparently attended by Werfel and Wertheimer as well, which after TGM's emigration almost cost Brod his job as a civil servant. See Max Brod, Eine Unterredung mit Professor Masaryk (A discussion with Professor Masaryk). In: Ernst Rychnovsky (ed.), *Masaryk und das Judentum* (Masaryk and Jews). Prag: Marsverlagsgesellschaft 1931, pp. 357–362, here pp. 358, 361.

112 Diary, 14 September 1915, and 6 October 1915. – See Kafka, *Tagebücher*, pp. 751, 766.

113 See Jiří Langer, Vzpomínka na Kafku (A Memoir of Kafka). In: Jiří Langer, *Studie, recenze, články, dopisy* (Papers, Reviews, Articles, Letters). Prague: Sefer 1995, pp. 139–141, here p. 140. See also Hartmut Binder, Kafkas Hebräischstudien. Ein biographisch-interpretatorischer Versuch (Kafka's study of Hebrew: A biographically interpretative approach). In: *Jahrbuch der deutschen Schillergesellschaft* 11 (1967), pp. 527–556, here p. 530.

114 Diary, 6 October 1915. – See Kafka, *Tagebücher*, pp. 766–768.

115 For the date see Milan Tvrdík, Franz Kafka und Jiří (Georg) Langer. Zur Problematik des Verhältnisses Kafkas zur tschechischen Kultur (Franz Kafka and Jiří (Georg) Langer: On Kafka's relation to Czech culture). In: Klaus Schenk (ed.), *Moderne in der deutschen und der tschechischen Literatur* (Modern in the German and Czech Literature). Tübingen, Basel: Francke Verlag 2000, pp. 189–199, here p. 199.

116 Franz Kafka, *The Diaries of Franz Kafka, 1914–1923*. Translated by Martin Greenberg. New York: Schocken 1949.

117 Franz Kafka to Max Brod, 14 November 1917. – See Brod – Kafka, *Eine Freundschaft*, p. 193f.

118 Kafka, *The Diaries of Franz Kafka, 1914–1923*, p. 394.

send his friend a review copy of *Betrachtung* (Contemplation). In a letter of 22 April 1914, František Langer, then editor of *Umělecký měsíčník* (Art Monthly) tells Kafka of his intention to 'publish a few translations from the book'.[119] The project came to nothing as the periodical was closed down in the same year; but in 1913 Langer had mentioned Kafka twice in its pages. Discussing the *Der jüngste Tag* series, he particularly appreciates Kafka's fragment 'The Stoker', published in May 1913.[120]

Langer also recalled, in a 1964 television interview, receiving from Kafka a copy of *The Metamorphosis* and giving him his own book *Zlatá Venuše* (Golden Venus).[121] Brod even sees parallels between Langer's drama *Periferie* (The Periphery) and Kafka's *The Trial*.[122] Although Langer recalls attending meetings at the Arco coffee house (Otto Pick translated both his and Čapek's stage works), he claims to have had only a poor command of German.[123] Whether he and Kafka discussed their literary interests in Czech, however, we will probably never know.

MODERNÍ REVUE

If Otokar Březina, who owed his literary and social success to his publications in the *Moderní revue* at the turn of the century, was as significant an influence on the Prague German writers as has been claimed, we must give careful but cautious consideration to Hugo Siebenschein's controversial remark that 'Kafka and his closest friends enjoyed cordial relations with Arnošt Procházka and the poets associated with the *Moderní revue* (Modern Revue)'.[124] This comment has not been discussed by German Kafka scholars, or if so its significance has been played down on the grounds of insufficient evidence. Kafka may or may not, they say, have been acquainted with the *Moderní revue* writers.[125]

---

119 Kafka, *Briefe 1902–1924*, p. 127.

120 *Umělecký měsíčník* 2 (1912/1913, pp. 223–224), and *Umělecký měsíčník* 3 (1913/1914, pp. 30–31). See Josef Čermák, Die Kafka-Rezeption in Böhmen (1913–1949) (Kafka's reception in Bohemia 1913–1949). *Germanoslavica* 1/1–2 (1994), pp. 127–144, here p. 127f.

121 See Josef Čermák, Recepce Franze Kafky v Čechách (1913–1963) (Reception of Franz Kafka in Bohemia 1913–1963). In: *Kafkova zpráva o světě* (Kafka's Report on the World). Prague: Nakladatelství Franze Kafky 2000, 14–36, here p. 16.

122 See Max Brod, *Der Prager Kreis* (The Prague Circle). Stuttgart et al.: W. Kohlhammer 1966, pp. 98, 155.

123 Čermák, Recepce Franze Kafky v Čechách, p. 16.

124 Hugo Siebenschein, Prostředí a čas. Poznámky k osobnosti a dílu Franze Kafky (Milieu and time: Remarks on the personality and oeuvre of Franz Kafka). In: *Franz Kafka a Praha. Vzpomínky, úvahy, dokumenty* (Franz Kafka and Prague. Memories, Reflections, Papers). Prague: Žikeš 1947, pp. 7–24, here p. 22.

125 See Kautman, Franz Kafka p. 50.

In the light of references in Kafka's letters and diaries, however, and the books in his library, there is not the slightest reason to doubt the truth of Siebenschein's observation. Consider the diary entry of 6 November 1910[126] in which Kafka mentions Paul Claudel (1868–1955), who from 1909 to 1911 was consul general in Prague. The French poet and playwright was well known among the young German intelligentsia[127] and was a personal friend of Miloš Marten (1883–1917), who dedicated his dialogue *Nad městem* (Above the City, 1915) to Claudel.[128] In the years around 1910 Miloš Marten (along with Arnošt Procházka and Jiří Karásek ze Lvovic) was a leading light in the *Moderní revue.* The diary entry, added to what we know about Marten, indicates that in all likelihood Kafka moved in the same intellectual circles as the *Moderní revue* writers.

That Kafka knew Claudel is evident from a brief reference in a letter dated 19 July 1920 to Milena Jesenská, who at the time was translating Claudel's essay 'Arthur Rimbaud'.[129] Of course Kafka's main interest was in Milena herself, but the phrase 'this was exactly what' suggests that he was far from indifferent to Claudel:

> Back then I read Claudel's essay immediately, but just once and too quickly; my enthusiasm, however, was neither directed at Claudel nor at Rimbaud. I didn't want to write about it until after I had read it a second time, nonetheless I was very glad this was exactly what you chose to translate. Is it complete?[130]

This is not the only time Kafka mentions the *Moderní revue*. Most significantly, he alludes to it in a letter to Brod,[131] where he quotes from the Czech newspaper *Čas*:

> Her pure, clear, emotional little voice did indeed sound pleasant.[132]

---

126 Kafka, *Tagebücher*, p. 121.

127 Čermák notes that Claudel was invited to the 'Lese- und Redehalle der deutschen Studenten in Prag' (Reading and Lecture Hall of German Students in Prague) – the circle surrounding Franz Werfel. See Josef Čermák, Junge Jahre in Prag. Ein Beitrag zum Freundeskreis Franz Werfels (Early years in Prague: A contribution to the circle of friends around Franz Werfel). In: Klaas-Hinrich Ehlers et al. (eds), *Brücken nach Prag. Deutschsprachige Literatur im kulturellen Kontext der Donaumonarchie und der Tschechoslowakei* (Bridges to Prague: German-written Literature in the Cultural Context of the Habsburg Monarchy and Czechoslovakia). Frankfurt am Main: Peter Lang 2000, pp. 125–162.

128 Published in Czech in 1917; French edition 1925.

129 Milena Jesenská's translation of Arthur Rimbaud appeared in *Tribuna* 2, 8 July 1920.

130 Franz Kafka, *Letters to Milena.* Translated by Philip Boem. New York: Schocken 1990, p. 97.

131 See Brod – Kafka, *Eine Freundschaft*, p. 73. This letter has hitherto been dated to 10 March 1910. But the sequence of events dictates that it cannot have been written before 15 March, when the article Kafka quotes appeared in print.

132 See article in *Čas* 22, No. 74, 15 March 1910, p. 3, entitled 'Literární večer' (Literary evening). For translation see Kafka, *Letters to Friends, Family, and Editors*, p. 64.

The line quoted by Kafka refers to the actress in the title role of *Milá sedmi loupežníků* (Sweetheart of Seven Thieves) by Viktor Dyk, in whose honour a literary evening was held on 11 March 1910 for invited guests – although Kafka can hardly have been among them. Sybil Smolová was by all accounts a remarkable young lady; of interest here, however, is the fact that both Brod and Kafka knew her by name and knew her as an actress (Kafka refers to her as '*die Smolová*'[133]), just as they were familiar with Viktor Dyk and his literary circle. Kafka takes Dyk's part, for example, by distancing himself from a biassed review:

> And that after they have already heaped praise on the predictable filth of the rest of the evening.[134]

This is interesting for two reasons. First, Viktor Dyk (1877–1931) had belonged to the exclusive *Moderní revue* circle in the early years of the century (also using the pseudonyms Peterka and R. Vilde); his debut as a playwright was with the 'Intimate Free Stage' group, whose leading members were closely involved with the *Moderní revue* circle. Second, the actress Sybil Smolová (?1886–1972, baptized Anneta Smolová) made her stage debut on 15 February 1910 in the dramatic poem *Apollonius z Tyany* (Apollonius of Tyana) by Jiří Karásek ze Lvovic, that is to say only a month or so before the literary evening alluded to in Kafka's letter. She was nevertheless not unknown to Kafka and Brod despite the fact that her debut took place in the exclusive circle of the *Moderní revue*, which after a long hiatus resumed its public program with that very performance.

The dramatic poem *Apollonius z Tyany* 'was first performed by students of the drama section of the Vinohrady Academicians in Prague. They decided to put on a series of "literary profile" evenings devoted to modern Czech writers. The first of these took place on 15 February in the large auditorium of the National House in Royal Vinohrady and was dedicated to Jiří Karásek ze Lvovic.'[135] A short introduction by Miloš Marten preceded the performance. The house was full, although apart from the invited critics and playwrights (among them Gabriela Preissová) the audience consisted mostly of 'kindred spirits'.[136] These 'soirées d'auteurs' put on by the *Moderní revue* were by their

---

133 Brod – Kafka, *Eine Freundschaft*, p. 73.

134 Kafka, *Letters to Friends, Family, and Editors*, p. 64.

135 Lumír Kuchař, *Dialogy o kráse a smrti. Studie a materiály k české literatuře přelomu 19. a 20. století* (Dialogues on Beauty and Death: Studies and Documents on the Czech Literature of the 19th century Fin de Siècle). Ed. by Marek Nekula. Brno: Host 1999, p. 32.

136 See Kuchař, *Dialogy*, p. 32. Gabriela Preissová (1862–1946) was known to Brod and Kafka as the author of the drama on which Janáček based the libretto of *Její pastorkyně* (Jenufa), first performed in 1904 in Brno. Following its success in Prague in 1916 Max Brod produced a German translation, with the title *Jenufa*, which was published to coincide with the Vienna premiere on

very nature exclusive (though on this occasion the independent reviews were not entirely kind.)[137]

Another literary evening was held on 2 March 1910. But according to *Přehled* and *Čas*, Smolová performed neither there nor anywhere else. Thus her second stage appearance was probably not until the literary evening devoted to Viktor Dyk mentioned above. Yet even before that performance - which Kafka could not have attended - the name Smolová meant something to both him and Brod. The only explanation seems to be that, thanks to Brod's contacts in the theatre, they did indeed see Smolová's first stage performance; either that, or she caused such a sensation that she was copiously discussed in their circle of friends. That circle, however, must have included people sympathetic to, or at least knowledgeable about, the events put on by *Moderní revue*, which were accessible mostly by invitation only. A likely candidate here would be Otto Pick, Dyk's translator, who was in regular written and personal contact with the playwright.[138] Here it may be worth noting that from February 1909 Max Brod worked for the Post Office Directorate in Prague,[139] where Jiří Karásek ze Lvovic was also employed.

The second hypothesis regarding how Kafka 'knew' Smolová seems the more likely. By all accounts she made a powerful impression: Miloš Marten, who met her at the premiere of *Apollonius z Tyany* and is credited with inventing her stage name Sybil, dedicated not only his short story *Cortigiana* to her, but notably the novella collection *Dravci* (Predators), subtitled *Rozhovor jedné noci* (Conversation of One Night). František Zavřel (1879–1915) was also struck by her, recommending her to Max Reinhardt, whom he had met in Berlin, and accompanying her thither. When Smolová absconded to Munich, Zavřel went after her and, far from persuading her to return to Berlin, urged her to go to Paris. Others, such as Václav Tille, Karel Hugo Hilar and Max Brod (who corresponded with Smolová), hoped to win her for the Prague stage,[140] but by now she was making a career in film in Berlin. Yet however strong the impression she had made at her staged reading, only a handful of people - at least some of whom had been in the audience that evening - can have heard of and talked about the young actress at that time. The critics' reaction to her first public performance had on the whole been positive, though it was

---

16 February 1918. Kafka did not know Preissová personally, but refers to her in letters to Brod dated on 30 June and 5 July 1922, at a time when they were considering visiting her in Planá nad Lužnicí, where Kafka was also staying. See Brod - Kafka, *Eine Freundschaft*, pp. 373, 375f.

137 *Čas*, 17 February 1910. p. 3; *Přehled*, 18 February 1910, p. 396.

138 See Literární archiv Památníku národního písemnictví (Literary Archive of Museum of Czech Literature).

139 See Brod - Kafka, *Eine Freundschaft*, pp. 58, 463.

140 Kuchař, *Dialogy*, p. 92.

hardly mindless adulation.[141] Brod was more enthusiastic in his recollections, declaring he and Kafka 'loved her'.[142]

These were not the only contacts Kafka had with the *Moderní revue* circle. Another admirer of Sybil Smolová was Arnošt Dvořák (1881–1933), who dedicated several of his plays to her. He had at one point also been associated with the *Moderní revue*, as well as with *Nový kult*. His historical drama *Král Václav IV* (King Wenceslas IV, 1910; first performance 1911), often described as a 'crowd drama', was produced in Leipzig in 1914 as *Der Volkskönig* (The People's King) in a translation by Brod, and in Prague at the Vinohrady Municipal Theatre, directed by František Zavřel. Kafka certainly knew the play, at least as a text, as he mentions it in a letter to Brod on 7 August 1920.[143] Moreover, Zavřel's fellow-editor on the theatre periodical *Scéna* in 1913–14, Arnošt Dvořák, was the translator of Werfel's *Bocksgesang* (Goat Song), published in Czech (*Kozlí zpěv*) in 1923, and of Chekhov's story 'On the road' (Czech: *Na velké cestě*), which was published by Staša Jílovská, a friend of Milena Jesenská, in 1920. Kafka refers to this book in a letter to Jesenská.[144]

This brought the Jesenská connection full circle, since Milena's aunt Růžena Jesenská, whose articles Kafka read,[145] had also been close to the *Moderní revue* circle in the early years of the century.[146]

Siebenschein's assertion about Kafka's contacts with the *Moderní revue* seems very plausible, bearing in mind that the journal not only brought important European writers to the notice of Czech readers, but also devoted considerable space to Prague German literature and culture. Thus we see in *Moderní revue* the publication in German of Rilke's poem *Der Kirchhof*; and in the closely affiliated periodical and later publishing house *Symposion* (which counted among its contributors Hugo Kosterka, Arnošt Procházka and Jiří Karásek ze Lvovic), Leppin's *Die Thüren des Lebens* (The Doors of Life, Prague 1901), also in German, as part of their 'Deutsche Serie' (German Serie).[147] It is significant that at a time of growing nationalism a Czech literary periodical should choose to publish in German, thus breaking a major cultural taboo. It shows, at least in the case of the *Moderní revue*, that the boundaries of language and culture in Prague were not only porous but fluid. Siebenschein's

---

141 See Kuchař, *Dialogy*, p. 34.
142 Max Brod, *Pražský kruh* (The Prague Circle). Prague: Akropolis 1993, p. 47.
143 See Brod – Kafka, *Eine Freundschaft*, p. 283.
144 See Kafka, *Briefe an Milena*, p. 314.
145 See Kafka, *Briefe an Milena*, pp. 82, 305.
146 See Robert B. Pynsent, Láska a slečna Jesenská (Love and Miss Jesenská). *Moderní revue 1894–1925*. Prague: Torst 1995, pp. 167–187.
147 See Marek Nekula, Franz Kafka und der Kreis um die Zeitschrift *Moderní revue*. Nebst einigen Bemerkungen zu Kafka und Florians *Dobré dílo* (Franz Kafka and the circle around the journal *Moderní revue*. With remarks on Kafka and Florian's *Dobré dílo*). In: *brücken. Germanistisches Jahrbuch Tschechien – Slowakei*. NF 7 (2000), pp. 153–166.

KMEN

LITERÁRNÍ TÝDENNÍK

ROČNÍK IV. V Praze, dne 22. dubna 1920. ČÍSLO 6.

Franz Kafka: Topič

Fragment

Se svolením autorovým přeložila Milena Jesenská

Když 16letý Karel Rosman, který byl svými chudými rodiči poslán do Ameriky, poněvadž ho svedla služka a měla s ním dítě, vjel již v zpomaleném parníku do newyorského přístavu, spatřil sochu Svobody, kterou již dávno pozoroval, jakoby ve světle náhle prudším. Její paže s mečem trčela jaksi nově vstříc a kolem její postavy vanul volný vzduch.

»Tak vysoko,« řekl si, a v tom, vůbec nemysle na odchod, byl stále rostoucím množstvím nosičů pomalu posunut až k zábradlí.

Jakýsi mladý muž, s nímž se byl při jízdě povrchně seznámil, řekl, předcházeje ho: »Nu, což pak nemáte pražádné chuti, abyste vystoupil?« »Jsem přece již hotov,« řekl Karel usmívaje se, a zdvihl z dobré nálady a poněvadž byl silný chlapec, kufr na ramena. Když však pohlédl za svým známým, který se již vzdaloval s ostatními a mával při tom hůlkou, s úlekem zpozoroval, že zapomněl dole v lodi svůj deštník. Rychle poprosil známého, aby mu laskavě u jeho zavazadla okamžik posečkal, čímž muž nebyl příliš obšťastněn, přehlédl ještě situaci, aby se při návratu vyznal, a pospíchal pryč.

S lítostí nalezl dole zavřenu chodbu, která by jeho cestu byla velice zkrátila, což patrně souviselo s vyloďováním cestujících, a bylo mu namáhavě si hledati cestu nespočetnými malými místnostmi, po krátkých schodech, které stále za sebou následovaly, korridory, neustále se zahýbajícími, prázdným pokojem s opuštěným psacím stolem, až skutečně, poněvadž touto cestou šel teprve jednou nebo dvakrát a vždy ve větší společnosti, úplně zabloudil. Ve své bezradnosti, poněvadž nepotkával lidí a slyšel jen nad sebou šoupání tisíce lidských nohou a pozoroval z dálky jakoby dech, poslední pracování již zastavovaných strojů, počal bez přemýšlení tlouci na první malá dvířka, na která při svém bloudění narazil.

»Vždyť je otevřeno,« ozvalo se uvnitř a Karel otevřel dvéře s poctivým oddechnutím. »Proč tlučete tak zběsile do dveří?« řekl ohromný člověk a skoro se po Karlovi ani neohlédl. Jakýmsi malým, svrchním oknem padalo ponuré, nahoře na lodi již dávno opotřebované světlo v žalostnou kabinu a v ní stáli těsně vedle sebe postel, skříň, židle a muž, jakoby složeni ve skladišti. »Zabloudil jsem,« řekl Karel, »ani jsem toho tak za jízdy nepozoroval, ale to je strašně veliká loď.« »To je pravda,« řekl muž s jistou pýchou, nepřestav se při tom nimrati se zámkem malého kufru, který oběma rukama vždy znovu přitlačil a čekal při tom na sklapnutí závory. »Ale pojďte přece dovnitř,« pokračoval muž, »nebudete přece státi venku.« »Nevyrušuji?« ptal se Karel. »Ale jak pak byste rušil?« »Jste Němec?« pokusil se Karel zabezpečiti, poněvadž mnoho slyšel o nebezpečí, které hrozí v Americe nově příchozím, obzvláště od Irů. »I jsem, jsem,« řekl muž. Karel ještě váhal. Tu muž náhle uchopil kliku a přisunul dveřmi, které rychle zavřel, Karla k sobě dovnitř. »Nemohu vystát, dívá-li se sem

Translation of Franz Kafka's fragment The Stoker by Milena Jesenská
Kmen 4 (1920), No. 6

perceived influence of Arnošt Procházka, however, is less apparent. A close study of the *Moderní revue* writers may reveal certain parallels in terms of motif; but the nature of Kafka's writing is far removed from theirs.

THE LEFT AND MILENA JESENSKÁ

The widely held conviction that Kafka was particularly close to the Czech political left stems largely from the fact that during his lifetime Milena Jesenská's translations of his stories appeared in left-wing periodicals such as *Kmen*, *Tribuna* and *Cesta*.[148] Other translations, by Milena Illová, were published in the social-democrat *Právo lidu*.[149] The Czech left-wing press also carried appreciations of Kafka's work (Stanislav Kostka Neumann in *Kmen*[150] and *Rudé právo*[151]), as well as his obituary (in *Komunistická revue*[152]). Various 'testimonials' (see Mareš, Janouch, Kácha) that he had contacts with Czech anarchists and attended their meetings for about a year, starting in October 1909, also played a part in accentuating Kafka's leftist sympathies. Yet despite the undisputed interest in Kafka's work shown by the Czech left in the early 20th century,[153] which was partly connected with his translator Milena Jesenská and with the socialist convictions of some of the people he knew (the Café Herrenhof group,[154] Max Brod,[155] Otto Pick), it is debatable, to say the least, whether Kafka had any active contact with Czech anarchists in the years around 1910.

---

148 See Franz Kafka, *Topič* (The Stoker). *Kmen* 4, No. 6, 22 April 1920, pp. 61–72; Franz Kafka, *Nešťastný* (Unhappiness). *Tribuna* 2, No. 166, 16 July 1920, pp. 1–2; Franz Kafka, *Náhlá procházka, Výlet do hor, Neštěstí mládence, Kupec, Cesta domů, Ti, kteří běží mimo* (The sudden walk, Excursion into the mountains, Bachelor's ill luck, The tradesman, The way home, Passers-by). *Kmen* 4, No. 26, 9 September 1920, pp. 308–310; Franz Kafka, *Zpráva pro akademii* (A report to an Academy). *Tribuna* 2, No. 227, 26 September 1920, pp. 1–4; Franz Kafka, *Závodníkům na uváženou* (Reflections for gentlemen-jockeys). *Tribuna* 4, Christmas supplement, 24 December 1922, p. 8; Franz Kafka, *Soud* (The judgment). *Cesta* 5 (1923), No. 26/27, pp. 369–372.

149 See Franz Kafka, *Před zákonem* (Before the law), *Právo lidu* 29, No. 253, 24 October 1920. Sunday supplement No. 43.

150 *Kmen* 4, No. 6, 22 April 1920.

151 *Rudé právo*, *Dělnická besídka*, 24 August 1924.

152 *Komunistická revue*, 1924, p. 479.

153 For Kafka's reception by the Czech left, see esp. Čermák, Die Kafka-Rezeption in Böhmen, p. 130 f. *Germanoslavica* 1/1–2 (1994), pp. 127–144, here p. 130f.

154 See e.g. Alena Wagnerová, *Milena Jesenská. Biographie* (Milena Jesenská: A Biography). Berlin: Bollmann 1994.

155 See e.g. Marek Nekula, Theodor Lessing und Max Brod. Eine mißlungene Begegnung (Theodor Lessing and Max Brod: A failed encounter). In: *brücken. Germanistisches Jahrbuch Tschechien – Slowakei*. NF 5 (1997), pp. 115–122.

Prochazka, and later Binder, argue against any such involvement.[156] First there is the fact that at about that time Kafka became the co-founder of an asbestos factory, and any contact with anarchist elements would have been in stark contradiction to his social position. Yet there is no mention of any conflict in his diary (which at the time he kept quite assiduously), an omission that would have been inconceivable, or at least very surprising, given what we know of Kafka's personality. It would have been equally surprising for Max Brod not to know anything of such contacts, as he was very close to Kafka at that time. Later Brod was to write of his association with Michal Kácha (1874–1940):

> With another group of Czechs seated at the table in this big inn room sat another German guest, who looked very thin, and very young, although he was apparently over thirty. He didn't utter a word the whole evening, only looked on attentively with his great grey gleaming eyes, which stood out in strange contrast to his brown face under his thick coal-black hair. It was Franz Kafka the writer. He often came and attended this gathering quite peacefully. Kácha liked him, and called him a 'kliďas', that is, a 'close-mouth'.[157]

We may ask whether Kácha would really have liked such a listener, who could easily have been mistaken for a secret policeman. It is also surprising that the police, who had disbanded the *Klub mladých* in October 1910, were never alerted to Kafka by any of their informants. On the contrary, when he was setting up the asbestos factory they issued him with a certificate of no criminal record; and on more than one occasion during the war they provided him with a passport.[158]

Prochazka and Binder have already found a number of inconsistencies in various 'eyewitness' accounts – all published at a later date – by Michal Mareš (1946), Gustav Janouch (1951), Michal Kácha, and Max Brod (1938/1954, 3rd edition) – which tend to compromise their reliability. For instance, Kafka

---

156 See Willy Prochazka, Kafka's association with Jaroslav Hašek and the Czech anarchists. *Modern Austrian Literature* 11 (1978), No. 3–4, pp. 275–287, Binder, *Kafka. Ein Leben in Prag*, p. 115 f.

157 Max Brod, *Franz Kafka: A Biography*. Translated by G. Humphreys Roberts and Richard Winston. New York: Da Capo, 1995, p. 86.

158 The 'Club of the Young' had been in trouble with the police since 1905 and was disbanded (after prior surveillance) in 1910. Kafka was on a number of occasions issued with a certificate of no criminal record: in 1906, when applying for the civil service post he briefly held at the *Zemský soud* (county court); in 1907, on joining Assicurazioni Generali; in 1910, on his lifetime civil service appointment; in 1911, on becoming a partner in the factory; and repeatedly in connection with his foreign trips (1915, 1916 and 1917). This would have been highly unlikely had he attended the Club's meetings regularly. See related material in the Literární archiv Památníku národního písemnictví (Literary Archive of Museum of Czech Literature). Bauer points out that some of these documents are signed by Commissar Slavíček, the very man who banned the Club. See Johann Bauer [Čermák, Josef] *Kafka und Prag* (Kafka and Prague). Stuttgart: Belser 1971, pp. 106 f., 116.

cannot possibly have known František Gellner, Karel Toman, Fráňa Šrámek, Stanislav Kostka Neumann, Michal Mareš and Jaroslav Hašek from his attendance at the Club, as Brod later claimed.[159] Gellner lived in Munich from 1905–1908, and then in Paris; Toman, in his 1906 volume *Melancholická pouť* (Melancholy Pilgrimage), was already distancing himself from anarchism; and Šrámek and Kafka were yet to meet. Neumann, who left Prague in 1904 and from 1905 lived in Řečkovice and later at Bílovice near Brno, was familiar with Kafka's name through Milena Jesenská but does not recall meeting him in that period. Hašek turned away from anarchism in 1907 and in 1910 married the eminently respectable Jarmila Mayerová.[160] In any case it is unlikely that Kafka knew Hašek personally, either then or at a later date. František Langer, who knew Kafka and attended the anarchist events and election meetings of Hašek's quasi-illegal Progress Party (*Strana pokroku*) where Kafka is alleged to have met the future creator of Švejk, does not remember ever seeing Kafka there.[161] Michal Mareš (1893–1971), whose Czech book *Policejní šťára* (A Police Raid) Kafka praised[162] and whom Kafka himself discounted as a witness of any import,[163] could not have been a member of the Club by reason of his age. In the case of Gustav Janouch (1903–1968) we should ask ourselves whether Kafka, given his critical attitude towards Janouch,[164] would have shared with him such private and for him as a public servant incriminating information regarding his (alleged) anarchist past. All this would seem to rule out any affinity or acquaintance between Kafka and the Czech anarchists.

Solid evidence of Kafka's links with the Czech Left can thus be found only among those who translated him and wrote about him. The search for that reception takes us, via Ernst Pollak, to Milena Jesenská, whose translations of Kafka appeared in the left-wing press partly because that is where her political sympathies[165] and those of her husband and his circle lay, and partly because of the cosmopolitan outlook of the intellectual left.

Kafka's reception among Czechs has been repeatedly and thoroughly examined elsewhere,[166] and is not the subject of this study. But we cannot completely ignore the first Czech reactions to his writings. We know from

159 See Brod, *Franz Kafka*, p. 91.

160 Jarmila Mayerová Hašková (1887–1931), journalist and writer of fiction, mostly for children.

161 See Čermák, Recepce Franze Kafky, p. 17.

162 Kafka to Milena Jesenská, Sept. 1921. See Kafka, *Briefe an Milena*, p. 306.

163 According to a letter to Milena Jesenská, Kafka calls him a *pitomec* (fool, buffoon). Franz Kafka to Milena Jesenská, 22 July 1920. – See Kafka, *Briefe an Milena*, p. 137.

164 Kafka to Robert Klopstock, mid-September 1921. – See Franz Kafka, *Briefe 1902–1924* (Letters 1902–1924). Ed. by Max Brod. Frankfurt am Main: S. Fischer 1958, p. 352. For the limited reliability of Janouch's testimony, see also Marek Nekula, Poznámky (Comments). In: Gustav Janouch, *Hovory s Kafkou* (Conversations with Kafka). Translated by Eva Kolářová, edited and commented by Marek Nekula, epilogue by Veronika Tuckerová. Prague: Torst 2009, pp. 223–252.

165 For his social milieu, opinions and activities at that time see Wagnerová, *Milena Jesenská*.

166 Most recently Čermák, Recepce Franze Kafky.

his correspondence with Milena and Ottla that Kafka followed Milena's work with keen (if not entirely regular) interest,[167] so we may assume he was familiar with the contents of at least those issues of the Czech periodicals in which her translations and reviews appeared. Those publications were all left-leaning. First among them was *Kmen* (1917–1922), which was edited by Stanislav Kostka Neumann from 1919 until its amalgamation with *Červen*[168] (1918–1921) – also an important source for Kafka. *Červen*'s place was filled by *Proletkult* (1922–1924).[169] It was in these magazines that he came across 'the first good original piece', making a note of its author Vladislav Vančura (1891–1942) and mentioning him in a letter to Milena Jesenská.[170] From Kafka's letters to Milena it is also abundantly clear that he read the newspapers and magazines she published in very carefully, noticing even a short piece like 'Židé a komunism' (Jews and Communism) containing an attack on his ex-classmate Rudolf Illový, which he cites in a letter to Milena.[171]

Thus in issue No. 23 of *Kmen* (19 August 1920), in which the first instalment of Jesenská's translation of a study of Hölderlin by Gustav Landauer appeared, Kafka could also read Vančura's 'Vzpomeň si na něco veselého!' (Remember something cheerful!), as well as texts by Josef Hora, Čestmír Jeřábek, Ivan Kastner and František Němec; in *Kmen* No. 24 (26 August 1920) there were pieces by Jindřich Hořejší, Zdeňek Kalista, Eduard Kučera and Albert Gleizes on dadaism; and in *Kmen* No. 25 (2 September 1920) texts by Tolstoy ('Cizinec a mužik', Jesenská's translation of 'The stranger and the peasant'), Zdeněk Kalista again, Anatoly Vasilyevich Lunacharsky, and others; and in No. 26 (9 September 1920), besides Jesenská's translations of his own stories, he would have found Franz Werfel, Max Krell, Ivan Kastner and Miloš Jirko. In this way, through reading articles, new prose and reviews, Kafka got to know many Czech avant-garde writers and artists, in a context where his own works were presented for the first time in a language other than German alongside texts by Franz Werfel, Hugo Sonnenschein and others.

The name of Karel Čapek also appears in Kafka for the first time in connection with Milena Jesenská, when he sends her a 'little volume' ('*Bändchen*')

---

167 E.g. Franz Kafka to Milena Jesenská, April 1920, 21 July 1920, 26 August 1920, 2 September 1920, September 1920 (*Kmen*), 22 October 1920 (*Červen*). See Kafka, *Briefe an Milena*, pp. 8, 135, 228, 245, 277, 284; Franz Kafka, *Letters to Milena*. Translated by Philip Boem. New York: Schocken 1990, pp. 4–8, 101, 168, 181. See also Franz Kafka to Ottla, 8 May 1920, from Merano. – See Kafka, *Briefe an Ottla*, p. 87.

168 From 1919–1920 Michael Kácha worked on the paper as a subeditor, and from 1921 as editor. He was succeeded by S.K. Neumann.

169 Published by the Communist Party of Czechoslovakia, *Proletkult* was also edited by S.K. Neumann.

170 Franz Kafka to Milena Jesenská, 26 August 1920. – See Kafka, *Briefe an Milena*, p. 228. Vančura's work was not published in book form until 1923.

171 Franz Kafka to Milena Jesenská, 22 October 1920. – See Kafka, *Briefe an Milena*, p. 284.

she has asked for[172]. But he must certainly have come across him before that, if only because Čapek had been involved as an editor in the *Jüngste tschechische Lyrik* anthology of 1916, which was discussed above. He was another Czech writer who was translated into German relatively quickly – his *Der Räuber* (*Loupežník*; The Robber) was given a public reading in German at the Mozarteum on 29 March 1920.[173] Not only was Čapek represented in the compendium *Tschechische Erzähler* (Czech Storytellers, 1921), edited by Otto Pick; his drama *R.U.R.* appeared in instalments in the *Prager Presse* in a German version entitled *W.U.R.*, translated by Otto Pick, who also worked on the newspaper.[174] Although at the time of the Mozarteum reading Kafka was in Matliary in the Tatra Mountains, he can hardly have failed to notice a writer who had established himself so successfully in his own immediate intellectual circle. The correspondence with Milena Jesenská provides tangible evidence for a fact that even without her would be evident enough: Kafka had a thorough knowledge of contemporary Czech literature, which he acquired through the medium of the Czech language.

FLORIAN AND *OPUS BONUM*

Given the early reception of Kafka's work it may come as a surprise to learn that the first Czech (and first foreign-language) book edition of his fiction was published by a group associated with the Catholic reformer Josef Florian (1873–1941), based at Stará Říše in South Moravia. Kafka may have been interesting for this group in the course of his perennial search for moral and spiritual truth. As to who brought Florian and Kafka together, the literature suggests several possible candidates.

Gustav Janouch claims it was he, thanks to his translation of *Ein Traum* (A Dream; Czech *Sen*), published as an introduction to Otto Coester's six etchings for *Proměna* (The Metamorphosis; Stará Říše, 1929), who initiated the first Czech book edition of the novella.[175] In the same year one of its translators, Ludvík Vrána, also published translations of eighteen stories from *Ein Landarzt* (A Country Doctor) and *Betrachtung* (Contemplation). Janouch also claims it was he who first made Kafka aware of *Opus Bonum* (in Czech *Dobré dílo*) by bringing him an anthology of French religious verse in Czech

172 Franz Kafka to Milena Jesenská, November 1920. – See Kafka, *Briefe an Milena*, p. 297. Čapek's play *Loupežník* (The Robber) appeared in 1920, as did his volume of criticism *Kritika slov* (Critique of Words), which Kafka probably also read.

173 *Prager Tagblatt* 45, No. 77, 31 March 1920, p. 4.

174 *Prager Presse* 1, No. 96, 3 June 1921.

175 Translated by Ludvík Vrána and F. Pastor, Stará Říše 1929.

translation[176] that had come out in the *Nova et Vetera* series.[177] It was Florian, on the other hand, who allegedly suggested that Janouch keep a record of his conversations with Kafka in the mid-1920s.[178]

Yet Josef Florian and his collaborators seem to have preferred a more direct form of contact with their authors. Jakub Deml, at one point a member of Florian's circle, was able to publish his authorized translation of Rilke's *Geschichten vom lieben Gott* (Stories about God, 1900/1904; Czech edition *Příběhy o Pánu Bohu*, 1906) without any special mediation. In view of this, Jiří Olič's notion that the proposal to translate Kafka,[179] as well as some of the funding, came from his 'schoolmate' Kamil Vaněk (1884–1964), would seem somewhat reckless. If there is any truth in it, then that 'schoolmate' must have been a relative of Zdenko Vaněk who, according to the class register of the German grammar school in Prague Old Town, was Czech, Catholic and born in 1881.[180] He was only in Kafka's class in the penultimate eighth year, excelling only in the optional Czech lessons – which of course Kafka also attended.

It would seem, however, that no such mediation was necessary. Florian's circle, which was by then well established in the Czech literary world and well known among the informed, certainly had need of sponsors, but not of agents. We know, for example, that Florian and his associates regularly read the *Prager Tagblatt* and cultivated personal contacts with its staff.[181]

Moreover, Josef Florian and Franz Kafka must have known of each other's existence before 1920, which also speaks against the scenarios presented by Janouch and Olič. In a letter to Milena on 9 July 1920, Kafka mentions Rudolf Jílovský (husband of Milena's friend Staša Jílovská[182]) and his planned trip to Brno to visit Florian. In another letter a few days later, writing about the Lucerna palace, he recalls the *Opus Bonum* window display that had at one time been in the arcade there.[183] From this it is clear that he knew of *Opus Bonum* before 1920 – and not necessarily through Milena Jesenská and her friends.

One thing is certain: Kafka's discovery of Josef Florian and his publishing and other activities did not happen in the way we have been made to believe. The reason is simple: on his walks around Prague Kafka kept his eyes open. When he spotted a display in the Lucerna arcade advertising *Dobré dílo* publi-

176 See Janouch, *Gespräche mit Kafka*, p. 70.
177 Published by Josef Florian in Stará Říše.
178 See Janouch, *Gespräche mit Kafka*, p. 70.
179 See Jiří Olič, *Čtení o Jakubu Demlovi* (Reading about Jakub Deml). Olomouc: Votobia 1993, p. 30.
180 See the chapter 'Franz Kafka at school', p. 139.
181 See Nekula, Theodor Lessing und seine Rezeption.
182 See Kafka, *Briefe an Milena*, p. 100.
183 See Kafka, *Briefe an Milena*, p. 107.

cations, his interest in the Czech cultural scene naturally made him commit the name to memory. The fact that from 1919 to 1922 a close friend of Milena Jesenská, Staša Jílovská, worked for Josef Florian as publisher and manager of his Prague office (she produced over twenty titles),[184] explains Kafka's increased interest in the group in around 1920.

If Josef Florian and his circle needed agents or mediators at all, then the most likely person in Kafka's case was Staša Jílovská. As early as in 1919 she wrote to Florian offering him 'a book by Franz Kafka, a German expressionist, the best, the translation of which someone is offering gratis'.[185] That 'someone' was most likely Milena Jesenská. But Florian had already heard the name Franz Kafka – he just hadn't paid him much attention.[186] Then on 23 February 1920 he wrote to Jílovská asking her to send a book 'by that Kafka'.[187] And in another letter on 19 November 1920 he ordered, among other titles, a copy of *In the Penal Colony*, adding the publishing details and price: '*In der Strafkolonie. Erzählung*. Kurt Wolff Verlag, München, 9 K 60'.[188] It was, moreover, the only German-language edition he asked for in that letter. Jílovská confirmed the order on 24 November with a promise to dispatch it in the next few days,[189] so we may assume he received it. This was the moment, it seems, when the foundations were laid for future translations and editions of Kafka: the translations by P. L. Vrána that appeared in Florian's *Archa* (The Ark) in 1929, and the book edition of *Proměna* (The Metamorphosis) translated by Vrána and F. Pastor, also published at Stará Říše in 1929.[190] That publication in turn led to editions by Josef Portman in Litomyšl.[191] It was there, in 1932, that excerpts from *The Trial* appeared in *Gedeon* (which called itself a 'Revue en miniature for the spiritual life of the present and for the friends of Palestine'),[192] one of whose contributors was Jakub Deml, a former close associate of Josef Flori-

184 See Petr F. Hájek, Kouzelné přátelství (A wonderful friendship). In: Josef Florian – Staša Jílovská, *Vzájemná korespondence 1919–1922* (Mutual Correspondence 1919–1922). Prague: Documenta 1993, pp. 7–10, here p. 7f.

185 Florian – Jílovská, *Vzájemná korespondence*, p. 96.

186 Josef Florian to Staša Jílovská, 31 December 1919. – See Florian – Jílovská, *Vzájemná korespondence*, p. 98.

187 Florian – Jílovská, *Vzájemná korespondence*, p. 112.

188 Florian – Jílovská, *Vzájemná korespondence*, p. 144.

189 See Florian – Jílovská, *Vzájemná korespondence*, p. 145.

190 See Nekula, Franz Kafka und der Kreis um die Zeitschrift *Moderní revue*, Čermák, Die Kafka-Rezeption in Böhmen, Čermák, Recepce Franze Kafky.

191 See Franz Kafka, *Starý list* (A Page from an Old Manuscript). Litomyšl: Portmann 1928; Franz Kafka, *Sen* (A Dream). Translated by Gustav Janouch, illustrations by Otto Coester. Stará Říše 1929; Franz Kafka *Proměna* (The Metamorphosis). Translated by L. Vrána and F. Pastor. Stará Říše 1929; Franz Kafka, *Zpráva pro akademii* (A Report to an Academy). Litomyšl: Portman 1929; Franz Kafka, *Venkovský lékař* (A Country Doctor). Litomyšl: Portman 1931.

192 This subtitle was changed several times.

an.[193] Similarly, the publication in the magazine *Středisko* in 1932/33 of the poem 'On the Death of a Poet: For Franz Kafka', by Jiří Langer (who translated it from Hebrew into Czech), can be linked to Florian and his circle.[194] Other Kafka editions by Catholic publishers go back to the same source.[195] But that would be another study altogether: Kafka as Reading and Myth.

PROOF-READING CZECH TRANSLATIONS

Kafka made a point of reading the Czech translations of his texts that were published in his own lifetime. A favourite (but by no means the only) piece of evidence for his ability to correct translations from German into Czech is his revision of Milena Jesenská's version of 'The Stoker', which is noteworthy in the way it demonstrates an active as well as a passive knowledge of Czech:

> Column I line 2 *arm* here also has the secondary meaning: pitiable, but without any special emphases of feeling, a sympathy without understanding that Karl has with his parents as well, perhaps *ubozí*
> l 9 *freie Lüfte* is a little more grand, but there's probably no alternative
> l 17 *z dobré nálady a poněvadž byl silný chlapec* should be removed entirely.[196]

Kafka is certainly right in saying that the Czech adjective *ubohý* (pitiable, miserable) is a closer semantic equivalent for the German *arm* in the first sentence of his text than *chudý* (poor). He explains why himself. The choice of the form *ubozí* (nominative plural), which refers to both parents, indicates that Kafka preferred the active verbal construction rather than the passive, that is, something like 'whom his poor parents had sent to America' rather than the passive 'who had been sent to America by his poor parents', where instrumental *ubohými* would be used in Czech.[197] Jesenská went for the second option, in other words for the more literal translation using the compound passive (the German is: *der von seinen armen Eltern nach Amerika geschickt worden war*[198]), which is further removed from habitual Czech usage than what Kafka suggests, partly because compound passive forms (even taking

---

193 See Marek Nekula, Jakub Deml zwischen 'Österreichisch', 'Tschechisch', 'Deutsch' (Jakub Deml between 'Austrian', 'Czech', 'German'). In: *brücken. Germanistisches Jahrbuch Tschechien – Slowakei.* NF 6 (1998), pp. 3–31, p. 59.

194 See Tvrdík, Franz Kafka und Jiří (Georg) Langer, here p. 199.

195 See Čermák, Die Kafka-Rezeption in Böhmen, p. 132f.

196 Franz Kafka to Milena Jesenská May 1920. – See Kafka, *Letters to Milena*, p. 13.

197 Kafka, Topič, p. 61.

198 Franz Kafka, *Ein Landarzt und andere Drucke zu Lebzeiten* (A Country Doctor and Other Texts Published in his Lifetime). Ed. by Hans-Gerd Koch. Frankfurt am Main: S. Fischer 1994, p. 55.

aspect into account) are less common in Czech than in German[199] and, at least here, would sound rather formal.

Kafka's dissatisfaction with the phrase *freie Lüfte* is also perfectly understandable. Jesenská translates his *und um ihre Gestalt wehten freie Lüfte* (around her form the free breezes blew)[200] as *kolem její postavy vanul volný vzduch.*[201] But since the 'figure' here is the *Freiheitsgöttin* (Goddess of Freedom), which Jesenská renders as *socha Svobody* (Statue of Liberty), it would seem that the most recent Czech translation of 'The Stoker' by Věra Koubová, who chooses the combination *svobodné povětří / bohyně Svobody*[202] ('free breezes' / 'Godess of Freedom'), better expresses the abstract sense of the German *frei* in *freie Lüfte*, with its obvious echo of *Freiheit*, than Jesenská's version.

Generally, Kafka's comments all go to show that his passive command of Czech was excellent while also indicating a good active command. The last note in the passage cited above is not a comment on the translation but a correction of his own text, which he wants to shorten, and illustrates Kafka's ability to work creatively on a Czech text:

> „Ich bin doch fertig", sagte Karl, ihn anlachend, und hob *aus Übermut, und weil er ein starker Junge war*, seinen Koffer auf die Achsel.[203]
>
> „Ale vždyť jsem hotov," usmál se na něj Karel a *z bujnosti a protože byl mladý a silný*, zvedl kufr na rameno.[204]
>
> 'I'm all ready,' said Karl with a smile, and *in his exuberance, and because he was a powerful youth, he* swung his suitcase onto his shoulder.[205]

Further evidence of Kafka's exceptional passive knowledge of Czech is his grasp of the subtle differences between Czech equivalents of the German *Platz* – *místo* ('place'), but also *náměstí* ('square') – and of the use of the spatial prepositions *v* (*in* / in) and *na* (*an, auf* / at, on) in the Czech translation of his short story 'The tradesman:[206]

---

199 František Štícha et al., *Akademická gramatika spisovné češtiny* (Academic Grammar of Standard Czech). Prague: Academia 2013, pp. 618 ff., 631 ff.

200 Kafka, *Ein Landarzt*, p. 55. Franz Kafka, Selected Stories. Translated and edited by Stanley Corngold. New York, London: J. J. Norton 2005, p. 13.

201 Kafka, Topič, p. 61.

202 Franz Kafka, *Povídky I. Proměna a jiné texty vydané za života* (Short Stories I. The Metamorphosis and other Texts Published in his Lifetime). Translated by Vladimír Kafka, Marek Nekula, Věra Koubová, Josef Čermák. Prague: Nakladatelství Franze Kafky 1999, p. 59.

203 Kafka, *Ein Landarzt*, p. 55. My emphases.

204 Kafka, *Povídky* I, p. 59. My emphases.

205 Franz Kafka, *Stories 1904–1924*. Translated by J. A. Underwood, foreword by Jorge Luis Borges. London: Abacus 1995, p. 59. My emphases.

206 Kafka, *Náhlá procházka...*, p. 309.

Just so you see I was reading it for mistakes: instead of *bolí uvnitř v čele a v spáncích – uvnitř na...* or something like that – the thought is namely that just as claws can work on the forehead from the outside, this can also happen on the inside; *potírajíce se* means to become confused? To thwart one another? – Right after that, instead of *volné místo*, it might be better to say *náměstí* – *pronásledujte jen*, I don't know whether *nur* is *jen* here, you see this *nur* is a Prague-Jewish *nur*, signifying a challenge like 'go ahead and do it' – the final words aren't translated literally. You separate the maidservant from the man, whereas in German they merge.[207]

His reservations about the suitability of Jesenká's *potírajíce se* ('fighting each other') for the German *durcheinander gehen* in the sentence *Doch genießet die Aussicht des Fensters, wenn die Prozessionen aus allen drei Straßen kommen, einander nicht ausweichen, durcheinander gehn und zwischen ihren letzten Reihen den freien Platz wieder entstehen lassen* (But enjoy yourselves there looking out of the window, see the processions converging at once, not giving way to each other and leaving the open space free again.)[208] are aptly and adequately expressed in his suggestion of an alternative phrase: *einander durchkreuzen? / kříží se navzájem?* (lit. 'cross [pass through] each other').

His doubts about the use of *jen* (only) as a modal particle in the context *Pronásledujte jen toho nenápadného muže*[209] for *Verfolget nur den unscheinbaren Mann*[210] (lit. 'Only follow that inconspicuous-looking man') are also justified, as the use of this particle (when it is used at all) requires a different word order in colloquial Czech than does the German *nur*, with *jen* at the beginning of the sentence, often followed by *klidně* (= German *ruhig*), as in Koubová's translation of 'The Stoker': *Jen klidně pronásledujte toho nenápadného muže!*[211] (roughly: 'Go right ahead and follow that inconspicuous man'). The word order used by Jesenská is not impossible, but the effect is too formal for direct speech.

The final sentence of the passage quoted above also makes it clear that Jesenská's translation (listed third below) contains some semantic inaccuracies, particularly in her rendering of the German *während* (while):

'*Dann* muß ich aussteigen, den Aufzug hinunterlassen, an der Türglocke läuten, *und* das Mädchen öffnet die Tür, *während ich grüße*.'[212]

---

207 Franz Kafka to Milena Jesenská, September 1920. Kafka, *Letters to Milena*, p. 207 f.

208 Kafka, *Ein Landarzt*, p. 23.

209 Kafka, *Náhlá procházka...*, p. 309.

210 Kafka, *Ein Landarzt*, p. 24. Franz Kafka, *Short Stories*. Ed. by Nahum N. Glatzer. London: Vintage 1999, p. 386.

211 Kafka, *Povídky* I, 23. See also Marek Nekula, *System der Partikeln im Deutschen und Tschechischen unter besonderer Berücksichtigung der Abtönungspartikeln* (The System of Particles in German and Czech with special Respect to Modal Particles). Tübingen: Niemeyer 1996, p. 54.

212 Kafka, *Ein Landarzt*, p. 24. My emphases.

> 'Pak musím vystoupit, poslat výtah dolů, zazvonit u dveří, a služebná otvírá, *zatímco já zdravím*.'[213] (literally: '*Then* I must get out, send the lift down, ring the doorbell, and the maid opens the door *while* I *greet* [her] [i.e. say Good evening].')

> *Nyní* musím vystoupiti, spustiti zdviž, zvoniti na zvonek u dveří; služka otvírá dveře *a já vcházím*.'[214] (literally: '*Now* I must get out, send the lift down, ring the doorbell; the maid opens the door *and* I *enter*.')

In this context we should also mention Kafka's reaction to another of Milena Jesenská's translations, although in this quotation his linguistic knowledge can only be inferred:

> The essay is much better than in German, although it still has some holes – or rather entering it is like entering a swamp, it's so difficult having to pull out your foot at every step. Recently a reader of *Tribuna* conjectured that I must have done a lot of research in the lunatic asylum. 'Only in my own', I said, whereupon he still tried to make a compliment out of 'my own lunatic asylum'. (There are 2 or 3 small misunderstandings in the translation. / I'm holding onto the translation for a little while.)[215]

The editor of Kafka's letters to Milena tells us the 'essay' in question was Gustav Landauer's article on Hölderlin, which was 'no easy reading even for Germans' and consequently caused Jesenská some difficulties. This relatively long piece appeared in instalments in *Kmen*.[216] Demanding though the text may have been, Kafka was capable of making a critical evaluation of Jesenská's translation and pointing out various mistakes, which he may have then discussed with her when they met in Gmünd on 14–15 August 1920.

But Kafka's correspondence with Milena Jesenská provides evidence of his considerable knowledge of Czech not only in his comments on her translations and his ability to detect errors, including misprints, in Czech – as for example when he asks Milena what the word '*pammatikální*' means (it should have read '*gramatikální*' = 'grammatical').[217] Kafka also reads, cites and comments – mostly on the letters themselves, responding sensitively and considerately to Milena's sometimes infelicitous formulations:

> You write: 'Ano máš pravdu, mám ho ráda. Ale F., i tebe mám ráda' (Yes, you are right, I do love him. But F., I also love you) – I am reading this sentence very exactly, pausing

213 Kafka, *Povídky* I, p. 23. My emphases.
214 Kafka, *Náhlá procházka*..., p. 309. My emphases.
215 Kafka, *Letters to Milena*, p. 137
216 Gustav Landauer, Friedrich Hölderlin. *Kmen* 4, No. 23 (19 Aug. 1920), pp. 269–274, No. 24 (26 Aug. 1920), pp. 283–286, No. 25 (2 Sept. 1920), pp. 294–297.
217 See Kafka, *Briefe an Milena*, p. 130.

in particular at the 'also' – it's all correct. You would not be Milena if it weren't correct and what would I be if you weren't, and it's also better that you write it from Vienna than say it in Prague. All this I perfectly understand, maybe better than you and yet out of some weakness I can't get over the sentence, it reads endlessly, and finally I'm transcribing it here for you to see as well and for us to read together, temple to temple. (Your hair against my temple.)[218]

CONCLUSION

We may conclude that Kafka's knowledge of Czech literature and culture should not be underestimated. That applies equally to the classics of the 19th century, which Kafka was introduced to in his Czech lessons at school, and to contemporary literature, as besides regularly reading the Czech press he also kept himself well-informed about the Czech arts scene and was familiar even with non-mainstream groups such as *Moderní revue* and *Dobré dílo*. Yet his judgment of Czech literature and culture, insofar as it embodied the ideals of modernism, was based on aesthetic rather than national criteria. The Czech language, which allowed him to acquire an intimate knowledge of Czech culture, also became a means of access to other literatures and cultures. Finally, any description of Kafka's knowledge of Czech would be incomplete without mentioning his ability to read and interpret Czech texts critically, often (in the case of translations) with reference to their German originals. With this capacity and skill he was able not only to evaluate translations from German into Czech and suggest corrections to Czech versions of his own texts, but also – as we saw in the case of translations by Max Brod (*Jenufa*) and Rudolf Fuchs – to revise texts translated from Czech into German.

218 Kafka, *Letters to Milena*, p. 84.

DIVIDED CITY: FRANZ KAFKA'S READINGS OF PRAGUE

INTRODUCTION

During the second half of the 19th century and the early years of the 20th, a number of monuments appeared on Prague's squares, embankments and hilltops that were linked with national ideology. They were erected by nationalist-minded groups with the aim of increasing their visibility in the public sphere and winning over those whose support was only lukewarm. Language and ethnicity took precedence over other values and shaped not only the programs of political parties, but decisions on the individual level such as choosing a school for one's children. Yet while the Czech nationalists campaigned for parity between the two languages and communities in Bohemia, the Germans wanted to preserve the status quo. Over time, nationalists on both sides increasingly desired separation, particularly in the urban environment.

One way of controlling public space was to hold meetings and demonstrations, including 'national funerals'. The first of these, in 1847, was that of Josef Jungmann. In the 1860s national funerals came to play an important part in rallying support for the nationalist cause and enhancing its organization. Another option for appropriating public space, as already noted, was to erect monuments and grand public buildings or name (or rename) streets and squares after eminent figures in the national movement. The transformation of public space went hand in hand with the transformation of the public sphere. According to Jürgen Habermas, the representative public of the feudal age evolved into a participative public that grew out of bourgeois salons (and later cafés), museums, galleries, concert halls and theatres staging bourgeois dramas that were commented on through the nascent genre of criticism.[1] An important element in the formation of the modern public was literary culture, which as well as books comprised literary journals, press reviews, publishing houses and reading circles.

Habermas dates the creation of a public sphere in Paris to the years between 1680 and 1730. A similar process took place later in Bohemia and

1 See Jürgen Habermas, *The Structural Transformation of the Public Sphere: An Inquiry into a Category of Bourgeois Society*. Translated by Thomas Burger with the assistance of Frederick Lawrence. Cambridge/Mass.: MIT Press 1989, pp. 31–56.

Prague, though more slowly in the Czech community than in the German-speaking. The mobilization of a Czech nationally oriented public in the Prague public sphere together with the creation of monuments and public buildings gained momentum towards the end of the century with a whole series of projects dedicated to the nationalist cause: the Palacký Bridge, the Czech National Theatre, the Slavonic pantheon Slavín, the new Museum building, the Municipal House, and the monuments to František Palacký and Jan Hus, to name the most prominent. Post-1918, German monuments in Prague were deliberately neglected, new ones were not allowed, and some were even removed or destroyed.[2] The Jewish Town was largely destroyed during the reconstruction of Prague at the turn of the century and architectonically integrated into the city as a whole.

Conceptually, Prague's monuments can be read as 'texts' that interlink national themes, values and symbols (the Libuše legend, Hussitism) with public spaces and with each other, providing an impulse and a setting for the mobilization and manifestation of nationalist support. Through them, the Czech national movement took possession of public space and put across its message to its 'readers'. Through these 'messages' – and of course through the imaginative force of Czech literature – Prague gradually defined itself as an icon of Czechness, or Czecho-Slavism, and became its intricately structured 'monument'. This was an alternative Prague that one could identify with – but also criticize or simply reject.

KAFKA'S 'SMALL PRAGUE'

In this chapter, I will attempt to elucidate Franz Kafka's reading and narration of Prague. In this endeavour, I consider both his literary and non-literary texts and place particular emphases on his correspondence with friends. The topography of Prague appears in Kafka's diaries and letters in two forms: 1) as a localization in references to people, things and events; and 2) as the subject of Kafka's observations and deliberations. Here I am less concerned with Prague as a referential space than with the significance Kafka attaches to it.

It should be said at the outset that Prague is mentioned far less often in Kafka's diaries and letters than its importance for him would lead us to expect. This may be simply because the city formed the invisible

2 See Cynthia Paces, *Prague Panoramas: National Memory and Sacred Space in the Twentieth Century*. Pittsburgh: University of Pittsburgh Press 2009; Marek Nekula, Prague Funerals: How Czech national symbols conquered and defended public space. In: Julie Buckler – Emily D. Johnson (eds), *Rites of Place: Public Commemoration in Russia and Eastern Europe*. Evanston/Illinois: Northwestern UP 2013, pp. 35–57.

backdrop of his daily life. Quoting Kafka, Josef Čermák actually sees Prague as Kafka's synonym for the habitual and commonplace:[3]

> If you, Felice, are in any way to blame for our common misfortune (omitting for the moment my own share, which is monumental), it is for your insistence on keeping me in Prague, although you ought to have realized that it was precisely the office and Prague that would lead to my – thus our – eventual ruin. I don't say you wanted to keep me here deliberately, this is not what I think; your ideas about possible ways of life are more courageous and more flexible than mine (I am up to the waist in Austrian officialdom, and over and above that in my own personal inhibitions), so you did not have any compelling urge to consider the future carefully. All the same you ought to have been able to assess or at least to sense this in me, even against myself, even contrary to my own words. [...] What happened instead? Instead we went to buy furniture in Berlin for an official in Prague. / Heavy furniture which looked as if, once in position, it could never be removed. Its very solidity is what you appreciated most. The sideboard in particular – a perfect tombstone, or the memorial to the life of a Prague official – oppressed me profoundly. If during our visit to the furniture store a funeral bell had begun tolling in the distance, it wouldn't have been inappropriate. I wanted to be with you, Felice, of course with you, but free to express my powers which you, in my opinion at least, cannot really have respected if you could consider stifling them with all that furniture.[4]

Their rarity makes such explicit references to Prague all the more significant and deserving of attention. Some critics even see Prague as the referential space and time rather than the fictional chronotope of Kafka's literary texts. Pavel Eisner, as well as the authors of the Czech monograph *Franz Kafka and Prague* and some contributors to the first Kafka conference at Liblice in 1963, all interpreted Kafka's work – as discussed in the first chapter – and Prague German literature as a whole from the 'from the Prague perspective.'[5]

Especially Franz Kafka's *literary* texts rarely refer explicitly to Prague's topography, as for example in the cathedral scene in *The Trial*.[6] Kafka

---

3 Josef Čermák, Kafka a Praha (Kafka and Prague). In: Walter Koschmal – Marek Nekula – Joachim Rogall (eds), *Češi a Němci. Dějiny – kultura – politika* (Czech and Germans. History – Culture – Politics). Praha: Paseka 2001, pp. 158–170, here p. 169.

4 Franz Kafka to Felice, probably mid-February 1916 (March in the English edition). Franz Kafka, *Letters to Felice*. Translated by James Stern and Elizabeth Duckworth. London: Vintage 1999 (first publ. by Schocken, New York 1967), p. 501.

5 See Pavel Eisner, Německá literatura na půdě ČSR od r. 1848 do našich dnů (German Literature in Czechoslovakia: from 1848 to the present). In: *Československá vlastivěda* (Encyclopaedic information on Czechoslovakia), Vol. VII: *Písemnictví* (Literature), Prague: Sfinx 1933, pp. 325–377; *Franz Kafka a Praha. Vzpomínky, úvahy, dokumenty* (Franz Kafka and Prague. Memories, Reflections, Papers). Prague: Žikeš 1947; Eduard Goldstücker – František Kautman – Pavel Reiman (eds), *Franz Kafka: liblická konference 1963* (Franz Kafka: Liblice Conference 1963). Prague: Academia 1963.

6 For a more detailed study see also Čermák, Kafka a Praha, pp. 217–235.

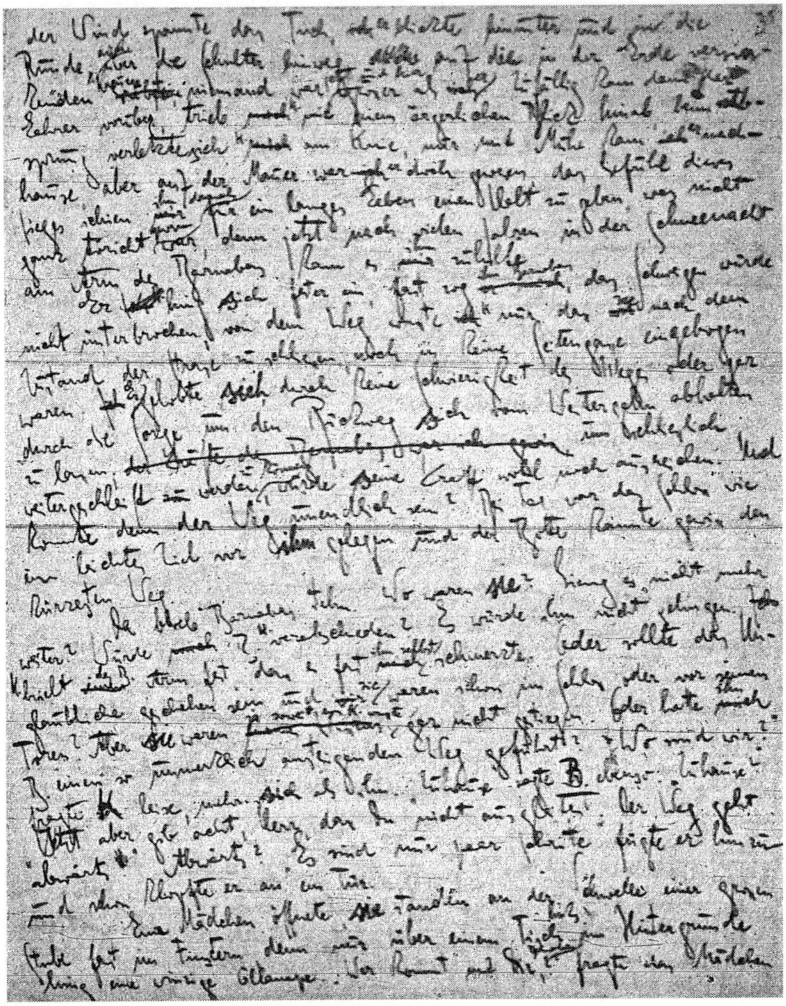

Manuscript of Franz Kafka's novel *The Castle* with correction from *Grabsteine* (gravestones) to *Kreuze* (crosses) etc.
Archiv Kritische Kafka-Ausgabe.

plays – as Malcolm Pasley phrases it – his 'semi-private games', but in his stories he also avoids being over-specific. We may observe this shift away from the private and local atmosphere in the novel *The Castle*. When Kafka revised the original manuscript he replaced the first-person narrator with a third-person narrator; he also replaced 'collapsing tombstones', which could be associated with the Old Jewish Cemetery in Prague, with 'collapsing crosses', and 'members of the community' with 'citizens'. Similarly, the experience of a local national fight for linguistically distinct spaces is transformed into a story about the confusion of tongues and thus made universal. Here the biblical myth becomes an allegory of a society divided along ethno-national lines.

In his *non*-literary texts, however, Kafka does make some explicit references to Prague. This is hardly surprising, since Kafka was born and bred in the city. He studied in Prague, worked there for fifteen years and spent most of his relatively short life there. Kafka's thoughts never left Prague, even when he was living somewhere else. In December 1923, for example, when he was living in Berlin, he wrote the following (in Czech) in a note addressed to his sister Ottla and her husband Josef David:

> And Ottla, please explain to our parents that I can only write once or twice a week; postage is already as expensive as it is *at home*. I am, however, enclosing Czech stamps for you to help you out a bit.[7]

The Czech words '*u nás*' (at home, in our country) mean Prague, where Kafka had remained in thought even though he was in Berlin.

By then Prague was already the capital of the newly founded Czechoslovakia. It became 'Greater Prague' in 1920 after new legislation incorporated all the Czech suburbs. The small German-speaking minority living in the Old Town in the centre of this Central European metropolis thus became smaller and more inconspicuous than it had been before Czechoslovak independence in 1918. From Kafka's point of view, however, Prague was not as large as the Czech majority seemed to think. From the window of his parents' apartment in the Oppelt House on the Old Town Square he could survey the entire area in which he lived (parts of the Old Town and the remains of the Old Jewish Ghetto in his mental map). Shortly after World War I, he outlined this space for his friend Friedrich Thieberger with a small movement of his index finger:

> Once when we were standing at the window and looking down on the Old Town Square, he pointed to the buildings and said: 'My high school was here, the university there in the building you can see and a little further to the left my office.' He made a few small circles with his finger. 'My entire life is enclosed in this small circle.[8]

While Kafka may have indicated such a small space with his finger, he in fact lived and moved in a larger area of Prague, and many other places, streets and districts appear in his correspondence and diaries or are associated with

---

7 Franz Kafka, *Briefe an Ottla und die Familie* (Letters to Ottla and Family). Ed. by Hartmut Binder and Klaus Wagenbach. Frankfurt am Main: S. Fischer 1974, p. 151. My emphases.

8 Friedrich Thieberger, Kafka und die Thiebergers (Kafka and the Thiebergers). In: Hans-Gerd Koch (ed.), *'Als Kafka mir entgegen kam…' Erinnerungen an Franz Kafka* ('As Kafka approached me.' Recollections of Franz Kafka). Berlin: Wagenbach 1995, pp. 128–134, here p. 133.

him by his contemporaries. Kafka worked in the Workers' Accident Insurance Company for the Kingdom of Bohemia in Prague on Na Poříčí Street, attended the German New Theatre in Vinohrady and the Czech National Theatre on the bank of the Vltava, climbed up Petřín hill, crossed the Charles Bridge to Prague Castle or to Kampa island. With his sisters he visited not only Troja, where he later went to work in the garden, but also Letná and Podskalí; he climbed up to Vyšehrad, went to the public swimming school on the bank of the Vltava, rowed on the Vltava, was responsible for the family factory in Žižkov, etc.[9] He was also familiar with the environs of the city, as we know from his postcards to his friends and family.

The story told by Thieberger shows, however, that these are not the referential places Kafka understands as Prague. He points to and writes his Prague with a slight movement of his finger. That small movement of Kafka's finger, stressing the words 'enclosed in this small circle' is rather Kafka's reading and narrating of Prague. His gesture and words may evoke the opposition between the small German and German-speaking Jewish minority in Prague's Old Town and the 'Greater Prague', in which the 'ethnic Czechs' had a twenty to one majority in most districts and the nationalist Czech middle classes controlled the city hall.

THE NARRATIVE OF BABYLON AND THE GREAT WALL OF CHINA

Friedrich Thieberger's story of Kafka's index finger may be particularly appealing because it shows that Franz Kafka ascribes to his space a semantic relevance. But it is perhaps too simplistic to believe that Kafka's Prague is a *specific* 'small' space, or as Paul Eisner phrased it, a 'triple' social, national and confessional ghetto which entraps Kafka. In fact, Kafka never lived in a real Jewish ghetto. The Prague ghetto ceased to exist legally after 1848, and the area was largely demolished and rebuilt as part of the general urban modernization around 1900. Eisner's postulate appears problematic also because Kafka obtained a regular education in Czech, had a good job in the public sphere and participated in German, Czech and Jewish culture in Ger-

9 See Franz Kafka, *Tagebücher* (Diaries). Ed. by Hans-Gerd Koch, Michael Müller and Malcolm Pasley. 4 vols. Frankfurt am Main: S. Fischer 1990; Franz Kafka, *Briefe* (Letters). Vol. 1–4. Ed. by Hans-Gerd Koch. Frankfurt am Main: S. Fischer Verlag 1999, 2001, 2005, 2013; Hartmut Binder, *Kafka-Handbuch in zwei Bänden* (A Kafka Manual in two Volumes). Stuttgart: Kröner 1979; Klaus Wagenbach, *Kafkas Prag. Ein Reiselesebuch*. Berlin: Wagenbach [7]2004 (English version: *Kafka's Prague: A Travel Reader*. Translated by Shaun Whiteside. Woodstock, New York: The Overlook Press 1996); Hans-Gerd Koch (ed.), *„Als Kafka mir entgegen kam…": Erinnerungen an Franz Kafka* ('As Kafka approached me.' Recollections of Franz Kafka). Berlin: Wagenbach 1995, etc.

man, Czech, Yiddish and Hebrew. Rather, the foundations of Kafka's ghetto were antisemitism (both individual and institutional) and the fear of violent pogroms, about which he read and which he and his friend Max Brod experienced in Prague. The fear of the violence he experienced in his native city never left his thoughts – no matter where he actually was, in Vienna, Munich, Flüelen, Paris or Berlin. Kafka would be able to answer the question in *Prager Presse* (Prague News): 'Why did you leave Prague?'[10] with the words: 'I never left Prague', which could be taken to mean, 'I never lost my fear of the pogroms'. He found this fear also in Berlin, where he had hoped to lose it, as he wrote in a Czech text addressed to his brother-in-law Josef David:

> Dear Pepa, be so good and write me a few lines should anything particular happen at home. [...] What are you doing now you don't have anyone to scare about going to Berlin. Scare me, Pepa? That's like *Eulen nach Athen tragen* ('taking owls to Athens' i.e. coals to Newcastle). And here it really is terrible living in the inner city, struggling to survive, reading the papers. None of which I do, of course, I wouldn't last half a day, but out here it's nice, just now and then some flash of news or fear finds it way to me which I then have to fight, but is it any different in Prague? How many dangers lurk there every day for the timid soul?[11]

The strong discursive polarization between Germans and Czechs along perceived linguistic-national lines, as well as anti-German sentiments, were a contributing factor to the pogroms in Prague, just as the language question had provoked the Badeni crisis in 1897. The Czech-German conflict over language occupied both Kafka's and Max Brod's thoughts. During a visit to Switzerland in August 1911, Brod noted in his diary:

> In the men's bathhouse. Very crowded. There are signs in an unusually large number of languages – the Swiss solution to the question of language. Everything is made confusing so that even a chauvinist doesn't know what's going on. First he finds German to the left, then to the right, German in connection with French or Italian or both or even with English, and German sometimes is missing completely. In Flüelen, it was prohibited in German-Italian to go on the train tracks. The slow passing of cars was in German-French. – Switzerland is certainly a school for statesmen![12]

---

10 See Kurt Krolop, *Studien zur Prager deutschen Literatur. Festschrift zum 75. Geburtstag* (Studies on Prague German Literature). Ed. by Klaas-Hinrich Ehlers, Steffen Höhne, Marek Nekula. Vienna: Edition Praesens 2005, pp. 89–102.

11 Franz Kafka to Josef David, 3 October 1923. – See Kafka, *Briefe an Ottla und die Familie*, p. 135 f.

12 Max Brod in Franz Kafka, *Reisetagebücher in der Fassung der Handschrift* (Travel Diaries Based on the Handwritten Manuscripts). Ed. by Hans-Gerd Koch. Frankfurt am Main: S. Fischer 1994, p. 123.

Franz Kafka makes a laconic remark on the same topic:

> Max: Confusion of Tongues – the solution to national problems. The chauvinist doesn't know what is going on anymore.[13]

Kafka considers the language situation in Switzerland and the German-French language conflict to be a form of the Confusion of Tongues at Babel, a situation he was familiar with from Prague and Bohemia generally. In the Old Testament, the story of the Tower of Babel represents the fragmentation of a linguistic, cultural and territorial whole into individual languages and clans:

> Now the whole world had one language and a common speech. 2 As men moved east-
> ward, they found a plain in Shinar and settled there.
> 3 They said to each other, 'Come, let's make bricks and bake them thoroughly.' They
> used brick instead of stone, and tar for mortar. 4 Then they said, 'Come, let us build
> ourselves a city, with a tower that reaches to the heavens, so that we may make a name
> for ourselves and not be scattered over the face of the whole earth.'
> 5 But the LORD came down to see the city and the tower that the men were build-
> ing. 6 The LORD said, 'If as one people speaking the same language they have begun to
> do this, then nothing they plan to do will be impossible for them. 7 Come, let us go down
> and confuse their language so they will not understand each other.'
> 8 So the LORD scattered them from there over all the earth, and they stopped build-
> ing the city. 9 That is why it was called Babel – because there the LORD confused the
> language of the whole world. From there the LORD scattered them over the face of the
> whole earth.[14]

The case of Bohemia was similar. Its territory was – or was perceived to be – divided into two exclusive (linguistic) worlds. Kafka returned to the Babel motif in September 1920 in his story 'The city coat of arms'. Some time earlier, in February, the Czechoslovak language law and constitution had added fuel to the fire of the 'Babylonian' divisions in public life. The 'Czechoslovak' language (which meant both Czech and Slovak) became the official language of the new state. All other languages, especially German, were partially restricted in their use. The tender wound of language-based nationalism that had pained the Habsburg monarchy was suddenly torn open again.

It is not surprising, then, that Kafka read the Praguian coat of arms as the Tower of Babel, and vice versa:

---

13 Kafka, *Tagebücher*, p. 950.

14 Genesis 11: 1–9.

> [...] the second or third generation had already recognized the senselessness of building a heaven-reaching tower, but by that time everybody was too deeply involved to leave the town. All the legends and songs that came to birth in the city are filled with longing for a prophesied day when the city would be destroyed by five successive blows from a gigantic fist. It is for that reason too that the city has a closed fist on its coat of arms.[15]

Prague's coat of arms also contains a huge gauntleted fist that can divide and destroy a city. There are, it is true, some differences between the Prague coat of arms and that of Babel in the story. Prague's fist holds a sword, Babel's does not. The fist in Prague's coat of arms symbolizes defensive strength, whereas the Babel fist stands for destruction.[16] Yet despite these differences the parallel is clear. Kafka does something similar in 'The Stoker', the first chapter of the novel *The Man Who Disappeared*, also known as 'Amerika'. The 'Statue der Freiheitsgöttin' (literally 'statue of the Goddess of Freedom') holding a 'sword', 'as if the goddess had just raised it, and the wind blew about her body without constraint',[17] is a very explicit allusion to the Statue of Liberty in New York – and is translated as such for example by Stanley Corngold[18]. The fact that the real statue is holding a burning torch does not detract from the parallel.

Unlike in the Bible story, the languages in 'The city coat of arms' are made confusing and divided even before the Tower of Babel is built. Kafka mentions 'signposts', 'interpreters' and separate 'accommodation' for the 'workmen from various countries', as well as 'conflicts' and 'bloody fights'.[19] In other words, Kafka's Babel is already divided. And in this it evokes the divided Czech and German worlds in Bohemia, and especially in its capital, Prague, where the Czech and German communities existed side by side, sometimes

---

15 Franz Kafka, *The Complete Short Stories of Franz Kafka*. Ed. by Nahum N. Glazer. London: Random House Vintage 1999, p. 434.

16 See also Hans Dieter Zimmermann, Der Turmbau zu Babel (Building of the Tower of Babel). In: Hans Dieter Zimmermann, *Der babylonische Dolmetscher: Zu Franz Kafka und Robert Walser* (The Babylonian Translator: on Franz Kafka and Robert Walser). Frankfurt am Main: Suhrkamp 1985, pp. 61–66, p. 64.

17 See Franz Kafka, *Ein Landarzt und andere Drucke zu Lebzeiten* (A Country Doctor and Other Texts Published in his Lifetime). Ed. by Hans-Gerd Koch. Vol. 1, Frankfurt am Main: S. Fischer 1994, p. 55. Translation: Franz Kafka, *Stories 1904–1924*. Translated by J. A. Underwood, foreword by Jorge Luis Borges. London: Abacus 1995, p. 59.

18 See Franz Kafka, *Selected Stories*. Edited and translated by Stanley Corngold. New York, London: W. W. Norton & Co. 2005, p. 12.

19 Franz Kafka, *Zur Frage der Gesetze und andere Schriften aus dem Nachlaß in der Fassung der Handschrift* (On the Question of Laws and Other Literary Remains Based on the Handwritten Manuscripts). Ed. by Hans-Gerd Koch. Frankfurt am Main: S. Fischer 1994, pp. 143–144; Kafka, *The Complete Short Stories*, p. 433. For more on the differences between the Bible story and Kafka see Zimmermann, Der Turmbau zu Babel, pp. 61–62.

peacefully but often also attacking each other in public discourse and perpetuating this discord through independent cultural and economic institutions and school systems.

Kafka had considered the true extent of the Tower of Babel's foundations three years earlier, in 1917, in his story 'Building of the Great Wall of China'. The foundations had to be enormous due to the tower's height. The Tower of Babel was supposed to reach heaven; it was also the tower from which heaven could be stormed. Kafka's word 'Himmelsturmbau' could be read in two ways in the German original: as 'Himmel-Sturm-Bau' but also as 'Himmels-Turm-Bau', that is, as a building from which heaven can be stormed, or as a tower reaching up to heaven.[20] Kafka's own 'Tower of Babel', the Workers' Accident Insurance Company for the Kingdom of *Bohemia* in Prague, reaching to the heaven of Bohemian government administration ('Statthalterei'), was at this time – around 1917 – planning to change its 'Bohemian' character and divide according to language into a German and a Czech company, to reinforce through this 'Great Wall' the stability of the entire state,[21] just as Charles University (1882) and other institutions had been divided some time earlier.

In Kafka's story 'Building of the Great Wall of China', a scholar questions the reason for the Tower of Babel's destruction. He does not believe that the failure of the project was an act of providence, as it is presented in the Old Testament. He believes that the plan was doomed to fail due to the weakness of the foundations ('the construction foundered, and was destined to founder, on the weakness of its foundations'). He says:

> the Great Wall would create, for the first time in human history, a solid foundation for a *new* Tower of Babel. Ergo: first the Wall and then the Tower.[22]

In the context of the story, the narrator's doubts about the scholar's assertions are logical and understandable:

> At the time, his book was in everyone's hands, but I admit that even today I do not really know how he thought this Tower would be built. The Wall, which did not even describe a circle but only a sort of quarter- or semi-quarter, was supposed to provide the foundation for a Tower?[23]

---

20 Kafka, *Zur Frage der Gesetze* , p. 143, 147; see also Zimmermann, Der Turmbau zu Babel, p. 62; Peter Demetz, Praha a Babylón (Prague and Babel). In: Peter Demetz, *České slunce a moravský měsíc* (Czech Sun and Moravian Moon). Ostrava: Tilia 1997, pp. 76–77.

21 See Marek Nekula, *Franz Kafkas Sprachen. „...in einem Stockwerk des innern babylonischen Turmes..."* (Franz Kafka's Languages. '... on one floor of the inner Tower of Babel...'). Tübingen: Niemeyer 2003, pp. 163–173.

22 Kafka, *Selected Stories*, p. 116. My emphases.

23 Kafka, *Selected Stories*, p. 116.

How could the Great Wall serve as a foundation for the Tower of Babel, given its shape?

If we read this story through the lens of New Historicism in the discursive context of the Czech-German linguistic-national division in Bohemia, bearing in mind that the 'Great Wall' was a common metaphor for this division, the Great Wall now appears as a 'true' foundation for the *new* Tower of Babel, rather than an absurd exaggeration:

> If anyone built the Great Wall, it wasn't us. It is true that some of our intellectual leaders led us to be closer to Roman and Slavonic culture because they recognized the danger of the German mind's influence on Czech culture [...] But there was no hatred of German culture in our country, there was only a healthy instinct for survival. Our nation would already have ceased to exist and we would have become Czech-speaking Germans, had we accepted the influence, the culture and the mind of our neighbour without reservation. We say yes to having contacts, but we say no to surrender.[24]

This is the Czech writer Viktor Dyk's reply in the Czech literary journal *Lumír* to Franz Werfel's article 'Note on a celebration of Wedekind', which had appeared on 18 April 1913 in the *Prager Tagblatt* (Prague Daily News). Viktor Dyk was already well known to Brod and Kafka in 1910. Czechs and most Germans were aware of Dyk's strong nationalism and his phrase 'I know our task is to either make Bohemia Czech or die'.[25]

If the 'Great Wall' is a metaphor for division along linguistic lines in contemporary national discourse, then the idea of the 'Great Wall' as the Tower of Babel's foundation appears quite logical. The linguistic boundary between German and Czech in the Bohemia of this time can now be understood territorially and functionally as a Great Wall that both Czechs and Germans were industriously building. The division of nations will follow as a natural consequence of the division of language and its 'foundations'. The story of the Confusion of Tongues at Babel, which leads to the division of the world into different countries, also reflects this separation. In Bohemia this resulted – or was expected to result – in the division of the once 'transnational' Bohemian society along ethno-national lines into German and Czech communities. Although in the Bible this absolute division comes only after divine intervention, in Prague it was a goal of nationalist politics, which sought to eliminate all moments of transition between language and national territories. Of course,

---

24 Viktor Dyk, Němci v Čechách a české umění (Germans in Bohemia and Czech art). *Lumír – měsíční revue pro literaturu, umění a společnost* 42 (1914), May, No. 8, pp. 331–336, p. 332. See also Krolop, *Studien zur Prager deutschen Literatur*, pp. 81–84.

25 Podiven (= Milan Otáhal, Petr Pithart, Petr Příhoda), *Češi v dějinách nové doby (Pokus o zrcadlo)* (The Czechs in the History of Modern Times: An Attempt at a Mirror). Prague: Rozmluvy 1991, p. 364.

there were no such clear borders in everyday linguistic practice. But they were, to various degrees, 'under construction' in the individual and official spheres, and in different territories. It is in this light that we should understand one of the narrator's somewhat absurd assertions about the Great Wall of China, that it was built in parts – separate sections that did not form a whole. And we can also understand why Kafka rejected the Czech-Slavonic/German polarization associated with a monolingual interpretation of the world and one's – or rather Odradek's – identity in the story 'The householder's concern'.[26]

Against the metaphoric backdrop of the Great Wall, the division along linguistic lines – a linguistic border within Bohemia – can be seen as substantial enough to serve as the foundation for a new 'Tower of Babel', as mentioned in the Travel Diaries, where it means language-based national separatism. It is also substantial enough to serve as the foundation for the 'new' tower to storm heaven ('Himmels-Turm-Bau' as 'Himmel-Sturm-Bau') and destroy the 'old' divine order – the Austrian empire and its rule over Bohemia. In all of these cases (Babel, 'Great Austria',[27] Bohemia) we see a violent destruction of a once homogenous territorial whole along its linguistic borders. However, this division was already present in their foundations: the multilingual Austrian empire 'is' a Babylon.

If the metaphorical Great Wall of the internal linguistic border is the foundation on which the division, the Tower of Babel, is metaphorically built, then the whole of Bohemia would be included in this Tower of Babel. The word 'city' ('Stadt') in Kafka's story 'The city coat of arms' may thus be read as 'state' ('Staat'). This is not only a pars-pro-toto figure (city for state), which is commonly associated with capital cities; it also connects narratives of the city (Babylon and Prague) with narratives of the state (China and Bohemia). Kafka frequently applies this strategy of double naming and reading to signal, for example, that the officials 'Sordini' and 'Sortini' in the novel *The Castle* can be understood as the same person, or at least as manifestations of one model. We saw this reading strategy also in the story 'Building the Great Wall of China' with the reading of the word 'Himmelsturmbau' as 'Himmels-Turm-Bau' and/or 'Himmel-Sturm-Bau'.[28]

---

26 See Marek Nekula, Franz Kafkas Sprachen und Identität (Franz Kafka's languages and identity). In: Marek Nekula – Walter Koschmal (eds), *Juden zwischen Deutschen und Tschechen. Sprachliche, literarische und kulturelle Identitäten* (Jews between German and Czechs: Linguistic, Literary and Cultural Identities). Munich: Oldenbourg 2006, pp. 135–158.

27 See Franz Kafka, *Beim Bau der chinesischen Mauer und andere Schriften aus dem Nachlaß in der Fassung der Handschrift* (Building of the Great Wall of China and Other Literary Remains Based on the Handwritten Manuscripts). Ed. by Hans-Gerd Koch. Frankfurt am Main: S. Fischer 1994, p. 64.

28 For the Czech-German double reading of the name 'Klamm' in *The Castle* see Hans Dieter Zimmermann, Das Labyrinth der Welt: Kafka und Comenius (The Labyrinth of the World: Kafka and Comenius). In: Klaas-Hinrich Ehlers et al. (eds), *Brücken nach Prag. Deutschsprachige Literatur im kulturellen Kontext der Donaumonarchie und der Tschechoslowakei* (Bridges to Prague: Ger-

The metaphorical Great Wall of China, separation along linguistic and national lines, and Babylonian fragmentation divided the Bohemian Lands both territorially and functionally. It is irrelevant whether in the 'city' ('Stadt') Kafka was recalling the old Habsburg 'state' ('Staat') or whether he meant the new Czechoslovak 'state' ('Staat'). The second interpretation seems more probable considering that the story was written in 1920 and in the future tense. Czechoslovakia, just like the Habsburg state, will collapse as a result of linguistically oriented nationalism. Its destruction 'by a huge fist in five short blows' will also be anticipated by some people with great 'longing'.[29]

This longing for self-destruction may appear rather unhealthy. In a letter to Max Brod, Kafka connects his own states of anxiety with the motif of the Tower of Babel and the confusion of tongues when he mentions his 'inner Tower of Babel'.[30] Incidentally, Kafka considered this anxiety to be the real reason for his illness in 1917, which was accompanied by serious thoughts of suicide. After the crisis in his relationship with Milena Jesenská, a personal crisis exacerbated by the pogroms of 1918 and 1920, these states of anxiety culminated in a nervous breakdown.

PRAGUE STEEPED IN MYTH

The Prague that Kafka knew so well and read as a new Babel – as he did the whole of divided Bohemia – was swept by language-based nationalism. This division was clearly visible in the Prague public sphere, which gradually came to be dominated by national monuments and grand 'representative' buildings, as we mentioned at the start of this chapter. Some historic monuments were now read as national monuments, notably the Charles Bridge,

---

man-written Literature in the Cultural Context of the Habsburg Monarchy and Czechoslovakia). Frankfurt am Main: Peter Lang 2000, pp. 309–319; for readings of the name 'Odradek' in the story 'The householder's concern' see in this book the chapter 'The "being" of Odradek: Franz Kafka in his Jewish context', p. 37 f.

29 We can also read it as a longing for the apocalypse, after which the new messianic world will arise. See Zimmermann, Der Turmbau zu Babel.

30 Franz Kafka to Max Brod, 29 August 1917. – See Max Brod – Franz Kafka, *Eine Freundschaft. Briefwechsel* (A Friendship: Correspondence). Ed. by Malcolm Pasley. Vol. 2. Frankfurt am Main: S. Fischer 1989, p. 159. Kafka also connects his writing process with the motif of the Tower of Babel, seeing a parallel between writing and building the Tower. He did not, of course, compose his texts as integrally constructed novels as we typically find in 19th century fiction. His texts are horizontally scattered fragments, as is typical for modern texts such as Rilke's 'Die Aufzeichnung des Malte Laurids Brigge'. Such fragments are the scattered foundation blocks of the Tower of Babel, which is formed by the partially built Great Wall as mentioned in Kafka's text 'Building the The Great Wall of China'. Nor does the castle in Kafka's text *The Castle* appear in the unified form of a castle (with a tower); rather it is scattered throughout buildings in the village.

Prague Castle and Vyšehrad.[31] In the latter part of the 19th century, the Prague public space was claimed by both Czech (Slavonic) and German nationalists, a fact reflected in the following well-known passage from a letter Kafka wrote in 1902:

> Prague doesn't let go. Either one of us. This old crone has claws. One has to yield, or else. We would have to set fire to it on two sides, at the Vyšehrad and at the Hradčany, then it would be possible for us to get away.[32]

We can recognize two elements in this quote. Prague appears as a mythic Siren,[33] and Prague's Castle and Vyšehrad hill are placed in a semantic opposition. The 'Czech' (Slavonic) Vyšehrad can be seen as an opposition to Prague Castle, which at this time was often seen as a symbol of official (Habsburg, 'German') authority.

Vyšehrad is a large hill in Prague above the River Vltava. Since the time of national rebirth, it had been seen as the sacred core of a Slavonic/Czech territory. In the *Green Mountain Manuscript*, written in Czech, it was closely associated with Libuše, a female ancestor of the Přemyslid (Slavonic/Czech) dynasty and of the Bohemian, Slavonic/Czech state, who prophesied the coming fame ('sláva'!) of Slavonic Prague.[34] Indeed, legend has it that she founded the city. Both the first Přemyslid king Vratislav and some later Přemyslid princes reigned from Vyšehrad. This mythic dimension of Vyšehrad explains why it was chosen as the site of the Czech pantheon Slavín. The Czech writer Julius Zeyer was the first person to be buried in the Slavín

---

31 See Marek Nekula, Die deutsche Walhalla und der tschechische Slavín (The German Walhalla and the Czech Pantheon Slavín). In: *brücken. Germanistisches Jahrbuch Tschechien – Slowakei.* NF 9–10 (2003), pp. 87–106; Michaela Marek, 'Monumentalbauten' und Städtebau als Spiegel des gesellschaftlichen Wandels in der 2. Hälfte des 19. Jahrhunderts (Monuments and urbanization as a reflection of social change in the second half of the 19th century). In: Ferdinand Seibt (ed.), *Böhmen im 19. Jahrhundert: Vom Klassizismus zur Moderne* (Bohemia in the 19th Century: From Classicism to Modernity). Frankfurt am Main, Berlin: Propyläen 1995, pp. 149–233, 390–411; Michaela Marek, *Kunst und Identitätspolitik. Architektur und Bildkünste im Prozess der tschechischen Nationsbildung* (Art and Identity Politics: Architecture and Visual Arts in the Process of Czech National Building). Weimar, Cologne, Vienna: Böhlau 2004; Zdeněk Hojda – Jiří Pokorný, *Pomníky a zapomníky* (Monuments and Memory Lost). Prague, Litomyšl: Paseka 1997; Roman Prahl, Výtvarné umění v divadle (Visual art in the theatre). In: Zdeňka Benešová et al. (eds), *Národní divadlo – historie a současnost budovy. History and Present Day of the Building. Geschichte und Gegenwart des Hauses*, Prague: Národní divadlo 1999, pp. 107–125.

32 Franz Kafka to Oskar Pollak, 20 December 1902. Franz Kafka, *Letters to Friends, Family, and Editors.* Translated by Richard and Clara Winston from the German original. New York: Schocken Books 1977, p. 5 f.

33 Note especially the word 'claws' ('Krallen') in this letter and in the later story 'The silence of the Sirens'. – See also Michel Reffet, Franz Kafka und der Mythos (Franz Kafka and Myth). In: *brücken. Germanistisches Jahrbuch Tschechien – Slowakei.* NF 9–10 (2003), pp. 155–168.

34 See Marek Nekula, Constructing Slavonic Prague: The 'Green Mountain Manuscript' and public space in discourse. *Bohemia* 52 (2012), pp. 22–36.

crypt in 1901, one year before Kafka wrote his sentence about Vyšehrad and Prague Castle. In his story *Inultus*, Zeyer connected the Czech myth of national death and rebirth with the story of the suffering, death and resurrection of Jesus Christ. The resurrection in Christ and the resurrection in language come together in the inscription on the crypt: 'Although they have died, they still *speak*' – not 'live', as Christians would say. Already in 1863, the tombstone of Václav Hanka in the Slavín crypt had been decorated with a similar inscription that manifested the ideology of Czech national rebirth and equates language and nation: 'Nations will not die as long as their language continues to live'. Kafka knew the modern Czech myth of national death and rebirth, which played a key role in the narrative division of Bohemian society into ethno-national communities and connected it symbolically with Vyšehrad.

He encountered this ideology not only at Slavín but also earlier in his Czech classes at the German grammar school on the Old Town Square, as well as in other contexts. One of them was the Czech National Theatre, which Kafka visited repeatedly. The national myths, as well as an imagined separate national space, are inscribed in the paintings in the foyer of the theatre. The resurrection myth is depicted in the triptych on the foyer ceiling. A separate linguistic space emerges in the lunettes around the foyer. Here, in a series of scenes named after specific locations in Bohemia, we see various episodes in the life of the 'Slavonic hero', who patrols the confines of the Czech 'national space', defending it against hostile nations and with his movement thus also 'narrating' the nation's geographical boundaries: the first of the lunettes is actually entitled 'Narration', the second 'Guardian of the Frontier'. The hero's journey ends in the last lunette, named Žalov ('Place of Grief'). The resting-place of the nation's great, Slavín, was also known as Žalov, to which it is conceptually and architecturally related. In both cases, the name Žalov emphasizes grief rather than pride in the deeds of the nation's heroes. On his visits to Slavín, Kafka will certainly have noticed František Bílek's statue *Grief* on the tomb of Václav Beneš Třebízský.[35]

We now come to the second part of the opposition, the second place Kafka wanted to set on fire. Hradčany is the Castle District, built on a large hill that dominates Prague on the other side of the Vltava. The emperors Charles IV and Rudolf II made it their capital, the latter residing here during his visits to Prague from Vienna. Up until 1918, the Castle was thus a symbol of official (Habsburg, 'German') authority, especially for the German-speaking community. Kafka too, like other Germans living in Prague, considered the Castle of

35 See Brod – Kafka, *Eine Freundschaft*, p. 401; Nekula, Die deutsche Walhalla und der tschechische Slavín.

Prague to be the 'emperor's castle'.[36] In similar fashion, the Czech National Theatre, symbol of a successful Czech national rebirth, was understood with respect to its national iconography and political program (autonomy for Bohemia, equality for Germans and Czechs) as antipodal to Prague Castle. The roof of the Czech National Theater could be read as an allusion to the roof of the Belvedere on the other side of the river near the Castle. In Prague public space the Czech National Theater with its monolingual ideology thus stands in semantic opposition to Prague Castle and confidently measures up against the 'German' Emperor's Castle, trying likewise to appropriate it this way.

These two hills loaded with national, monolingual semantics – Vyšehrad with the Czech/Slavonic pantheon Slavín on the right and Hradčany with the Emperor's Castle on the left bank of the Vltava – enclose the city of Prague, which Kafka sketched with a slight movement of his index finger as a small circle in which he feels trapped. Kafka, who also constructs an intertextual connection between Prague (with 'claws') and Sirens (with 'claws') in the story 'The silence of the Sirens', reads Prague as a Siren that he cannot escape. This mythic reading of Prague allows us to understand these two hills in Prague as Scylla and Charybdis, between which Odysseus had to navigate in the *Odyssey* when he was escaping from the Sirens.

Thus, just as the myth of Scylla and Charybdis teaches us that escape is impossible, it is impossible to escape the Siren Prague, who encircles the narrator and appears misleadingly pleasant but at the same time represents the fear of violence and pogroms. In fact it is as impossible to escape from Scylla and Charybdis as from the German-Czech battle over language with its monolingual ideology that dominated public discourse, institutions and public space in Bohemia and Prague. The only way out is an act of desperation: to set fire to Prague as Kafka proposed in the letter to Oskar Pollak. Without Odysseus's tricks, the only alternative is to sink into the swirling water between Scylla and Charybdis. Kafka describes this submersion into water in the story 'The judgment' (1912/1917), which I will return to later.

KAFKA'S READING OF NATIONAL MONUMENTS

We can already see, however, that Kafka does more than merely reflect on the issues of national polarization along linguistic lines, the German-Czech language conflict and the national annexation of public space by national monuments – he emphatically rejects them. In a letter to Max Brod, Kafka

36 Translation from the Czech original. See Franz Kafka to Růžena Hejná (Wettenglová), 1 October 1917. – See Kafka, *Briefe April 1914–1917* (Letters April 1914–1917). Ed. by Hans-Gerd Koch. Frankfurt am Main: S. Fischer 2005, p. 341.

evaluates a monument with a very strong nationalistic program. His critique is motivated not by the monument's subject but by the lack of aesthetic value that results from blind nationalism:

> It is a wanton and senseless impoverishment of Prague and Bohemia that mediocre stuff like Šaloun's *Hus* or wretched stuff like Sucharda's Palacký are erected with all honours [...].[37]

The monument to František Palacký, the nineteenth-century Czech historian and leader of the Czech national movement, on the Palacký Bridge was, by virtue of its theme, placement and iconography, not only a reflection and expression of Czech national ideology but also a public place where monolingual national agitation could be staged and motivated. And it was certainly with these aims in mind that the monument was erected in 1912 and unveiled during the 6th meeting of the patriotic Sokol gymnastics movement in Prague.[38]

The Palacký Bridge was built from stone in the Czech colours of protest (white-red-blue), named after Palacký and adorned with statues of ur-Slavonic 'heroes'. Early Slavonic (Czech) history and the present are thus connected. On one of the bridgeheads stood a statue of the mythical Libuše and Přemysl; on the other, a monument to František Palacký himself. In discussing the *Green Mountain Manuscript*, Palacký described the age of Libuše as a time of autonomous and democratic Slavonic paganism that preceded the arrival of western Christianity from Germanic Bavaria and Saxony, projecting the values of cultural and political autonomy and democratic equality into Libuše's era as well as into the era of Hussitism and the Reformation. According to Palacký, these values defined the course of Czech history and thus set out the political program for contemporary Czech politics (from Libuše's era through the era of Hussitism to the national rebirth and the present). So Palacký's name became in this special and simplified sense a byword for Czech national politics based on a monolingual national ideology and territorial claims ('The Bohemian/Czech Lands for the Czechs'), as expressed in the lunettes in the foyer of the Czech National Theatre.

The Palacký Bridge, the second stone bridge in Prague after the Charles Bridge, became engaged in a polemical dialogue with its mediaeval counter-

37 Franz Kafka to Max Brod, 30 July 1922. – See Kafka, *Letters to Friends, Family, and Editors*, p. 347.

38 In a speech given at the inauguration of the monument to Palacký, Karel Kramář, a prominent Czech politician of the day, called for equality of Czechs and Germans in Bohemia and legal autonomy for Bohemia. See also Hojda – Pokorný, *Pomníky a zapomníky*, p. 102. 'Sokol' is a sports association. In the 19th century it was a mass organization for nationalistic Czechs with some cultural goals (books, periodicals, public readings, etc.). It was also noticeably paramilitary in character, at least in the 19th century.

part based on its iconography. The statues on the Charles Bridge (and consequently the bridge as a whole) were at this time read as an icon of the Counter-reformation after the Battle of White Mountain (1620), of domination by the Catholic Habsburg dynasty (or any foreign power), of the empire (Reich) and of German culture. This is why the German population could identify with this bridge and why it was unacceptable to 19th century Czech nationalist ideology (František Palacký, Jaroslav Goll)[39] – an ideology founded on an anti-Catholic, Protestant (democratic) understanding of the 'national rebirth' that had overcome the nation's 'death' (period of darkness) after the Battle of White Mountain and the subsequent recatholicization and Germanization of the country.

As with Vyšehrad and the Emperor's Castle, the two bridges display opposing iconographies. Kafka must have been aware of this on his walks through Prague. Like other German-speaking Praguians in the city, he began his walks at the Charles Bridge,[40] crossed over to the predominantly German Lesser Town with its monument to the Austrian marshal Radetzky (which was torn down after 1918), and walked up to the Castle. By contrast, Czechs from the New Town or the predominantly Czech suburbs of Nusle or Podskalí would go for walks to Vyšehrad; and if they went there from the Czech district of Smíchov, they would cross the Palacký Bridge.

Between 25 and 29 May 1920 Kafka writes in a letter to Milena Jesenská:

> Some years ago I often went rowing on the Moldau [= Vltava] in a maňas (small boat), I would row upstream and then float down with the current underneath the bridges, completely stretched out.[41]

Knowing how acutely aware Kafka was of Prague's national iconography, we can imagine that when he sees the bridges from underneath, it is as if he were seeing the ideologies concealed within their iconography.

Against this background, the bridge motif that ends Kafka's 'The judgment' deserves particular attention. Kafka wrote this story in September 1912, only two months after the monument to Palacký was placed at the head of Palacký Bridge. At roughly the same time, occasioned by the census

39 See Marek Nekula, Prager Brücken und der nationale Diskurs in Böhmen (Prague bridges and the national discourse in Bohemia). In: *brücken. Germanistisches Jahrbuch Tschechien – Slowakei.* NF 12 (2004), pp. 163–186. 'German' professors commissioned a statue of the Emperor Charles IV on the bridgehead of the Charles Bridge in 1848 and thus gave Charles IV a role in the national discourse of the 19th century.

40 See Nelly Engel, Franz Kafka als 'boyfriend' (Franz Kafka as a boyfriend). In: Hans-Gerd Koch (ed.), *„Als Kafka mir entgegen kam…": Erinnerungen an Franz Kafka* ('As Kafka approached me'. Recollections of Franz Kafka). Berlin: Wagenbach 1995, pp. 118–124.

41 Franz Kafka, *Letters to Milena*. Translated and with an introduction by Philip Boehm. New York: Schocken Books 1990, p. 16.

of 1910, his family was pondering the question of its own national identity, while Kafka himself was commenting in his Travel Diaries on the complexity of the language situation in Switzerland viewed from the perspective of the language conflict in Bohemia, as I mentioned at the start of this chapter. This was also shortly after Kafka's Jewish 'rebirth' at around the end of 1911. Kafka's story could be read as a polemic against the program of assimilation, which the generation of fathers stood for, the bridge motif being a polemic against German and Czech national self-portrayals.

Hartmut Binder connects the bridge in 'The judgment' with the Svatopluk Čech Bridge, which was built between 1905 and 1908.[42] For Kafka's contemporaries this bridge symbolized the opening up of the rebuilt Jewish ghetto onto the banks of modernity. Kafka, however, associates this bridge with failure and suicide. While the statues on the Charles and Palacký Bridges embody opposing fossilized national agendas, which German and Czech nationalist students loudly defended in street battles, the fleeting shadow of the suicide Georg Bendemann darts quietly over the 'Jewish' bridge in the 'The judgment'. In 'a simply endless stream of traffic', Georg Bendemann falls quietly, covered by the noise of a passing bus, from the bridge parapet into the river[43] after his revolt against his father has failed, not unlike his former friend whose attempt to become a part of the 'colony of his compatriots in Russia' (which could mean the Jews), also came to naught.[44] Whereas in the first instance the allusion is to the policy of Jewish assimilation personified by Kafka's father, the second hints at the limits of Zionism. By committing suicide, Bendemann points to a third solution to the insoluble dilemma of being a Jew faced with the Scylla and Charybdis of German and Czech nationalism accompanied by antisemitism, which in 1918–20 came to an ugly head in pogroms on the streets of Prague and, as Kafka observed in a letter to Milena written between 17 and 20 November 1920, poisoned the atmosphere of the city:

> I've been spending every afternoon outside on the streets, wallowing in antisemitic hate. The other day I heard someone call the Jews 'prašivé plemeno' ('a mangy race').[45]

In his literary texts, however, the echoes of the discourse of the day are less audible – though audible nonetheless. Although the story 'Gracchus the hunter' (1917) is associated with Riva in Italy, the very name Gracchus (= jackdaw = *kavka*/Kafka) relocates it in Prague, thus evoking the monuments and their functions in the public space of the city:

---

42 See Binder, *Kafka-Handbuch in zwei Bänden*.

43 See Kafka, *Ein Landarzt*, p. 52. – Kafka, *Stories 1904–1924*, p. 56. See also Kafka, *The Complete Short Stories*, p. 88.

44 See Kafka, *Ein Landarzt*, p. 39. – See also Kafka, *Stories 1904–1924*, p. 45.

45 Kafka, *Letters to Milena*, p. 212.

> Two boys were sitting on the harbour wall playing with dice. A man was reading a newspaper on the steps of the monument, resting in the shadow of a hero who was flourishing his sword. A girl was filling her bucket at the fountain. A fruit-seller was lying beside his wares, gazing at the lake. [...] A man in a top hat tied with a band of black crêpe now descended one of the narrow and very steep lanes that led to the harbour. He glanced around vigilantly, everything seemed to distress him, his mouth twisted at the sight of some offal in a corner. Fruit skins were lying on the steps of the monument; he swept them off in passing with his stick.[46]

At first sight the monument appears as an unmarked, semantically 'dead' and empty part of an everyday scene: two boys play around it, discarded fruit peel lies on its steps. Yet at the same time the ideological semantics of the monument are potentially present in the irritable gesture of the old man, for whom the fruit skins are an insult to its importance – which is in turn evoked and reinforced by the newspaper the man is reading on the steps of the monument 'in the shadow of a hero who was flourishing his sword'. The depiction of the setting is so non-specific that it could be in any other city, except that it would be a different hero with a different sword pointing in a different direction, but in both cases dividing the world by nationalism.

So it is that, in those of Kafka's literary texts that take up the thread of contemporary public discourse, the small circle Thieberger watched him draw with his index finger is confronted with a space and a world divided by the Great Wall of China, the Babel of linguistic confusion, and the Scylla and Charybdis of Czech and German nationalism represented by (inter alia) the opposing icons of Vyšehrad and Prague Castle, and the monuments of warriors whose weapons cast their shadows on the printed media where public debate is conducted. In doing so he realigns the axis of Czech-German polarity, generalizing it into myth and thus lending his local 'Prague' stories universal validity.

46 Kafka, *The Complete Short Stories*, p. 326 f.

BIBLIOGRAPHY

André Alt, *Franz Kafka. Der ewige Sohn. Eine Biographie* (Franz Kafka. The Eternal Son. A Biography). Munich: Beck 2005.

Hans Peter Althaus, *Mauscheln. Ein Wort als Waffe* (Mauscheln: A Word as Weapon). Berlin, New York: de Gruyter 2002.

Hermann Bahr, Vorwort (Foreword). In: Fráňa Šrámek, *Flammen* (Flames). Leipzig: Ernst Rowohlt Verlag 1913, 5–7.

Hermann Bahr – Jaroslav Kvapil: *Briefe, Texte, Dokumente* (Letters, Texts, Documents). Ed. by Kurt Ifkovits. Berlin et al.: P. Lang 2007.

Jan Balhar et al., *Český jazykový atlas* (Atlas of the Czech Language). Vol. 4. Prague: Academia 2002.

František X. Bašík, *Vyučil jsem se u Kafků: Praha a Mladá Boleslav na konci 19. století očima dospívajícího muže* (I was an Apprentice in the Kafka Store: Prague and Mladá Boleslav at the end of 19th Century through the Eyes of an Adolescent). Prague: Prostor 2003.

Moritz Bassler (ed.), *New Historicism.* Tübingen: Francke 2001.

Johann Bauer [Josef Čermák], *Kafka und Prag* (Kafka and Prague). Stuttgart: Belser 1971.

Verena Bauer, Regionalismen in Franz Kafkas Deutsch (Amtliche Schriften, Tagebücher, Briefe). Ein Projektbericht (Regionalisms in Franz Kafka's German (Office writings, diaries, letters). Project report). Project Report). In: *brücken. Germanistisches Jahrbuch Tschechien – Slowakei.* NF 14 (2006), pp. 341–372.

Verena Bauer, 'Schwimmen zwischen Sprachen' – Franz Kafka und Prag. Sprachliche Variabilität im Kontext städtisch geprägter Identitätsangebote und institutioneller Zwänge ('Swimming between languages' – Franz Kafka and Prague. Language variability in context of urban identities and institutional pressures). In: Katarzyna Lasatowicz (ed.), *Städtische Räume als kulturelle Identitätsstrukturen: Schlesien und andere Vergleichsregionen* (Urban Spaces as Cultural Identity Structure: Silesia and other Comparative Regions). Berlin: trafo 2007, pp. 155–172.

Verena Bauer, Regionalismen in Franz Kafkas Deutsch – reflektiert vor dem Hintergrund des städtischen Kontextes Prags (Regionalisms in Franz Kafka's German – Against the background of the urban Prague context). In: Marek Nekula – Verena Bauer – Albrecht Greule (eds), *Deutsch in multilingualen Stadtzentren Mittel- und Osteuropas: Um die Jahrhundertwende vom 19. zum 20. Jahrhundert* (German in Multinational Cities in Central and East Europe. Around the Fin de Siècle from the 19th to the 20th Century). Vienna: Praesens 2008, pp. 45–78.

Peter Becher – Steffen Höhne – Marek Nekula (eds), *Kafka und Prag* (Kafka and Prague). Weimar, Cologne, Vienna: Böhlau 2012.

Evelyn Torton Beck, *Kafka and the Yiddish Theater. Its Impact on His Work.* Madison: University of Wisconsin Press 1971.

Franz J. Beranek, *Atlas der sudetendeutschen Umgangssprache* (Atlas of German Common Language in Sudetian Area). Vol. I. Marburg: Elwert 1970.

Hugo Bergmann, Schulzeit und Studium (School and student years). In: Hans-Gerd Koch (ed.), *„Als Kafka mir entgegen kam..." Erinnerungen an Franz Kafka* ('As Kafka approached me.' Recollections of Franz Kafka). Berlin: Wagenbach 1995, pp. 13–24.

Petr A. Bílek, Obraz Boženy Němcové – pár poznámek k jeho emblematické funkci (The image of Božena Němcová – some remarks on its emblematic function). In: Karel Piorecký (ed.), *Božena Němcová a její Babička* (Božena Němcová and her *Babička*). Prague: Ústav pro českou literaturu 2006, pp. 11–23.

Hartmut Binder, Franz Kafka und die Wochenzeitschrift *Selbstwehr* (Franz Kafka and the weekly *Selbstwehr*). *Deutsche Vierteljahrsschrift für Literaturwissenschaft und Geistesgeschichte* 41 (1967), Vol. 2 (May), pp. 283–304.

Hartmut Binder, Kafkas Hebräischstudien. Ein biographisch-interpretatorischer Versuch (Kafka's study of Hebrew: A biographically interpretative approach). In: *Jahrbuch der deutschen Schillergesellschaft* 11 (1967), pp. 527–556.

Hartmut Binder, Kafkas Briefscherze (Kafka's letter jokes). In: *Jahrbuch der deutschen Schillergesellschaft* 13 (1969), pp. 536–559.

Hartmut Binder, *Kafka-Kommentar zu den Romanen, Rezensionen, Aphorismen und zum Brief an den Vater* (Commentaries on Kafka' Novels, Reviews, Aphorisms and Letter to Father). Munich: Winkler Verlag 1976.

Hartmut Binder, *Kafka-Handbuch in zwei Bänden* (A Kafka Manual in two Volumes). Stuttgart: Kröner 1979.

Hartmut Binder, *Kafka. Ein Leben in Prag* (Kafka. A Life in Prague). München: Mahnert-Lueg 1982.

Hartmut Binder, *Kafka-Kommentar zu sämtlichen Erzählungen* (Commentaries on Kafka's Complete Stories). Munich: Winkler [3]1986.

Hartmut Binder, Kindheit in Prag. Kafkas Volksschuljahre (Childhood in Prague: Kafka's Years at Volksschule). In: Harry Järv (ed.), *Humanismen*. Stockholm: Atlantis 1987, pp. 63–115.

Hartmut Binder, Entlarvung einer Chimäre: Die deutsche Sprachinsel Prag (Unmasking a chimera: German island in Prague). In: Maurice Godé, Jacques Le Rider, Françoise Mayer (eds), *Allemands, Juifs et Tchèques à Prague de 1890 à 1924. / Deutsche, Juden und Tschechen in Prag 1890–1924*. Montpellier: Bibliothèque d'Études Germaniques et Centre-Européennes 1994, pp. 183–209.

Hartmut Binder, Paul Eisners dreifaches Ghetto (Paul Eisner's triple ghetto). In: Michel Reffet (ed.), *Le monde de Franz Werfel et la morale des nations. / Die Welt Franz Werfels und die Moral der Völker*. Berlin et al.: P. Lang 2000, pp. 17–137.

Hartmut Binder, *Wo Kafka und seine Freunde zu Gast waren. Prager Kaffeehäuser und Vergnügungsstätten in historischen Bilddokumenten* (Where Kafka and his Friends met: Prague Cafés and Etablissements in Historical Pictorial Documents). Prague, Furth im Wald: Vitalis 2000.

Hartmut Binder, *Kafkas Welt. Eine Lebenschronik in Bildern*: (Kafka's World: Chronicle of his Life in Pictures). Reinbek b. Hamburg: Rowohlt 2008.

Hartmut Binder (ed.), *Prager Profile. Vergessene Autoren im Schatten Kafkas* (Prague Profiles. Forgotten Writers in the Shadow of Franz Kafka). Berlin: Gebr. Mann Verlag 1991.

Salomo A. Birnbaum, *Grammatik der jiddischen Sprache* (Yiddish Grammar). Hamburg: Buske 1988.

Boris Blahak, „...wo die Menschen schreien, als brenne der Boden". Italienbilder bei Franz Kafka („...where the people cry, as if the earth would burn". Images of Italy in Franz Kafka). *Halbjahresschrift für südosteuropäische Geschichte, Literatur und Politik* 19 (2007), pp. 84–97.

Boris Blahak, Zum Erscheinungsbild von Franz Kafkas gesprochenem Deutsch. Die Autokorrekturen in den Manuskripten der literarischen Werke liefern Indizien für ‚austrophone' Mündlichkeit. (On an appearance of Franz Kafka's spoken German: Autocorrections in manuscripts of literary works give indices to 'austrophone' orality) In: Marek Nekula – Verena Bauer – Albrecht Greule (eds), *Deutsch in multilingualen Stadtzentren Mittel- und Osteuropas. Um die Jahrhundertwende vom 19. zum 20. Jahrhundert* (German in Multinational Cities in Central and East Europe. Around the Fin de Siècle from the 19th to the 20th Century). Vienna: Praesens 2008, pp. 79–98.

Boris Blahak, 'Deutsch, das wir von unsern undeutschen Müttern noch im Ohre haben'. Sedimente des Westjiddischen in Franz Kafkas Literatursprache' ('German that we have in our ears from our un-German mothers': West-Yiddish sediments in Franz Kafka's literary language). In: *brücken. Germanistisches Jahrbuch Tschechien – Slowakei.* NF 18 (2010), pp. 293–321.

Boris Blahak, „ich habe ja ganz an meinen Koffer vergessen". Divergenzen zwischen ‚reichsdeutscher', österreichischer und Prager Normauffassung um 1910 am Beispiel von Franz Kafkas Sprachmanagement im Schriftdeutschen ('I fully forgot my suitcase.': Divergence between German, Austrian and Praguian norm around 1900, exemplified on Franz Kafka's language management of standard German). *Brünner Hefte zu Deutsch als Fremdsprache* 4, 2011, issue 1/2, pp. 14–42.

Boris Blahak, *Franz Kafkas Literatursprache: Deutsch im Kontext des Prager Multilingualismus* (Franz Kafka's Literary Language: German in Context of Prague Multilingualism). Cologne, Weimar, Vienna: Böhlau 2015.

Herbert Blank, *V Kafkově knihovně* (In Kafka's Library). Prague: Nakladatelství Franze Kafky 2004.

Eduard Blocher, Zweisprachigkeit: Vorteile und Nachteile (Bilingualism: Advantages and disadvantages). In: Wilhelm Rein (ed.), *Enzyklopädisches Handbuch der Pädagogik* (Encyclopaedic Handbook of Pedagogy). Vol. 10. Langensalza: Beyer & Söhne [1909] [2]1910, pp. 665–670.

Hans Blüher, *Secessio Judaica. Philosophische Grundlegung der historischen Situation des Judentums und der antisemitischen Bewegung* (Secessio Judaica. Philosophical Foundation of the Historical Situation of Judaism and the Antisemitic Movement). Berlin: Der Weiße Ritter-Verlag 1922.

Alfred Bodenheimer, A sign of sickness and a symbol of health: Kafka's Hebrew notebooks. In: Mark Gelber (ed.), *Kafka, Zionism, and Beyond.* Tübingen: Niemeyer 2004, pp. 259–270.

Jonathan Bolton (ed.), *New Historicism.* Brno: Host 2007.

Jürgen Born, *Kafkas Bibliothek. Ein beschreibendes Verzeichnis* (Kafka's Library: A Descriptive Index). Frankfurt am Main: S. Fischer 1990.

Jürgen Born, *„Daß zwei in mir kämpfen…" und andere Aufsätze zu Franz Kafka* ('Two combatants at war within me …' and Other Papers on Franz Kafka). Furth im Wald, Prague: Vitalis 2000.

Alef Botros, *Kafka. Ein jüdischer Schriftsteller aus arabischer Sicht* (Kafka. A Jewish Author from the Arabic point of View). Wiesbaden: Reichert 2009.

Pierre Bourdieu, *Rules of Art: Genesis and Structure of the Literary Field.* Stanford University Press 1996.

Michael Brenner, *Kleine jüdische Geschichte* (A Short Jewish History). Munich: Beck 2008.

Emil Brix, *Die Umgangssprachen in Altösterreich zwischen Agitation und Assimilation: Die Sprachenstatistik in den zisleithanischen Volkszählungen 1880 bis 1910* (Common Languages in Old Austria between Agitation and Assimilation: Language Statistics in the Austrian Censuses, 1880–1910). Vienna, Cologne, Graz: Böhlau 1982.

Max Brod, Literarischer Abend des Klubs jüdischer Frauen und Mädchen (A literary evening in the Club for Jewish Women and Girls). *Selbstwehr* 12 (1918) [4 January], p. 4 f.

Max Brod, *Im Kampf um das Judentum. Politische Essays* (In the Struggle for Jewishness: Political Essays). Vienna, Berlin: R. Löwit Verlag 1920.

Max Brod, *Sozialismus im Zionismus* (Socialism and Zionism). Vienna, Berlin: R. Löwit Verlag 1920.

Max Brod, Eine Unterredung mit Professor Masaryk (A discussion with Professor Masaryk). In: Ernst Rychnovsky (ed.), *Masaryk und das Judentum* (Masaryk and Jews). Prag: Marsverlagsgesellschaft 1931, pp. 357–362.

Max Brod, *Franz Kafka: Eine Biographie* (Franz Kafka: A Biography). Frankfurt am Main: S. Fischer Verlag 1954.

Max Brod, *The Castle*: Its genesis. In: Angel Flores – Homer Swander (eds), *Franz Kafka Today.* Madison: University of Wisconsin Press 1958, pp. 161–164.

Max Brod, *Streitbares Leben. Autobiographie* (Disputatious Life: An Autobiography). Munich: Kindler 1960.

Max Brod, *Franz Kafka. Eine Biographie* (Franz Kafka: A Biography). Frankfurt am Main: S. Fischer 1963.

Max Brod, *Der Prager Kreis* (The Prague Circle). Stuttgart et al.: W. Kohlhammer 1966.

Max Brod, *Pražský kruh* (The Prague Circle). Prague: Akropolis 1993.

Max Brod, *Franz Kafka: A Biography*. Translated by G. Humphreys Roberts and Richard Winston. New York: Da Capo, 1995.

Max Brod – Franz Kafka, *Eine Freundschaft. Briefwechsel* (A Friendship: Correspondence). Ed. by Malcolm Pasley. Vol. 2. Frankfurt am Main: S. Fischer 1989.

Walter Bulst, Bedenken eines Philologen (Concerns of a philologist). *Studium generale* 7 (1954), pp. 321–323.

Miloslav Bureš, Franz Kafka u nás (Franz Kafka with us [a list of the old and planned translations]). *Svobodné slovo*, 9.7.1963, p. 3.

Hannelore Burger, *Sprachenrecht und Sprachgerechtigkeit im österreichischen Unterrichtswesen 1867–1918* (Language Law and Language Justice in the Austrian School System). Vienna: Verlag der Österreichischen Akademie der Wissenschaften 1995.

František Čapka – Květoslava Santlerová, *Z dějin vývoje písma* (From the History of the Evolution of Writing System). Brno: Masarykova univerzita 1998.

Kateřina Čapková, *Češi, Němci, Židé? Národní identita Židů v Čechách, 1918–1938* (Czechs, Germans, Jews? National Identity in Bohemia, 1918–1938). Prague: Paseka 2005.

Kateřina Čapková, Tschechisch, Deutsch, Jüdisch – wo ist der Unterschied? Komplexität von nationalen Identitäten der böhmischen Juden 1918–1938 (Czech, German, Jewish – where is the difference? Complexity of national identities of Bohemian Jews 1918–1938). In: Marek Nekula – Walter Koschmal (eds), *Juden zwischen Deutschen und Tschechen. Sprachliche, literarische und kulturelle Identitäten* (Jews between Germans and Czechs: Linguistic, Literary and Cultural Identities). Munich: Oldenbourg 2006, pp. 73–84.

Kateřina Čapková, Raum und Zeit als Faktoren der nationalen Identifikation der Prager Juden (Space and time as factors of national identification of Prague Jews). In: Peter Becher – Anna Knechtel (eds), *Praha – Prag 1900–1945: Literatur zweier Sprachen* (Prague 1900–1945: Literature of two Languages). Passsau: Stutz.

Kateřina Čapková, *Czechs, Germans, Jews? National Identity and the Jews of Bohemia*. New York, Oxford: Berghahn Books 2012.

Kateřina Čapková, 'Ich akzeptiere den Komplex, der ich bin'. Zionisten um Franz Kafka ('I accept the complex which I am.' Zionists around Franz Kafka). In: Peter Becher – Steffen Höhne – Marek Nekula (eds), *Kafka und Prag* (Kafka and Prague). Weimar, Cologne, Vienna: Böhlau 2012, pp. 79–95.

Maria Luise Caputo-Mayr – Julius Michael Herz, *Franz Kafka: Internationale Bibliographie* (Franz Kafka: An International Bibliography). Vol. 1–2. Munich: De Gruyter/Saur 1997 & 2000.

Josef Čermák, Franz Kafka, umělec naší doby (Franz Kafka, artist of our age). *Práce*, 3.7.1963, p. 4.

Josef Čermák, Zpráva o neznámých kafkovských dokumentech (Report on unknown Kafka documents). In: Eduard Goldstücker – František Kautman – Pavel Reiman (eds), *Franz Kafka: liblická konference 1963* (Franz Kafka: Liblice Conference 1963). Prague: ČSAV 1963, pp. 249–252.

Josef Čermák, Česká kultura a Franz Kafka: Recepce Kafkova díla v letech 1920–1948 (Czech Culture and Franz Kafka: Reception of Kafka's work 1920–1948). *Česká literatura* 16 (1968), pp. 463–473.

Josef Čermák, Franz Kafkas Sorgen mit der tschechischen Sprache (Franz Kafka's Concerns with Czech). In: Kurt Krolop – Hans Dieter Zimmermann (eds), *Kafka und Prag* (Kafka and Prague). Berlin, New York: de Gruyter 1994, pp. 59–66.

Josef Čermák, Die Kafka-Rezeption in Böhmen (1913–1949) (Kafka's reception in Bohemia 1913–1949). In: Kurt Krolop – Hans Dieter Zimmermann (eds), *Kafka und Prag* (Kafka and Prague). Berlin, New York: de Gruyter 1994, pp. 217–237.

Josef Čermák, Die Kafka-Rezeption in Böhmen (1913–1949) (Kafka's reception in Bohemia 1913–1949). *Germanoslavica* 1 (1994), pp. 1–2, pp. 127–144.

Josef Čermák, Recepce Franze Kafky v Čechách (1913–1963) (Franz Kafka's reception in Bohemia (1913–1963). In: *Kafkova zpráva o světě* (Kafka's Report on the World). Prague: Nakladatelství Franze Kafky 2000, pp. 14–36.

Josef Čermák, Junge Jahre in Prag. Ein Beitrag zum Freundeskreis Franz Werfels (Early life in Prague: A contribution to a circle of friends around Franz Werfel). In: Klaas-Hinrich Ehlers et al. (eds), *Brücken nach Prag. Deutschsprachige Literatur im kulturellen Kontext der Donaumonarchie und der Tschechoslowakei* (Bridges to Prague: German-written Literature in the Cultural Context of the Habsburg Monarchy and Czechoslovakia). Frankfurt am Main: P. Lang 2000, pp. 125–162.

Josef Čermák, Kafka und Prag (Kafka and Prague). In: Walter Koschmal – Marek Nekula – Joachim Rogall (eds), *Deutsche und Tschechen. Geschichte – Kultur – Politik* (Germans and Czechs: History – Culture – Politics). Munich: Beck 2001, pp. 217–235.

Václav Černý, *První sešit o existencialismu* (The First Book on Existentialism). Prague: Václav Petr 1948.

Václav Černý, Hrsť poznámok o kafkovskom románe a o Kafkovskom svete (Some comments on Kafka's novel and on Kafka's world). *Slovenské pohľady* 79 (1963), No. 10, pp. 80–95.

Václav Černý, *Paměti 1945–1972* (Memoires 1945–1972). Brno: Atlantis 1992.

Karel Charvát – Edvard Ouředníček, *Lehrgang der böhmischen Sprache für deutsche Mittelschulen* (Course in Czech Language for German Secondary Schools). Olomouc: Ed. Hölzel. Vol. 1, 1891; Vol. 2, 1893; Vol. 3, 1895.

Peter Demetz, Spekulationen über Prager Jiddisch (Speculations on Prague Yiddish). In: Peter Demetz, *Böhmen böhmisch. Essays* (Bohemian Bohemia: Essays). Vienna: Zsolnay 2006, pp. 9–27.

Gary B. Cohen, *The Politics of Ethnic Survival: Germans in Prague 1861–1914*. Princeton: Princeton University Press 1981.

Gary B. Cohen, *Němci v Praze 1861–1914* (Germans in Prague 1861–1914). Prague: Karolinum 2000.

Charles Darwin, *On the Origin of Species by Means of Natural Selection*. London: J. Murray [1859] 1861.

Charles Darwin, *The Descent of Man and Selection in Relation to Sex*. London: D. Appleton 1872.

Ivan Diviš, Franz Kafka. *Literární noviny* 12 (1963), No. 27, p. 7.

Giles Deleuze – Félix Guattari, *Kafka. Pour une littérature mineure*. Paris: Les Éditions de Minuit 1975.

Giles Deleuze – Félix Guattari, *Kafka: Toward a Minor Literature*. Minneapolis: University of Minnesota Press 1986.

Peter Demetz, Praha a Babylón (Prague and Babel). In: Peter Demetz, *České slunce a moravský měsíc* (Czech Sun and Moravian Moon). Ostrava: Tilia 1997, pp. 76–77.

Oskar Donath, *Židé a židovství v české literatuře 19. a 20. století* (Jews and Jewishness in the Czech Literature of the 19th and 20th Century). 2 vol. Brno: Privately printed 1930.

Oskar Donath, *Jüdisches in der neuen tschechischen Literatur* (Jewishness in the New Czech Literature). Prag: Privately printed 1931.

Ivan Dubský, Kafkova Amerika (Kafka's *Amerika*). *Kultura* 6 (1962), 12, p. 4.

Ivan Dubský, Amerika aneb Nezvěstný (Kafka's *Amerika* or *The Man who Disappeared*). *Host do domu* 9 (1962), 4, p. 181f.

Ivan Dubský, Návrat Franze Kafky (The return of Franz Kafka). *Kulturní tvorba* 1 (1963), No. 26, p. 8.

Ivan Dubský – Mojmír Hrbek, O Franzi Kafkovi (On Franz Kafka). *Nový život* 8 (1956), pp. 415–435.

Ivan Dubský – Mojmír Hrbek, Kafkův Proces (Kafka's *The Trial*). *Květen* 3 (1958), pp. 620–623.

Viktor Dyk, Němci v Čechách a české umění (Germans in Bohemia and Czech art). *Lumír – měsíční revue pro literaturu, umění a společnost* 42 (1914), May, no 8, pp. 331–336.

Eckhard Eggers, Zur Rolle Regensburgs bei der Entstehung des Jiddischen (On a role of Regensburg in the origin of Yiddish). In: Susanne Näßl (ed.), *Regensburger Deutsch. Zwölfhundertjahre Deutschsprachigkeit in Regensburg* (German in Regensburg: More than twelve Hundred Years of Germanness in Regensburg). Frankfurt am Main et al.: P. Lang 2002, pp. 127–137.

Pavel Eisner, *Milenky. Německý básník a česká žena* (Lovers. The German Writer and the Czech Woman). Prague: Dolínek 1930.

Pavel Eisner, Německá literatura na půdě ČSR od r. 1848 do našich dnů (German literature on Czechoslovak territory: from 1848 to the present). In: *Československá vlastivěda* (Encyclopae-

dic Information on Czechoslovakia). Vol. VII: *Písemnictví* (Literature). Prague: Sfinx 1933, pp. 325–377.
Pavel Eisner, Franz Kafka. *Světová literatura* 3 (1957), pp. 109–129.
Nelly Engel, Franz Kafka als 'boyfriend' (Franz Kafka as a boyfriend). In: Hans-Gerd Koch (ed.), *„Als Kafka mir entgegen kam...": Erinnerungen an Franz Kafka* ('As Kafka approached me.' Recollections of Franz Kafka). Berlin: Wagenbach 1995, pp. 118–124.
Manfred Engel – Dieter Lamping (eds), *Franz Kafka und die Weltliteratur* (Franz Kafka and World Literature). Göttingen: Vandenhoeck & Ruprecht 2006.
Manfred Engel – Bernd Auerochs (eds), *Kafka-Handbuch: Leben – Werk – Wirkung* (A Kafka Manual: Life – Oeuvre – Impact). Stuttgart, Weimar: Metzler 2010.
Howard Fast, *Literatura a skutečnost* (Literature and Reality). Translation by Zd. Kirschner and Jaroslav Bílý. Prague: Svoboda 1951.
Ernst Fischer, Jaro, vlaštovky a Franz Kafka (Spring, the swallows and Franz Kafka). *Literární noviny* 12 (1963), No. 41, p. 9.
Ingrid Fleischmann (= Stöhr), Sprachen an deutschen Prager Volksschulen (Languages in elementary schools in Prague). In: Marek Nekula – Ingrid Fleischmann – Albrecht Greule (eds), *Franz Kafka im sprachnationalen Kontext seiner Zeit. Sprache und nationale Identität in öffentlichen Institutionen der böhmischen Länder* (Franz Kafka in the National Context of his Time. Language and National Identity in the Public Institutions of the Bohemian Crown Lands). Cologne, Weimar: Böhlau 2007, pp. 183–212.
Ivo Fleischmann, Kafkova Amerika (Kafka's *Amerika*). *Literární noviny* 11 (1962), No. 16, pp. 368–369.
Ivo Fleischmann, O čem psal Franz Kafka? (What did Franz Kafka write about?). *Literární noviny* 12 (1963), No. 13, pp. 4–5.
Ivo Fleischmann (ed.), Franz Kafka a náš svět (Kafka and our world). Articles by Eduard Goldstücker, Ernst Fischer, Roger Garaudy, Ivan Sviták. *Literární noviny* 12 (1963), No. 23, p. 3.
Josef Florian – Staša Jílovská, *Vzájemná korespondence 1919–1922* (Mutual Correspondence 1919–1922). Prague: Documenta 1993.
Hanuš Frank – Karel Šmejkal, Po stopách Franze Kafky do jižních Čech (On the trail of Franz Kafka in South Bohemia). Anna Pouzarová's memoirs recorded by Hanuš Frank and Karel Šmejkal. *Práce*, 16.2.1964, p. 5.
Michal Frankl, *„Emancipace od židů." Český antisemitismus na konci 19. století* ('Emancipation from Jews.' Czech Antisemitism at the End of 19th Century). Prague, Litomyšl: Paseka 2007.
Michal Frankl, *„Prag ist nunmehr antisemitisch." Tschechischer Antisemitismus am Ende des 19. Jahrhunderts* ('Prague is henceforth antisemitic.' Czech Antisemitism at the end of 19th Century). Berlin: Metropol 2011.
Michal Frankl – Jindřich Toman (eds), *Jan Neruda a Židé. Texty a kontexty* (Jan Neruda and Jews: Texts and Contexts). Prague: Akropolis 2012.
Emanuel Frynta, *Franz Kafka lebte in Prag* (Franz Kafka Lived in Prague). With photographs by Jan Lukas. Translation into German by Lotte Elsner. Prague: Artia 1960.
Rudolf Fuchs, *Die Prager Aposteluhr. Gedichte, Prosa, Briefe* (The Prague Astronomical Clock: Poems, Prose, Letters). Ed. by Ilse Seehase. Halle, Leipzig: Mitteldeutscher Verlag 1985.
Louis Fürnberg, Život a smrt Franze Kafky (The life and death of Franz Kafka). Translation by Valter Feldstein. *Plamen* 5 (1963), No. 7, p. 108.
Roger Garaudy, Kafka a doktor Pangloss (Kafka and Dr. Pangloss). *Literární noviny* 12 (1963), No. 40, p. 9.
Roger Garaudy, O filosofii, Picassovi a Kafkovi (On philosophy, Picasso and Kafka; interview). *Plamen* 5 (1963), No. 8, pp. 1–3.
Mark Gelber, Kafka und zionistische Deutungen (Kafka and Zionist interpretations). In: Bettina von Jagow – Oliver Jahraus (eds), *Kafka-Handbuch: Leben – Werk – Wirkung* (A Kafka Manual : Life – Oeuvre – Impact). Göttingen: Vandenhoeck & Ruprecht 2008, pp. 293–303.
Axel Gellhaus, 'Das Schweigen der Sirenen.' Poetische Sprachreflexion in der Prosa Franz Kafkas ("The silence of the Sirens': Poetic language reflections in Franz Kafka's stories). In: Axel Gellhaus – Horst Sitta (eds), *Reflexionen über Sprache aus literatur- und sprachwissenschaftlicher*

Sicht (Reflections of Language from the Point of View of Linguistics and the Theory of Literature). Tübingen: Niemeyer 2000, pp. 13–39.

Eduard Goldstücker, Předtucha zániku: K profilu pražské německé poezie před půlstoletím (Premonition of doom: On the profile of German poetry in Prague 50 years ago). *Plamen* 2 (1960), pp. 92–96.

Eduard Goldstücker, Vyděděnci a temný obraz světa (Outcasts and their dark image of the world). *Plamen* 3 (1961), No. 10, pp. 66–69.

Eduard Goldstücker, Kafkův 'Topič' (Kafka's 'The Stoker'). *Tvorba* 27 (1962), No. 16, pp. 368–369.

Eduard Goldstücker, Jak je to s Franzem Kafkou? (How is it with Franz Kafka?). *Literární noviny* 12 (1963), No. 7, p. 4.

Eduard Goldstücker, O přístupu ke Kafkovi (On the approach to Kafka). *Literární noviny* 12 (1963), No. 11, pp. 4–5.

Eduard Goldstücker, Lidské poselství hledajícího člověka (Human legacy in search of people). *Rudé právo*, 3.7.1963, p. 5.

Eduard Goldstücker, Dnešní potřeby, zítřejší perspektivy (Today's needs, tomorrow's perspectives). *Literární noviny* 12 (1963), No. 40, p. 9.

Eduard Goldstücker, Kafka, oni a my (Kafka, them and us). *Literární noviny* 13 (1964), No. 26, p. 1.

Eduard Goldstücker, Kafkas 'Der Heizer'. Versuch einer Interpretation (Kafka's 'The Stoker': An attempt for an interpretation). *Germanistica Pragensia* 2 (1964), pp. 49–64.

Eduard Goldstücker, Doslov (Afterword). In: Franz Kafka, *Zámek* (The Castle). Prague: Mladá fronta 1964, pp. 306–313.

Eduard Goldstücker, Über Franz Kafka aus der Prager Sicht (On Franz Kafka from the Prague perspective). Translation by Kurt Krolop. In: Eduard Goldstücker – František Kautman – Paul Reimann (eds), *Franz Kafka aus Prager Sicht 1963* (Franz Kafka from the Prague Perspective 1963). Prague: ČSAV 1965, p. 23–43.

Eduard Goldstücker, *Na téma Franz Kafka. Články a studie* (On the Subject of Franz Kafka: Essays and Papers). Prague: Československý spisovatel 1964.

Eduard Goldstücker, *Prozesse. Erfahrungen eines Mitteleuropäers* (Trials: Experiences of a Central European). Munich: Knaus 1989.

Eduard Goldstücker, *Vzpomínky* (Memoirs) Vol. 2: 1945–1968. Prague: G plus G 2005.

Eduard Goldstücker – František Kautman – Pavel Reiman (eds), *Franz Kafka: liblická konference 1963* (Franz Kafka: Liblice Conference 1963). Prague: ČSAV 1963.

Eduard Goldstücker – František Kautman – Paul Reiman (eds), *Franz Kafka aus Prager Sicht 1963* (Franz Kafka from the Prague Perspective 1963). Prague: ČSAV 1965.

Růžena Grebeníčková, Gogolovy 'metamorphosis' na Západě (Gogol's 'metamorphosis' in the West). *Plamen* 2 (1960), pp. 126–128.

Jacob Grimm, *Deutsches Wörterbuch* (German Dictionary). Vol. 10. Leipzig: Verlag S. Hirzel 1919.

F. Ulbrich Grochtmann, *Anarchosyndikalismus, Bolschewismus und Proletkult in der Tschechoslowakei 1918–1924. Der Dichter Stanislav Kostka Neumann als Publizist in der tschechoslowakischen Arbeiterbewegung* (Anarchosyndicalism, Bolshevism and Prolekult in the Czechoslovakia 1918–1924: The Poet Stanislav Kostka Neumann as Publicist in the Czechoslovak Proletarian Movement). Munich: Lerche 1979.

Jan Grossman, Kafkova divadelnost? (Kafka's theatricality?). *Divadlo* 9 (1964), pp. 1–17.

Gm [= Pavel Grym], Kafkův hrdina v labyrintu světa (Kafka's hero in the labyrinth of the world). *Lidová demokracie*, 16.2.1962, p. 3.

Jürgen Habermas, *The Structural Transformation of the Public Sphere: An Inquiry into a Category of Bourgeois Society*. Translated by Thomas Burger by assistance of Frederick Lawrence. Cambridge/Mass.: MIT Press 1989.

Jiří Hájek, Spor o Franze Kafku (The dispute over Franz Kafka). *Tvorba* 24, 8.1.1959, No. 2, pp. 31–32.

Jiří Hájek, Neznámé dopisy Franze Kafky (Unknown letters by Franz Kafka). *Plamen* 5 (1963), No. 6, pp. 84–94.

Jiří Hájek, Kafka a marxistické literární myšlení (Kafka and Marxist literary thought). *Plamen* 5 (1963), No. 7, pp. 131–132.

Jiří Hájek, Alfréd Kurella a Franz Kafka, aneb o podmínkách principiální polemiky (Alfred Kurella and Franz Kafka, or on the conditions for a controversy over principles). *Plamen* 5 (1963), No. 10, 131.

Petr F. Hájek, Kouzelné přátelství (Wonderful friendship). In: Josef Florian – Staša Jílovská, *Vzájemná korespondence 1919–1922* (Mutual Correspondence 1919–1922). Prague: Documenta 1993, pp. 7–10.

Marie Halířová – Hana Larvová (eds), *František Bílek (1872–1941)*. Prague: Národní galerie 2001.

Aage A. Hansen-Löve, Vor dem Gesetz (Before the law). In: Michael Müller, (ed.), *Interpretationen. Franz Kafka. Romane und Erzählungen* (Interpretations. Franz Kafka. Novels and Short Stories). Stuttgart: Reclam 1994, pp. 146–157.

Ekkehard W. Haring, Leben und Persönlichkeit (Biography and personality). In: Manfred Engel – Bernd Auerochs (eds), *Kafka-Handbuch. Leben – Werk – Wirkung* (A Kafka Manual: Biography – Oeuvre – Impact). Stuttgart, Weimar: Metzler 2010, pp. 1–27.

Hugo Hermann, *In jenen Tagen* (In those Days). Jerusalem: self-publication 1938.

Stephan Hermlin, Die Abrüstung der Kultur. Rede auf dem Weltfriedenkongreß in Moskau (Demilitarization of the culture: Speech for the world peace conference in Moskau). *Sinn und Form* 14 (1962), pp. 805–815.

Klaus Hermsdorf, Werfels und Kafkas Verhältnis zur tschechischen Literatur (Werfel's and Kafka's relation to Czech literature). *Germanistica Pragensia* 2 (1964), pp. 39–47.

Steffen Höhne, 1968, Prag und die DDR-Germanistik. Zur Verflechtung von Ideologie und Politik in der Kafka-Rezeption (1968, Prague and GDR German Studies: Ideology a politics in Kafka's reception). In: Wolfgang Adam – Holger Dainat – Günter Schandera (eds), *Wissenschaft und Systemveränderung: Rezeptionsforschung in Ost und West – eine konvergente Entwicklung?* (Scholarship and System Change? Reception Research in East and West: A Convergent Development?) Heidelberg: Winter 2003, pp. 225–244.

Steffen Höhne (ed.), *August Sauer (1855–1926) – ein Intellektueller in Prag im Spannungsfeld von Kultur- und Wissenschaftspolitik* (August Sauer: An Intellectual in Prague between Cultural and Scholarly Politics). Cologne, Weimar, Vienna: Böhlau 2011.

Zdeněk Hojda and Jiří Pokorný, *Pomníky a zapomníky* (Monuments and Memory Lost). Prague, Litomyšl: Paseka 1997.

Wilma Iggers, *Die Juden in Böhmen und Mähren. Ein historisches Lesebuch* (Jews in Bohemia and Moravia: A Historical Reader). Munich: Beck 1986.

Wolfgang Iser, *Der Akt des Lesens* (The Act of Reading). Munich: Fink 1976.

Jahresbericht über das Deutsche Staats-Gymnasium mit deutscher Unterrichtssprache in Prag-Altstadt für das Schuljahr... (Annual School Reports on German State Grammar school with German as Instruction Language in Old Prague...). Vol. 22.–29. Prag 1894–1901: K.u.k. Hofbuchdruckerei A. Haase.

Jaroslava Janáčková, Alena Macurová et al., *Řeč dopisů, řeč v dopisech Boženy Němcové* (Language of Letters, Language in Božena Němcová's Letters). Prague: ISV nakladatelství 2001.

Gustav Janouch, *Gespräche mit Kafka* (Conversations with Kafka). Frankfurt am Main: S. Fischer 1951.

Gustav Janouch, *Gespräche mit Kafka. Aufzeichnungen und Erinnerungen* (Conversations with Kafka. Notes and Memoirs). Extended edition. Frankfurt am Main: S. Fischer [1968] 1981.

Hans Robert Jauss, *Literaturgeschichte als Provokation der Literaturwissenschaft* (Historiography of Literature as a Provocation of the Theory of Literature) Constance: Universitätsverlag 1967.

Čestmír Jeřábek, Jubileum pražského básníka (Anniversary of the Prague writer). *Host do domu* 5 (1958), pp. 334–335.

Čestmír Jeřábek, Kafkův Proces česky (Kafka's *The Trial* in Czech). *Host do domu* 5 (1958), pp. 373–374.

Josef Jungmann, O jazyku českém rozmlouvání první (The first dialogue on Czech language). In: Josef Jungmann, *Vybrané spisy původní a přeložené* (Selected Writings: Original and Translations). Ed. by Karel Hikl. Prague: Vojtěch Hrách [1806] 1918, pp. 39–45.

Franz Kafka, Topič (The Stoker). *Kmen* 4, No. 6, 22 April 1920, pp. 61–72.
Franz Kafka, Nešťastný (Unhappiness). *Tribuna* 2, No. 166, 16 July 1920, pp. 1–2.
Franz Kafka, Náhlá procházka, Výlet do hor, Neštěstí mládence, Kupec, Cesta domů, Ti, kteří běží mimo (The sudden walk, Excursion into the mountains, Bachelor's ill luck, The tradesman, The way home, Passers-by). *Kmen* 4, No. 26, 9 September 1920, pp. 308–310.
Franz Kafka, Zpráva pro akademii (A report to an Academy). In *Tribuna* 2, No. 227, 26 September 1920, pp. 1–4.
Franz Kafka, Před zákonem (Before the law), *Právo lidu* 29, No. 253, 24 October 1920. Sunday supplement No. 43.
Franz Kafka, Závodníkům na uváženou (Reflections for gentlemen-jockeys). *Tribuna* 4, Christmas supplement, 24 December 1922, p. 8.
Franz Kafka, Soud (The judgment). *Cesta* 5 (1923), No. 26/27, pp. 369–372.
Franz Kafka, *Starý list* (A Page from an Old Manuscript). Litomyšl: Portman 1928.
Franz Kafka, *Sen* (A Dream). Translated by Gustav Janouch, Graphik von O. Coestera. Stará Říše 1929.
Franz Kafka, *Proměna* (The Metamorphosis). Translated by L. Vrána and F. Pastor. Stará Říše 1929.
Franz Kafka, *Zpráva pro akademii* (A Report to an Academy). Litomyšl: Portman 1929.
Franz Kafka, *Venkovský lékař* (A Country Doctor). Litomyšl: Portman 1931.
Franz Kafka, *The Diaries of Franz Kafka 1910–1913*. Edited by Max Brod and translated by Joseph Kresh. New York: Schocken 1948.
Franz Kafka, *The Diaries of Franz Kafka, 1914–1923*. Translated by Martin Greenberg. New York: Schocken 1949.
Franz Kafka, *Briefe an Milena* (Letters to Milena). Frankfurt am Main: Fischer 1952.
Franz Kafka, *Letters to Milena*. Edited by Willi Haas. Translated by Tania and James Stern. New York: Schocken Books [1953] 1965.
Franz Kafka, *Dearest Father. Stories and Other Writings*. Translated by Ernst Kaiser and Eithne Wilkins. New York: Schocken 1954.
Franz Kafka, Doupě (The burrow). *Světová literatura* 3 (1957), pp. 132–153.
Franz Kafka, *Proces* (The Trial). Translation and afterword by Pavel Eisner. Prague: Československý spisovatel 1958.
Franz Kafka, *Briefe 1902–1924* (Letters 1902–1924). Ed. by Max Brod. Frankfurt am Main: S. Fischer 1958.
Franz Kafka, *Amerika* (The Man who Disappeared). Translation by Dagmar Eisnerová, foreword by Pavel Reiman. Prague: SNKLU 1962.
Franz Kafka, Dopis otci (Letter to his Father). Translation by Dagmar Eisnerová and Pavel Eisner, introduced by Klaus Hermsdorf. *Světová literatura* 7 (1962), No. 6, pp. 84–112.
Franz Kafka, *Proměna* (The Metamorphosis). Translation by Zbyněk Sekal and afterword by Josef Čermák. Prague: SNKLU 1963.
Franz Kafka, Neznámé dopisy Franze Kafky (Unknown letters by Franz Kafka). Translation by Aloys Skoumal. Introduced by Jiří Hájek. *Plamen* 5 (1963), No. 6, pp. 84–94.
Franz Kafka, Kafka inconnu. Translation by O. Beneš and Paul Lecler. In: *La vie tchécoslovaque* 11 (1963), No. 10, pp. 26–27.
Franz Kafka, Poselství Franze Kafky (Legacy of Franz Kafka). With translations of First Sorrow and Poseidon by Jiří Gruša. *Mladý svět* 5 (1963), No. 27, pp. 10–11.
Franz Kafka, *Briefe an Milena* (Letters to Milena). Edited and with an afterword by Willy Haas. Frankfurt am Main: S. Fischer 1966.
Franz Kafka, *Briefe an Felice und andere Korrespondenz aus der Verlobungszeit* (Letters to Felice and other Correspondence from the Time of Engagement). Ed. by E. Heller and Jürgen Born. Frankfurt am Main: S. Fischer 1967.
Franz Kafka, *Letters to Felice*. Translated by James Stern and Elizabeth Duckworth. New York: Schocken 1967.
Franz Kafka, *Briefe an Ottla und die Familie* (Letters to Ottla and Family). Edited by Hartmut Binder and Klaus Wagenbach. Frankfurt am Main: S. Fischer [1974] 1975.

Franz Kafka, *Letters to Friends, Family, and Editors*. Translated by Richard and Clara Winston. New York: Schocken Books 1977.
Franz Kafka, *Letters to Ottla and Family*. Translated by Richard and Clara Winston. New York: Schocken Books 1982.
Franz Kafka, *Amtliche Schriften* (Office Writings). Edited by Klaus Hermsdorf. Berlin: Akademie-Verlag 1984.
Franz Kafka, *Tagebücher* (Diaries). Ed. by Hans-Gerd Koch, Michael Müller, Malcolm Pasley. Vol. 1. Frankfurt am Main: S. Fischer 1990.
Franz Kafka, *Letters to Milena*. Translated by Philip Boem. New York: Schocken 1990.
Franz Kafka, *Nachgelassene Schriften und Fragmente* (Literary Remains and Fragments). Ed. by Malcolm Pasley. Vol. 1. Frankfurt am Main: S. Fischer 1993.
Franz Kafka, *Ein Landarzt und andere Drucke zu Lebzeiten* (A Country Doctor. Texts Published in his Lifetime). Ed. by Hans-Gerd Koch. Frankfurt am Main: S. Fischer 1994.
Franz Kafka, *Zur Frage der Gesetze und andere Schriften aus dem Nachlaß in der Fassung der Handschrift* (On the Question of Laws and other Literary Remains Based on the Handwritten Manuscripts). Ed. by Hans-Gerd Koch. Frankfurt am Main: S. Fischer 1994.
Franz Kafka, *Beschreibung eines Kampfes und andere Schriften aus dem Nachlaß in der Fassung der Handschrift* (Description of a Struggle and Other Literary Remains Based on the Handwritten Manuscripts). Ed. by Hans-Gerd Koch. Frankfurt am Main: S. Fischer 1994.
Franz Kafka, *Beim Bau der chinesischen Mauer und andere Schriften aus dem Nachlaß in der Fassung der Handschrift* (Building of the Great Wall of China and other Literary Remains Based on the Handwritten Manuscripts). Ed. by Hans-Gerd Koch. Frankfurt am Main: S. Fischer 1994.
Franz Kafka: *Tagebücher 1914–1923 in der Fassung der Handschrift* (Diaries 1914–1923 Based on the Handwritten Manuscripts). Ed. by Hans-Gerd Koch. Frankfurt am Main: S. Fischer 1994.
Franz Kafka, *Reisetagebücher in der Fassung der Handschrift* (Travel Diaries Based on Handwritten Manuscripts). Ed. by Hans-Gerd Koch. Frankfurt am Main: S. Fischer 1994.
Franz Kafka, *Stories 1904–1924*. Translated by J. A. Underwood, with a foreword by Jorge Luis Borges. London: Abacus 1995.
Franz Kafka, *Dopisy Ottle a rodině* (Letters to Ottla and Family). Translation, annotation and afterword by Vojtěch Saudek. Prague: Aurora 1996.
Franz Kafka, *Briefe an Milena* (Letters to Milena). Extended new edition. Ed. by Jürgen Born and Michael Müller. Frankfurt am Main: S. Fischer 1998.
Franz Kafka, *Briefe 1900–1913* (Letters 1900–1913). Ed. by Hans-Gerd Koch. Frankfurt am Main: S. Fischer 1999.
Franz Kafka, *Povídky I. Proměna a jiné texty vydané za života* (Short Stories I. The Metamorphosis and other Texts Published during the Life). Translated by Vladimír Kafka, Marek Nekula, Věra Koubová, Josef Čermák. Prague: Nakladatelství Franze Kafky 1999.
Franz Kafka, *The Complete Short Stories of Franz Kafka*. Ed. by Nahum N. Glazer. London: Random House Vintage 1999.
Franz Kafka, *Letters to Felice*. Translated by James Stern and Elizabeth Duckworth. London: Vintage 1999.
Franz Kafka, *Briefe 1913 – März 1914* (Letters 1913 – March 1914). Ed. by Hans-Gerd Koch. Frankfurt am Main: S. Fischer 2001.
Franz Kafka, *Amtliche Schriften* (Office Writings). Ed. by Klaus Hermsdorf and Benno Wagner. Frankfurt am Main 2004.
Franz Kafka, *Dopisy rodině* (Letters to Family). Translation by Vojtěch Saudek. Edited and commentary by Václav Maidl and Marek Nekula. Prague: Nakladatelství Franze Kafky 2005.
Franz Kafka, *Selected Stories*. Translated and edited by Stanley Corngold. New York, London: J. J. Norton 2005.
Franz Kafka, *Briefe April 1914–1917* (Letters April 1914–1917). Edited by Hans-Gerd Koch. Frankfurt am Main: S. Fischer 2005.
Franz Kafka, *Dopisy přátelům* (Letters to Friends). Translated by Věra Koubová. Ed. by Hans-

-Gerd Koch, Věra Koubová, Michaela Jacobsenová and Marek Nekula. Prague: Nakladatelství F. Kafky 2007.
Franz Kafka, *Briefe 1918–1920* (Letters 1918–1920). Edited by Hans-Gerd Koch. Frankfurt am Main: S. Fischer 2013.
Franz Kafka a Praha. Vzpomínky, úvahy, dokumenty (Franz Kafka and Prague. Memories, Reflections, Papers). Prague: Žikeš 1947.
Kalendář česko-židovský, since 1881.
Agneša Kalinová, Kafka v Bergamu (Kafka in Bergamo). *Literární noviny* 11 (1962), No. 40, p. 8.
Dr. M. K. [= Miroslav Kaňák], Ztracený a znovu nalezený (Lost and rediscovered). *Český zápas* 46 (1963), No. 34–35, p. 8.
František Kautman, Franz Kafka a česká literatura (Franz Kafka and Czech literature). In: Eduard Goldstücker – František Kautman – Pavel Reiman (eds), *Franz Kafka: liblická konference 1963* (Franz Kafka: Liblice Conference 1963). Prague: ČSAV 1963, pp. 39–75.
František Kautman, Ještě jednou Franz Kafka z pražské perspektivy (Franz Kafka, once again from the Prague perspective). *Plamen* 6 (1964), No. 8, pp. 165–166.
František Kautman, Boje o Kafku včera a dnes (Disputes over Kafka then and now). *Literární noviny* 14 (1964), No. 27, p. 5
František Kautman, Pražská německá literatura (German literature in Prague). *Literární noviny* 14 (1964), No. 48, p. 4.
František Kautman, Franz Kafka und die tschechische Literatur (Franz Kafka and Czech literature). In: Eduard Goldstücker – František Kautman – Paul Reimann (eds), *Franz Kafka aus Prager Sicht 1963* (Franz Kafka from the Prague Perspective 1963). Prague: ČSAV 1965, pp. 44–77.
František Kautman, Franz Kafka a Čechy (Franz Kafka and Bohemia). *Literární archiv* 1 (1966), pp. 179–197.
Hillel J. Kieval, *The Making of Czech Jewry. National Conflict and Jewish Society in Bohemia, 1870–1918.* New Oxford, Oxford: Oxford University Press 1988.
Andreas Kilcher, Kafka, Scholem und die Politik der jüdischen Sprachen (Kafka, Scholem and the politics of Jewish languages). In: Christoph Miething (ed.), *Politik und Religion im Judentum* (Politics and Religion in Judaism). Tübingen: Niemeyer 1999, pp. 79–115.
Andreas B. Kilcher, Kafka und das Judentum (Kafka and Jewishness). In: Bettina von Jagow – Oliver Jahraus (eds), *Kafka-Handbuch: Leben – Werk – Wirkung* (A Kafka Manual: Life – Oeuvre – Impact). Göttingen: Vandenhoeck & Ruprecht 2008, pp. 194–211.
Andreas Kilcher, Kafkas Proteus: Verhandlungen mit Odradek (Kafka's Proteus: Negotiation with Odradek). In: Irmgard M. Wirtz (ed.), *Kafka verschrieben* (Committed to Kafka). Göttingen, Zürich: Wallstein 2010, pp. 97–116.
Alfred Klepsch, *Westjiddisches Wörterbuch. Auf der Basis dialektologischer Erhebungen in Mittelfranken* (West Yiddish Dictionary: Based on Dialectological Research in Middle Franconia). Tübingen: Niemeyer 2004.
Clemens Knobloch, *Geschichte der psychologischen Sprachauffassung in Deutschland von 1850 bis 1920* (History of Psychological Conceptions of Language in Germany from 1850 until 1920). Tübingen: Niemeyer 1988.
Hans-Gerd Koch, Ein Bericht für eine Akademie (A report to an Academy). In: Michael Müller (ed.), *Franz Kafka. Romane und Erzählungen* (Franz Kafka: Novels and Stories). Stuttgart: Reclam 1994, pp. 173–196.
Hans-Gerd Koch (ed.), *„Als Kafka mir entgegen kam...": Erinnerungen an Franz Kafka* ('As Kafka approached me.' Recollections of Franz Kafka). Berlin: Wagenbach 1995.
Ines Koeltzsch, Liblice. In: Dan Diner (ed.), *Enzyklopädie jüdischer Geschichte und Kultur* (Encyclopaedia of Jewish History and Culture). Vol. 3 (He – Lu). Stuttgart, Weimar: Metzler 2012, pp. 511–515.
Albert Kohn, *Die Notablenversammlung der Israeliten Böhmens in Prag, ihre Berathungen und Beschlüsse. Mit statistischen Tabellen über die israelitischen Gemeinden, Synagogen, Schulen und Rabbinate in Böhmen* (Collection of Notable Bohemian Jews in Prague, their Sessions and

Decisions, Statistical Tables on Jewish Municipal Authorities, Synagogues, Schools and Rabbinates in Bohemia). Vienna: Verlag von Leopold Sommer, 1852.

Jiří Kořalka, Das Nationalitätenproblem in den böhmischen Ländern 1848–1918 (Problem of nationality in Bohemian Lands 1848–1918). *Österreichische Osthefte* 5 (1991), pp. 1–11.

Jiří Kořalka, *Tschechen im Habsburgerreich und in Europa 1815–1914* (Czechs in the Habsburg Empire and in Europe 1815–1914). Vienna, Munich: Oldenbourg 1991.

Walter Koschmal, *Der Dichternomade: Jiří Mordechai Langer ein tschechisch-jüdischer Autor* (A Nomad Poet: Jiří Mordechai Langer – a Czech-Jewish Author). Cologne, Weimar, Vienna: Böhlau 2010.

Karel Kosík, Hašek a Kafka neboli groteskní svět (Hašek and Kafka, or the grotesque world). *Plamen* 5 (1963), No. 6, pp. 95–102.

Karel Kosík, *Století Markéty Samsové* (Century of Markéta Samsa). Prague: Český spisovatel 1993.

Jan Evangelista Kosina – František Bartoš, *Malá Slovesnosť, kterou za knihu učebnou a čitací pro vyšší třídy škol středních* (Short Poetics, which Can be Used as Textbook and Reader for High Secondary Schools). Brno: Karl Winker 1876; [3]1883; [4]1893.

Oskar Kosta, Hledání a bloudění Franze Kafky (The searching and wandering of Franz Kafka). *Nový život* 10 (1958), pp. 784–786.

Emanuel Kovář, *O původě lidské mluvy* (On the Origin of Human Speech). Prague: Bursík a Kohout 1898.

Zdeněk Kožmín, Marxistická monografie o Kafkovi (Marxist monograph on Kafka). *Host do domu* 7 (1962), pp. 223–225.

F. R. Kraus, K 80. narozeninám Franze Kafky (On Franz Kafka's 80th birthday). In: *Věstník židovských náboženských obcí v Československu* 25 (1963), No. 7, p. 6.

J. S. Kraus, Německo-židovské školy v Čechách (German-Jewish schools in Bohemia). In: *Kalendář česko-židovský na rok 1882/1883*, 117–125.

Detlef Kremer, Ein *Landarzt* (A Country Doctor). In: Michael Müller (ed.), *Interpretationen. Franz Kafka. Romane und Erzählungen* (Interpretations. Franz Kafka. Novels and Short Stories). Stuttgart: Reclam 1994, pp. 197–214.

Jan Křen, *Konfliktgemeinschaft. Tschechen und Deutsche 1780–1918* (Conflictive Community: Czechs and Germans 1780–1918). 2nd edition. Munich: Oldenbourg 2000.

Václav K. Krofta, Im Amt mit Franz Kafka (In the office with Franz Kafka). In: Hans-Gerd Koch (ed.), *„Als Kafka mir entgegen kam..." Erinnerungen an Franz Kafka* ('As Kafka approached me.' Recollections of Franz Kafka). Berlin: Wagenbach 1995, pp. 92–94.

Kurt Krolop, Zu den Erinnerungen Anna Lichtensterns an Franz Kafka. Ke vzpomínkám Anny Lichtensternové na Franze Kafku (On Anna Lichtenstern's recollections of Franz Kafka). *Germanistica Pragensia* 5 (1968), pp. 21–60.

Kurt Krolop, Prager Autoren im Lichte der 'Fackel' (Prager writers in the light of 'Die Fackel'). *Prager deutschsprachige Literatur zur Zeit Kafkas* (Prague German-Written Literature in Kafka's Time). Ed. by Österreichische Franz-Kafka-Gesellschaft Wien-Klosterneuburg. Vienna: Braunmüller 1989, 92–117.

Kurt Krolop, Sprachprobleme bei der Lektüre des ‚Prozesses' (Language problems in reading of 'The Trial'). *Wissenschaftliche Zeitschrift der Martin-Luther-Universität Halle-Wittenberg* 41 (1992), vol. 1, pp. 49–57.

Kurt Krolop, *Studien zur Prager deutschen Literatur. Festschrift zum 75. Geburtstag* (Studies on Prague German Literature). Ed. by Klaas-Hinrich Ehlers, Steffen Höhne, Marek Nekula. Vienna: Edition Praesens 2005.

Jaroslav Kučera, *Minderheit im Nationalstaat. Die Sprachenfrage in den tschechisch-deutschen Beziehungen 1918–1938* (Minority in the National State: The Language Question in the Czech – German Relationship, 1918–1938). Munich: R. Oldenbourg 1999.

Lumír Kuchař, *Dialogy o kráse a smrti. Studie a materiály k české literatuře přelomu 19. a 20. století* (Dialogues on Beauty and Death: Studies and Documents to the Czech Literature of Fin de Siècle from the 19th and 20th Century). Ed. by Marek Nekula. Brno: Host 1999.

Jiří Kuděla, Germanizace židovských jmen v Čechách (Germanization of Jewish names in Bohemia). *Židovská ročenka*, 2005, pp. 23–39.

Jiří Kuděla, Galician and East European refugees in the historic lands: 1914–16. *Review for the History of Czechoslovak Jews* 4 (1991–92), pp. 15–32.

Milan Kundera, *Kastrující stín svatého Garty* (The Castrating Shadow of Saint Garta). Brno: Atlantis 2006.

Alfred Kurella, Jaro, vlaštovky a Franz Kafka (Spring, the swallows and Franz Kafka). *Literární noviny* 12 (1963), No. 40, p. 8.

Alexej Kusák, *Tance kolem Kafky: Liblická konference 1963 – vzpomínky a dokumenty po 40 letech* (The Dance around Kafka: the Liblice Conference of 1963 – Memories and Papers 40 years on). Prague: Akropolis 2003.

Vladimir V. Kusin, *The Intellectual Origins of the Prague Spring. The Development of Reformist Ideas in Czechoslovakia 1956–1967*. Cambridge (MA): Cambridge University Press 2002.

Gustav Landauer, Friedrich Hölderlin. *Kmen* 4, No. 23 (19 Aug. 1920), pp. 269–274, No. 24 (26 Aug. 1920), pp. 283–286, No. 25 (2 Sept. 1920), pp. 294–297.

Jiří Langer, Vzpomínka na Kafku (A memoir of Kafka). In: Jiří Langer, *Studie, recenze, články, dopisy* (Papers, Reviews, Articles, Letters). Prague: Sefer 1995, p. 139–140. (Hebrew original in the magazine *Hege*, 23.2.1941, resp. 27. ševat 5701).

Moritz Lazarus, *Geist und Sprache. Eine psychologische Monographie* (Mind and Language: A Psychological Monograph). Berlin: F. Fümmler 1884 [1st ed. 1856/7].

Friedrich von der Leyen, *Deutsche Dichtung* (German Literature). Jena: Diederichs 1922.

William Burley Lockwood, *Lehrbuch der modernen jiddischen Sprache* (Textbook of Modern Yiddish). Hamburg: Buske 1995.

Heinrich Loewe, Der Nationalismus (Nationalism). In: *Zion. Monatsschrift für die nationalen Interessen des Judentums* 2 (1895), pp. 33–41.

Ronald Lötzsch, *Jiddisches Wörterbuch* (Yiddish Dictionary). Mannheim, Leipzig, Vienna, Zürich: Dudenverlag 1992.

Jaromír Loužil, Dopisy Franze Kafky Dělnické úrazové pojišťovně pro Čechy v Praze (Franz Kafka's letters to the Worker's Accident Insurance Company). In: *Sborník Národního muzea v Praze*, Row C, Literary history 8 (1963), No. 2, pp. 57–83.

Robert Luft, Sind die böhmischen Deutschen Deutsche? Oder: Die Nationalität und das weiße Pferd! (Are Bohemian Germans Germans?) *Bohemia* 35 (1994), 403–409.

Robert Luft, Sprache und Nationalität an Prager Gymnasien um 1900 (Language and nationality at Prague grammar schools around 1900). In: Klaas-Hinrich Ehlers et al. (eds), *Brücken nach Prag. Deutschsprachige Literatur im kulturellen Kontext der Donaumonarchie und der Tschechoslowakei* (Bridges to Prague: German-written Literature in the Cultural Context of the Habsburg Monarchy and Czechoslovakia). Frankfurt am Main: P. Lang 2000, pp. 105–122.

Věra Macháčková, Konference o díle Franze Kafky (Conference on the work of Franz Kafka). *Rudé právo*, 31.5.1963, p. 3.

Vladimír Macura, *Znamení zrodu: české národní obrození jako kulturní typ* (Signs of Rebirth: Czech National Rebirth as Cultural Type). Jinočany: H & H 1995.

Marie Majerová, Zahajovací projev (Opening speech). In: Eduard Goldstücker – František Kautman – Pavel Reiman (eds), *Franz Kafka: liblická konference 1963* (Franz Kafka: Liblice Conference 1963). Prague: ČSAV 1963, p. 9.

Michaela Marek, 'Monumentalbauten' und Städtebau als Spiegel des gesellschaftlichen Wandels in der 2. Hälfte des 19. Jahrhunderts (Monuments and urbanization as a reflection of social change in second half of the 19th century). In: Ferdinand Seibt (ed.), *Böhmen im 19. Jahrhundert: Vom Klassizismus zur Moderne* (Bohemia in the 19th Century: From Classicism to Modernity). Frankfurt am Main, Berlin: Propyläen 1995, pp. 149–233, 390–411.

Michaela Marek, *Kunst und Identitätspolitik. Architektur und Bildkünste im Prozess der tschechischen Nationsbildung* (Art and Identity Politics: Architecture and Visual Arts in Process of Czech National Building). Weimar, Cologne, Vienna: Böhlau 2004.

Anton Marty, *Über den Ursprung der Sprache* (On the Origin of Language). Würzburg: A. Stuber 1875.

Anton Marty, *Untersuchungen zur Grundlegung der allgemeinen Grammatik und Sprachphilosophie* (Investigations into the Foundation of General Grammar and Language Philosophy). Halle: M. Niemeyer 1908.

Josef Masařík, *Böhmische Schulgrammatik. Für deutsche Mittelschulen und Lehrer-Bildungsanstalten bearbeitet* (Czech Grammar for Schools: Prepared for German Secondary Schools and Institutes for Teacher Education). 6th revised edition. Prague: F. Tempsky 1894.

Guido Massino, *Franz Kafka, Jicchak Löwy und das jiddische Theater. "diese nicht niederzudrückende Feuer des Löwy"* (Franz Kafka, Yitzchak Löwy and the Yiddish Theatre: 'This irrepressible fire of Löwy). Frankfut am Main: Stroemfeld, Nexus 2007.

Fritz Mauthner, *Die Sprache* (Language). Frankfurt am Main 1907.

Fritz Mauthner, *Prager Jugendjahre: Erinnerungen* (Youth in Prague: Memoirs). Munich: Müller [1918] 1969.

Puah Menzel-Ben-Tovim, Ich war Kafkas Hebräischlehrerin (I was Kafka's Hebrew teacher). In: Hans-Gerd Koch (ed.), *„Als Kafka mir entgegen kam..." Erinnerungen an Franz Kafka* ('As Kafka approached me.' Recollections of Franz Kafka). Berlin: Wagenbach 1995, pp. 165–167.

Antonín Měšťan, Slované u Franze Kafky (Slavs in Franz Kafka's oeuvre). In: Antonín Měšťan, *Česká literatura mezi Němci a Slovany* (Czech Literature between Germans and Slavs). Prague: Academia 2002, pp. 38–67.

Vl. Moulíková, K nedožitým osmdesátinám Franze Kafky (On Franz Kafka's 80th birthday anniversary). *Vlasta* 17 (1963), No. 34, p. 6 f.

Bert Nagel, *Kafka und die Weltliteratur. Zusammenhänge und Wechselwirkungen* (Kafka and World Literature: Contexts and Impacts). Munich: Winkler 1983.

Jiří J. K. Nebeský, Nové obrázky z Kafkova dětství (New images of Kafka's childhood). *Host* 17 (2001), No. 7, 64–68.

Marek Nekula, *System der Partikeln im Deutschen und Tschechischen unter besonderer Berücksichtigung der Abtönungspartikeln* (The System of Particles in German and Czech with special Respect to Modal Particles). Tübingen: Niemeyer 1996.

Marek Nekula, Theodor Lessing und seine Rezeption in der Tschechoslowakei (Theodor Lessing and his reception in Czechoslovakia). In: *brücken. Germanistisches Jahrbuch Tschechien – Slowakei*. NF 4 (1996), pp. 57–103.

Marek Nekula, Theodor Lessing und Max Brod. Eine mißlungene Begegnung (Theodor Lessing and Max Brod: A failed encounter). In: *brücken. Germanistisches Jahrbuch Tschechien – Slowakei*. NF 5 (1997), pp. 115–122.

Marek Nekula, Jakub Deml zwischen 'Österreichisch', 'Tschechisch', 'Deutsch' (Jakub Deml between 'Austrian', 'Czech', 'German'). In: *brücken. Germanistisches Jahrbuch Tschechien – Slowakei*. NF 6 (1998), pp. 3–31.

Marek Nekula, Franz Kafka ve škole. Výuka a znalosti češtiny (Franz Kafka at school. His Czech lessons and knowledge of Czech). In: *Kafkova zpráva o světě. Sborník ze semináře Společnosti Franze Kafky 20.–21. října 1999* (Kafka's Report on the World. Proceedings from the Franz-Kafka-Society Seminar, 20–21 October 1999). Prague: Nakladatelství Franze Kafky 2000, pp. 59–78.

Marek Nekula, Franz Kafka und der Kreis um die Zeitschrift *Moderní revue*. Nebst einigen Bemerkungen zu Kafka und Florians *Dobré dílo* (Franz Kafka and the circle around the journal *Moderní revue*. With remarks on Kafka and Florian's *Dobré dílo*). In: *brücken. Germanistisches Jahrbuch Tschechien – Slowakei*. NF 7 (2000), pp. 153–166.

Marek Nekula, Franz Kafka als Beamter der Arbeiter-Unfall-Versicherungs-Anstalt für Böhmen in Prag (Franz Kafka as an official in the Worker's Accident Insurance Company for Bohemia in Prague). *Brünner Beiträge zur Germanistik und Nordistik* 15 (2001), pp. 113–140.

Marek Nekula, Ad Nové obrázky z Kafkova dětství (Ad New images of Kafka's childhood). *Host* 10 (2001), 74.

Marek Nekula, Deutsch und Tschechisch in der Familie Kafka (German and Czech in the family

Kafka). In: Dieter Cherubim – Karlheinz Jakob – Angelika Linke (eds), *Neue deutsche Sprachgeschichte. Mentalitäts-, kultur- und sozialgeschichtliche Zusammenhänge* (New German History of Language: Mentality, Culture and Social History). Berlin, New York: W. de Gruyter 2002, pp. 379–415.

Marek Nekula, Franz Kafkas tschechische Lektüre im Kontext (Kafka's Czech reading in context). *Bohemia* 43 (2002), No. 2, pp. 346–380.

Marek Nekula, *„...v jednom poschodí vnitřní babylonské věže..." Jazyky Franze Kafky* ('...on one Floor of the Inner Tower of Babel...': Franz Kafka's Languages). Prague: Nakladatelství Franze Kafky 2003.

Marek Nekula, *Franz Kafkas Sprachen „...in einem Stockwerk des innern babylonischen Turms..."* (Franz Kafka's Languages. '...on one Floor of the Inner Tower of Babel...'). Tübingen: Niemeyer 2003.

Marek Nekula, Die deutsche Walhalla und der tschechische Slavín (The German Walhalla and the Czech pantheon Slavín). In: *brücken. Germanistisches Jahrbuch Tschechien – Slowakei.* NF 9–10 (2003), pp. 87–106.

Marek Nekula, Prager Brücken und der nationale Diskurs in Böhmen (Prague bridges and the national discourse in Bohemia). In: *brücken. Germanistisches Jahrbuch Tschechien – Slowakei.* NF 12 (2004), pp. 163–186.

Marek Nekula, Franz Kafkas Sprachen und Identität (Franz Kafka's languages and identity). In: Marek Nekula – Walter Koschmal (eds), *Juden zwischen Deutschen und Tschechen. Sprachliche, literarische und kulturelle Identitäten* (Jews between German and Czechs: Linguistic, Literary and Cultural Identities). Munich: Oldenbourg 2006, pp. 135–158.

Marek Nekula, Franz Kafkas Sprachen und Sprachlosigkeit (Franz Kafka's languages and the absence of language). In: *brücken. Germanistisches Jahrbuch Tschechien – Slowakei.* NF 15 (2007), pp. 99–130.

Marek Nekula, The divided city: Prague's public space and Franz Kafka's readings of Prague. In: Marek Nekula, Ingrid Fleischmann – Albrecht Greule (eds), *Franz Kafka im sprachnationalen Kontext seiner Zeit. Sprache und nationale Identität in öffentlichen Institutionen der böhmischen Länder* (Franz Kafka in the National Context of his Time. Language and National Identity in the Public Institutions of the Bohemian Crown Lands). Weimar, Cologne: Böhlau 2007, pp. 85–106.

Marek Nekula, Franz Kafka's Languages: Monolingualism, bilingualism, or multilingualism of a Prague Jew? In: Marek Nekula – Verena Bauer – Albrecht Greule (eds), *Deutsch in multilingualen Stadtzentren Mittel- und Osteuropas. Um die Jahrhundertwende vom 19. zum 20. Jahrhundert* (German in Multinational Cities in Central and East Europe. Around the Fin de Siècle from the 19th to the 20th Century). Vienna: Praesens 2008, pp. 15–44.

Marek Nekula, Poznámky (Comments). In: Gustav Janouch, *Hovory s Kafkou* (Conversations with Kafka). Translated by Eva Kolářová, edited and commented by Marek Nekula, epilogue by Veronika Tuckerová. Prague: Torst 2009, pp. 223–252.

Marek Nekula, Kafkas 'organische' Sprache: Sprachdiskurs als Kampfdiskurs (Kafka's organical language: Language discourse as struggle discourse). In: Manfred Engel – Ritchie Robertson (eds), *Kafka, Prag und der Erste Weltkrieg. Kafka, Prague, and the First World War.* Würzburg: Königshausen & Neumann 2012, pp. 237–256.

Marek Nekula, Constructing Slavonic Prague: The 'Green Mountain Manuscript' and public space in discourse. *Bohemia* 52 (2012), pp. 22–36.

Marek Nekula, Prague funerals: How Czech national symbols conquered and defended public space. In: Julie Buckler – Emily D. Johnson (eds), *Rites of Place: Public Commemoration in Russia and Eastern Europe.* Evanston/Illinois: Northwestern UP 2013, pp. 35–57.

Marek Nekula, Einblendung und Ausblendung: Tschechoslowakische Kafka-Rezeption und Erstveröffentlichungen von Kafkas tschechischen Texten (From the shadow into light: Czechoslovak reception of Franz Kafka and the first publishing of his Czech texts). In: Steffen Höhne – Ludger Udolph (eds), *Franz Kafka – Wirkung, Wirkungsverhinderung* (Franz Kafka – Reception and Reception Blocks). Cologne, Weimar, Vienna: Böhlau 2014, pp. 61–91.

Marek Nekula, *Smrt a zmrtvýchvstání národa: Sen o Slavíně v české literatuře a kultuře* (Death and Resurrection of a Nation: Dream on Pantheon Slavín in the Czech Literature and Culture). Prague: Karolinum 2016.

Marek Nekula – Walter Koschmal (eds), *Juden zwischen Deutschen und Tschechen. Sprachliche und kulturelle Identitäten 1800–1945* (Jews between German and Czechs: Linguistic, Literary and Cultural Identities). Munich: Oldenbourg 2006.

Marek Nekula – Ingrid Fleischmann – Albrecht Greule (eds), *Franz Kafka im sprachnationalen Kontext seiner Zeit. Sprache und nationale Identität in öffentlichen Institutionen der böhmischen Länder* (Franz Kafka in the National Context of his Time. Language and National Identity in the Public Institutions of the Bohemian Crown Lands). Weimar, Cologne: Böhlau 2007.

Marek Nekula – Verena Bauer – Albrecht Greule (eds), *Deutsch in multilingualen Stadtzentren Mittel- und Osteuropas. Um die Jahrhundertwende vom 19. zum 20. Jahrhundert* (German in Multinational Cities in Central and East Europe. Around the Fin de Siècle from the 19th to the 20th Century). Vienna: Praesens 2008.

Marek Nekula – Lucie Rychnovská, Smetanova čeština v dobovém kontextu (Smetana's Czech in historical context). *Hudební věda* 47 (2010), No. 1, pp. 43–76.

Marek Nekula – Lucie Rychnovská, Bedřich Smetana's Use of the Czech Language. *Musicalia. Journal of the Czech Museum of Music* 1 (2012), No. 1–2, pp. 6–38.

Ladislav Nezdařil, *Česká poezie v německých překladech* (Czech Poetry in German Translations). Prague: Academia 1985.

Anthony Northey, *Kafkas Mischpoche* (Kafka's Mishpoche). Berlin: Wagenbach 1988.

Anthony Northey, Die Kafkas: Juden? Christen? Tschechen? Deutsche? (The Kafkas: Jews? Christians? Czechs? Germans?) In: Kurt Krolop – Hans Dieter Zimmermann (eds), *Kafka und Prag. Colloquium im Goethe-Institut Prag. 24.–27. November 1992* (Kafka and Prague: Colloquium in the Goethe Institute in Prague, 24–27 November 1992). Berlin, New York: de Gruyter 1994, pp. 11–32.

Bohumil Nuska – Jiří Pernes, *Kafkův Proces a Švihova aféra* (Kafka's *The Trial* and Šviha's Affair). Prague: Barrister & Principal 2000.

Jiří Olič, *Čtení o Jakubu Demlovi* (Reading about Jakub Deml). Olomouc: Votobia 1993.

Cynthia Paces, *Prague Panoramas: National Memory and Sacred Space in the Twentieth Century.* Pittsburgh: University of Pittsburgh Press 2009.

Ernst Pawel, *The Nightmare of Reason: A Life of Franz Kafka.* New York: Farrar, Straus, Giroux 1984.

Zdeněk Pešat, Kafkův návrat domů a literární věda (Kafka's homecoming and literary studies). *Literární noviny* 12 (1963), No. 17, p. 5.

Jiří Pešek, *Od aglomerace k velkoměstu. Praha a středoevropské metropole 1850–1920* (From an Agglomeration to the Capital City: Prague and Central European Capital Cities 1850–1920). Prague: Scriptorium 1999.

A. Petřina, Jako v Kafkově 'Procesu' (As in Kafka's 'The Trial'). *Rudé právo* 43, 10.8.1963, No. 219, p. 3.

Hana Pichová, The Lineup for Meat: The Stalin statue in Prague. *PMLA* (*Journal of* Modern Language Association of America) 123 (2008), 3, pp. 614–630.

Meyer Isser Pinès, *Historie de la littérature judéo-allemande.* Paris: Iouve & Co 1911.

Podiven (= Milan Otáhal, Petr Pithart, Petr Příhoda), *Češi v dějinách nové doby. Pokus o zrcadlo* (The Czechs in the History of Modern Times: An Attempt at a Mirror). Prague: Rozmluvy 1991.

Miloš Pojar (ed.), *Hilsnerova aféra a česká společnost 1899–1999* (The Hilsner Affair and Czech Society 1899–1999). Prague: Židovské muzeum 1999.

Heinz Politzer, Problematik und Probleme der Kafka-Forschung (Themes and problems in Kafka research). *Monatshefte für deutschen Unterricht, deutsche Sprache und Literatur* 42 (1950), pp. 273–280.

Věra Poppova, Výročí Franze Kafky (Franz Kafka's anniversary). *Lidová demokracie,* 3.7.1963, p. 3.

Anna Pouzarová, Ze vzpomínek vychovatelky v rodině Franze Kafky (From the memoirs of the governess in Franz Kafka's family). Recorded by Hanuš Frank and Karel Šmejkal. *Plamen* 6 (1964), pp. 104–107.

Anna Pouzarová, Als Erzieherin in der Familie Kafka (Governess in the Kafka family). In: Hans-Gerd Koch (ed.), *„Als Kafka mir entgegen kam..." Erinnerungen an Franz Kafka* ('As Kafka approached me.' Recollections of Franz Kafka). Berlin: Wagenbach 1995, pp. 55–65.

Roman Prahl, Výtvarné umění v divadle (Visual art in the theatre). In: Zdeňka Benešová et al. (eds), *Národní divadlo – historie a současnost budovy. History and Present Day of the Building. Geschichte und Gegenwart des Hauses*. Prague: Národní divadlo 1999, pp. 107–125.

Willy Prochazka, Kafka's association with Jaroslav Hašek and the Czech anarchists. *Modern Austrian Literature* 11 (1978), No. 3–4, pp. 275–287.

Antonín Profous, *Místní jména v Čechách. Jejich vznik, původní význam a změny* (Bohemian Toponyms: The Origins and Changes of their Meanings). Vol. 1. Prague: ČSAV 1954.

Robert B. Pynsent, Láska a slečna Jesenská (Love and Miss Jesenská). In: Otto M. Urban – Luboš Merhaut (eds), *Moderní revue 1894–1925*. Prague: Torst 1995, pp. 167–187.

Michel Reffet, Franz Kafka und der Mythos (Franz Kafka and myth). In: *brücken. Germanistisches Jahrbuch Tschechien – Slowakei*. NF 9–10 (2003), pp. 155–168.

Michal Reiman, Die Kafka-Konferenz von 1963 (Kafka's conference 1963). In: Michaela Marek – Dušan Kováč – Jiří Pešek – Roman Prahl (eds), *Kultur als Vehikel und als Opponent politischer Absichten. Kulturkontakte zwischen Deutschen, Tschechen und Slowaken von der Mitte des 19. Jahrhunderts bis in die 1980er Jahre* (Culture as Medium and Opponent of Political Programs: Cultural Contact between Germans, Czechs and Slovaks from the middle of 19th Century to the 1980s). Essen: Klartext 2010, pp. 107–113.

Pavel Reiman, Společenská problematika v Kafkových románech (On the social issues in Kafka's novels). *Nová mysl* 1 (1958), pp. 52–63.

Pavel Reiman, 'Proces' Franze Kafky (Franz Kafka's *The Trial*). In: Franz Kafka, *Proces* (The Trial). Prague: Československý spisovatel 1958, pp. 207–225.

Pavel Reiman, Úvod (Foreword). In: Franz Kafka, *Amerika*. Prague: SNKLU 1962, pp. 7–23.

Pavel Reiman, Kafka a dnešek (Kafka today). In: Eduard Goldstücker – František Kautman – Pavel Reiman (eds), *Franz Kafka: liblická konference 1963* (Franz Kafka: Liblice Conference 1963). Prague: ČSAV 1963, pp. 13–20.

Pavel Reiman, O fragmentárnosti Kafkova díla (On the fragmentarity of Kafka's oeuvre). In: Eduard Goldstücker – František Kautman – Pavel Reiman (eds), *Franz Kafka: liblická konference 1963*. Prague: ČSAV 1963, pp. 213–218;

Pavel Reiman, Závěrečné slovo (Closing words). In: Eduard Goldstücker – František Kautman – Pavel Reiman (eds), *Franz Kafka: liblická konference 1963*. Prague: ČSAV 1963 pp. 275–277.

Ritchie Robertson, *Kafka, Judaism, Politics, and Literature*. Oxford: Clarendon Press 1985.

Ján Rozner, Případ Kafka? Nad českým vydáním Procesu (The case of Kafka? On the Czech edition of *The Trial*). *Slovenské pohľady* 75 (1959), No. 2, pp. 125–140.

William C. Rubinstein, Kafka's *Jackals and Arabs*. *Monatshefte* 1 (1967), pp. 13–18.

Ernst Rychnovsky (ed.), *Masaryk und das Judentum* (Masaryk and Jews). Prague: Marsverlagsgesellschaft 1931.

Vítězslav Rzounek, Poznámka o pojetí stranickosti v epice (Remarks on the concept of party-mindedness in epic literature). *Česká literatura* 11 (1963), No. 3, pp. 188–192.

Jean-Paul Sartre, La démilitarisation de la culture: Extrait du discours à Moscou devant le Congrès mondial pour le désarmement générale et la paix. *France-Observateur*, 17.7.1962, pp. 12–14.

August Schleicher, *Die Darwinsche Theorie und die Sprachwissenschaft – offenes Sendschreiben an Herrn Dr. Ernst Haeckel* (Darwin's Theory and Linguistics – An Open Letter to Dr. Ernst Haeckel). Weimar: H. Böhlau 1863.

Carsten Schmidt, *Kafkas fast unbekannter Freund: Leben und Werk von Felix Weltsch. Philosoph, Journalist und Zionist* (Kafka's Nearly Unknown Friend: The Life and Work of Felix Weltsch. Philosopher, Journalist and Zionist). Würzburg: Königshausen u. Neumann 2010.

Monika Schmitz-Emans, *Poetiken der Verwandlung* (Poetics of Metamorphosis). Innsbruck, Vienna, Bozen: Studienverlag 2008.

Seznam míst v království Českém (Index of Villages and Towns in the Kingdom of Bohemia). Prague: Místodržitelská tiskárna (Governor's Printing Press) 1907.

Ilse Seehase, Drei Mitteilungen Kafkas und ihr Umfeld (Three messages from Kafka and their context). *Zeitschrift für Germanistik* 8 (1987), No. 2, pp. 178–183.

Dimitry Shumsky, Czechs, Germans, Arabs, Jews. Franz Kafka's 'Jackals and Arabs' between Bohemia and Palestine. *Association for Jewish Studies Review* 33 (2009), No. 1, pp. 71–100.

Dimitry Shumsky, *Zweisprachigkeit und binationale Idee: Der Prager Zionismus 1900–1930* (Bilingualism and the Idea of Binationalism: Prague Zionism 1900–1930). Göttingen: Vandenhoeck & Ruprecht 2012.

Hugo Siebenschein, Prostředí a čas. Poznámky k osobnosti a dílu Franze Kafky (Milieu and time: Remarks on the personality and oeuvre of Franz Kafka). In: *Franz Kafka a Praha. Vzpomínky, úvahy, dokumenty* (Franz Kafka and Prague. Memories, Reflections, Papers). Prague: Žikeš 1947, pp. 7–24.

Hugo Siebenschein, *Česko-německý slovník* (Czech-German Dictionary), vol 2. Prague: Státní pedagogické nakladatelství 1983.

Michael K. Silver, Josephinian reforms. In: *The YIVO Encyclopedia of Jews in Eastern Europe* (on line).

Miriam Singer, Hebräischstunden mit Kafka (Hebrew lessons with Kafka). In: Hans-Gerd Koch (ed.), *„Als Kafka mir entgegen kam..." Erinnerungen an Franz Kafka* ('As Kafka approached me.' Recollections of Franz Kafka). Berlin: Wagenbach 1995, pp. 140–143.

Dušan Šlosar, Slovotvorba (Word formation). In: Petr Karlík – Marek Nekula – Zdenka Rusínová (eds), *Příruční mluvnice češtiny* (Handbook of Czech-Grammar). Prague: Nakladatelství Lidové noviny 1996, pp. 109–225.

Johann Gottfried Sommer, *Das Königreich Böhmen statistisch-topographisch dargestellt* (The Kingdom Bohemia from Statistical and Topographical Perspective). Vol. 8, Prague: Sommer 1840.

Scott Spector, *Prague Territories. National Conflict and Cultural Innovation in Franz Kafka's Fin de Siècle*. Berkeley, Los Angeles, London: University of California Press 2000.

Barbora Šrámková, *Max Brod und seine tschechische Kultur* (Max Brod and his Czech Culture). Wuppertal: Arco 2009.

Reiner Stach, *Kafka. Die Jahre der Erkenntnis* (Kafka: Years of Insight). Frankfurt am Main: S. Fischer 2008.

August Stein, O židovské obci v Čechách (On the Jewish community in Bohemia). In: *Kalendář česko-židovský na rok 1887/1888*, pp. 131–165.

Moritz Steinschneider, *Die hebräischen Übersetzungen des Mittelalters und die Juden als Dolmetscher* (Hebrew Translations of Middle Ages and the Jews as Translators). Berlin: Kommissionsverlag des Bibliographischen Bureaus 1893

Heymann Steinthal, *Grammatik, Logik und Psychologie, ihre Prinzipien und ihr Verhältnis zueinander* (Grammar, Logic and Psychology, their Principles and their Relation to each Other). Berlin: F. Dümmler 1855.

František Štícha et al., *Akademická gramatika spisovné češtiny* (Academic Grammar of Standard Czech). Prague: Academia 2013.

Christoph Stölz, *Kafkas böses Böhmen. Zur Sozialgeschichte eines Prager Juden* (Kafka's Villainous Bohemia: On Social History of Prague Jews). Munich: Text + Kritik 1975.

Ingrid Stöhr, *Zweisprachigkeit in Böhmen. Deutsche Volksschulen und Gymnasien im Prag der Kafka-Zeit* (Bilingualism in Bohemia: German Elementary and Grammar Schools in the Prague of Kafka's Time). Cologne, Weimar, Vienna: Böhlau 2010.

Ingrid Stöhr, Franz Kafkas deutsch-tschechische Zweisprachigkeit im Prager schulischen Kontext (Franz Kafka's German-Czech bilingualism in Prague school context). In: Peter Becher – Steffen Höhne – Marek Nekula (eds), *Kafka und Prag. Literatur-, kultur-, sozial- und sprachwissenschaftliche Kontexte* (Kafka and Prague: Contexts of Literature, Culture, Social Studies and Linguistics). Weimar, Cologne, Vienna: Böhlau 2012, pp. 207–229.

Gustav Strakosch-Grassmann, *Geschichte des österreichischen Unterrichtswesens* (History of the Austrian School System). Vienna: Pichler 1905.

David Suchoff, *Kafka's Jewish Languages: The Hidden Openness of Tradition.* Philadelphia: University of Pennsylvania Press 2012.

Oleg Sus, Kafka – zmatení jazyků (Kafka – the confusion of tongues). *Host do domu* 6 (1959), pp. 139–140.

Martin Svatoš, *Písemná pozůstalost. Franz Kafka (1883–1924)* (Written Remains: Franz Kafka). Prague: Literární archiv Památníku národního písemnictví 1984.

Martin Svatoš, Pozůstalostní spis Franze Kafky (Documentation of remains of Franz Kafka). *Documenta Pragensia* 15 (1997), pp. 301–338.

Simona Švingrová: *Tschechisch oder Deutsch? Auf dem Weg von Konkurrenz zu Dominanz. Zum Einsatz von innerer und äußerer Amtssprache in der Arbeiter-Unfall-Versicherungs-Anstalt im Prag der Kafka-Zeit (1908–1922)* (Czech or German? On the Way from Rivality to Dominance. On Use of the Internal and External Official Language in Worker's Accident Insurance Company in Prague of Kafka's Time, 1908–1922). Prague: Charles University 2010.

Simona Švingrová, Die Rolle der sprachlichen Qualifikation bei der Karriere eines (k.k.) Beamten: Franz Kafka und seine Kollegen bei der AUVA (Role of language qualification of an Austrian official: Franz Kafka and his colleagues in the Worker's Accident Insurance Company). In: Peter Becher – Steffen Höhne – Marek Nekula (eds), *Kafka und Prag. Literatur-, kultur-, sozial- und sprachwissenschaftliche Kontexte* (Kafka and Prague: Contexts of Literature, Culture, Social Studies and Linguistics). Weimar, Cologne, Vienna: Böhlau 2012, pp. 185–205.

Simona Švingrová – Marek Nekula, Die Sprachenfrage in Böhmen nach 1900. Der tatsächliche Gebrauch der deutschen und tschechischen Amtssprache am Beispiel der Arbeiter-Unfall-Versicherungs-Anstalt in Prag (The language question in Bohemia after 1900. The real use of German and Czech official language demonstrated on the Worker's Accident Insurance Company). In: Steffen Höhne – Ludger Udolph (eds), *Deutsche – Tschechen – Böhmen: Kulturelle Integration und Desintegration im 20. Jahrhundert* (German – Czechs – Bohemians: Cultural Integration and Desintegration in the 20th Century). Weimar, Cologne, Vienna: Böhlau 2010, 73–90.

Josef Svoboda, Bez víry? (Without faith?). *Křesťanská revue* 25 (1958), pp. 283–285.

Svatoslav Svoboda, Franz Kafka. *Mladá fronta*, 3.7.1963, p. 5.

Friedrich Thieberger, Kafka und die Thiebergers (Kafka and the Thiebergers). In: Hans-Gerd Koch (ed.), *„Als Kafka mir entgegen kam..." Erinnerungen an Franz Kafka* ('As Kafka approached me.' Recollections of Franz Kafka). Berlin: Wagenbach 1995, pp. 121–127; Berlin: Wagenbach 2005, pp. 128–134.

Karl Tieftrunk, *Böhmisches Lesebuch für Deutsche insbesondere für Schüler an deutschen Mittelschulen. Česká čítanka, zvláště pro žáky na gymnasiích a realních školách* (Czech Reader for Germans, especially for Pupils on German Secondary Schools). Vol. 1. Prague: F. L. Kober ^{4}1881, ^{5}1886, ^{6}1889, ^{7}1896; vol. 2. Prague: F. L. Kober ^{3}1884, ^{4}1893.

Jens Tismar, Kafkas 'Schakale und Araber' im zionistischen Kontext betrachtet (Kafka's 'Jackals and Arabs' from Zionist point of view). In: *Jahrbuch der deutschen Schillergesellschaft* 19 (1975), pp. 311–313.

Jindřich Toman, Mumlání, špatná čeština a nedostatek poetického citu. Židé v kontextu českého nacionalismu, 30. a 40. léta 19. století (Mauscheln, incorrect Czech and the lack of poetic sense: Jews in context of Czech nationalism, 1830s and 1840s). In: Zdeněk Hojda – Marta Ottlová – Roman Prahl (eds), *Slovanství a česká kultura 19. století* (Slavonic World and Czech Culture in the 19th Century). Prague: KLP 2006, pp. 352–360.

Pavel Trost, Das späte Prager Deutsch. Pozdní pražská němčina (Late Prague German). *Germanistica Pragensia* 1 (1962), pp. 31–39.

Pavel Trost, Franz Kafka und das Prager Deutsch (Franz Kafka and 'Prague German'). *Germanistica Pragensia* 2 (1964), 29–37.

Pavel Trost, Der Name Kafka (The proper name Kafka). *Beiträge zur Namenforschung* 18 (1983), No. 1, 52–53.

Antonín Truhlář, *Výbor z literatury české. Doba nová* (Anthology of Czech Literature: Modern Period). 3 vol. Prague: Bursík & Kohout 1886, [2]1892, [3]1898.

Veronika Tuckerová, *Reading Kafka in Prague: The Reception of Franz Kafka between the East and the West during the Cold War.* New York: Columbia University 2012.

Veronika Tuckerová, Reading Kafka Writing Vita: The Trials of the Kafka Scholar Eduard Goldstucker, *New German Critique* 124 (2015), pp. 129–162

Milan Tvrdík, Franz Kafka und Jiří (Georg) Langer. Zur Problematik des Verhältnisses Kafkas zur tschechischen Kultur (Franz Kafka and Jiří (Georg) Langer: On Kafka's relation to the Czech culture). In: Klaus Schenk (ed.), *Moderne in der deutschen und der tschechischen Literatur* (Modern in the German and Czech Literature). Tübingen, Basel: Francke Verlag 2000, pp. 189–199.

Johannes Urzidil, Von Odkolek zu Odradek (From Odkolek to Odradek). *Schweizer Monatshefte* 50 (1970), No. 1, pp. 957–972.

Silvio Vietta, *Ästhetik der Moderne: Literatur und Bild* (Aesthetics of Modern: Literature and Image). Munich: Fink 2001.

Manfred Voigt, *„Wir sollen alle kleine Fichtes werden!" Johann Gottlieb Fichte als Prophet der Kultur-Zionisten* ('We all should become like Fichte!' Johann Gottlieb Fichte as Prophet of Cultural Zionism). Berlin, Vienna: Philo Verlag 2003.

Vlastimil Vrabec, Fantastický svět Franze Kafky (The fantastical world of Franz Kafka). *Svobodné slovo*, 2.7.1963, p. 3.

Výroční zpráva cís. král. vyššího gymnasia českého na Novém Městě v Praze (Annual Report of Emperor's and King's High Grammar School in Prague New Town). Prague. 1892–97.

Klaus Wagenbach, *Franz Kafka. Eine Biographie seiner Jugend 1883–1912* (Franz Kafka: A Biography of his Youth 1883–1912). Bern: Francke 1958; Berlin Wagenbach 2006.

Klaus Wagenbach, *Franz Kafka.* Reinbek bei Hamburg: Rowohlt [1964] 1991.

Klaus Wagenbach, *Franz Kafka.* Prague: Mladá fronta [1965] 1993.

Klaus Wagenbach, *Kafka's Prague: A Travel Reader*. Translated by Shaun Whiteside. Woodstock, New York: The Overlook Press 1996.

Klaus Wagenbach, *Kafkas Prag. Ein Reiselesebuch* (Kafka's Prague: A Travel Reader). Berlin: Wagenbach [7]2004.

Benno Wagner, „Sprechen kann man mit den Nomaden nicht". Sprache, Gesetz und Verwaltung bei Otto Bauer und Franz Kafka ('It is impossible to speak with nomads'. Language, Law and Administration in Otto Bauer and Franz Kafka). In: Marek Nekula – Ingrid Fleischmann – Albrecht Greule (eds), *Franz Kafka im sprachnationalen Kontext seiner Zeit. Sprache und nationale Identität in öffentlichen Institutionen der böhmischen Länder* (Franz Kafka in the National Context of his Time. Language and National Identity in the Public Institutions of the Bohemian Crown Lands). Cologne, Weimar, Vienna: Böhlau 2007, pp. 109–128.

Benno Wagner, Fürsprache – Widerstreit – Dialog: Karl Kraus, Franz Kafka und das Schreiben gegen den Krieg (Recommendation – conflict – dialogue: Karl Kraus, Franz Kafka and the writing against the war). In: Manfred Engel – Ritchie Robertson (eds), *Kafka, Prag und der Erste Weltkrieg. Kafka, Prague, and the First World War*. Würzburg: Königshausen & Neumann 2012, 257–272.

Jan Wagner, Dopis Franze Kafky inž. Františku Kholovi v Literárním archivu (Franz Kafka's letter to Ing. František Khol in Literary Archiv). *Sborník národního muzea v Praze. Acta musei nationalis Pragae* 8 (1963), Serie C, vol. 8, No. 2, p. 84.

Alena Wagnerová, *„Im Hauptquartier des Lärms." Die Familie Kafka aus Prag* ('In the Headquarter of Noise': The Family Kafka from Prague). Berlin: Bollmann 1997.

Werner Weinberg, *Die Reste des Jüdischdeutschen* (The Remains of Yiddish). Stuttgart: Kohlhammer 1969.

Franz Werfel, Vorrede (Foreword). In: Petr Bezruč, *Die schlesischen Lieder* (The Silesian Songs). Leipzig: Kurt Wolff Verlag 1917, pp. 5–22.

Hugo Wetscherek (ed.), *Kafkas letzter Freund: Der Nachlaß Robert Klopstock (1899–1972). Mit kommentierter Erstveröffentlichung von 38 teils ungedruckten Briefen Franz Kafkas* (Kafka's Last

Friend: The Literary Remains of Robert Klopstock. With First Oprint of 38 Partially Unpublished Letters Including Commentary). In collaboration with Ch. Frey and M. Peche. Vienna: Inlibris Verlag 2003.

Robert Wistrich, Georg von Schönerer and the genesis of modern Austrian antisemitism. *Wiener Library Bulletin* 29 (1976), pp. 20–29.

Rudolf M. Wlaschek, *Juden in Böhmen. Beiträge zur Geschichte des europäischen Judentums im 19. und 20. Jahrhundert* (Jews in Bohemia: Contributions to the History of European Jewry in the 19th and 20th Century). Munich: Oldenbourg 1997.

Siegmund A. Wolf, *Jiddisches Wörterbuch: Wortschatz des deutschen Grundbestands der jiddischen Sprache mit Leseprobe* (Yiddish Dictionary: Vocabulary of the German Basis in Yiddish with a Reading Example). Hamburg: Buske ²1993.

Jan Zábrana, *Celý život: Výbor z deníků. 5. listopadu 1976 – červenec 1984* (A Whole Life: Selected Passages from the Diaries, 5 November 1976 – July 1984). Vol. 2. Prague: Torst 1992.

Josef Žalud, Zákonná ustanovení ohledně židů v Rakousku od r. 1867 (Legal regulations concerning Jews in Austria since 1867). In: *Kalendář česko-židovský na rok 1882/1883*, 96–104.

Tara Zarah, Bilingualism and the nationalist 'Kampf um Kinder' in the Bohemian Lands, 1900– 1938. In: Marek Nekula – Ingrid Fleischmann – Albrecht Greule (eds), *Franz Kafka im sprachnationalen Kontext seiner Zeit. Sprache und nationale Identität in öffentlichen Institutionen der böhmischen Länder* (Franz Kafka in the National Context of his Time. Language and National Identity in the Public Institutions of the Bohemian Crown Lands). Weimar: Böhlau 2007, pp. 229–244.

Jaromír Zeman: 'Neue' Entwicklungstendenzen in der deutschen Syntax (New tendencies in the development of German syntax). *Brünner Beiträge zur Germanistik und Nordistik* 21 (2007), R 12, pp. 46–49.

Zf, O Kafkovi trochu jinak (Harry Järve's bibliography of Kafka scholarship). *Lidová demokracie*, 8. 4. 1962, p. 5.

Hans Dieter Zimmermann, Der Turmbau zu Babel (Building of the Tower of Babel). In: Hans Dieter Zimmermann, *Der babylonische Dolmetscher: Zu Franz Kafka und Robert Walser* (The Babylonian Translator: on Franz Kafka and Robert Walser). Frankfurt am Main: Suhrkamp 1985, pp. 61–66.

Hans Dieter Zimmermann, Das Labyrinth der Welt: Kafka und Comenius (The Labyrinth of the World: Kafka and Comenius). In: Klaas-Hinrich Ehlers et al. (eds), *Brücken nach Prag. Deutschsprachige Literatur im kulturellen Kontext der Donaumonarchie und der Tschechoslowakei* (Bridges to Prague: German-written Literature in the Cultural Context of the Habsburg Monarchy and Czechoslovakia). Frankfurt am Main: P. Lang 2000, pp. 309–319.

Hans Dieter Zimmermann, Franz Kafka liest Božena Němcová (Franz Kafka reads Božena Němcová). In: *brücken – Germanistisches Jahrbuch* N.F. 15 (2007), pp. 182–192.

Hanns Zischler, *Kafka geht ins Kino* (Kafka Goes to the Cinema). Reinbek b. Hamburg: Rowohlt 1996.

Peter Zusi, Kafka and Czech literature. In: Caroline Duttlinger (ed.), *Kafka in Context*. Cambridge University Press 2016, in print.

INDEX

EDITORIAL NOTE

1. Suppression and distortion: Franz Kafka 'from the Prague perspective'

Based on text first published in German: Einblendung und Ausblendung: Tschechoslowakische Kafka-Rezeption und Erstveröffentlichungen von Kafkas tschechischen Texten. In: Steffen Höhne – Ludger Udolph (eds), *Franz Kafka – Wirkung, Wirkungsverhinderung, Nicht-Wirkung*. Cologne/Weimar/Vienna: Böhlau 2014, pp. 61–91. (= Intellektuelles Prag 4)

Translated by Carly McLaughlin

2. The 'being' of Odradek: Franz Kafka in his Jewish context

Based on the second and third chapter of my monograph first published in Czech and German: *„...v jednom poschodí vnitřní babylonské věže..." Jazyky Franze Kafky*. Prague: Nakladatelství Franze Kafky, 2003 & *Franz Kafkas Sprachen: „...in einem Stockwerk des innern babylonischen Turmes..."*. Tübingen: Niemeyer 2003.

Translated by Robert Russell

3. Franz Kafka's languages

Partially based on text first published in English: Franz Kafka's languages. Monolingualism, bilingualism, or multilingualism of a Prague Jew? In: Marek Nekula – Verena Bauer – Albrecht Greule (eds), *Deutsch in multilingualen Stadtzentren Mittel- und Osteuropas. Um die Jahrhundertwende vom 19. zum 20. Jahrhundert*. Vienna: Praesens 2008, pp. 15–44.

Final English text edited by Anna Bryson-Gustová

4. Kafka's 'organic' language: Language as a weapon.

First published in German: Kafkas »organische« Sprache: Sprachdiskurs als Kampfdiskurs. In: Manfred Engel – Ritchie Robertson (eds), *Kafka, Prague, and the First World War*. Würzburg: Königshausen & Neumann, 2012, pp. 237–256. (= Kafka Oxford Studies 2)

Translated by Carly McLaughlin

5. Franz Kafka at school: Kafka's education in Czech language and literature

Based on the fifth chapter of my monograph first published in Czech and German: *„...v jednom poschodí vnitřní babylonské věže..." Jazyky Franze*

Kafky. Prague: Nakladatelství Franze Kafky, 2003 & *Franz Kafkas Sprachen: „...in einem Stockwerk des innern babylonischen Turmes...“*. Tübingen: Niemeyer 2003.

Translated by Robert Russell

6. Kafka's Czech reading in context

First published in German: Franz Kafkas tschechische Lektüre im Kontext. In: *Bohemia* 43 (2002), Heft 2, pp. 346–380.

Translated by Robert Russell

7. Divided city: Franz Kafka's readings of Prague

Based on text first published in English: The divided city: Prague's public space and Franz Kafka's readings of Prague. In: Marek Nekula – Ingrid Fleischmann – Albrecht Greule (eds), *Franz Kafka im sprachnationalen Kontext seiner Zeit. Sprache und nationale Identität in öffentlichen Institutionen der böhmischen Länder.* Weimar, Cologne: Böhlau 2007, pp. 85–106.

Final English text edited by Robert Russell

MAREK NEKULA

FRANZ KAFKA AND HIS PRAGUE CONTEXTS: STUDIES IN LANGUAGE AND LITERATURE

Published by Charles University in Prague
Karolinum Press
Ovocný trh 3, 116 36 Praha 1, Czech Republic
www.karolinum.cz
Prague 2016
Translation by Robert Russell, Carly McLaughlin
Cover and layout by Jan Šerých
Copyediting by Martin Janeček
Typeset and printed by Karolinum Press
First English edition

ISBN 978-80-246- 2935-3
ISBN 978-80-246-2992-6 (pdf)